# Italian

3rd Edition

## by Giuseppe Cavatorta, PhD, and Teresa L. Picarazzi, PhD

# Italian For Dummies®, 3rd Edition

Published by: **John Wiley & Sons, Inc.**, 111 River Street, Hoboken, NJ 07030-5774, www.wiley.com



For general information on our other products and services, please contact our Customer Care Department within the U.S. at 877-762-2974, outside the U.S. at 317-572-3993, or fax 317-572-4002. For technical support, please visit https://hub.wiley.com/community/support/dummies.

Wiley publishes in a variety of print and electronic formats and by print-on-demand. Some material included with standard print versions of this book may not be included in e-books or in print-on-demand. If this book refers to media that is not included in the version you purchased, you may download this material at http://booksupport.wiley.com. For more information about Wiley products, visit www.wiley.com.

Library of Congress Control Number: 2025945491

ISBN 978-1-394-32146-9 (pbk); ISBN 978-1-394-32148-3 (ebk); ISBN 978-1-394-32147-6 (ebk)

Printed and bound by CPI Group (UK) Ltd, Croydon, CR0 4YY

C9781394321469_071125

# Table of Contents

# Introduction

The current era is fascinating, one that interconnects everyone with others all around the world. With globalization and technology as the driving forces, you find yourselves getting in closer and closer contact with more and more people. As a result, knowing how to say at least a few words in a language such as Italian is becoming an ever-more-vital tool.

Whatever your reason for wanting to learn some Italian, *Italian For Dummies* is a terrific choice because it gives you the skills you need for basic communication in Italian. We aren't promising fluency here, but basic communicative competency that will allow you to be understood. If you need to greet someone, purchase a ticket, or order off a menu in Italian, you need look no further than this book.

## About This Book

This isn't a class that you have to drag yourself to twice a week for a specified period of time. You can use *Italian For Dummies* however you want to, whether your goal is to learn some words and phrases to help you get around when you visit Italy, or you just want to be able to say "Hello, how are you?" to your Italian-speaking neighbor. Go through this book at your own pace, reading as much or as little at a time as you like. You don't have to follow the chapters in order, either; just read the sections that interest you.

*Note:* If you've never taken Italian before, you may want to read the chapters in Part 1 before you tackle the later chapters.

## Conventions Used in This Book

To make this book easy for you to navigate, we've set up a few conventions:

>> Italian terms are set in **boldface** to make them stand out.

>> Pronunciation is set in parentheses following the Italian term and the stressed syllables are *italicized*.

- **>>** English translations are also set in italics. You can find them set in parentheses following the pronunciation of Italian terms or sentences.

- **>>** Verb conjugations (lists that show you the forms of a verb) are given in tables in this order of six persons: "I," "you (singular, informal)," "he/she/it/you (singular, formal)," "we," "you (plural/informal)," and "they/you (plural, formal)" form. Pronunciations follow in the second column. Following is an example using the verb **parlare** (pahr-*lah*-reh) *(to speak)*. The translations in the third column have all three forms, but for the sake of space, I only give you the first:

| Conjugation | Pronunciation | Translation |
| --- | --- | --- |
| **io parlo** | *ee*-oh *pahr*-loh | *I speak, I do speak, I am speaking* |
| **tu parli** | tooh *pahr*-lee | *you (informal) speak* |
| **lui/lei/Lei parla** | *looh*-ee/ley/ley *pahr*-lah | *he/she/you (formal) speak* |
| **noi parliamo** | noi pahr-*lyah*-moh | *we speak* |
| **voi parlate** | voi par-*lah*-teh | *you (plural informal) speak* |
| **loro parlano** | *loh*-roh *pahr*-lah-noh | *they/you (plural formal) speak* |

Language learning is a peculiar beast, so this book includes a few elements that other *For Dummies* books don't. Following are the new elements you'll find:

- **>> Talkin' the Talk dialogues:** The best way to learn a language is to see and hear how it's used in conversation, so we include dialogues throughout the book under the heading "Talkin' the Talk." Listen to and repeat these dialogues as often as you like. Both the online audio tracks and the text can help you approximate authentic pronunciation. You can find the online audio tracks at `www.dummies.com/go/italianfd3e`.

- **>> Words to Know blackboards:** Identifying key words and phrases is also important in language learning, so we group important words in a chapter on a chalkboard with the heading "Words to Know."

- **>> Fun & Games activities:** You can use the Fun & Games activities at end of most chapters to reinforce some chapter concepts you've learned. These word games are fun ways to gauge your progress.

Also note that because each language has its own ways of expressing ideas, the English translations that we provide for the Italian terms may not always be literal. We want you to know the gist of what's being said. For example, the phrase **Mi dica** (mee dee-kah) can be translated literally as the formal imperative *Tell me,* but the phrase is commonly used to mean *(How) Can I help you?*

# Foolish Assumptions

To write this book, we make some assumptions about who you are and what you hope to gain from it:

>> You know little to no Italian — or if you took it in school, you don't recall much.

>> You're not looking for a book that will make you fluent in Italian; you just want to know some words, phrases, and sentence constructions so that you can communicate basic information in Italian.

>> You don't want to have to memorize long lists of vocabulary words or a bunch of boring grammar rules.

If these statements apply to you, you've found the right book!

# Icons Used in This Book

You may be looking for particular information while reading this book. To make certain types of information easier for you to find, we've placed the following icons in the left-hand margins throughout the book:

This icon highlights tips that can make learning Italian easier.

To ensure that you don't forget important information, this icon serves as a reminder, like a string tied around your finger.

Languages are full of quirks that may trip you up if you're not prepared for them. This icon points to discussions of these unusual grammar rules.

If you're looking for information and advice about culture and travel, look for these icons.

The online audio tracks that accompany this book give you the opportunity to listen to real Italian speakers. This icon marks the Talkin' the Talk dialogues that you can listen to online; just go to www.dummies.com/go/italianfd3e.

## Beyond This Book

In addition to what you're reading right now, this book comes with a free, access-anywhere Cheat Sheet containing phrases and tips for learning Italian faster. To get this Cheat Sheet, go to www.dummies.com and type "Italian For Dummies Cheat Sheet" in the search box.

## Where to Go from Here

Learning a language is all about jumping in and giving it a try (no matter how bad your pronunciation is at first). So take the leap! Start at the beginning, pick a chapter that interests you, or listen to a few dialogues online. Skip the parts that distract you and take you away from Italian (such as the pronunciation spellings and translations after you've been through them once): The more you think in Italian, the more natural it will come to you. Before long, you'll be able to respond, **"Sì!"** when people ask, **"Parla italiano?"**

# 1

# Getting Started with Italian

# Chapter **1**

# Saying Italian Like It Is

You probably know that Italian is a Romance language, which means that Italian, just like Spanish, French, Portuguese, and some other languages, is a "child" of Latin. There was a time when Latin was the official language in a large part of Europe because the Romans ruled so much of the area. Before the Romans came, people spoke their own languages, and the mixture of these original tongues with Latin produced many of the languages and dialects still in use today.

If you know one of these Romance languages, you can often understand parts of another. But just as members of the same family can look very similar but have totally different personalities, so it is with these languages. People in different areas speak in very different ways due to historical or social reasons, and even though Italian is the official language, Italy has a rich variety of dialects. Some dialects differ so much from standard Italian that people from different regions can't understand each other.

Despite the number of different accents and dialects, you'll be happy to discover that everybody understands the Italian you speak and you'll understand theirs. (Italians don't usually speak in their dialect with people outside their region.) This chapter introduces you to the world of Italian.

# You Already Know Some Italian!

Although Italians are very proud of their language, they have allowed some English words such as *gadget, jogging, weekend,* and *shock* to enter it. They often use the word *okay,* and since computers have entered their lives, they say **"cliccare sul mouse"** (kleek-*kah*-reh soohl mouse) *(to click the mouse).* Finally, there's **lo zapping** (loh zapping), which means continuously switching TV channels with the remote. These are only a few of the flood of English words that have entered the Italian language.

In the same way, many Italian words are known in English–speaking countries. Can you think of some? Consider the following words:

- **pizza** (*peet*-tsah)

- **pasta** (*pah*-stah)

- **spaghetti** (spah-*geht*-tee)

- **tortellini** (tohr-tehl-*lee*-nee)

- **mozzarella** (moht-tsah-*rehl*-lah)

- **espresso** (eh-*sprehs*-soh)

- **cappuccino** (kahp-pooh-*chee*-noh)

- **panino** (pah-*nee*-noh): For one sandwich: for two or more, the word is **panini** (pah-*nee*-nee)

- **biscotti** (bee-*skoht*-tee) (cookies): One cookie is a **biscotto** (bee-*skoht*-toh)

- **tiramisù** (tee-rah-mee-*sooh*)

Incidentally, did you know that tiramisù literally means *pull me up?* The name comes from the boost of energy you get from the strong Italian espresso and eggs in it. You may have heard words not directly related to food, such as the following:

- **amore** (ah-*moh*-reh): This is the word for *love* that so many Italian songs talk about.

- **avanti** (ah-*vahn*-tee): You use this word as *come in!, come on!,* or *get a move on!*

- **bambino** (bahm-*bee*-noh): This means *child* or *boy.* The word for *girl* is **bambina** (bahm-*bee*-nah).

- **bravo!** (*brah*-voh): Say this to a man. For a woman, use **brava!** (*brah*-vah), and for a group, **bravi!** (*brah*-vee) or **brave!** (*brah*-veh) if it's all women.

>> **ciao!** (chow): **Ciao** means *hello* and *good-bye.*

>> **scusi** (*skooh*-zee): This word stands for *excuse me* and *sorry* and is addressed to persons you don't know or to whom you speak formally. You say **"scusa"** (*skooh*-zah) to people you know and to children.

You've heard at least some of these words, haven't you? This is just a little taste of all the various words and expressions you'll get to know in this book.

## Cognates

In addition to the words that have crept into the language directly, Italian and English have many cognates. A *cognate* is a word in one language that has the same origin as a word in another one and may sound similar. The following words can give you an immediate sense of what cognates are:

>> **aeroporto** (ah-eh-roh-*pohr*-toh) *(airport)*

>> **attenzione** (aht-tehn-*tsyoh*-neh) *(attention)*

>> **comunicazione** (koh-mooh-nee-kah-*tsyoh*-neh) *(communication)*

>> **importante** (eem-pohr-*tahn*-teh) *(important)*

>> **incredibile** (een-kreh-*dee*-bee-leh) *(incredible)*

You understand much more Italian than you think you do. Italian and English are full of cognates. To demonstrate, read this little story with some Italian words and see how easy it is for you to understand.

It seems **impossibile** (eem-pohs-*see*-bee-leh) to him that he is now at the **aeroporto** (ah-eh-roh-*pohr*-toh) in Rome. When he goes out on the street, he first calls a **taxi** (*tah*-ksee). He opens his bag to see if he has the **medicine** (meh-dee-*chee*-neh) that the **dottore** (doht-*toh*-reh) prescribed for him. Going through this **terribile traffico** (tehr-*ree*-bee-leh *trahf*-fee-koh), he passes a **cattedrale** (kaht-teh-*drah*-leh), some **monumenti** (moh-nooh-*mehn*-tee), and many **palazzi** (pah-*laht*-tsee). He knows that this is going to be a **fantastico** (fahn-*tah*-stee-koh) journey.

# Sounding Italian: The Essentials

Italian gives your tongue plenty of chances to do acrobatics — and that's part of the fun. The language introduces you to some new and exciting sounds. In this section, we walk you through some basic pronunciation guidelines to help you speak Italian like a native speaker.

Throughout this book, you find the pronunciation of Italian words in parentheses. The next few sections contain helpful hints on how to read and use these pronunciations — in other words, how to pronounce Italian words. Here's the deal: We need to agree on what letters stand for which sounds, so stick with this pronunciation code as you go through the book.

In the pronunciations, we separate the syllables with a hyphen, like this: **casa** (*kah*-zah) *(house)*. The stressed syllable, that is, the part of the word where you place the emphasis is italicized. If you acquire the correct pronunciation, starting with the alphabet, you may even be able to forgo the pronunciation spelling provided, and read it like a real Italian.

## The alphabet

**PLAY THIS**

What better way is there to start speaking a language than to familiarize yourself with its alphabet! Table 1-1 shows you all the letters as well as how each of them sounds. It's essential to learn how to pronounce the Italian alphabet so that you'll be able to pronounce all of the new words you will be learning. Listen to and repeat what you hear in Track 1 of the audio files as many times as you need to in order to get down the right sounds. In the long run, this will help you be understood when you communicate in Italian. Note that there are only 21 letters in the Italian alphabet: Missing are j, k, w, x, and y (which have crept into some Italian words).

**TABLE 1-1**

### The Italian Alphabet (ahl-fah-*beh*-toh)

| Letter | Pronunciation | Letter | Pronunciation |
|--------|---------------|--------|---------------|
| a | ah | b | bee |
| c | chee | d | dee |
| e | eh | f | *ehf*-feh |
| g | jee | h | *ahk*-kah |
| i | ee | j | ee *loohn*-gah |
| k | *kahp*-pah | l | *ehl*-leh |
| m | *ehm*-meh | n | *ehn*-neh |
| o | oh | p | pee |
| q | kooh | r | *ehr*-reh |

| Letter | Pronunciation | Letter | Pronunciation |
| --- | --- | --- | --- |
| s | *ehs*-seh | t | tee |
| u | ooh | v | vooh |
| w | *dohp*-pyah-vooh | x | eeks |
| y | *eep*-see-lohn | z | *dzeh*-tah |

# Vowels

We start with the tough ones: vowels. The sounds aren't that new, but the connection between the written letter and the actual pronunciation isn't quite the same as it is in English.

Italian has five written vowels: a, e, i, o, and u. The following sections tell you how to pronounce each of them.

## The vowel "a"

In Italian, the letter **a** has just one pronunciation. It sounds like the **a** in the English word father. The Italian **a** is always pronounced this way.

To help you avoid slipping into the various **a** sounds used in English, we transcribe the Italian **a** as (ah) like in **casa.** Here are a few more examples:

>> **albero** (*ahl*-beh-roh) *(tree)*

>> **marmellata** (mahr-mehl-*lah*-tah) *(jam)*

>> **sale** (*sah*-leh) *(salt)*

## The vowel "e"

Try to think of the sound in the English word let. This sound comes very close to the Italian **e**. In this book, we transcribe the **e** sound as (eh). For example:

>> **sole** (*soh*-leh) *(sun)*

>> **peso** (*peh*-zoh) *(weight)*

>> **bere** (*beh*-reh) *(to drink)*

## The vowel "i"

The Italian **i** is simply pronounced (ee), as in the English word see. Here are some examples:

>> **cinema** (*chee*-neh-mah) (*cinema*)

>> **bimbo** (*beem*-boh) (*little boy*)

>> **vita** (*vee*-tah) (*life*)

## The vowel "o"

The Italian **o** is pronounced as in the English (from the Italian) piano. We therefore list the pronunciation as (oh). Try it out on the following words:

>> **domani** (doh-*mah*-nee) (*tomorrow*)

>> **piccolo** (*peek*-koh-loh) (*little; small*)

>> **dolce** (*dohl*-cheh) (*sweet*)

## The vowel "u"

The Italian **u** sounds always like the English (ooh), as in zoo. Therefore, we use (ooh) to transcribe the Italian u. Here are some sample words:

>> **tu** (tooh) (*you*)

>> **luna** (*looh*-nah) (*moon*)

>> **frutta** (*frooht*-tah) (*fruit*)

## Pronunciation peculiarities

You'll come across some sounds and spellings that aren't so familiar, for example:

>> oi as in oink: **noi** (noi) (*we*)

>> ahy as in ice: **dai** (dahy) (*you give*)

>> ey as in aid: **lei** (ley) (*she*)

>> yeh as in yes: **grazie** (*grah*-tsyeh) (*thank you*)

# Consonants

Italian has the same consonants that English does. You pronounce most of them the same way in Italian as you pronounce them in English, but others have noteworthy differences. We start with the easy ones and look at those that are pronounced identically:

>> **b:** As in **bene** (*beh*-neh) *(well)*

>> **d:** As in **dare** (*dah*-reh) *(to give)*

>> **f:** As in **fare** (*fah*-reh) *(to make)*

>> **l:** As in **ladro** (*lah*-droh) *(thief)*

>> **m:** As in **madre** (*mah*-dreh) *(mother)*

>> **n:** As in **no** (noh) *(no)*

>> **p:** As in **padre** (*pah*-dreh) *(father)*

>> **t:** As in **treno** (*treh*-noh) *(train)*

Make certain to exaggerate the t when it's doubled, like in the word **spaghetti** (spah-*geht*-tee) as in the last name Getty.

>> **v:** As in **vino** (*vee*-noh) *(wine)*

Finally, some consonants that aren't part of the Italian alphabet except in foreign words have entered the language such as the following:

>> **j:** It appears mostly in foreign words such as *jogging* and *jeans* where it keeps the same original English pronunciation like the **j** in *jeep.*

>> **k:** Like **j**, it appears mostly in foreign words; you find it in words like *okay, ketchup,* and *kiwi.*

>> **w:** As with **j** and **k**, it appears in foreign words — often from English words — like *whisky, windsurf,* and *wafer.*

>> **x:** It doesn't really exist in Italian, with the difference that the few words derive mostly from Greek. Examples include **xenofobia** (kseh-noh-foh-*bee*-ah) *(xenophobia)* and **xilofono** (ksee-*loh*-foh-noh) *(xylophone).*

>> **y:** The letter y normally appears only in foreign words, like *yogurt, hobby,* and *yacht.*

# The consonant "c"

>> The Italian c has two sounds, depending on which letter follows it:

>> **Hard c:** When **c** is followed by **a, o, u,** or any consonant, you pronounce it as in the English word cat**.** We transcribe this as (k). Examples include **casa, colpa** (*kohl*-pah) *(guilt),* and **cuore** (*kwoh*-reh) *(heart).*

REMEMBER

To obtain the "k" sound before **e** and **i,** you must put an **h** between the **c** and the **e** or the **c** and the **i.** Examples include **che** (keh) *(what),* **Chianti** (*kyan*-tee) (a type of Italian red wine), and **Pinocchio** (pee-*nohk*-kyoh*) (Pinocchio*).

>> **Soft c:** When **c** is followed by **e** or **i,** you pronounce it as you do the first and last sound in the English word *church*; therefore, we give you the pronunciation (ch). Examples include **cena** (*cheh*-nah) *(dinner),* **città** (cheet-*tah*) *(city),* and **certo** (*chehr*-toh) *(certainly).*

REMEMBER

To obtain the "ch" sound before **a, o,** or **u,** you have to insert an i. This **i,** however, serves only to create the "ch" sound; you don't pronounce it. Examples include **ciambella** (chahm-*behl*-lah) *(donut),* **cioccolata** (chok-koh-*lah*-tah) *(chocolate),* and **ciuccio** (*chooch*-choh) *(baby's pacifier).*

This pronunciation scheme might seem terribly complicated, but in the end, it's not that difficult. Here another way to think about it — a little memory aid:

Follow this pattern:

C + i, e = pronounced like "ch"

C+ h, a, o, u, any other consonant = pronounced like "k"

# The consonant "g"

>> The Italian **g** follows the same pattern as the letter **c.** Therefore, we present it the same way:

>> **Hard g:** When **g** is followed by **a, o, u,** or any consonant, you pronounce it as you pronounce the **g** in the English word *good.* We transcribe this pronunciation as *(g).* Examples include **gamba** (*gahm*-bah) *(leg),* **gomma** (*gohm*-mah) *(rubber),* and **guerra** (*gwehr*-rah) *(war).*

REMEMBER

To obtain the "g" sound before **e** or **i,** you must put an **h** between the letter **g** and the **e** or **g** and i. Examples include **spaghetti** (spah-*geht*-tee) *(spaghetti),* **ghiaccio** (*gyahch*-choh) *(ice),* and **funghi** (*foohn*-gee) *(mushrooms).*

>> **Soft g:** When **g** is followed by **e** or **i,** you pronounce it as you do the first sound in the English word **job;** therefore, we give you the pronunciation as *(j).* Examples include **gentile** (jehn-*tee*-leh) *(kind),* **gita** (*jee*-tah) *(day trip),* and **gelato** (jeh-*lah*-toh) *(ice cream).*

To obtain the "j" sound before **a, o,** or **u,** you have to insert an **i.** The **i** serves only to indicate the proper sound; you don't pronounce it. Examples include **giacca** (*jahk*-kah) *(jacket),* **gioco** (*joh*-koh) *(game),* and **giudice** (*jooh*-dee-cheh) *(judge).*

Here's another little pattern to help you remember these pronunciations:

g + i, e = pronounced like "j"

g+ h, a, o, u, any other consonant = pronounced like "g"

## The consonant "h"

The consonant **h** has only one function: namely, to change the sound of **c** and **g** before the vowels **e** and **i.** It also appears in foreign words such as *hotel, hamburger,* and *hobby,* and in some forms of the conjugated verb **avere** (ah-*veh*-reh) *(to have),* but it's always silent.

## The consonant "q"

The consonant **q** exists only in combination with u followed by another vowel; that is, you always find **qu.** The **q** is pronounced like a hard **k,** and **qu** sounds like (kw), as in the English word *quick.* Examples include **quattro** (*kwaht*-troh) *(four),* **questo** (*kweh*-stoh) *(this),* and **quadro** (*kwah*-droh) *(picture, painting).*

## The consonant "r"

The Italian **r** isn't pronounced at the back of the mouth like in English but rolled or trilled at the *alveolar ridge* — the area right behind your front teeth. It takes practice. In the beginning, you may find this pronunciation tricky, but practice makes perfect!

Here are some words to help you practice:

>> **radio** (*rah*-dyoh) *(radio)*

>> **per favore** (pehr fah-*voh*-reh) *(please)*

>> **prego** (*preh*-goh) *(you're welcome)*

## The consonant "s"

The Italian **s** is sometimes pronounced like the English **s,** as in *so.* In this case, we give you the pronunciation as (s). Examples include **pasta** (*pah*-stah) *(pasta)* and **solo** (*soh*-loh) *(only).* In other cases, it's pronounced like the English **z,** as in *zero;*

in these cases, we list the pronunciation as (z). Examples include **chiesa** (*kyeh*-zah) (*church*), and **gelosia** (jeh-loh-*zee*-ah) (*jealousy*). The pronunciation depends on its position within a word and the surrounding letters. But don't worry too much — you'll naturally pick up the difference as you acquire more words and hear them spoken.

## The consonant "z"

A single **z** is pronounced (dz) — the sound is very similar to the English **z** in zoo, with a **d** added at the beginning, as in **zanzara** (*dzahn*-dzah-rah) (*mosquito*). Just try it. When the **z** is doubled, you pronounce it more sharply, like (t-ts), as in **tazza** (*taht*-tsah) (*cup; mug*). Furthermore, when **z** is followed by the letter **i,** it also has a ts sound, like in the word **nazione** (nah-*tsyoh*-neh) (*nation*).

## Double consonants

When you encounter double consonants in Italian, you have to pronounce each instance of the consonant or lengthen the sound. The difficult part is that there's no pause between the consonants.

Doubling the consonant usually changes the meaning of the word. So, to make sure that your Italian is understandable, emphasize doubled consonants well. To make you pronounce words with double consonants correctly, we write the first consonant at the end of one syllable and the other one at the beginning of the following one, as in these examples:

>> **nono** (*noh*-noh) (*ninth*)

>> **nonno** (*nohn*-noh) (*grandfather*)

>> **capello** (kah-*pehl*-loh) (*a single strand of hair*)

>> **cappello** (kahp-*pehl*-loh) (*hat*)

Try it once again:

>> **bello** (*behl*-loh) (*beautiful*)

>> **caffè** (kahf-*feh*) (*coffee*)

>> **occhio** (*ohk*-kyoh) (*eye*)

>> **spiaggia** (*spyahj*-jah) (*beach*)

## Consonant clusters

Certain consonant clusters have special sounds in Italian. Here they are:

>> **gn** is pronounced as the English "ny." The sound is actually the same as in a Spanish word I'm sure you know: **señorita** (seh-nyoh-*ree*-tah) *(miss)*, or better yet, an Italian word like **gnocchi** (*nyohk*-kee).

>> **gl**, when followed by "i," is pronounced in somewhat like the **-ill** in the English word *million* in words like **gli** (lyee) *(the)* and **famiglia** (fah-*mee*-lyah) *(family)*. Be careful not to pronounce it like the **gl** sound in *glue*.

>> **sc** follows the same rules of the soft and hard "c" from the previous section. It's pronounced as in the English scooter when it comes before **a, o, u, h** or *any other consonant* — that is, as in **scala** (*skah*-lah) *(staircase/ladder)*, **sconto** (*skohn*-toh) *(discount)*, and **scuola** (*skwoh*-lah) *(school)*. Before **e** and **i**, it's pronounced like the *sh* in *cash*. Examples of this pronunciation include **scena** (*sheh*-nah) *(scene)*, **discesa** (dee-*sheh*-zah) *(descent)*, and **scimmia** (*sheem*-myah) *(monkey)*.

# Kickstarting your Italian with keywords

Every language has expressions that you use so often that they almost become routine. For example, when you give something to somebody and he or she says, "Thank you," you automatically reply, "You're welcome!" This type of popular expression is an inseparable part of every language. When you know these expressions and how to use them, you're on the way to really speaking Italian.

**PLAY THIS**

The following are some of the most common popular expressions in Italian (Track 2):

>> **Buongiorno!** (bwohn-*johr*-noh) *(Good morning!)*

>> **Mi chiamo . . .** (mee *kyah*-moh) *(My name is . . .)*

>> **Non capisco!** (nohn kah-*pee*-skoh) *(I don't understand!)*

>> **Parla inglese?** (pahr-lah een-gleh-zeh) *(Do you speak English?)*

>> **Come si dice . . . ?** (koh-meh see *dee*-cheh) *(How do you say . . .?)*

>> **Cosa vuol dire . . . ?** (koh-zah vwohl *dee*-reh) *(What does . . . mean?)*

>> **Per favore/per piacere.** (pehr-fah-*voh*-reh/pehr pyah-*cheh*-reh) *(Please.)*

>> **Scusa!** (*skooh*-zah) *(Excuse me!)* (Informal)

>> **Scusi!** (*skooh*-zee) *(Excuse me!)* (Formal)

>> **Mi dispiace!** (mee dee-*spyah*-cheh) *(I'm sorry!)*

>> **Permesso?** (pehr-mehs-soh) *(May I pass/come in?)*

Italians use this expression when entering a room or when passing through a crowd.

>> **Andiamo!** (ahn-dyah-moh) *(Let's go!)*

>> **Va bene!** (vah beh-neh) *(Okay!)*

# Stressing Words Properly

Stress is the audible emphasis that you place on a syllable when speaking. In every word, one syllable is stressed more than the others. (Just a reminder: In this book we *italicize* the stressed syllable.)

Some words give you a hint as to where to place the stress: They have an accent grave (`) or acute (´) above the last vowel. Here are some examples:

>> **caffè** (kahf-*feh*) *(coffee)*

>> **città** (cheet-*tah*) *(city)*

>> **lunedì** (looh-neh-*dee*) *(Monday)*

>> **perché** (pehr-*keh*) *(why)*

>> **però** (peh-*roh*) *(but)*

>> **università** (ooh-nee-vehr-see-*tah*) *(university)*

>> **virtù** (veer-*tooh*) *(virtue)*

Written accents are used in Italian only if the accent is on the last vowel of the word. If there's no marked accent, it's not obvious which is the stressed syllable. A useful tip is that most Italian words have the stress on the next-to-last syllable.

>> The accent tells you where to stress the word.

>> Fortunately, only a few words are spelled the same way and only an accent distinguishes them. But this small difference can be a very important because the meaning of the word changes, as in the following example:

**e** (eh) *(and)* and **è** (eh) *(he/she/it is)* are distinguished only by the accent.

REMEMBER

# Chapter **2**
# Jumping Into the Basics of Italian

This chapter takes a look at some basic Italian grammar and leads you through the building blocks of sentences. Consider these blocks as challenging scaffolding that helps you to construct your sentences, piece by piece. In this chapter, we walk you through gender and number, as well as how to conjugate enough verbs to get you immediately on the road to communicating in Italian.

## Setting Up Simple Sentences

Becoming a fluent speaker of a foreign language takes a lot of work. Simply communicating or making yourself understood in another language is much easier. Even if you only know a few words, you can usually communicate successfully in common situations such as at a restaurant or a hotel.

Forming simple sentences is, well, simple. The basic sentence structure of Italian is subject–verb–object — the same as in English. Nouns in Italian are gender specific. In the following examples, you can see how this structure works:

>> **Carla parla inglese.** (*kahr*-lah *pahr*-lah een-*gleh*-zeh) *(Carla speaks English.)*

>> **Pietro ha una macchina.** (*pyeh*-troh ah *ooh*-nah *mahk*-kee-nah) *(Pietro has a car.)*

>> **L'Italia è un bel paese.** (lee-*tah*-lyah eh oohn behl pah-*eh*-zeh) *(Italy is a beautiful country.)*

# Dealing with Gender and Number (Articles, Nouns, and Adjectives)

Gender drives the construction of definite and indefinite articles, nouns, and adjectives. It is essential to learn the gender of nouns as soon as you encounter them, because that will determine what article and adjective you're going to use with them — these are all interconnected. Luckily most of this grammar follows some very cool schemata that you can plug in anywhere once you have it down. The more you commit these to memory, the easier it will be to effectively create sentences.

## Gender and number

All nouns have a specific gender (masculine or feminine) and number (singular or plural). Understanding these characteristics is essential for constructing and interpreting sentences, ensuring proper verb agreement and correctly using articles and adjectives. The good news is that nouns follow a predictable pattern. The following shows you how to form the singular and plural of masculine and feminine nouns. See if you can infer the rules just by looking at this chart.

| | | |
|---|---|---|
| Masculine nouns singular | **-o** (oh) | **un libro** (oohn *lee*-broh) *(a/one book)* |
| Feminine nouns singular | **-a** (ah) | **una casa** (*ooh*-nah *kah*-zah) *(a/one house)* |
| Masculine nouns plural | **-i** (ee) | **due libri** (*dooh*-eh *lee*-bree) *(two books)* |
| Feminine nouns plural | **-e** (eh) | **due case** (*dooh*-eh *kah*-zeh) *(two houses)* |

| Masculine/feminine nouns singular | **-e** (eh) | **un ristorante** (m) (oohn reeh-stoh-*rhan*-teh) (*a/one restaurant*)<br><br>**una stazione** (f) (*ooh*-nah stah- *tsyoh*-neh) (*a/one train station*) |
| Masculine/feminine nouns plural | **-i** (ee) | **due ristoranti** (*dooh*-eh reeh-stoh- *rhan*-tee) (*two restaurants*)<br><br>**due stazioni** (*dooh*-eh stah-*tsyoh*-nee) (*two train stations*) |

So, the rules are as follows:

>> Masculine nouns usually end in **-o** in the singular and **-i** in the plural.

>> Feminine nouns usually end in **-a** in the singular and **-e** in the plural.

>> Masculine and feminine nouns that end in -**e** in the singular, end in -**i** in the plural. It's a good idea to memorize the gender of these nouns.

   Any noun ending in **–ione** (like **nazione** [nah-*ts*yoh-neh]) is feminine.

TIP

That was pretty painless, wasn't it? Are you ready for some exceptions in the way of invariable nouns? These nouns only have one form: That is, they are the same in both the singular and plural forms. See if you can guess the rules for these as you go through the following bullets.

| | |
|---|---|
| **un caffè** (m) (oohn kahf-*feh*) (*one coffee*) | **due caffè** (*dooh*-eh kahf-*feh*) (*two coffees*) |
| **un bar** (m) (oohn bahr) (*one bar*) | **due bar** (*dooh*-eh bahr) (*two bars*) |
| **una bici** (f) (*ooh*-nah *bee*-chee) (*one bike*) | **due bici** (*dooh*-eh *bee*-chee) (*two bikes*) |

The rules for the three main types of invariable nouns follow:

>> Nouns that end in an accented final vowel, such as **caffè** and **città** (cheet-*tah*) (*city*), are invariable.

>> Nouns that end in a consonant (these are rare and usually come from English), such as **bar** and **film** (feelm) (*film, movie*) are invariable.

>> Nouns that are abbreviations, such as **bici** (*bee*-chee), **foto** (*foh*-toh) *(photo)*, and **cinema** (*chee*-neh-mah) *(movie theater)* are invariable. The full words **(bicicletta, fotografia, cinematografo),** when used, follow the standard rules for forming the plural of regular nouns.

## Indefinite articles

Did you notice that the **articoli indeterminativi** (lyee ahr-tee-*koh*-lee een-deh-tehr-meen-ah-*tee*-vee) for "one" or "a/an" precede all the previously mentioned nouns? They're always singular. Also, Italian indefinite articles agree in gender. And the one you choose also has to consider the first letter of the noun that it precedes. Table 2-1 shows you the indefinite articles, along with examples that show how they combine with masculine and feminine nouns.

**TABLE 2-1**  ## Indefinite Articles

| Maschili (mahs-*kee*-lee) *(Masculine)* | Femminili (fehm-meen-*nee*-lee) *(Feminine)* |
| --- | --- |
| **un ragazzo** (oohn rah-*gahts*-tsoh) *(a boy)* | **una ragazza** (*ooh*-nah rah-*gahts*-tsah) *(a girl)* |
| **un amico** (oohn ah-*mee*-koh) *(a [boy]friend)* | **un'amica** (oohn-ah-*mee*-kah) *(a [girl]friend)* |
| **uno zio** (*ooh*-noh *dzee*-oh) *(an uncle)* | **una zia** (*ooh*-nah *dzee*-ah) *(an aunt)* |
| **uno studente** (*ooh*-noh stooh-*dehn*-teh) *(a [male] student)* | **una studentessa** (*ooh*-nah stooh-dehn-*tehs*-sah) *(a [female] student)* |

Did you make a special note of the letters that the nouns begin with? So, the rules for indefinite articles go like this:

**un** before all masculine nouns beginning with vowels and consonants

**uno** before all masculine nouns beginning with **s+ consonant, z, gn, ps: zio** (*dzee*-oh) *(uncle)*; **gnomo** (*nyoh*-moh) *(gnome)*; **psicologo** (psee-*koh*-loh-goh); **studente** (stooh-*dehn*-teh) *(student)*

**una** before all feminine nouns beginning with a consonant

**un'** before all feminine nouns beginning with a vowel

## Definite articles

Of course, you don't go around talking about singular things all the time. In English the definite article has only one form *the.* Italian is one of those languages that require a definite article before the noun in most cases and differs from English usage. For example, you need to use the definite article before the names of certain countries and geographical areas. If you want to say, "Sicily is interesting," you need to precede Sicily with an article: **"La Sicilia è interessante"** (lah see-*chee*-lyah eh een-teh-rehs-*sahn*-teh). The same goes for nouns that refer to universal concepts or general categories: "Love is blind" **(L'amore è cieco)** (lah-*moh*-reh eh *cheh*-koh) or "Flowers are beautiful" **(I fiori sono belli.)** (ee *fyoh*-ree *soh*-noh *behl*-lee).

Table 2-2 shows the list of articles that you should try to commit to memory. As you can see, the Italian definite articles have different forms depending on the number and gender of the nouns they precede. Just like with the indefinite articles, the letter that starts the noun also determines what article to use.

**TABLE 2-2**    **Definite Articles (Articoli determinativi) (ahr-*tee*-koh-lee deh-tehr-mee-nah-*tee*-vee)**

| Maschili (mahs-*kee*-lee) *(Masculine)* | | Femminili (fehm-mee-*nee*-lee) *(Feminine)* | |
| --- | --- | --- | --- |
| Singular | Plural | Singular | Plural |
| **lo** *(loh)* | **gli** *(lyee)* | **l'** *(l)* | **le** *(leh)* |
| **l'** | | **la** *(lah)* | |
| **il** *(eel)* | **i** *(ee)* | | |

Here are some examples of definite articles. Can you identify a pattern?

> **lo zio/gli zii** (loh *dzee*-oh, lyee *dzee*-ee) *(uncle, uncles)* **lo studente, gli studenti** (loh stooh-*dehn*-teh, lyee stooh-*dehn*-tee) *(student, students)* **l'amico/gli amici** (lah-*mee*-koh, lyee ah-*mee*-keh) *(male friend, friends)*
>
> **il libro/i libri** (eel *lee*-broh, ee *lee*-bree) *(book, books)*
>
> **l'amica/le amiche** (lah-*mee*-kah, leh ah-*mee*-keh) *(female friend, friends)*
>
> **la casa/le case** (lah *kah*-zah/leh *kah*-zeh) *(house, houses)*

## Adjectives

The gender feature of nouns extends to other grammatical categories, including pronouns and adjectives. First, we look at the adjectives.

An adjective is a word that modifies a noun — whether a person, a thing, a place, or idea — giving the noun a specific quality or characteristic. (You can read more about adjectives in Chapters 3, 8, and 16.) There are two groups of adjectives in Italian:

>> The first group has four endings: masculine, singular **-o,** masculine plural **-i,** feminine singular **-a,** feminine plural **-e.** See how the adjective **italiano** (ee-tah-*lyah*-noh) *(Italian)* works in these four forms:

- **il ragazzo italiano** (eel rah-*gahts*-tsoh ee-tah-*lyah*-noh) *(the Italian boy)*

- **i ragazzi italiani** (ee rah-*gahts*-tsee ee-tah-*lyah*-nee) *(the Italian boys)*

- **la ragazza italiana** (lah rah-*gahts*-tsah ee-tah-*lyah*-nah) *(the Italian girl)*

- **le ragazze italiane** (leh rah-*gahts*-tseh ee-tah-*lyah*-neh) *(the Italian girls)*

>> The second group has two endings: the masculine and feminine singular form ends in **-e,** the masculine and feminine plural form ends in **-i** forms. See how the adjective **interessante** (een-teh-rehs-*sahn*-teh) *(interesting)* works:

- **il libro interessante** (eel *lee*-broh een-teh-rehs-*sahn*-teh) *(the interesting book)*

- **i libri interessanti** (ee *lee*-bree een-teh-rehs-*sahn*-tee) *(the interesting books)*

- **l'amica interessante** (lah- *mee*-kah een-teh-rehs-*sahn*-teh) *(the interesting friend)*

- **le amiche interessanti** (leh ah-*mee*-keh een-teh-rehs-*sahn*-tee) *(the interesting friends)*

In Italian, the position of the adjective isn't as rigid as it is in English. In most cases, the adjective follows the noun. Nevertheless, there are some adjectives which can precede the noun, such as **bello** (*behl*–loh) *(beautiful)*, **buono** (*bwoh*–noh) *(good)*, and **cattivo** (kaht–*tee*–voh) *(bad)*.

## WORDS TO KNOW

| | | |
|---|---|---|
| **ristorante [m]** | reeh-stoh-*rahn*-teh | *restaurant* |
| **ragazzo/a [m/f]** | rah-*gaht*-tsoh/tsah | *boy/girl* |
| **studente [m]** | stooh-*dehn*-teh | *student (male)* |
| **studentessa [f]** | stooh-dehn-*tehs*-sah | *student (female)* |
| **zio/a [m/f]** | *dzee*-oh/ah | *uncle/aunt* |
| **casa [f]** | *kah*-zah | *house/home* |

| libro [m] | *lee*-broh | *book* |
|---|---|---|
| amica [f/sing.] | ah-*mee*-kah | *girlfriend* |
| amiche [f/pl.] | ah-*mee*-keh | *girlfriends* |
| amico [m/sing.] | ah-*mee*-koh | *friend (male)* |
| amici [m/pl.] | ah-*mee*-chee | *male friends or mixed gender friends* |
| caffè (m) | kahf-*feh* | *coffee* |
| bici (f) | *bee*-chee | *bike* |

# Talking about Pronouns

A pronoun replaces, as the word itself says, a noun. When you talk about Jim, for example, you can replace his name with *he.* You often use pronouns to avoid repetition. Here we delve deeper into what you need to know about pronouns.

## Personal pronouns

Several types of personal pronouns exist. The most important ones for you are the subject pronouns, which refer to *I, you, he, she, it, we,* or *they.* Every verb form refers to one of these pronouns, as the following section points out. Table 2-3 lists the subject pronouns.

**TABLE 2-3**

### Subject Pronouns

| Pronoun | Pronunciation | Translation |
|---|---|---|
| **io** | *ee*-oh | *I* |
| **tu** | tooh | *you* |
| **lui** | *looh*-ee | *he/it* |
| **lei** | ley | *she/it* |
| **noi** | noi | *we* |
| **voi** | voi | *you (all)* |
| **loro** | *loh*-roh | *they* |

Italians often drop subject pronouns because the verb ending shows what the subject is. Use a personal pronoun only for contrast, for emphasis, or when the pronoun stands alone:

>> Contrast: **Tu mangi la pizza, ma io mangio un panino.** (tooh *mahn*-jee lah *peets*-tsah, mah *ee*-oh m*ahn*-joh oohn pah-*neeh*-noh) *(You're eating pizza, but I am eating a sandwich.)*

>> Emphasis: **Vieni anche tu alla festa?** (*vyeh*-nee *ahn*-keh tooh *ahl*-lah *feh*-stah) *(Are you coming to the party, too?)*

>> Isolated position: **"Chi è?" "Sono io."** (kee eh *soh*-noh *ee*-oh) *("Who's there?" "It's me.")*

## Saying "you": Formal and informal

You probably already know that many foreign languages contain both formal and informal ways of addressing people. If you didn't know before, now you do! In Italian, you need to respect this important characteristic. Use the informal pronoun **tu** (tooh) *(you)* with good friends, young people, children, and your family members. However, when you speak to a person you don't know well (a superior, shopkeeper, server, teacher, professor, and so on), address them formally — that is, with **lei** (ley) *(you)*. When you become more familiar with someone, you may change from formal to informal. According to custom, the elder person initiates the use of **tu.**

**Tu** requires the verb form of the second person singular — for example, **tu sei** (tooh sey) *(you are)*. **Lei** requires the verb form of the third person singular — **lei è** (ley eh) *(you are [formal singular])*.

The following examples show the two forms of you:

>> **Tu,** you informal: **Ciao, come stai?** (chow *koh*-meh stahy?) *(Hi, how are you?)*

>> **Lei,** you formal: **Buongiorno, come sta?** (bwohn-*johr*-noh *koh*-meh stah) *(Good morning, how are you?)*

## Being inclusive? Still a long way to go . . .

Italian is a gendered language, so knowing which nouns are masculine or feminine and then making sure adjectives agree accordingly in order to communicate effectively is important. Despite pressure from advocacy groups to adopt gender-neutral pronouns and endings for nouns and adjectives, no official steps have been taken so far to implement these changes.

In certain areas of the United States, however, especially in inclusive schools and universities, people more frequently express their preferred pronoun according to the gender with which they identify (*she, her, hers*; *he, his, his*; *they, their, theirs*). Although this practice isn't as common in Italy yet as it is in the United States, some schools have launched something called *carriera ALIAS,* which encourages students and faculty to declare their pronoun preference by choosing between **lui** and **lei** (but not **loro**).

When students choose *they, their, theirs* as pronouns, you may ask them to choose between masculine and feminine endings in the Italian classroom because otherwise verb and adjective agreement just doesn't work. The asterisk * or the *schwa* that many Italianists in the United States use is an effective way to get around privileging one gender over the other when writing to a group of people.

# Exploring Verbs

There seems to be an infinite number of verbs in Italian. They truly are the glue to bind the different parts of speech together. Some people try to get by using only infinitives (the verbs before you conjugate them), but we want you to make sense and feel confident when speaking, so study the regular and irregular verbs patterns in this chapter (and also Appendix B), and you'll be on your way to speaking in the present, past, and future tenses. Getting a good handle on them gives you a solid basis from which to build your sentences, communicate, and be understood!

## Introducing regular and irregular verbs

What's the difference between regular and irregular verbs? Regular verbs follow a certain pattern in their conjugation: They behave the same way as other verbs in the same category. Therefore, you can predict a regular verb's form in any part of any tense. On the other hand, you can't predict irregular verbs in this way — they behave a bit like individualists.

### Regular verbs

You can divide Italian verbs into three categories, according to their ending in the infinitive form. They are, **-are,** as in **parlare** (pahr-*lah*-reh) *(to speak)*; **-ere,** as in **vivere** (*vee*-veh-reh) *(to live)*; and **-ire,** as in **partire** (pahr-*tee*-reh) *(to leave)*. Verbs in these categories can be regular as well as irregular. Notice the subject pronouns that go with the verbs: We place them here to remind you which verb form you need.

These translate in the present tense as, for example: *I speak, I do speak, I am speaking, I'm going to speak* (if it's not too much in the future) — it depends on the context. We translate the first person of all of the verbs that follow: the other persons follow suit.

The following shows you the conjugation of three regular verbs:

| Conjugation | Pronunciation | Translation |
| --- | --- | --- |
| **parl-are** | pahr-*lah*-reh | *to speak* |
| **io parlo** | ee-oh *pahr*-loh | *I speak, I do speak, I'm speaking* |
| **tu parli** | tooh *pahr*-lee | |
| **lui/lei parla** | *looh*-ee/ley *pahr*-lah | |
| **noi parliamo** | noi pahr-*lyah*-moh | |
| **voi parlate** | voi pahr-*lah*-teh | |
| **loro parlano** | *loh*-roh *pahr*-lah-noh | |
| **viv-ere** | *vee*-veh-reh | *to live* |
| **io vivo** | ee-oh *vee*-voh | *I live, I do live, I'm living* |
| **tu vivi** | tooh *vee*-vee | |
| **lui/lei vive** | *looh*-ee/ley *vee*-veh | |
| **noi viviamo** | noi vee-*vyah*-moh | |
| **voi vivete** | voi vee-*veh*-teh | |
| **loro vivono** | *loh*-roh *vee*-voh-noh | |
| **part-ire** | pahr-*tee*-reh | *to leave, to depart* |
| **io parto** | ee-oh *pahr*-toh | *I leave, I do leave, I am leaving* |
| **tu parti** | tooh *pahr*-tee | |
| **lui/lei parte** | *looh*-ee/ley *pahr*-teh | |
| **noi partiamo** | noi pahr-*tyah*-moh | |
| **voi partite** | voi pahr-*tee*-teh | |
| **loro partono** | *loh*-roh *pahr*-toh-noh | |

You can apply these patterns to every regular verb, such as **arrivare** (ahr-ree-*vah*-reh) *(to arrive)*, **ascoltare** (ahs-kohl-*tah*-reh) *(to listen to)*, **ripetere** (ree-*peh*-teh-reh) *(to repeat)*, **prendere** (*prehn*-deh-reh) *(to take or to have when ordering in a restaurant)*, and **aprire** (ah-*pree*-reh) *(to open)*. Some regular verbs behave a bit differently, but this doesn't render them irregular. For some -ire verbs you insert the letters -isc- between the root and the ending (for all persons except **noi** and **voi**), as in this example of **capire** (kah-*pee*-reh) *(to understand)*:

| Conjugation | Pronunciation | Translation |
| --- | --- | --- |
| **io capisco** | *ee*-oh kah-*pee*-skoh | *I understand, I do understand, I am understanding* |
| **tu capisci** | tooh kah-*pee*-shee | |
| **lui/lei capisce** | *looh*-ee/ley kah-*pee*-sheh | |
| **noi capiamo** | noi kah-*pyah*-moh | |
| **voi capite** | voi kah-*pee*-teh | |
| **loro capiscono** | *loh*-roh kah-*pee*-skoh-noh | |

Other verbs that behave similarly are **finire** (fee-*nee*-reh) *(to finish, end)* and **preferire** (preh-feh-*ree*-reh) *(to prefer)*. For more verbs that follow this -isc- pattern, check out Appendix A, and for lots more on Italian verbs in general, pick up a copy of *Italian Verbs For Dummies* by Teresa (John Wiley & Sons, Inc.).

## Irregular verbs

Irregular verbs don't follow the standard conjugation patterns of regular verbs ending in -are, -ere, or –ire.

### AVERE AND ESSERE

Two important verbs, which you often use as helping verbs, are irregular — **avere** (ah-*veh*-reh) *(to have)* and **essere** (*ehs*-seh-reh) *(to be)*.

| Conjugation | Pronunciation | Translation |
| --- | --- | --- |
| **avere** | ah-*veh*-reh | *to have* |
| **io ho** | *ee*-oh oh | *I have, I do have* |
| **tu hai** | tooh ahy | |
| **lui/lei ha** | *looh*-ee/ley ah | |

| Conjugation | Pronunciation | Translation |
| --- | --- | --- |
| **noi abbiamo** | noi ahb-*byah*-moh | |
| **voi avete** | voi ah-*veh*-teh | |
| **loro hanno** | *loh*-roh *ahn*-noh | |
| **essere** | *ehs*-seh-reh | *to be* |
| **io sono** | *ee*-oh *soh*-noh | *I am* |
| **tu sei** | tooh sey | |
| **lui/lei è** | *looh*-ee/ley eh | |
| **noi siamo** | noi *syah*-moh | |
| **voi siete** | voi *syeh*-teh | |
| **loro sono** | *loh*-roh *soh*-noh | |

# Talkin' the Talk

Cindy is visiting Florence for the first time. She's gotten lost, and so she asks a traffic cop, a **vigile urbano** (*vee*-jee-leh oohr-*bah*-noh), how to find her hotel. (Track 3)

**PLAY THIS**

Cindy:     **Scusi, ho una domanda.**
*skooh*-zee oh *ooh*-nah doh-*mahn*-dah
*Excuse me, I have a question.*

            **Parla inglese?**
*pahr*-lah een-*gleh*-zeh
*Do you speak English?*

Vigile:     **No, ma Lei parla italiano!**
noh mah ley *pahr*-lah ee-tah-*lyah*-noh
*No, but you speak Italian!*

Cindy:     **Parlo poco ma capisco di più.**
*pahr*-loh *poh*-koh mah kah-*pee*-koh dee pyooh
*I speak a little, but I understand more.*

            **Mi sono persa.**
mee *soh*-noh *pehr*-sah
*I'm lost.*

| Vigile: | **Dove deve andare?** |
| | *doh*-veh *deh*-veh ahn-*dah*-reh |
| | *Where do you need to go?* |
| Cindy: | **Non posso trovare il mio albergo.** |
| | nohn *pohs*-soh troh-*vah*-reh il *mee*-oh ahl-*behr*-goh |
| | *I can't find my hotel.* |
| Vigile: | **Ha una piantina di Firenze?** |
| | ah *ooh*-nah pyahn-*tee*-nah dee fee-*rehn*-tseh |
| | *Do you have a map of Florence?* |
| Cindy: | **Si, ecco quella che ho.** |
| | see *ehk*-koh-kwel-lah keh oh |
| | *Yes, here's what I have.* |

**TIP**

**Ecco!** (*ehk*–koh) (*Here you go! Here it is!*) is used only when pointing something out. You frequently hear this expression in a hotel: **Ecco la sua chiave** (*ehk*–koh lah *sooh*–ah *kyah*–veh) (*Here is your key*), and in a bar: **Ecco i due cappuccini!** (*ehk*–koh ee *dooh*–eh kahp–pooh–*chee*–nee) (*Here are the two cappuccinos!*).

### IDIOMATIC USES OF AVERE

Even though the verb **avere** means *to have*, it's frequently after *to be hungry, to be thirsty, to be hot, to be cold, to be a certain age*. In Italian, these terms literally mean to have hunger, to have thirst, to have heat, to have years. Table 2-4 lists some common idiomatic expressions with **avere.**

**TABLE 2-4**

## Idiomatic Uses of Avere

| Expression | Pronunciation | Translation |
|---|---|---|
| **avere fame** | ah-*veh*-reh *fah*-meh | *to be hungry* |
| **avere sete** | ah-*veh*-reh *seh*-teh | *to be thirsty* |
| **avere caldo** | ah-*veh*-reh *kahl*-doh | *to be hot* |
| **avere freddo** | ah-*veh*-reh *frehd*-doh | *to be cold* |
| **avere sonno** | ah-*veh*-reh *sohn*-noh | *to be sleepy* |
| **avere voglia di** | ah-*veh*-reh *vohl*-yah dee | *to feel like, to have a craving for* |
| **avere bisogno di** | ah-*veh*-reh bee-*zoh*-nyoh dee | *to need/to need to* |

*(continued)*

| Expression | Pronunciation | Translation |
|---|---|---|
| **avere torto** | ah-*veh*-reh *tohr*-toh | *to be wrong* |
| **avere ragione** | ah-*veh*-reh rah-*joh*-neh | *to be right* |
| **avere . . . anni** | ah-*veh*-reh *ahn*-nee | *to be . . . years old* |

### MORE COMMON IRREGULAR VERBS

Other common irregular verbs are **andare** (ahn-*dah*-reh) (*to go*), **venire** (veh-*nee*-reh) (*to come*), **dire** (*dee*-reh) (*to say or tell*), **fare** (*fah*-reh) (*to do or make*), **dare** (*dah*-reh) (*to give*), and **uscire** (ooh-*shee*-reh) (*to go out*):

| Conjugation | Pronunciation | Translation |
|---|---|---|
| **andare** | ahn-*dah*-reh | *to go* |
| **io vado** | *ee*-oh *vah*-doh | *I go, I do go, I'm going* |
| **tu vai** | tooh vahy | |
| **lui/lei va** | *looh*-ee/ley vah | |
| **noi andiamo** | noi ahn-*dyah*-moh | |
| **voi andate** | voi ahn-*dah*-teh | |
| **loro vanno** | *loh*-roh *vahn*-noh | |
| **venire** | veh-*nee*-reh | *to come* |
| **io vengo** | *ee*-oh *vehn*-goh | *I come, I do come, I'm coming* |
| **tu vieni** | tooh *vyeh*-nee | |
| **lui/lei viene** | *looh*-ee/ley *vyeh*-neh | |
| **noi veniamo** | noi veh-*nyah*-moh | |
| **voi venite** | voi veh-*nee*-teh | |
| **loro vengono** | *loh*-roh *vehn*-goh-noh | |
| **dire** | *dee*-reh | *to say or tell* |
| **io dico** | *ee*-oh *dee*-koh | *I say, I do say, I'm saying* |
| **tu dici** | tooh *dee*-chee | |
| **lui/lei dice** | *looh*-ee/ley *dee*-cheh | |
| **noi diciamo** | noi dee-*chah*-moh | |

| Conjugation | Pronunciation | Translation |
| --- | --- | --- |
| **voi dite** | voi *dee*-teh | |
| **loro dicono** | *loh*-roh *dee*-koh-noh | |
| **fare** | *fah*-reh | *to do or make* |
| **io faccio** | ee-oh *fahch*-choh | *I make, I do make, I'm making* |
| **tu fai** | tooh fahy | |
| **lui/lei fa** | *looh*-ee/ley fah | |
| **noi facciamo** | noi fahch-*chah*-moh | |
| **voi fate** | voi *fah*-teh | |
| **loro fanno** | *loh*-roh *fahn*-noh | |

Like the verb **avere,** Table 2–5 shows that the verb **fare** (*fah*–reh) (*to do or make*) has some interesting idiomatic uses that don't translate word for word.

**TABLE 2-5**     ## Idiomatic Uses of Fare

| Expression | Pronunciation | Translation |
| --- | --- | --- |
| **fare una domanda** | *fah*-reh *ooh*-nah doh-*mahn*-dah | *to ask a question* |
| **fare una passeggiata** | *fah*-reh *ooh*-nah pahs-sehj-*jah*-tah | *to take a walk/to go for a walk* |
| **fare un giro** | *fah*-reh oohn *jee*-roh | *to go for a ride* |
| **fare una foto/un selfie** | *fah*-reh *ooh*-nah *foh*-toh oohn *sehl*-fee | *to take a picture/a selfie* |
| **fare colazione** | *fah*-reh koh-lah-*tsyoh*-neh | *to have breakfast* |
| **fare la spesa/lo shopping** | *fah*-reh lah *speh*-zah/loh *shohp*-peeng | *to go grocery shopping/shopping* |
| **fare bel/cattivo tempo** | *fah*-reh behl kaht-*tee*-voh *tehm*-poh | *to be nice/bad (for weather)* |
| **fare caldo/freddo** | *fah*-reh *kahl*-doh *frehd*-doh | *to be hot/cold out* |

Note that weather expressions that use **fare** are conjugated impersonally in the third person singular. In this context, **fa** in the expression **fa bel tempo,** simply means *it is*, where *it* stands for the weather.

Here are a few more irregular verbs:

| Conjugation | Pronunciation | Translation |
| --- | --- | --- |
| **dare** | *dah*-reh | *to give* |
| **io do** | doh | *I give, I do give, I'm giving* |
| **tu dai** | dahy | |
| **lui/lei dà** | *looh*-ee/ley dah | |
| **noi diamo** | noi *dyah*-moh | |
| **voi date** | voi *dah*-teh | |
| **loro danno** | *loh*-roh *dahn*-noh | |
| **uscire** | ooh-*shee*-reh | *to go out, to exit, to leave the house* |
| **io esco** | *ee*-oh *eh*-skoh | *I go out, I do go out, I'm going out* |
| **tu esci** | tooh *eh*-shee | |
| **lui/lei esce** | *looh*-ee/ley *ehsh*-eh | |
| **noi usciamo** | noi ooh-*shah*-moh | |
| **voi uscite** | voi ooh-*shee*-teh | |
| **loro escono** | *loh*-roh *eh*-skoh-noh | |

# Talkin' the Talk

**PLAY THIS**

Fabio has just called Giacomo to chat and catch up on things. (Track 4)

**Fabio:** **Ciao Giacomo, sono Fabio.**
chow *jah*-koh-moh *soh*-noh *fah*-byoh
*Hi Giacomo, it's Fabio.*

**Giacomo:** **Ciao Fabio, come va?**
chow *fah*-byoh koh-*meh* vah
*Hi Fabio, how's it going?*

**Fabio:** **Benone! Studio molto in questi giorni.**
beh-*noh*-neh *stooh*-dyoh *mohl*-toh een *kweh*-stee *johr*-nee
*Great! I'm studying a lot these days.*

**Giacomo:** **Cosa fai stasera?**
*koh*-zah fahy stah-*seh*-rah
*What are you doing tonight?*

| Fabio: | **Esco con Anna. Prima facciamo una passeggiata e poi andiamo a fare la spesa.** |
|---|---|

*eh*-skoh kohn *ahn*-nah *preeh*-mah fahch-*chah*-moh *ooh*-na pahs-seh-*jah*-tah eh poi ahn-*dyah*-moh ah fah-reh lah *speh*-zah

*I'm going out with Anna. First we are going for a walk and then we are going grocery shopping.*

| Giacomo: | **Dove andate dopo?** |
|---|---|

*doh*-ve ahn-*dah*-te *doh*-poh

*Where are you going afterwards?*

| Fabio: | **Se fa bello, andiamo a mangiare in campagna.** |
|---|---|

seh fah *behl*-loh ahn-*dyah*-moh ah mahn-*jah*-reh een kahm-*pah*-nyah

*If the weather is nice, we're going to eat in the countryside.*

**Perché non venite anche tu e Daniela?**

pehr-*keh* nohn veh-*nee*-teh ahn-keh tooh eh dahn-yeh-lah

*Why don't you and Daniela come?*

| Giacomo: | **Buona idea! Vedo anche cosa dice Daniela.** |
|---|---|

*bwoh*-nah ee-*deh*-ah *veh*-dho *ahn*-keh *koh*-zah *dee*-cheh dhan-*yeh*-lah

*Good idea! I'll see what Daniela says.*

| Fabio: | **D'accordo — ciao, a dopo!** |
|---|---|

dahk-*kohr*-doh chow ah *doh*-poh

*Okay — see you later!*

# Having to, wanting to, being able to

Three modal verbs — **dovere** (doh–*veh*–reh) (*to have to, must*), **volere** (voh–*leh*–reh) (*to want*), **potere** (poh–*teh*–reh) (*to be able to, can, may*) — are kind of like helping verbs. When conjugated, they're often followed by the infinitive of another verb. For example:

>> **Devo fare la spesa.** (*deh*-voh *fah*-reh lah *speh*-zah) (*I have to go grocery shopping.*)

>> **Voglio dormire!** (*voh*-lyoh dohr-*mee*-reh) (*I want to sleep!*)

>> **Posso andare a bere?** (*pohs*-soh ahn-*dah*-reh ah *beh*-reh) (*May I go get a drink?*)

| Conjugation | Pronunciation | Translation |
| --- | --- | --- |
| **dovere** | doh-*veh*-reh | *to have to, must* |
| **io devo** | io *deh*-voh | *I have to, I must* |
| **tu devi** | tooh *deh*-vee | |
| **lui/lei deve** | *looh*-ee/ley *deh*-veh | |
| **noi dobbiamo** | noi dohb-*byah*-moh | |
| **voi dovete** | voi doh-*veh*-teh | |
| **loro devono** | *loh*-roh *deh*-voh-noh | |
| **volere** | voh-*leh*-reh | *to want* |
| **io voglio** | io *voh*-lyoh | *I want, I do want* |
| **tu vuoi** | tooh vwoi | |
| **lui/lei vuole** | *looh*-ee/ley *vwoh*-leh | |
| **noi vogliamo** | noi voh-*lyah*-moh | |
| **voi volete** | voi voh-*leh*-teh | |
| **loro vogliono** | *loh*-roh voh-*lyoh*-noh | |
| **potere** | poh-*teh*-reh | *to be able to, can, may* |
| **io posso** | ee-oh *pohs*-soh | *I'm able to, I can, I may* |
| **tu puoi** | tooh pwoi | |
| **lui/lei può** | *looh*-ee/ley pwoh | |
| **noi possiamo** | noi pohs-*syah*-moh | |
| **voi potete** | voi poh-*teh*-teh | |
| **loro possono** | *loh*-roh *pohs*-soh-noh | |

# Presenting the Simple Tenses: Past, Present, and Future

Clearly, people don't use just one tense. You may want to talk about what you did yesterday or what you're doing now or what you're going to do tomorrow. These four tenses — past, imperfect, present, and future — aren't advanced grammar — just basic stuff:

>> **Present tense:** This tense is used to describe an action that is happening now. Chapter 11 examines this tense in greater detail.

**Mangio un gelato.** (*mahn*-joh oohn jeh-*lah*-toh) *(I am eating/I eat an ice cream.)*

>> **Future tense:** This tense is used to describe actions that will happen later. Chapter 10 explores this tense in greater detail.

**Domani mangerò un gelato.** (doh-*mah*-nee mahn-*jeh*-roh oohn jeh-*lah*-toh) *(Tomorrow I'm going to eat an ice cream.)*

>> **Present perfect:** Use the present perfect to talk about a completed action in the past. Chapter 10 addresses this tense in greater detail.

**Ieri ho mangiato un gelato.** (*yeh*-ree oh mahn-*jah*-toh oohn jeh-*lah*-toh) *(Yesterday I ate an ice-cream.)*

>> **Imperfect tense:** This tense is used to describe how things were in the past like habits, ongoing situations, or background details. Most verbs in the imperfect tense follow a regular pattern. Chapter 17 discusses this tense in greater detail.

**Il gelato era buono.** (eel -jeh-*lah*-toh *eh*-rah *bwoh*-noh) *(The ice cream was good.)*

# Talkin' the Talk

Marco and Lucia are making possible plans for this evening.

**Marco:** **Ciao Lucia, cosa vuoi fare stasera?**
chow loo-*chee*-ah *koh*-zah vwoi *fah*-reh stah-*seh*-rah
*Hi Lucia, what do you want to do tonight?*

**Lucia:** **Vorrei andare al cinema, ma devo finire un progetto per domani.**
*vohr*-rey ahn-*dah*-reh ahl *chee*-neh-mah mah *deh*-voh fee-*nee*-reh oohn proh-*jeht*-toh pehr doh-*mah*-nee
*I'd like to go to the movies, but I have to finish a project for tomorrow.*

**Marco:** **Peccato! Allora, possiamo uscire domani?**
pehk-*kaht*-toh ahl-loh-rah pohs-*syah*-moh ooh-*shee*-reh doh-*mah*-nee
*That's too bad! Then, can we go out tomorrow?*

*(continued)*

*(continued)*

| Lucia: | **Sì, domani posso. A che ora?** |
|---|---|
| | see doh-*mah*-nee *pohs*-soh ah keh oh-rah |
| | *Yes, tomorrow I can. At what time?* |

| Marco: | **Possiamo vederci alle otto?** |
|---|---|
| | pohs-*syah*-moh veh-dehr-chee *ahl*-leh *oht*-toh |
| | *Can we meet at eight?* |

| Lucia: | **Perfetto!** |
|---|---|
| | pehr-*feht*-toh |
| | *Perfect!* |

## WORDS TO KNOW

| | | |
|---|---|---|
| **albergo [m]** | ahl-*behr*-goh | *hotel* |
| **piantina [f]** | pyahn-*tee*-nah | *map* |
| **gelato [m]** | jeh-*lah*-toh | *ice-cream* |
| **va bene** | vah *beh*-neh | *okay* |
| **d'accordo** | dahk-*kohr*-doh | *okay, agreed* |
| **ciao** | chow | *hi/bye* |
| **mi piace** | mee *pyah*-cheh | *I like (something singular)* |
| **mi piacciono** | mee *pyahch*-choh-noh | *I like (something plural)* |
| **anch'io** | ahn-*kee*-oh | *I also, me too* |
| **domanda [f]** | doh-*mahn*-dah | *question* |
| **stasera** | stah-*seh*-rah | *tonight* |
| **dove** | *doh*-veh | *where* |
| **quanti anni ha** | *kwahn*-tee *ahn*-nee ah | *how old is . . .?* |

# FUN & GAMES

The following contains several Italian words that we introduced in this chapter. Just find and circle the words from the list! See Appendix C for the answer key.

```
A  R  Q  D  R  P  U  F  C  M  N  D
V  O  L  E  R  E  A  A  T  G  H  O
E  S  A  D  H  C  O  M  L  Z  E  V
R  S  D  B  I  F  E  E  S  A  M  E
E  O  I  L  P  A  R  T  I  R  E  R
T  B  E  W  E  R  N  R  D  I  R  E
O  D  A  L  B  E  R  G  O  E  S  T
Z  S  M  Q  C  F  V  G  V  S  L  R
I  C  I  B  A  X  E  T  E  S  U  M
O  A  C  S  R  Z  K  R  D  E  B  O
T  P  A  U  S  A  E  U  P  R  A  D
U  I  T  A  L  I  A  N  O  E  J  L
F  R  A  G  A  Z  Z  A  N  T  K  A
Y  E  N  D  Q  U  A  L  R  I  L  C
```

| | |
|---|---|
| albergo | facile |
| amica | fame |
| avere | fare |
| bici | italiano |
| caldo | partire |
| capire | pausa |
| dire | ragazza |
| dove | rosso |
| dovere | sete |
| esame | volere |
| essere | zio |

*© John Wiley & Sons, Inc.*

# Chapter **3**

# Buongiorno Italia!

**B**uongiorno! (bwohn-*johr*-noh) *(Hello!)*

Have you ever counted the number of times you say hello in a single day? You probably say it more often than you realize. When you interact with people, you usually begin with a greeting — and that greeting can have an impact on the first impression you give. This chapter explains how to say hello and good-bye as well as how to follow up a greeting with some basic small talk.

## Looking at Common Greetings and Farewells

Italians like to have social contact and meet new people. Generally, they're easy-going and receptive to people trying to speak their language. At the same time, they tend to be very respectful and polite. Chapter 2 explores the differences between **tu** and **lei** when addressing someone in Italian.

A key aspect of Italian culture is the distinction between formal and informal speech. The way you greet someone depends on your relationship with them.

To give you a good start in greeting people in Italian, we want you to familiarize with the most common greetings and good-byes, followed by examples.

- **Ciao** (chow) *(Hello and good-bye)* (informal)

- **Salve** (*sahl*-veh) *(Hello and good-bye)*

  **Salve,** neutral, but more formal than **Ciao,** is a relic from Latin. In Caesar's time, the Romans used it a lot.

- **Buongiorno** (bwohn *johr*-noh) *(Good morning)*

  **Buongiorno** (Literally: Good day) is the most formal greeting. Whenever you're in doubt, use this word (if it's before 2 p.m.). You frequently hear it when you enter an Italian shop.

- **Buonasera** (*bwoh*-nah-*seh*-rah) *(Good afternoon; good evening)* (formal)

  You use **buonasera** after 2 p.m. to say both hello and good-bye. Just mind the time of day!

- **Buonanotte** (*bwoh*-nah-*noht*-teh) *(Good-night)*

  Use only when parting for the night and going to bed.

- **Buona giornata!** (*bwoh*-nah johr-*nah*-tah) *(Have a good day!)*

  You often use this phrase when you're leaving somebody or saying goodbye on the phone.

- **Buona serata!** (*bwoh*-nah seh-*rah*-tah) *(Have a good evening!)*

  Like **buona giornata,** you use **buona serata** when you're leaving someone or saying good-bye on the phone, if that person is your friend. The difference is that you use **buona serata,** according to Italian custom, after 2 p.m.

- **Arrivederci** (ahr-ree-veh-*dehr*-chee) *(Good-bye)*

## Replying to a greeting

When you reply to a greeting in English, you often say "How are you?" as a way of saying "Hello" — you don't expect an answer. In Italian, however, that's not the case; you answer back. Here are common ways to reply to particular greetings, formally and informally.

Here is a formal greeting and response:

- Greeting: **Buongiorno signora, come sta?**

  bwohn-*johr*-noh see-*nyoh*-rah *koh*-meh stah

  *Hello, ma'am, how are you?*

>> Response: **Benissimo, grazie, e Lei?**

beh-*nees*-see-moh *grah*-tseh eh ley

*Very well, thank you, and you?*

An alternative response is **molto bene** (*mohl*-toh *beh*-neh). Both expressions convey the same meaning.

If you know the person or people you're addressing, you can use this informal greeting:

>> Greeting: **Ciao, Roberto, come stai?**

chow roh-*behr*-toh *koh*-meh *stahy*

*Hi, Roberto, how are you?*

>> Response: **Bene, grazie, e tu?**

*beh*-neh *grah*-tsyeh eh *tooh*

*Fine, thanks, and you?*

Here's another typical, somewhat informal, greeting and reply:

>> Greeting: **Come va?**

*koh*-me *vah*

*How are things?/How's it going?*

>> *Response:* **Non c'è male.**

nohn cheh *mah*-leh

*Not bad.*

## Reuniting . . . not sure when

Sometimes, you want to say more than just good–bye and specify your next meeting. The following expressions are common and also can be used as good–byes on their own:

>> **A presto!** (ah *preh*-stoh) *(See you soon!)*

>> **A dopo!** (ah *doh*-poh) *(See you later!)*

>> **A domani!** (ah doh-*mah*-nee) *(See you tomorrow!)*

>> **Ci vediamo!** (chee veh-*dyah*-moh) *(See you!)*

# Making Introductions

Being able to introduce yourself to someone and to answer questions about who you are and where you're from is important.

**CULTURAL WISDOM**

Whether to use first or last names as well as formal and informal registers are important considerations. In a job situation, you usually use last names, whereas at private functions, people are more likely to tell you their first names. The fact that someone gives you his or her first name, however, does not necessarily mean that you should use the informal **tu** (tooh) (*you*); using a person's first name with the formal form of address is quite common. Usually, the older person proposes making the switch to the informal form.

The following sections explain the basics to introducing yourself and introducing others in Italian.

## Introducing yourself

We want to familiarize you with an important reflexive verb, **chiamarsi** (kyah-mahr-see) (*to call oneself*), which you use to introduce yourself and to ask others for their names. Table 3-1 shows this verb conjugation:

**TABLE 3-1**

### Using chiamarsi

| Conjugation | Pronunciation | English |
| --- | --- | --- |
| **io mi chiamo** | ee-oh mee *kyah*-mogh | *my name is* |
| **tu ti chiami** | tooh tee *kyah*-mee | *your name is* (informal) |
| **lei si chiama** | ley see *kyah*-mah | *your name is* (formal) |
| **lui/lei si chiama** | looh-ee/ley see *kyah*-mah | *his/her name is* |

So that you can get the ring of the verb **chiamarsi,** practice these easy examples. Just change your intonation and word order, and you can ask someone's name instead of telling them:

>> **Ciao (or Buongiorno), mi chiamo Eva.** (*chow/bwohn*-johr-*noh* mee *kyah*-moh *eh*-vah) *(Hello, my name is Eva.)*

>> **E tu come ti chiami?** (eh too *koh*-meh tee *kyah*-mee) *(And what's your name?)* (Informal)

>> **Lei, come si chiama?** (ley *koh*-meh see *kyah*-mah) *(What's your name?)* (Formal)

>> **Piacere!** (pyah-*cheh*-reh) (with a quick handshake) is one way of saying: *Nice to meet you!*

TIP

Incidentally, as in English, you can also introduce yourself simply by saying your name: **Io sono Pietro** (*ee*-oh *soh*-noh *pyeh*-troh) *(I'm Pietro)*. Finally, you can just simply state your name, without the **"Mi chiamo"** *(My name is)* or **"Sono,"** *(I am)* as in the sample dialogue that follows.

# Talkin' the Talk

The people in this dialogue are colleagues assigned to work on the same project. They introduce themselves to each other.

| | |
|---|---|
| **Mr. Messa:** | **Carlo Messa. Piacere!**<br>*kahr*-loh *mehs*-sah pyah-*cheh*-reh<br>*Carlo Messa, nice to meet you!* |
| **Mr. Rossi:** | **Piacere, Marco Rossi.**<br>pyah-*cheh*-reh *mahr*-koh *rohs*-see<br>*Nice to meet you, Marco Rossi.* |
| **Ms. Pertini:** | **Piacere, sono Paola Pertini.**<br>pyah-*cheh*-reh *soh*-noh *pah*-oh-lah pehr-*tee*-nee<br>*Nice to meet you, I'm Paola Pertini.* |
| **Ms. Salvi:** | **Lieta di conoscerLa. Anna Salvi.**<br>*lyeh*-tah dee koh-*noh*-shehr-lah *ahn*-nah *sahl*-vee<br>*Pleased to meet you, Anna Salvi.* |
| **Mr. Melis:** | **Mi chiamo Carlo Melis, piacere.**<br>mee *kyah*-moh *kahr*-loh *meh*-lees pyah-*cheh*-reh<br>*My name is Carlo Melis, nice to meet you.* |
| **Mr. Foschi:** | **Molto lieto, Silvio Foschi.**<br>*mohl*-toh *lyeh*-toh *seel*-vyoh *foh*-skee<br>*Very pleasd to meet you, Silvio Foschi.* |

Children and young people forego ceremony and introduce themselves more casually, though still politely — something like this:

>> Greeting: **Ciao! Sono Giulio.** (chow *soh*-noh *jooh*-lyoh) *(Hello! I'm Giulio.)*

>> Response: **E io sono Giulia, piacere.** (eh *ee*-oh *soh*-noh *jooh*-lyah pyah-*cheh*-reh) *(And I'm Giulia, nice to meet you.)*

The following example offers a very informal introduction, used only in a very casual situation, such as on the beach or at a club:

>> Greeting: **Come ti chiami?** *(koh*-meh tee-*kyah*-mee) *(What's your name?)*

>> Response: **Chiara. E tu?** *(kyah*-rah eh tooh) *(Chiara, and you?)*

>> *(looh*-kah) *(Luca.)*

# Introducing other people

Sometimes you not only have to introduce yourself, but you also introduce someone to your friends or to other people.

The following vocabulary may be helpful in making introductions. With it, you can indicate the relationship between you and the person you're introducing. Gesturing toward the person and simply saying **mio fratello** means, quite simply, "This is my brother."

>> **mio fratello** (*mee*-oh frah-*tehl*-loh) *(my brother)*

>> **mia sorella** (*mee*-ah soh-*rehl*-lah) *(my sister)*

>> **mia figlia** (*mee*-ah *fee*-lyah) *(my daughter)*

>> **mio figlio** (*mee*-oh *fee*-lyoh) *(my son)*

>> **mio marito** (*mee*-oh mah-*ree*-toh) *(my husband)*

>> **mia moglie** (*mee*-ah *moh*-lyeh) *(my wife)*

>> **mia madre** (*mee*-ah *mah*-dreh) *(my mother)*

>> **mio padre** (*mee*-oh *pah*-dreh) *(my father)*

>> **il mio amico/la mia amica** (eel *mee*-oh ah-*mee*-koh lah *mee*-ah ah-*mee*-kah) *(my [male] friend/my [female] friend)*

- **il mio ragazzo/la mia ragazza** (eel *mee*-oh rah-*gaht*-tsoh/lah *mee*-ah rah-*gaht*-tsah) *(my boyfriend/my girlfriend)*

- **il mio fidanzato/la mia fidanzata** (eel *mee*-oh fee-dahn-*tsah*-toh/lah *mee*-ah fee-dahn-*tsah*-tah) *(my fiancé/fiancée)*

- **il mio collega/la mia collega** (eel *mee*-oh kohl-*leh*-gah lah *mee*-ah kohl-*leh*-gah) *(my [male] colleague/my [female] colleague)*

To make life easier we give you here the verb **presentare** (preh–zehn–*tah*–reh) *(to introduce)* (see Chapter 2 for more on **–are** verb conjugations):

- **Ti presento mia moglie, Teresa.** (tee preh-*zehn*-toh *mee*-ah *moh*-lyeh teh-*reh*-sah) *(Let me introduce you to my wife, Teresa.)* (Informal)

- **Le presento mia suocera, Mary.** (leh preh-*zehn*-toh *mee*-ah *swoh*-cheh-rah) *(Let me introduce you to my mother-in-law, Mary.)* (Formal)

# Talkin' the Talk

The following dialogue, which represents a formal occasion, contains some typical expressions used during introductions. Here, Mrs. Ponti introduces a new colleague to one of her co-workers. Note the abbreviation for signora. (Track 5)

| | |
|---|---|
| **Sig.ra Ponti:** | **Buonasera signora Bruni . . . Signora Bruni, Le presento il signor Rossi.**<br>*bwoh*-nah-*seh*-rah see-*nyoh*-rah *brooh*-nee see-*nyoh*-rah *brooh*-nee leh preh-*zehn*-toh eel see-*nyohr* rohs-see<br>*Good afternoon, Mrs. Bruni . . . Mrs. Bruni, I'd like to introduce you to Mr. Rossi.* |
| **Sig.ra Bruni:** | **Lieta di conoscerla.**<br>*lyeh*-tah dee koh-*noh*-shehr-lah<br>*Pleased to meet you.* |
| **Sig. Rossi:** | **Il piacere è tutto mio!**<br>eel pyah-*cheh*-reh eh *tooht*-toh *mee*-oh<br>*The pleasure is all mine!* |

# Talkin' the Talk

Of course, friends can be informal with one another, as the next conversation shows. Here Teresa bumps into her old friend Marinella. Both are married now and introduce their husbands. (Track 6)

**Marinella:** **Ciao, Teresa, come stai?**
chow teh-*reh*-zah *koh*-meh stahy
*Hello, Teresa. How are you?*

**Teresa:** **Bene, grazie.**
*beh*-neh *grah*-tsyeh.
*Well, thank you.*

**Sono contenta di vederti!**
*soh*-noh con-*tehn*-tah dee veh-*dehr*-tee
*I'm happy to see you!*

**Marinella, ti presento mio marito Giancarlo.**
mah-ree-*nehl*-lah tee preh-*zehn*-toh *mee*-oh mah-*ree*-toh
jahn-*kahr*-loh
*Marinella, I'd like to introduce you to my husband, Giancarlo.*

**Marinella:** **Ciao, Giancarlo.**
chow jahn-*kahr*-loh
*Hello Giancarlo.*

**Giancarlo:** **Piacere.**
pyah-*cheh*-reh
*Nice to meet you.*

**Marinella:** **E questo è Gianni.**
eh *kweh*-stoh eh *jahn*-nee
*And this is Gianni.*

**Gianni:** **Piacere.**
pyah-*cheh*-reh
*Nice to meet you.*

# Getting Acquainted

Introducing yourself is the first step in getting to know someone. If you get a good feeling about the person and want to speak more, a conversation usually follows the introduction. This section tells you about the different topics you might talk about to get to know each other.

# Finding out whether someone speaks English

When in a foreign country, knowing how to ask if someone speaks English is important. In urgent situations, there may be no time to practice your Italian:

>> **Parli inglese?** (*pahr*-lee een-*gleh*-zeh) *(Do you speak English?)* (Informal)

>> **Parla inglese?** (*pahr*-lah een-*gleh*-seh) *(Do you speak English?)* (Formal)

A possible response to these questions is **Parlo un po'.** (*pahr*–loh oohn poh) (*I speak a little bit.*).

## Talkin' the Talk

Ilaria and Carmen have recently gotten to know each other. Because Carmen isn't Italian, although she lives in Italy, Ilaria is curious to know how many languages she speaks.

| | |
|---|---|
| **Ilaria:** | **Quante lingue parli?**<br>*kwahn*-teh *leen*-gweh *pahr*-lee<br>*How many languages do you speak?* |
| **Carmen:** | **Tre. Italiano, spagnolo e tedesco.**<br>treh ee-tah-*lyah*-noh spah-*nyoh*-loh eh teh-*deh*-skoh<br>*Three. Italian, Spanish, and German.* |
| **Ilaria:** | **E qual è la tua lingua madre?**<br>eh kwah-*leh* lah *tooh*-ah *leen*-gwah *mah*-dreh<br>*And what is your native language* (Literally: *mother tongue*)? |
| **Carmen:** | **Lo spagnolo.**<br>loh spah-*nyoh*-loh<br>*Spanish.* |
| **Ilaria:** | **Tua madre è spagnola?**<br>*tooh*-ah *mah*-dreh eh spah-*nyoh*-lah<br>*Is your mother Spanish?* |
| **Carmen:** | **Sì. E mio padre è austriaco.**<br>see eh *mee*-oh *pah*-dreh eh ow-*stree*-ah-koh<br>*Yes, and my father is Austrian.* |

# Talking about where you come from

You know how interesting meeting people from other countries and nationalities can be. Two common questions are useful to remember:

» **Da dove viene?** (dah *doh*-veh *vyeh*-neh) *(Where do you come from? Where are you coming from; in this instance, where are you from?)* (Formal)

» **Da dove vieni?** (dah *doh*-veh *vyeh*-nee) *(Where are you from?)* (Informal)

» **Di dov'è?** (dee doh-*veh*) *(Where are you from?)* (Formal)

» **Di dove sei?** (dee *doh*-veh sey) *(Where are you from?)* (Informal)

The answers are, respectively:

» **Vengo da . . .** (*vehn*-goh dah) *(I come from/I'm from)*

» **Sono di . . .** (*soh*-noh dee) *(I'm from . . .)*

Now you can play with these phrases. You can insert the names of continents, countries, cities, or places.

## Talkin' the Talk

Il signor Dadina is sitting in his favorite café in Ravenna drinking his coffee and notices somebody at the next table who is examining a map of the city's Byzantine churches. Il signor Dadina is a curious person:

| | |
|---|---|
| **Sig. Dadina:** | **Non è di qui, vedo. Di dov'è?**<br>nohn eh dee kwee *veh*-doh di doh-*veh*<br>*I can see you're not from here. Where are you from?* |
| **Sig. Tarroni:** | **Sono di Perugia.**<br>*soh*-noh dee peh-*rooh*-jah<br>*I'm from Perugia.* |
| **Sig. Belli:** | **Una bella città!**<br>*ooh*-nah *behl*-lah cheet-*tah*<br>*A beautiful city/town!* |
| **Sig. Verdi:** | **Sì, è piccola ma molto bella.**<br>see eh *peek*-koh-lah mah *mohl*-toh *behl*-lah<br>*Yes, it is small but very beautiful.* |

If you want to talk about provenance, the adjectives denoting nationalities come in handy. As you say in English, "Are you American?" you say the same in Italian:

>> **È americano/a?** (eh ah-meh-ree-*kah*-noh/nah) (*Are you American?*) Formal

>> **Sei americano/a?** (sey ah-meh-ree-*kah*-noh/nah) (*Are you American?*) Informal

After you know the basics for such a situation, you're ready to chat.

## Talkin' the Talk

Il signor Bennati, meets a Canadian, Mr. Walsh. Because they're strangers, their exchange is in the formal form.

| | |
|---|---|
| **Sig. Bennati:** | **Di dov'è?**<br>dee doh-*veh*<br>*Where are you from?* |
| **Mr. Walsh:** | **Sono canadese.**<br>*soh*-noh kah-nah-*deh*-zeh<br>*I'm Canadian.* |
| **Sig. Bennati:** | **Di dove esattamente?**<br>dee *doh*-veh eh-zaht-tah-*mehn*-teh<br>*From where, exactly?* |
| **Mr. Walsh:** | **Di Montreal. Lei è italiano?**<br>dee *mohn*-treh-ahl ley eh ee-tah-*lyah*-noh<br>*From Montreal. Are you Italian?* |
| **Sig. Bennati:** | **Sì, di Firenze.**<br>see dee fee-*rehn*-tseh<br>*Yes, from Florence.* |

In English, you must put the pronoun (*I, you, he, she, we,* and so on) in front of the verb. You may have noticed that this isn't the case in Italian. Because the verb form is different for each personal pronoun, you can easily leave out the pronoun — you understand who is meant from the verb ending and from the context. You use the pronoun only when the subject isn't clear enough or when you want to emphasize a fact — for example, **Loro sono americani, ma io sono italiano** (_loh_-roh *soh*-noh ah-meh-ree-*kah*-nee mah *ee*-oh *soh*-noh ee-tah-*lyah*-noh) (*They are American, but I am Italian*).

Use adjectives ending in **-o** (singular) and **-i** (plural) to refer to males, and adjectives ending in **-a** (singular) and **-e** (plural) to refer to females. Adjectives that end in **-e** in the singular refer to both males and females and end in the plural with **-i.**

Some adjectives indicating nationality end with **-e:** This form is both masculine and feminine. Table 3-2 gives some examples.

**TABLE 3-2**    ## Some Nationalities and Countries I

| Nationality/Country | Pronunciation | Translation |
| --- | --- | --- |
| **albanese/i Albania** | ahl-bah-*neh*-zeh/zee ahl-bah-*nee*-ah | *Albanian/Albanians Albania* |
| **canadese/i Canada** | kah-nah-*deh*-zeh/zee *kah*-nah-dah | *Canadian/Canadians Canada* |
| **cinese/i Cina** | chee-*neh*-zeh/zee *chee*-nah | *Chinese* (sing.pl.) *China* |
| **francese/i Francia** | frahn-*cheh*-zeh/zee *frahn*-chah | *French* (sing./pl.) *France* |
| **giapponese/i Giappone** | jahp-*poh*-neh-zeh/zee jahp-*poh*-neh | *Japanese* (sing/pl.) *Japan* |
| **inglese/i Inghilterra** | een-*gleh*-zeh/zee een-geel-*tehr*-rah | *English* (sing./pl.) *England* |
| **irlandese/i Irlanda** | eer-lahn-*deh*-zeh/zee eer-*lahn*-dah | *Irish* (sing./pl.) *Ireland* |
| **olandese/i Olanda** | oh-lahn-*deh*-zeh/zee oh-*lahn*-dah | *Dutch* (sing./pl.) *the Netherlands/ Holland* |
| **portoghese/i Portogallo** | pohr-toh-*geh*-zeh/zee pohr-toh-*gahl*-loh | *Portuguese* (sing./pl.) *Portugal* |
| **senegalese/i Senegal** | seh-neh-gah-*leh*-zeh/zee *seh*-neh-gahl | *Senegalese* (sing./pl.) *Senegal* |
| **svedese/i Svezia** | zveh-*deh*-zeh/zee *zveh*-tsyah | *Swedish* (sing./pl.) *Sweden* |

Table 3-3 shows other nationalities with four endings like **italiano**, and **americano** [o (m.s.), a (f.s.), i (m.p.), e (f.p.)].

Instead of saying **sono americano** (*soh*-noh ah-meh-ree-kah-noh) (*I'm American*), or even better **statunitense** (stah-too-nee-*tehn*-seh), you can also say **vengo dall'America/dagli Stati Uniti** (*vehn*-goh dahl-lah-*meh*-ree-kah *dah*-lyee stah-tee ooh-*nee*-tee) (*I'm from America/the United States*). The same is true for all countries.

## Some Nationalities and Countries II

| Nationality/Country | Pronunciation | Translation |
| --- | --- | --- |
| **americano/a/i/e** | ah-*meh*-ree-kah-noh/nah/nee/neh | *American/Americans* |
| **Stati Uniti d'America** | *stah*-tee ooh-*nee*-tee dah-*meh*-ree-kah | *United States of America* |
| **australiano/a/i/e** | ow-strah-*lyah*-noh/nah/nee/neh | *Australian/Australians* |
| **Australia** | ow-*strah*-lyah | *Australia* |
| **brasiliano/a/i/e** | brah-see-*lyah*-noh/nah/ nee/neh | *Brazilian/Brazilians* |
| **Brasile** | brah-*zee*-leh | *Brazil* |
| **greco/a/greci/greche** | *greh*-koh/*greh*-kah/*greh*-chee/*gre*-keh | *Greek/Greeks* |
| **Grecia** | *greh*-chah | *Greece* |
| **italiano/a/i/e** | ee-tah-*lyah*-noh/nah/nee/neh | *Italian/Italians* |
| **Italia** | ee-*tah*-lyah | *Italy* |
| **marocchino/a/i/e** | mah-rohk-*kee*-noh/nah/nee/neh | *Moroccan/Moroccans* |
| **Marocco** | mah-*rohk*-koh | *Morocco* |
| **messicano/a/i/e** | mehs-see-*kah*-noh/nah/nee/neh | *Mexican/Mexicans* |
| **Messico** | mehs-see-koh | *Mexico* |
| **polacco/a/polacchi/polacche** | poh-*lahk*-koh/kah/kee/keh | *Polish* (sing./pl.) |
| **Polonia** | poh-*loh*-nyah | *Poland* |
| **rumeno/a/i/e** | rooh-*meh*-noh/nah/nee/neh | *Romanian/Romanians* |
| **Romania** | roh-mah-*nee*-ah | *Romania* |
| **russo/a/i/e** | *roohs*-soh/sah/see/seh | *Russian/Russians* |
| **Russia** | *roos*-syah | *Russia* |
| **spagnolo/a/i/e** | spah-*nyoh*-loh/lah/lee/leh | *Spanish* (sing./pl.) |
| **Spagna** | *spah*-nyah | Spain |
| **svizzero/a/i/e** | *zveet*-tseh-roh/rah/ree/reh | *Swiss* (sing./pl.) |
| **Svizzera** | *zveet*-tseh-rah | *Switzerland* |
| **tedesco/a/tedeschi/tedesche** | teh-*deh*-skoh/kah/teh-*deh*-skee/keh | *German/Germans* |
| **Germania** | jehr-*mah*-nyah | *Germany* |

The following examples give you more practice with this construction:

>> **Veniamo dall'Italia.** (veh-_nyah_-moh dahl-lee-_tah_-lyah) *(We come from Italy/ We're from Italy.)*

>> **Vengono dalla Spagna.** (_vehn_-goh-noh _dahl_-lah _spah_-nyah) *(They come from Spain/They're from Spain.)*

>> **Vengo dal Giappone.** (_vehn_-goh dahl jahp-_poh_-neh) *(I come from Japan/I'm from Japan.)*

>> **Veniamo dal Canada.** (veh-_nyah_-moh dahl _kah_-nah-dah) *(We come from Canada/We're from Canada.)*

>> **Veniamo dagli U. S. A./Stati Uniti** (veh-_nyah_-moh _dah_-lyee ooh-_sah stah_-tee ooh-_nee_-tee) *(We come from the U. S. A./United States / We're from the U. S. A./ United States.)*

If you travel to Italy and make new friends, you may be asked these informal questions:

>> **Ti piace l'Italia?** (tee _pyah_-cheh lee-_tah_-lyah) *(Do you like Italy?)*

>> **Sei qui per la prima volta?** (sey kwee pehr lah _pree_-mah _vohl_-tah) *(Is this your first time here?)*

>> **Sei qui in vacanza?** (sey kwee een vah-_kahn_-tsah) *(Are you on vacation?)*

>> **Quanto rimani?** (_kwahn_-toh ree-_mah_-nee) *(How long are you staying?)*

# Extending and responding to invitations

GRAMMATICALLY
SPEAKING

You may be asked to join an Italian friend for a meal in a restaurant, or even at his/ her home after you've become friends. When you want to invite someone to din–ner, you can use the following phrases:

>> **Andiamo a cena insieme?** (ahn-_dyah_-moh ah _cheh_-nah een-_syeh_-meh) *(Should we go to dinner together?)*

>> **Posso invitarti stasera?** (_pohs_-soh een-vee-_tahr_-tee stah-_seh_-rah) *(Can I invite you out this evening?)* This usually means that the person asking is going to be treating.

To accept an invitation, you can use the following expressions:

>> **Volentieri, grazie!** (voh-lehn-*tyeh*-ree *grah*-tsyeh) *(I'd like to, thank you!)*

>> **Con piacere, grazie!** (kohn pyah-*cheh*-reh *grah*-tsyeh) *(With pleasure, thank you!)*

Of course, you can't accept every invitation you receive. Following are expressions you can use to decline an invitation:

>> **Mi dispiace ma non posso.** (mee dee-*spyah*-cheh mah nohn *pohs*-soh) *(I'm sorry, but I can't.)*

>> **Magari un'altra volta, grazie.** (mah-*gah*-ree oohn-*ahl*-trah *vohl*-tah *grah*-tsyeh) *(Perhaps another time, thank you.)*

>> **Mi dispiace, ho già un altro impegno.** (mee dee-*spyah*-cheh oh jah oohn *ahl*-troh eem-*peh*-nyoh) *(I'm sorry, but I already have another commitment.)*

# Talkin' the Talk

Francesca talks to Giovanni about the possibility to go out to dinner together that evening.

**Francesca:** **Ci vediamo per cena questa sera?**
chee veh-*dyah*-moh pehr *cheh*-nah *kweh*-stah *seh*-rah
*Are we meeting for dinner tonight?*

**Giovanni:** **Si, perchè no? Offro io, però.**
see pehr-*keh* noh *ohf*-froh *ee*-oh peh-*roh*
*Yes, why not? It's my treat, though.*

# FUN & GAMES

A chance meeting leads to a quick introduction in the short dialogue. Fill in the blanks in the Italian, using the following phrases. See Appendix C for the answer key.

le presento, il piacere, e lei, come sta, conoscerla

**Gayle:** **Buonasera, signora Frederick. _______?**

Good afternoon, Ms. Frederick. How are you?

**Ms. Frederick** **Benissimo, grazie, _______?**

Very well, thank you, and you?

**Gayle:** **Bene, grazie. _______ il mio amico, George.**

Fine, thanks. I'd like to introduce my friend, George.

**George:** **Lieto di _______, signora.**

Pleased to meet you, Ma'am.

**Ms. Frederick:** **_______ è mio.**

The pleasure is mine.

# Chapter **4**

# Getting Your Numbers and Time Straight

Numbers are a basic part of any language, so we include numbers early on in this chapter. You can't get away without knowing numbers, even in small talk. Somebody may ask you how old you are, how many days you're visiting, or whatever. You can see how numbers are used throughout this book, for example in Chapters 7 and 13.

## Practicing Using Numbers

Every language follows a certain scheme to formulate higher numbers. When you know the basics — the numbers from one to ten — you're halfway there.

In the Italian scheme, as in English, the higher value precedes the lower one, so that to say "22," you first say **venti** (*vehn*-tee) (*twenty*) and then **due** (*dooh*-eh) (*two*) and simply put them together: **ventidue** (*vehn*-tee-*dooh*-eh) (*twenty-two*). The same is true for higher numbers — like **trecentoventidue** (treh-*chehn*-toh-*vehn*-tee-*dooh*-eh) (*three hundred and twenty-two*) and **duemilatrecentoventidue** (*dooh*-eh-*mee*-lah-treh-*chehn*-toh-*vehn*-tee-*dooh*-eh) *(two thousand three hundred and twenty-two).*

One thing merits some further explanation: When two vowels meet (this happens with **uno** [*ooh*-noh] *[one]* and **otto** [*oht*-toh] *[eight]*), you eliminate the first vowel as in **vent**(i)**uno** (vehn-*tooh*-noh) *(twenty-one)* and **quarant**(a)**otto** (*kwah*-rahn-*toht*-toh) *(forty-eight)*. So far so good.

Numbers that end in **tre** (treh) *(three)* require an accent on the final *e*; this also means that the stress is on the final syllable: **trentatré** (trehn-tah-*treh*) *(thirty-three)*. The word for the number three is **tre** (treh) and when it stands alone, it has no written accent.

Every rule has exceptions, and there are some irregular numbers, which you simply have to memorize. The numbers from 11 to 19 follow their own rules: **undici** (oohn-dee-chee) *(eleven)*, **dodici** (*doh*-dee-chee) *(twelve)*, **tredici** (*treh*-dee-chee) *(thirteen)*, **quattordici** (kwaht-*tohr*-dee-chee) *(fourteen)*, **quindici** (*kween*-dee-chee) *(fifteen)*, **sedici** (*seh*-dee-chee) *(sixteen)*, **diciassette** (dee-chahs-*seht*-teh) *(seventeen)*, **diciotto** (dee-*choht*-toh) *(eighteen)*, and **diciannove** (dee-chahn-*noh*-veh) *(nineteen)*.

In Italian you can't express a decade in just one word — you use a phrase. To say "the seventies" you say "**gli anni settanta**" (lyee *ahn*-nee seht-*tahn*-tah). When you want to say "in the sixties," you have to say **negli anni sessanta** (*neh*-lyee *ahn*-nee sehs-*sahn*-tah).

One other thing to keep in mind is that the plural of **mille** (*meel*-leh) *(one thousand)* is **mila** (*mee*-lah), as in **duemila** (*dooh*-eh-*mee*-lah) *(two thousand)*.

Table 4-1 gives you enough numbers so that you can form the one you need.

Common usage for numbers that denote the centuries are

**Manzoni scrisse nell'Ottocento.** (mahn-*zoh*-nee *skrees*-seh nehl-*oht*-toh-*chehn*-toh) *(Manzoni wrote in the 1800s.)*

**Il Rinascimento va dal '400 al '500 (dal Quattrocento al Cinquecento).** (eel ree-*nah*-shee-*mehn*-toh vah dahl *kwaht*-troh-*chehn*-toh ahl *cheen*-kweh-*chehn*-toh) *(The Renaissance goes from the 15th to the 16th century — literally, from the 1400s to the 1500s.)*

## Numbers

| Italian | Pronunciation | Number |
|---|---|---|
| *From 1 to 30* | | |
| **zero** | *dzeh*-roh | 0 |
| **uno** | *ooh*-noh | 1 |
| **due** | *dooh*-eh | 2 |
| **tre** | treh | 3 |
| **quattro** | *kwaht*-troh | 4 |
| **cinque** | *cheen*-kweh | 5 |
| **sei** | sey | 6 |
| **sette** | *seht*-teh | 7 |
| **otto** | *oht*-toh | 8 |
| **nove** | *noh*-veh | 9 |
| **dieci** | *dyeh*-chee | 10 |
| **undici** | *oohn*-dee-chee | 11 |
| **dodici** | *doh*-dee-chee | 12 |
| **tredici** | *treh*-dee-chee | 13 |
| **quattordici** | kwaht-*tohr*-dee-chee | 14 |
| **quindici** | *kween*-dee-chee | 15 |
| **sedici** | *seh*-dee-chee | 16 |
| **diciassette** | dee-chahs-*seht*-teh | 17 |
| **diciotto** | dee-*choht*-toh | 18 |
| **diciannove** | dee-chahn-*noh*-veh | 19 |
| **venti** | *vehn*-tee | 20 |
| **ventuno** | vehn-*tooh*-noh | 21 |
| **ventidue** | *vehn*-tee-*dooh*-eh | 22 |
| **ventitré** | *vehn*-tee-*treh* | 23 |
| **ventiquattro** | *vehn*-tee-*kwaht*-troh | 24 |
| **venticinque** | *vehn*-tee-*cheen*-kweh | 25 |
| **ventisei** | *vehn*-tee-*sey* | 26 |

*(continued)*

| Italian | Pronunciation | Number |
|---|---|---|
| ***From 1 to 30*** | | |
| **ventisette** | *vehn*-tee-*seht*-teh | 27 |
| **ventotto** | *vehn-toht*-toh | 28 |
| **ventinove** | *vehn*-tee-*noh*-veh | 29 |
| **trenta** | *trehn*-tah | 30 |
| ***Numbers 40 to 100*** | | |
| **quaranta** | kwah-*rahn*-tah | 40 |
| **cinquanta** | cheen-*kwahn*-tah | 50 |
| **sessanta** | sehs-*sahn*-tah | 60 |
| **settanta** | seht-*tahn*-tah | 70 |
| **ottanta** | oht-*tahn*-tah | 80 |
| **novanta** | noh-*vahn*-tah | 90 |
| **cento** | *chehn*-toh | 100 |
| ***Numbers from 200 to 900*** | | |
| **duecento** | *dooh*-eh-*chehn*-toh | 200 |
| **trecento** | treh-*chehn*-toh | 300 |
| **quattrocento** | *kwaht*-troh-*chehn*-toh | 400 |
| **cinquecento** | *cheen*-kweh-*chehn*-toh | 500 |
| **seicento** | sey-*chehn*-toh | 600 |
| **settecento** | *seht*-teh-*chehn*-toh | 700 |
| **ottocento** | *oht*-toh-*chehn*-toh | 800 |
| **novecento** | *noh*-veh-*chehn*-toh | 900 |
| ***Higher numbers*** | | |
| **mille** | *meel*-leh | 1,000 |
| **duemila** | *dooh*-eh-*mee*-lah | 2,000 |
| **un milione** | oohn mee-*lyoh*-neh | 1,000,000 |
| **due milioni** | *dooh*-eh mee-*lyoh*-nee | 2,000,000 |
| **un miliardo** | oohn mee-*lyahr*-doh | 1,000,000,000 |

# Identifying Times of Day and Days of the Week

Arranging your social life — whether you want to go to a performance or invite someone to a party — requires knowing the days of the week and times of the day. Table 4-2 gives you the days of the week and the abbreviations for them. You can hear the days of the week on Track 7 on the online audio tracks.

**TABLE 4-2**

### Days of the Week

| Italian/Abbreviation | Pronunciation | Translation |
|---|---|---|
| **lunedì/lun** | looh-neh-*dee* | *Monday* |
| **martedì/mar** | mahr-teh-*dee* | *Tuesday* |
| **mercoledì/mer** | mehr-koh-leh-*dee* | *Wednesday* |
| **giovedì/gio** | joh-veh-*dee* | *Thursday* |
| **venerdì/ven** | veh-nehr-*dee* | *Friday* |
| **sabato/sab** | *sah*-bah-toh | *Saturday* |
| **domenica/dom** | doh-*meh*-nee-kah | *Sunday* |

The week begins on Monday in the Italian calendar.

You don't capitalize the days of the week or the months in Italian as you do in English.

Here are terms for *yesterday, today, tomorrow,* and *day after tomorrow:* **ieri** (*yeh*-ree), **oggi** (*oj*-jee), **domani** (doh-*mah*-nee), and **dopodomani** (*doh*-poh-doh-*mah*-nee).

There's a great song, "Domani il 21 aprile" that most of Italy's greatest contemporary singers put together in support of the people of Abruzzo after the earthquake of 2009. You can do an online search for the title of the song and sing along with it. This is a fun way to practice your pronunciation!

# Talkin' the Talk

Note the following teacher/student exchange in Italian 101:

**Teacher:**     **Se oggi è lunedì, che giorno è domani?**
seh *oj*-jee eh looh-neh-*dee* keh *johr*-noh eh doh-*mah*-nee
*If today is Monday, what day is tomorrow?*

**Student:**     **Domani è martedì.**
doh-*mah*-nee eh mahr-teh-*dee*
*Tomorrow is Tuesday.*

**Teacher:**     **Bravo. Oggi è giovedì: che giorno è domani?**
*brah*-voh *ohj*-jee eh joh-veh-*dee* keh *johr*-noh eh
doh-*mah*-nee
*Good job. Today is Thursday: what day is tomorrow?*

**Student:**     **Domani è venerdì.**
doh-*mah*-nee eh veh-nehr-*dee*
*Tomorrow is Friday.*

Now the teacher is talking to one of her colleagues.

**Teacher:**     **Quando parti per le vacanze?**
*kwahn*-doh *pahr*-tee pehr leh vah-*kahn*-tseh
*When are you leaving for vacation?*

**Colleague:**     **Sabato, dopodomani.**
*sah*-bah-toh *doh*-poh-doh-*mah*-nee
*Saturday, the day after tomorrow.*

GRAMMATICALLY
SPEAKING

You may find the Italian expression for "the day before yesterday" interesting. It's **l'altro ieri** (*lahl*-troh *yeh*-ree), which literally means "the other yesterday." Here are some of the ways you might use these expressions:

>> **Il concerto è martedì sera.** (eel kohn-*chehr*-toh eh mahr-teh-*dee seh*-rah) *(The concert is on Tuesday evening.)*

>> **Dov'eri ieri pomeriggio?** (doh-*veh*-ree *yeh*-ree poh-meh-*reej*-joh) *(Where were you yesterday afternoon?)*

>> **Il concerto è stato l'altro ieri. L'hai perso!** (eel kohn-*chehr*-toh eh *stah*-toh *lahl*-troh *yeh*-ree lahy *pehr*-soh) *(The concert was the day before yesterday. You missed it!)*

# Using the Calendar

If you want to plan a vacation, organize your life, remember your friends' birthdays, and also talk about your favorite holidays and seasons, then you need to know the months in Italian (see Table 4-3). You can hear them on Track 8 of the online audio tracks.

**TABLE 4-3**

## Months

| Italian | Pronunciation | Translation |
| --- | --- | --- |
| **gennaio** | gehn-*nah*-yoh | *January* |
| **febbraio** | fehb-*brah*-yoh | *February* |
| **marzo** | *mahr*-tsoh | *March* |
| **aprile** | ah-*pree*-leh | *April* |
| **maggio** | *mahj*-joh | *May* |
| **giugno** | *jooh*-nyoh | *June* |
| **luglio** | *looh*-lyoh | *July* |
| **agosto** | ah-*goh*-stoh | *August* |
| **settembre** | seht-*tehm*-breh | *September* |
| **ottobre** | oht-*toh*-breh | *October* |
| **novembre** | noh-*vehm*-breh | *November* |
| **dicembre** | dee-*chehm*-breh | *December* |

Here is a useful rhyme that most Italians learn some version of. This might help you to remember and pronounce some of the months and numbers. You can listen and repeat as much as you want!

**Trenta giorni ha novembre con aprile, giugno e settembre; di ventotto ce n'è uno. Tutti gli altri ne han trentuno.**

(*trehn*-tah *johr*-nee ah noh-*vehm*-breh kohn ah-*pree*-leh *jooh*-nyoh eh seht-*tehm*-breh dee vehn-*toht*-toh cheh neh *ooh*-noh *tooht*-tee lyee *ahl*-tree neh ahn *trehn*-tooh-noh)

*(Thirty days have November, April, June, and September; with 28 there is but one. All the rest have thirty-one.)*

# Asking about and Giving Dates

To ask for the date you say one of the following:

>> **Che giorno è oggi?** (keh *johr*-noh eh *ohj*-jee) *(What day is it today?/What is today's date?)*

>> **Quanti ne abbiamo oggi?** (*kwahn*-tee neh ahb-*byah*-moh *ohj*-jee) *(What is today's date?)*

Here is an important difference between saying the date in English and in Italian. The word order is reversed in Italian. To say the date you use this order: **è** (eh) (it's) + **il** (eel) (the) + number + month + (year, if necessary).

Here's an example.:

**Oggi è il dieci febbraio duemilaundici.** (*ohj*-jee eh eel *dyeh*-chee fehb-*brah*-yoh *dooh*-eh-*mee*-lah-*oohn*-dee-chee) *(Today is February 10, 2011.)*

To ask when something is occurring, just use the word **quando** (*qwahn*–doh) *(when)*.

**Quando parti per la Sicilia?** (*kwahn*-doh *pahr*-tee pehr lah see-*chee*-lyah) *(When are you leaving for Sicily?)*

To answer:

**Parto l'8 agosto.** (*pahr*-toh *loht*-toh ah-*goh*-stoh) *(I'm leaving August 8th.)*

To ask when someone was born:

**Quando sei nato/a?** (*kwahn*-doh sey *nah*-toh/tah) *(When were you born?)*

To answer:

**Sono nato/a il sette novembre millenovecentosessantuno.** (*soh*-noh *nah*-toh/tah eel *seht*-teh noh-*vehm*-breh *meel*-leh-*noh*-veh-*chehn*-toh-sehs-sahn-*tooh*-noh) *(I was born in 1961.)*

*Note:* If you're speaking to or about a male, the past participle is **nato** (ending in -**o**.) If you're speaking to or about a female, the past participle is **nata** (ending in -**a**.)

# Telling Time

When you write the time in Italian, you go from 1:00 to 24:00 (or 00:00). But generally when you speak, you use just 1 to 12, and if there's a doubt about a.m. or p.m., you can add **di mattina** (dee maht-*tee*-nah) *(in the morning)*, **di pomeriggio** (dee poh-meh-*reej*-joh) *(in the afternoon)*, or **di sera** (dee *seh*-rah) *(in the evening)*. The following sections focus on what you need to know about telling time.

## Asking for the time

You can ask for the time in two interchangeable ways:

>> **Che ora è?** (keh *oh*-rah eh) *(What time is it?)*

>> **Che ore sono?** (keh *oh*-reh *soh*-noh) *(What time is it?)*

Another way of asking politely for the time follows:

**Scusi, mi può dire l'ora, per favore?** (*skooh*-zee mee pwoh *dee*-reh *loh*-rah pehr fah-*voh*-reh) *(Excuse me, can you please tell me the time?)*

If the hour is singular, you answer with the singular verb:

>> **È l'una.** (eh *looh*-nah) *(It's one o'clock.)*

>> **È mezzanotte.** (eh *mehd*-dzah-noht-teh) *(It's midnight.)*

>> **È mezzogiorno.** (eh *mehd*-dzoh-*johr*-noh) *(It's noon.)*

If the time is plural (for instance, more than one), just change your verb from è (eh) (it is) to **sono** (*soh*-noh) ("*they are*," literally, to reflect the plural **ore** [*oh*-reh] — hours.)

>> **Sono le due.** (*soh*-noh leh *dooh*-eh) *(It's two o'clock.)*

>> **Sono le diciotto.** (*soh*-noh leh dee-*choht*-toh) *(It's six p.m.)*

Did you notice the use of military time in the previous example? In Italy, the 24-hour clock is always used for movie times or plane and train schedules.

You can also add on, when necessary, minutes, such as in the examples that follow:

- » **e tredici** (eh *treh*-dee-chee) *[thirteen (minutes) past]*

- » **e un quarto** (eh oohn *qwahr*-toh) *(a quarter past)*

- » **e mezzo** (eh *mehd*-dzoh) *(half past)*

- » **e tre quarti** (eh treh *kwahr*-tee) *(three-quarters past)*

- » **meno un quarto** (*meh*-noh oohn *qwahr*-toh) *(a quarter to)*

## Asking what time something begins

Of course, sometimes you want to take the conversation about time a little farther. Frequently you need to ask what time something begins. Just begin your question with **A che ora?** Look here:

- » **A che ora inizia la partita?** (ah keh *oh*-rah ee-*nee*-tsyah lah pahr-*tee*-tah) *(What time does the game begin?)*

- » **A mezzogiorno/mezzanotte.** (ah *mehd*-dzoh-*johr*-noh/*mehdz*-zah-*noht*-teh) *(At noon/midnight)*

- » **All'una.** (ahl-*looh*-nah) *(At one.)*

- » **Alle dieci.** (*ahl*-leh *dyeh*-chee) *(At ten.)*

(Note that the preposition **a** contracts with the definite article that precedes the number.)

## USING THE 24-HOUR CLOCK

All schedules and posted times in Italy use a 24-hour clock — from trains and planes to movies and concerts. It's a good idea to review how the 24-hour clock works, especially when you're at a train or bus station. The word for clock and watch is **orologio** (oh-roh-*loh*-joh). So, from midnight to 12:00 noon, the hours are the same, but at 1 p.m. it becomes 13 hours, or **le tredici** (leh *treh*-dee-chee). 2 p.m. becomes **le quattordici** (leh kwaht-*tohr*-dee-chee), and so on.

So imagine you arrive at the train station and want to know what time the trains heading down to Naples are. Here are some options: **6:37 (le sei e trentasette)** (leh sey eh *trehn*-tah-*seht*-teh) *(6:37 a.m.)*; **17:23 (le diciassette e ventitré)** (leh dee-chahs-*seht*-teh eh vehn-tee-*treh*) *(5:23 p.m.).*

Giancarlo and Daniele, two Roman university students, are in piazza Navona chatting about a concert being held at the Circus Maximus tomorrow.

| | |
|---|---|
| **Giancarlo:** | **Sai a che ora c'è il concerto di Elton John domani?** |
| | sahy ah keh *oh*-rah cheh eel kon-*chehr*-toh dee Elton John doh-*mah*-nee |
| | *Do you know what time the Elton John concert is tomorrow?* |
| **Daniele:** | **Certo! Inizia alle 10 di sera.** |
| | *chehr*-toh ee-*nee*-tsyah *ahl*-leh *dyeh*-chee dee *seh*-rah. |
| | *Of course! It starts at 10 p.m.* |
| **Giancarlo:** | **A proposito, che ore sono adesso?** |
| | ah proh-*poh*-zee-toh keh *oh*-reh *soh*-noh ah-*dehs*-soh |
| | *By the way, what time is it now?* |
| **Daniele:** | **Sono le due e mezzo in punto.** |
| | *soh*-noh leh *dooh*-eh eh *mehd*-dzoh een *poohn*-toh |
| | *It's 2:30 on the dot.* |
| **Giancarlo:** | **Oddio! Sono in ritardo per l'esame!** |
| | oh *dee*-oh *soh*-noh een ree-*tahr*-doh pehr leh-*zah*-meh |
| | *Goodness!* (Literally: *Oh God!*) *I'm late for the exam!* |

# Chatting about the Weather

Whenever you're in conversational trouble and don't know what to say, you can always talk about the weather: "It's very hot today, isn't it?" Or you can ask, "Is spring your rainy season?" Talking about the weather can save your conversation in many situations!

Because the weather is such an important topic, you want to be armed with the necessary vocabulary. In this section, we talk about the **quattro stagioni** (*kwaht-troh stah–joh–nee*) (*four seasons*).

## WEATHER WISE

Italy is a fortunate country, at least as far as weather is concerned. During at least three of the four seasons, it has a mild climate and gets a lot of sun.

Summers are for the most part warm — sometimes too hot. The winters can be very cold, but snow is rare, except in the mountains of northern and central Italy, but as far south as Calabria.

Summer in the cities is generally terribly hot, so most Italians take their vacation in August and flee to cooler places: the sea or the lakes or the mountains. As a matter of fact, in August, it is hard to find many residents in the big cities. The only people you are likely to find are tourists and those Italians who have to work.

The fact that both the famous concertos by Antonio Vivaldi (ahn-*toh*-nyoh vee-*vahl*-dee) and an oh-so-good pizza are named **Quattro Stagioni** is no accident. Both are subdivided into four parts, and each part refers to one season.

>> **primavera** (pree-mah-*veh*-rah) *(spring)*

>> **estate** (eh-*stah*-teh) *(summer)*

>> **autunno** (ow-*toohn*-noh) *(autumn; fall)*

>> **inverno** (in-*vehr*-noh) *(winter)*

# Talkin' the Talk

Mr. Brancato and Ms. Roe, seatmates on a plane, are talking about the weather. (Track 9)

| | |
|---|---|
| **Ms. Roe:** | **Le piace Milano?**<br>leh *pyah*-cheh mee-*lah*-noh<br>*Do you like Milan?* |
| **Sig. Brancato:** | **Sì, ma non il clima.**<br>see mah nohn eel *klee*-mah<br>*Yes, but not the climate.* |

| **Ms. Roe:** | **Fa molto freddo?** |
| | fah *mohl*-toh *frehd*-doh |
| | *Is it very cold?* |
| **Sig. Brancato:** | **In inverno sì.** |
| | een een-*vehr*-noh see |
| | *In winter yes.* |
| **Ms. Roe:** | **E piove molto, no?** |
| | eh *pyoh*-veh *mohl*-toh noh |
| | *And it rains a lot, doesn't it?* |
| **Sig. Brancato:** | **Sì, e c'è sempre la nebbia.** |
| | see eh cheh *sehm*-preh lah *nehb*-byah |
| | *Yes, and there is always fog.* |
| **Ms. Roe:** | **Com' è il clima a Palermo?** |
| | kohm-*eh* eel *klee*-mah ah pah-*lehr*-moh |
| | *What's Palermo's climate like?* |
| **Sig. Brancato:** | **Temperato, mediterraneo.** |
| | tehm-peh-*rah*-toh meh-dee-tehr-*rah*-neh-oh |
| | *Temperate, Mediterranean.* |
| **Ms. Roe:** | **Non fa mai freddo?** |
| | nohn fah mahy *frehd*-doh |
| | *Is it ever cold?* |
| **Sig. Brancato:** | **Quasi mai.** |
| | *kwah*-zee mahy |
| | *Almost never.* |

**CULTURAL WISDOM**

An expression that shows a cultural difference is **Una rondine non fa primavera** (*ooh*-nah-*rohn*-dee-neh nohn fah pree-mah-*veh*-rah) *(One swallow does not a summer make)*. Note the difference; in English, the expression refers to summer; in Italian it refers to spring. This difference may be due to the fact that the birds come earlier in Italy and later to other countries.

# Talkin' the Talk

Our friends il signor Brancato and Ms. Roe, airplane seatmates, are still talking about the weather.

| | |
|---|---|
| **Ms. Roe:** | **E l'estate a Milano com'è?**<br>e leh-*stah*-teh ah mee-*lah*-noh coh-*meh*<br>*What's the summer like in Milan?* |
| **Sig. Brancato:** | **Molto calda e lunga.**<br>*mohl*-toh *kahl*-dah eh *loohn*-gah<br>*Very hot and long.* |
| **Ms. Roe:** | **E la primavera?**<br>eh lah pree-mah-*veh*-rah<br>*And the spring?* |
| **Sig. Brancato:** | **La mia stagione preferita.**<br>lah *mee*-ah stah-*joh*-neh preh-feh-*ree*-tah<br>*My favorite season.* |
| **Ms. Roe:** | **Davvero?**<br>dahv-*veh*-roh<br>*Really?* |
| **Sig. Brancato:** | **Sì, perché è mite.**<br>see pehr-*keh* eh *mee*-teh<br>*Yes, because it's mild.* |
| **Ms. Roe:** | **Come l'estate in Canada.**<br>*koh*-meh leh-*stah*-teh een *kah*-nah-dah<br>*Like summer in Canada.* |

When you're talking about the weather, the following expressions, which are very idiomatic, will make you sound like a native speaker:

>> **Fa un caldo terribile!** (fah oohn *kahl*-doh tehr-*ree*-bee-leh) (*It's terribly hot!*)

>> **Oggi il sole spacca le pietre!** (*ohj*-jee eel *soh*-leh *spahk*-kah leh *pyeh*-treh) (It's hot enough to fry an egg! [Literally: *The sun today is splitting the stones!*])

>> **Fa un freddo cane!** (fah oohn *frehd*-doh *kah*-neh) (*It's very cold!*)

>> **Fa freddo/caldo da morire!** (fah *frehd*-doh/*kahl*-doh dah moh-*ree*-reh) (*It's freezing cold/It's unbearably hot!*)

# Talkin' the Talk

Back in the plane, there's small talk about the weather as the plane goes in for its landing.

**Voice over the loudspeaker:** **Signore e Signori!**
see-*nyoh*-reh eh see-*nyoh*-ree
*Ladies and Gentlemen!*

**Sig. Brancato:** **Che succede?**
kee sooh-*cheh*-deh
*What's up?*

**Voice:** **Stiamo atterrando a Milano Malpensa.**
*styah*-moh aht-tehr-*rahn*-doh ah mee-*lah*-noh
mahl-*pehn*-sah
*We're landing now at Milan Malpensa.*

**Sig. Brancato:** **Meno male!**
*meh*-noh *mah*-leh
*Thank goodness!*

**Voice:** **Il cielo è coperto.**
eel *cheh*-loh eh koh-*pehr*-toh
*The sky is overcast.*

**Ms. Roe:** **Come al solito!**
*koh*-meh ahl *soh*-lee-toh
*As usual!*

**Voice:** **E la temperatura è di cinque gradi.**
eh lah tehm-peh-rah-*tooh*-rah eh dee *cheen*-kweh
*grah*-dee
*And the temperature is 5 degrees.*

You probably know that in Europe the Celsius scale is used to measure temperature. So, in the preceding dialogue, "five degrees" converts to 41 degrees Fahrenheit. Refer to the next section for more about Celsius and the metric system.

## WORDS TO KNOW

| come al solito | *koh*-meh ahl *soh*-lee-toh | *as usual* |
| --- | --- | --- |
| **umido [m]** | *ooh*-mee-doh | *humid* |
| **tempo incerto [m]** | *tehm*-poh een-*chehr*-toh | *uncertain weather* |
| **nebbia [f]** | *nehb*-byah | *fog* |
| **mite** | *mee*-teh | *mild* |
| **visibilità [f]** | vee-zee-bee-lee-*tah* | *visibility* |
| **gradi [m/pl.]** | *grah*-dee | *degrees* |
| **piove** | *pyoh*-veh | *It's raining* |

**Piove sul bagnato** (*pyoh*-veh soohl bah–*nyah*-toh) (Literally: *It rains on the wet[ground]*) is an idiomatic expression that Italians use when something negative happens to someone already in a bad situation, or when something positive happens to someone who doesn't really need it. For example, if a millionaire wins the lottery, you might say **piove sul bagnato** to indicate your feeling that you should have won instead.

There's a lovely song about rain, called "Piove," by Jovanotti. Look up the song online, listen to it, and sing along to practice your Italian!!

# Familiarizing Yourself with the Metric System

The whole world uses the metric system, with the exception of the United States, Liberia, and Myanmar, so it's a good idea to review this very common system of measurement. You'll need it to understand directions, order bread and cheese at a market, understand your pharmacy prescription, and even figure out how to make your favorite Italian dishes if you're looking up a recipe on `www.giallozaffer-ano.it`. We discuss temperature, length and distance, and weight here.

## Temperature

First, we discuss **temperature** (tehm-peh-rah-*too*-reh) *(temperature)* as well. Although the United States uses Fahrenheit, most of the world — including Italy — uses **gradi Celsius** *(grah*-dee *chel*-syoos) *(Celsius degrees)*. So, whether you're checking your oven, a thermometer, or the weather, the temperature is in Celsius. The conversion between the two isn't hard — but most people still turn to the internet for a quick and easy answer. A common oven temperature in Italy is 180 degrees C, which corresponds to the medium heat setting of 350 degrees F.

If you're just looking for a quick estimate — especially for weather — a handy trick is to multiply the Celsius temperature by 2 and add 30. It's not exact, but it's usually close enough. For example, 20 degrees C becomes 70 degrees F with this shortcut (actual: 68 degrees F).

## Length and distance

Measures of length go up incrementally as follows. We're only listing the main ones, and you can find scores of conversion sites online if you'd like to take this farther:

>> **millimetro** (meel-*lee*-meh-troh) *(millimeter)*

>> **centimetro** (chehn-*tee*-meh-troh) *(centimeter)*

>> **metro** (*meh*-troh) *(meter)*

>> **chilometro** (kee-*loh*-meh-troh) *(kilometer)*

To ask how far something is, you may say the following:

> **Quanto dista il Colosseo?** (kwahn-toh *dee*-stah eel koh-lohs-*seh*-oh) *(How far is the Colosseum?)*

And a typical response could be

> **Duecento metri a destra.** (*dooh*-eh-*chehn*-toh *meh*-tree ah *deh*-strah) *(200 meters on the right.)*

# Weight

If you're worried about how much weight you're gaining, you can easily pop into a pharmacy in Italy and weigh yourself on one of their scales. (This is usually free or it could cost up to **cinquanta centesimi** (cheen-*qwahn*-tah chehn-*teh*-zee-mee) *(50 cents)*. You will get your weight in chili (kee-lee) *(kilos)*, which you then have to multiply by 2.2, if you're from the United States and use pounds.

Similarly, if you decide you need to buy some very expensive dried **funghi porcini** (*foohn*-gee pohr-*chee*-nee) **(porcini mushrooms)** or **tartufi** (tahr-*tooh*-fee) *(truffles)*, you will ask for those by weight, in this case **grammi** (grahm-mee) *(grams)*.

So, incrementally, measures of weight go as follows:

>> **milligrammo** (meel-lee-grahm-moh) *(milligram)*

>> **grammo** (*grahm*-moh) *(gram)*

>> **ettográmmo** (eht-toh-*grahm*-moh) (*hectogram* = 100 grams)

>> **chilogrammo** (kee-loh-*grahm*-moh) (*kilogram* = 1000 grams)

>> **quintale** (kween-*tah*-leh) *(quintal)*

>> **tonnellata** (tohn-nehl-*lah*-tah) *(ton)*

When shopping for food, **ettogrammo** is often shortened to **etto** (*eht*-toh) *(100 grams)*. For example:

**Un etto/due etti di prosciutto, per favore.** (oohn *eht*-toh *dooh*-eh *eht*-tee dee proh-*shoot*-toh pehr fah-*voh*-reh) (*100 grams* [3.5 ounces, approx.]/*200 grams* [7 ounces, approx.] of prosciutto, please.)

To talk about the volume of liquids, you use the following:

>> **millilitro** (meel-lee-*lee*-troh) *(milliliter)*

>> **litro** (*lee*-troh) *(liter)*

>> **mezzo litro** (*mehd*-dzoh *lee*-troh) *(half liter)*

# Talkin' the Talk

Sarah, an American high school student with two years of Italian, is doing a home stay with an Italian family in Castellaneta this year. They're getting to know each other. Here's part of her first dinner conversation with her new host family. Is she glad she learned her numbers!

**Host Mom:** **Sarah, quanti fratelli hai?**
*sah*-rah *kwahn*-tee frah-*tehl*-lee ahy
*Sara, how many brothers and sisters do you have?*

**Sarah:** **Ho un fratello e due sorelle.**
oh oohn *frah*-tehl-loh eh *dooh*-eh soh-*rehl*-leh
*I have one brother and two sisters.*

**Host Mom:** **Quanti anni hanno?**
*kwahn*-tee *ahn*-nee *ahn*-noh
*How old are they?*

**Sarah:** **Mio fratello David ha dodici anni.**
*mee*-oh frah-*tehl*-loh David ah *doh*-dee-chee *ahn*-nee
*My brother David is 12.*

**Mia sorella Rebecca ne ha diciannove, e mia sorella Naomi ne ha 21.**
*mee*-ah soh-*rehl*-lah Rebecca neh ah dee-chahn-*noh*-veh eh *mee*-ah soh-*rehl*-lah Naomi neh ah vehn-*tooh*-noh.
*My sister Rebecca is 19 and my sister Naomi is 21.*

**Host Mom:** **E quand' è il tuo compleanno?**
eh kwahn-*deh* eel *tooh*-oh kohm-pleh-*ahn*-noh
*And when is your birthday?*

**Sarah:** **Il ventidue maggio.**
eel *vehn*-tee-*dooh*-eh *mahj*-joh
*May 22.*

**Host Mom:** **Quanto dista casa tua da New York?**
*kwahn*-toh *dee*-stah *kah*-zah *tooh*-ah dah New York?
*How far is your house from New York?*

**Sarah:** **Centoventi chilometri, più o meno.**
*chehn*-toh-*vehn*-tee kee-*loh*-meh-tree pyooh oh *meh*-noh
*120 kilometers, more or less.*

**O che bel cane! Che razza è?**
oh keh behl *kah*-neh keh *raht*-tsah eh
*Oh, what a beautiful dog! What kind of dog is he?*

*(continued)*

*(continued)*

| Host Mom: | **È un pastore maremmano.** |
|---|---|
| | eh oohn pah-*stoh*-reh mah-rehm-*mah*-noh |
| | *He's a Maremma sheepdog.* |
| Sarah: | **Quanto pesa?** |
| | *kwahn*-toh *peh*-zah |
| | *How much does he weigh?* |
| Host Mom: | **Trenta chili.** |
| | *trehn*-tah *kee*-lee |
| | *30 kilos.* |

## WORDS TO KNOW

| | | |
|---|---|---|
| **a proposito** | ah proh-*poh*-zee-toh | *by the way* |
| **anni [m/pl.]** | *ahn*-nee | *years* |
| **chilo [m]** | *kee*-loh | *kilo* |
| **compleanno [m]** | kohm-pleh-*ahn*-noh | *birthday* |
| **giorno [m]** | *johr*-noh | *day* |
| **mese [m]** | *meh*-zeh | *month* |
| **numero [m]** | *nooh*-meh-roh | *number* |
| **pastore [m]** | pah-*stoh*-reh | *shepherd* |
| **quanti** | *kwahn*-tee | *how many* |
| **quando** | *kwahn*-doh | *when* |
| **quanto** | *kwahn*-toh | *how much* |

# FUN & GAMES

Take a look at this picture and name the four seasons. For a more challenging task, name the months that comprise each of the seasons. See Appendix C for the answer key.

# 2

# Italian in Action

IN THIS CHAPTER

» **Exploring ordinal numbers**

» **Looking for an apartment**

» **Decorating your home**

» **Cleaning your house**

» **Getting around the kitchen**

# Chapter **5**
# Casa Dolce Casa (Home Sweet Home)

This chapter introduces you to the different vocabulary and situations associated with the house, from renting an apartment to furnishing it to setting the table and eating in it. Just as Italy leads the way in the fashion industry, so too does it enjoy a well-deserved reputation for its fine furnishings and interior spaces.

This chapter also walks you through some essential household chores like cleaning and setting the table, along with the vocabulary for some everyday utensils and appliances. We even give you a quick cooking lesson for a pasta recipe later in the chapter.

## Practicing Ordinal Numbers

When talking about the different floors of a building or you're trying to locate an item in the apartment, you need a command of **numeri ordinali** (*nooh*-meh-ree *ohr*-dee-*nah*-lee) (*ordinal numbers*). Because ordinal numbers are adjectives, they agree with the noun they modify. For example, you use the feminine forms when referring to **camera** (*kah*-meh-rah) (*room*) or **via** (*vee*-ah) (*street*), which are feminine nouns, and the masculine form when talking about a **piano** (*pyah*-noh) *(floor)*. Table 5-1 lists the ordinal numbers in the singular masculine form followed by the singular feminine form.

**TABLE 5-1**     **Ordinal Numbers**

| Italian | Pronunciation | Translation |
| --- | --- | --- |
| **il primo/la prima** | eel *pree*-moh/lah *pree*-mah | *the first* |
| **il secondo/la seconda** | eel seh-*kohn*-doh/lah seh-*kohn*-dah | *the second* |
| **il terzo/la terza** | eel *tehr*-tsoh/lah *tehr*-tsah | *the third* |
| **il quarto/la quarta** | eel *kwahr*-toh/lah *kwahr*-tah | *the fourth* |
| **il quinto/la quinta** | eel *kween*-toh/lah *kween*-tah | *the fifth* |
| **il sesto/la sesta** | eel *seh*-stoh/lah *seh*-stah | *the sixth* |
| **il settimo/la settima** | eel *seht*-tee-moh/lah *seht*-tee-mah | *the seventh* |
| **l'ottavo/l'ottava** | loht-*tah*-voh/loht-*tah*-vah | *the eighth* |
| **il nono/la nona** | eel *noh*-noh/lah *noh*-nah | *the ninth* |
| **il decimo/la decima** | eel *deh*-chee-moh/lah *deh*-chee-mah | *the tenth* |
| **il tredicesimo/la tredicesima** | eel treh-dee-*cheh*-zee-moh/lah treh-dee-*cheh*-zee-mah | *the thirteenth* |
| **Il venteslmo/la venteslmo** | eel vehn-*teh*-zee-moh/lah vehn-*teh*-zee-mah | *the twentieth* |
| **il quararantottesimo/la quarantottesima** | eel qwah-rahn-toht-*teh*-zee-moh/lah qwah-rahn-toht-*teh*-zee-mah | *the forty-eighth* |

**TIP**

After tenth, you take the cardinal number, drop the final vowel, and add **esimo/a/i/e** (*eh*-zee-moh/ah/ee/eh).

These examples show you how to use ordinal numbers in sentences:

>> **È la terza camera a sinistra.** (eh lah *tehr*-tsah *kah*-meh-*rah* ah see-*nee*-strah) *(It's the third room on the left.)*

>> **È la prima via a destra.** (eh lah *pree*-mah *vee*-ah ah deh-strah) *(It's the first street on the right.)*

>> **Sai se abitano all'undicesimo o al dodicesimo piano?** (sahy seh *ah*-bee-tah-noh ahl-loohn-dee-*cheh*-zee-moh oh ahl doh-dee-*cheh*-zee-moh *pyah*-noh) *(Do you know if they live on the eleventh or twelfth floor?)*

In Italy, there are different types of dwellings where people live, the most common being the **appartamento** (ahp-pahr-tah-*mehn*-toh). An apartment is usually in a **condominio** (kohn-doh-*mee*-nyoh) *(apartment building)* or an old refurbished palazzo (pah-*laht*-tsoh). A villa (*veel*-lah) is a free-standing house, usually in the town outskirts or in the countryside. Some people opt to live **in campagna** (een kahm-*pah*-nyah) *(the countryside)*. The suburban area of a city, often residential, is referred to as **periferia** (peh-ree-feh-*ree*-ah). What you refer to in the United States as a townhouse in Italy is called a **casa a schiera** (*kah*-zah ah *skyeh*-rah).

**CULTURAL WISDOM**

All Italian buildings begin with the **pianterreno** (pyahn-tehr-*reh*-noh) or ground floor. So, the first floor (**il primo piano**) (eel *pree*-moh *pyah*-noh) corresponds to a North American second floor, the second floor (**il secondo piano**) (eel seh-*kohn*-doh *pyah*-noh) corresponds to the third floor, and so on.

# Living in Your Home

Italians usually speak of **la casa** (lah *kah*-zah) *(the house; the home)*, even though they often mean **l'appartamento** (lahp-pahr-tah-*mehn*-toh) *(the apartment)*. Italians of all social classes often live in apartment buildings in small towns and large cities rather than in single-family dwellings in the suburbs. Houses can be rented as **monolocali** (moh-noh-loh-*kah*-lee) *(studio apartments)*, **bilocali** (bee-loh-*kah*-lee) *(two-room apartments)*, or as an **appartamento** with a specified number of **camere da letto** (*kah*-meh-reh dah *leht*-toh) *(bedrooms)*.

Here we discuss everything you need to know from finding a place to live to furnishing your new residence.

## Hunting for a place to live

**TIP**

When you're looking for an apartment or a house to rent for the summer, you need to know about the rooms in the house and the size of the apartment. The size is given in square meters.

You can turn to **un'agenzia immobiliare** (oohn-ah-jehn-*tsee*-ah eem-moh-bee-*lyah*-reh) *(a real estate agency)* for help or browse one of the many websites for rental homes, like www.airbnb.it or www.vrbo.com.

You need to know if the **casa** is **ammobiliata** (ahm-moh-bee-*lyah*-tah) *(furnished)*, because most short-term rentals are. If you're renting for the long term, many times the house will be completely empty without even a fridge. **L'aria condizionata** (*lah*-ryah kohn-dee-tsyoh-*nah*-tah) (*air conditioning*) is an important feature to look for in the summer months, although it isn't as common as it is in the United States.

These words can help you specify your wishes about the number and types of rooms as well as location and amenities.

>> **l'ascensore** (lah-shehn-*soh*-reh) (*the elevator*)

>> **l'angolo cottura** (*lahn*-goh-loh koht-*tooh*-rah) (*cooking area* — such as in a studio apartment)

>> **il bagno** (eel *bah*-nyoh) (*the bathroom*)

>> **il balcone** (eel bahl-*koh*-neh) (*the balcony*)

>> **la camera da letto** (lah *kah*-meh-rah dah *leht*-toh) (*the bedroom*)

>> **la cantina** (lah kahn-*tee*-nah) (*the cellar*)

>> **la cucina** (lah kooh-*chee*-nah) (*the kitchen*)

>> **la doccia** (lah *doch*-chah) (*the shower*)

>> **la finestra** (lah fee-*neh*-strah) (*the window*)

>> **il garage** (eel gah-*rahj*) (*the garage*)

>> **la mansarda** (mahn-*sahr*-dah) (*the attic*)

>> **la piscina** (lah pee-*shee*-nah) (*the pool*)

>> **il soggiorno** (eel sohj-*johr*-noh) (*the living room*)

>> **la stanza** (lah *stahn*-tsah) (*the room*)

>> **la sala da pranzo** (lah *sah*-lah dah *prahn*-zoh) (*the dining room*)

>> **lo studio** (loh *stooh*-dyoh) (*the office* or *study*)

>> **la vasca da bagno** (lah *vah*-skah dah *bah*-nyoh) (*the bathtub*)

Using the verb "to rent" may be somewhat confusing. The confusion comes from the fact that, in English, both **i padroni di casa** (ee pah-*droh*-nee dee *kah*-zah) (*landlords*) and **gli inquilini** (lyee een-kwee-*lee*-nee) (*tenants*) use the verb **affittare** (ahf-feet-*tah*-reh) (*to rent*). To avoid misunderstandings, landlords sometimes say **dare in affitto** (*dah*-reh een ahf-*feet*-toh) (*to rent out*) and tenants use **prendere in affitto** (*prehn*-deh-reh een ahf-*feet*-toh) (*to rent a place to live*). Other useful verbs for these types of actions might include **subaffittare** (soohb-ahf-fee-*tah*-reh) (*to sublet*), **traslocare** (trahz-loh-*kah*-reh) (*to change houses*), and **trasferirsi** (trahs-feh-*reer*-see) (*to move from place to place*).

# Talkin' the Talk

Flaminia is looking for an apartment, and Pietro helps her read through the web ads. After a few minutes, Pietro thinks he's found something interesting.

| | |
|---|---|
| **Pietro:** | **Affittasi appartamento zona centro.**<br>ahf-*feet*-tah-see ahp-pahr-tah-*mehn*-toh *dzoh*-nah *chehn*-troh<br>*Apartment for rent, city center.* |
| **Flaminia:** | **Continua!**<br>kohn-*tee*-nwah<br>*Go on!* |
| **Pietro:** | **Due stanze, balcone, garage.**<br>*dooh*-eh *stahn*-tseh bahl-*koh*-neh gah-*rahj*<br>*Two rooms, balcony, garage.* |
| **Flaminia:** | **Perfetto!**<br>pehr-*feht*-toh<br>*Perfect!* |
| **Pietro:** | **Tranquillo, in Via Treviso.**<br>trahn-*kweel*-loh een *vee*-ah treh-*vee*-zoh<br>*Quiet, on Treviso Street.* |
| **Flaminia:** | **Chiamo subito. Non è molto centrale.**<br>*kyah*-moh *sooh*-bee-toh nohn eh *mohl*-toh chehn-*trah*-leh<br>*I'll call immediately. It's not very centrally located.* |
| **Pietro:** | **No, ma costa sicuramente meno.**<br>noh mah *koh*-stah see-kooh-rah-*mehn*-teh *meh*-noh<br>*No, but it's definitely less expensive.* |
| **Flaminia:** | **È vero.**<br>eh *veh*-roh<br>*That's true!* |
| **Pietro:** | **Chiama!**<br>*kyah*-mah<br>*Call!* |

When you see a listing — whether online or elsewhere — that interests you, reacting immediately is always best because as Italians say **Chi tardi arriva male alloggia** (kee *tahr*-dee ahr-*ree*-vah *mah*-leh ahl-loh-jah) (*You snooze, you lose.*). You don't want to hear **Mi dispiace, è già affittato** (mee dee-*spyah*-cheh eh jah ahf-feet-*tah*-toh) (*I'm sorry, it's already rented.*).

You may want to know the following words when searching for an apartment (and any time you are considering making a purchase). **Caro** (*kah*-roh) means "expensive," and **economico** (eh-koh-*noh*-mee-koh) means "inexpensive," although Italians seldom use the word **economico**. Rather, most people say **costa poco** (*koh*-stah *poh*-koh) (*it costs little*) or **è a buon mercato** (eh ah bwohn mehr-*kah*-toh) (*it's not expensive*). When you want to compare costs, you say **costa meno** (*koh*-stah *meh*-noh) (*it costs less*) or **costa di più** (*koh*-stah dee pyooh) (*it costs more*). Other questions you might want to ask include: **A che piano è?** (ah keh *pyah*-noh eh) (*What floor is it on?*) and **C'è l'ascensore?** (cheh lah-shehn-*soh*-reh) (*Is there an elevator?*).

# Talkin' the Talk

Flaminia calls the landlord's number to find out more about the apartment.

| | |
|---|---|
| **Landlord:** | **Pronto!** |
| | *prohn*-toh |
| | *Hello!* |
| | |
| **Flaminia:** | **Buongiorno, chiamo per l'appartamento. Quant'è l'affitto?** |
| | bwohn-*johr*-noh *kyah*-moh pehr lahp-pahr-tah-*mehn*-toh kwahn-*teh* lah-*fit*-toh |
| | *Good morning! I'm calling about the apartment. How much is the rent?* |
| | |
| **Landlord:** | **600 euro al mese.** |
| | sey-*chehn*-toh *eh*-ooh-roh ahl *meh*-zeh |
| | *Six hundred euros per month.* |
| | |
| **Flaminia:** | **Riscaldamento e acqua sono compresi?** |
| | ree-skahl-dah-*mehn*-toh eh *ah-k*wah *soh*-noh kohm-*preh*-zee |
| | *Are heat and water included?* |
| | |
| **Landlord:** | **No, vengono pagati separatamente.** |
| | noh *vehn*-goh-noh pah-*gah*-tee seh-pah-rah-tah-*mehn*-teh |
| | *No, they are paid separately.* |
| | |
| **Flaminia:** | **Sono alte le bollette?** |
| | *soh*-noh *ahl*-teh leh bohl-*leht*-teh |
| | *Are the bills high?* |

| Landlord: | **Dipende dal consumo . . . come l'elettricità.**<br>dee-*pehn*-deh dahl kohn-*sooh*-moh *koh*-meh<br>leh-leht-tree-chee-*tah*<br>*It depends on your usage . . . the same goes for electricity.* |
| --- | --- |
| Flaminia: | **Quando lo posso vedere?**<br>*kwahn*-doh loh *pohs*-soh veh-*deh*-reh<br>*When can I see it?* |
| Landlord: | **Subito, se vuole.**<br>*sooh*-bee-toh seh *vwoh*-leh<br>*Immediately, if you want.* |

You'll probably have more questions if you decide to rent an apartment or buy a house/a flat. **Pagare in contanti** (pah-*gah*-reh een kohn-*tahn*-tee) (*Paying in cash*) is always a possibility, but in most cases, you may take out a **mutuo** (*mooh*-twoh) (*mortgage*) to pay little by little. When you buy a house in Italy, it's also important to have a good **avvocato** (*ahv*-voh-kah-toh) (*lawyer*). You'll also need a **notaio** (noh-*tah*-yoh) (*notary* – in Italy, a legal professional and public officer who specializes, among other things, in real estate transactions).

Table 5-2 lists some of the more common questions and some possible answers.

**TABLE 5-2**

## Common House-Hunting Questions and Answers

| Questions | Possible Answers |
| --- | --- |
| **È occupato?** (eh ohk-kooh-*pah*-toh)<br>(*Is it occupied?*) | **No, è libero.** (noh eh *lee*-beh-roh) (*No, it's vacant.*)<br><br>**Sì, per il momento.** (see pehr eel moh-*mehn*-toh) (*Yes, at the moment.*)<br><br>**Sarà libero fra sei mesi.** (sa-*rah lee*-beh-roh frah sey *meh*-zee) (*It will be vacant in six months.*) |
| **Bisogna lasciare un deposito?** (bee-*zoh*-nyah lah-*shah*-reh oohn deh-*poh*-zee-toh) (*Is it necessary to put down a deposit?*) | **Sì, un mese d'affitto.** (see oohn *meh*-zeh dahf-*feet*-toh) (*Yes, one month's rent.*)<br><br>**Sì, la cauzione** (see lah kow-*tsyoh*-neh) (*Yes, we require a security deposit.*) |
| **Paghi molto d'affitto?** (*pah*-gee *mohl*-toh dahf-*feet*-toh) (*Is your rent high?*) | **No, l'affitto è veramente basso.** (noh lahf-feet-toh eh veh-rah-*mehn*-teh *bahs*-soh) (*No, the rent is really low.*) |
| **La casa è tua?** (lah *kah*-sah eh *tooh*-ah)<br>(*Do you own your home?*) | **No, sono in affitto.** (noh *soh*-noh een ahf-*feet*-toh) (*No, I rent.*)<br><br>**Sì, l'ho comprata l'anno scorso.** (see loh kohm-*prah*-tah *lahn*-noh *skohr*-soh) (*Yes, I bought it last year.*)<br><br>**Ho fatto un mutuo.** (oh *faht*-toh oohn *mooh*-tooh-oh) (*I took out a mortgage.*) |

# Sprucing up your residence

When you finally find a place to live, you probably want to furnish it beautifully.

## Talkin' the Talk

Valerio has found a new apartment, **non ammobiliato** (nohn ahm-moh-bee-*lyah*-toh) *(unfurnished).* His friend Eugenia is asking him what he needs.

| | |
|---|---|
| **Valerio:** | **Ho trovato un appartamento! Devo comprare dei mobili.**<br>oh troh-*vah*-toh oohn ahp-pahr-tah-*mehn*-toh *deh*-voh kohm-*prah*-reh dey *moh*-bee-lee<br>*I just found an apartment! I have to buy some furniture.* |
| **Eugenia:** | **Tutto?**<br>*tooht*-toh<br>*Everything?* |
| **Valerio:** | **No, per la camera da letto, il letto e l'armadio.**<br>noh pehr lah *kah*-meh-rah dah *leht*-toh eel *leht*-toh eh lahr-*mah*-dyoh<br>*No, for the bedroom a bed and a wardrobe.* |
| **Eugenia:** | **Nient'altro?**<br>nyehn-*tahl*-troh<br>*Anything else?* |
| **Valerio:** | **Ho due comodini e una cassettiera.**<br>oh *dooh*-eh koh-moh-*dee*-nee eh *ooh*-nah kahs-seht-*tyeh*-rah<br>*I have two bedside tables and a chest of drawers.* |
| **Eugenia:** | **E per il soggiorno?**<br>eh pehr eel sohj-*johr*-noh<br>*And for the living room?* |
| **Valerio:** | **Ho una poltrona. Mi mancano ancora il divano e un tavolino.**<br>oh *ooh*-nah pohl-*troh*-nah mee *mahn*-kah-noh ahn-*koh*-rah eel dee-*vah*-noh eh oohn tah-voh-*lee*-noh<br>*I have an armchair. I still need a couch and a coffee table.* |

La signora Giorgetti wants to buy secondhand furniture. She sees an interest-ing ad:

> **Vendesi** (*vehn*-deh-see) *(For sale)*: **tavolo e due sedie** (*tah*-voh-loh eh *dooh*-eh *seh*-dyeh) *(table and two chairs)* **stile Liberty** (*stee*-leh *lee*-behr-tee) *(Liberty style)*

> **"Quello che cercavo!"** (*kwehl*-loh keh chehr-*kah*-voh) *("Just what I was looking for!")*, she exclaims. She immediately calls the number on the ad.

Of course, she needs answers to some questions:

- **Sono in buono stato?** (*soh*-noh een *bwoh*-noh *stah*-toh) *(Are they in good condition?)*
- **Quanto vuole?** (*kwahn*-toh *vwoh*-leh?) *(How much are you asking?)*
- **Posso venire a vederli?** (*pohs*-soh veh-nee-reh ah veh-*dehr*-lee) *(Can I come to see them?)*

## Furnishing your new pad

Table 5-3 divides the different pieces of **mobili** (*moh*-bee-lee) *(furniture)* and other items according to the rooms.

**TABLE 5-3**

### Room Furniture Translation

| | |
|---|---|
| **il soggiorno/il salotto** (eel soj-*johr*-noh)/ (eel sah-*loht*-toh) | *the living room* |
| **il divano** (eel dee-*vah*-noh) | *couch* |
| **la poltrona** (lah pohl-*troh*-nah) | *armchair* |
| **il tappeto** (eel tahp-*peht*-toh) | *rug* |
| **lo scaffale** (loh skahf-*fah*-leh) | *bookshelf* |
| **la cucina** (lah koo-*chee*-nah) | *the kitchen* |
| **il frigorifero** (eel free-goh-*ree*-feh-roh) | *refrigerator* |
| **la lavastoviglie** (lah lah-vah-stoh-*vee*-lyeh) | *dishwasher* |
| **il lavello** (eel lah-*vehl*-loh) | *kitchen sink* |
| **le sedie** (leh *seh*-dyeh) | *chairs* |
| **il tavolo** (eel *tah*-voh-loh) | *table* |

*(continued)*

| | |
|---|---|
| **la credenza** (lah creh-*dehn*-tsah) | *sideboard or cupboard* |
| **i pensili** (ee *pehn*-see-lee) | *kitchen cabinets* |
| **la camera da letto** (lah *kah*-meh-rah dah *leht*-toh) | ***the bedroom*** |
| **il letto** (eel *leht*-toh) | *bed* |
| **il comodino** (eel koh-moh-*dee*-noh) | *nightstand* |
| **l'armadio** (lahr-*mah*-dyoh) | *armoire* |
| **il comò** (eel koh-*moh*) | *dresser* |
| **i cuscini** (ee kooh-*shee*-nee) | *pillows* |
| **la lampada** (lah *lahm*-pah-dah) | *lamp* |
| **il lenzuolo/le lenzuola** (eel lehn-*zwoh*-lo/leh lehn-*zwoh*-lah) | *sheet/sheets* |
| **le tende** (leh *tehn*-deh) | *curtains* |
| **il bagno** (eel *bah*-nyoh) | ***the bathroom*** |
| **Il bidet** (eel bee-*deh*) | *bidet* |
| **la tazza** (lah *taht*-tsah) | *toilet bowl* |
| **Il lavandino** (eel lah-vahn-*dee*-noh) | *sink* |
| **la doccia** (lah *dohch*-chah) | *shower* |
| **la vasca da bagno** (lah *vah*-skah dah *bah*-nyoh) | *bathtub* |

## WORDS TO KNOW

| | | |
|---|---|---|
| **accanto** | ahk-*kahn*-toh | *next to* |
| **davanti a** | dah-*vahn*-tee ah | *in front of* |
| **dietro** | *dyeh*-troh | *behind* |
| **sopra** | *soh*-prah | *on top of* |
| **sotto** | *soht*-toh | *under* |
| **di fianco** | dee *fyahn*-koh | *on the side* |
| **dentro** | *dehn*-troh | *inside* |
| **fuori** | *fwoh*-ree | *outside* |

# Housekeeping in Style

Italians do love their **elettrodomestici** (eh–leht–troh–doh–*meh*–stee–chee) *(household appliances)*, and there are many sleek Italian brands for these things. Dryers are very rare in Italy because of the large amount of electricity they consume, but almost every household now has dishwashers. Some essential **elettrodomestici** include the following:

>> **l'aspirapolvere** (lah-spee-rah-*pohl*-veh-reh) *(vacuum cleaner)*

>> **la lavatrice** (lah lah-vah-*tree*-cheh) *(washing machine)*

>> **la lavastoviglie** (lah lah-vah-stoh-*vee*-lyeh) *(dishwasher)*

>> **il frullatore** (eel froohl-lah-*toh*-reh) *(blender)*

>> **il tostapane** (eeh toh-stah-*pah*-neh) *(toaster)*

>> **il frigorifero** (eel free-goh-*ree*-fehr-oh) *(refrigerator)*

>> **i fornelli** (ee fohr-*nehl*-lee) *(stovetop)*

>> **il forno** (eel *fohr*-noh) *(oven)*

>> **la cucina a gas/elettrica** (la koo-*chee*-nah ah gahz eh-*leht*-tree-kah) *(gas/ electric range)*

>> **il microonde** (eel mee-kroh-*ohn*-deh) *(microwave oven)*

# Talkin' the Talk

A mother and son are preparing for dinner. She asks him to set the table and sweep the floor in the **sala da pranzo** (*sah*-lah dah *prahn*-zoh) *(dining room)* before their guests arrive.

| | |
|---|---|
| **Mamma:** | **Salvatore, per favore, passa la scopa prima che arrivino gli ospiti.**<br>sahl-vah-*toh*-reh pehr fah-*voh*-reh *pahs*-sah lah *skoh*-pah *pree*-mah keh ahr-*ree*-vee-noh lyee *oh*-spee-tee<br>*Salvatore, please sweep before the guests arrive.* |
| **Salvatore:** | **Va bene, mamma.**<br>vah *beh*-neh *mahm*-mah<br>*Okay, Mom.* |

*(continued)*

*(continued)*

**Che altro?**
keh *ahl*-troh
*What else?*

**Mamma:** **Apparecchia il tavolo, tesoro.**
ahp-pah-*rek*-kyah eel *tah*-voh-loh teh-*zoh*-roh
*Set the table, sweetheart.*

**Salvatore:** **Cosa ci metto?**
*koh*-zah chee *meht*-toh
*What should I put out?*

**Mamma:** **Metti la tovaglia con i limoni con i suoi tovaglioli.**
*meht*-tee lah toh-*vah*-lyah kohn ee lee-*moh*-nee kohn ee
swoi toh-vah-*lyoh*-lee
*Put out the tablecloth with the lemons and matching napkins.*

**Salvatore:** **Quali piatti?**
*kwah*-lee *pyaht*-tee
*What dishes?*

**Mamma:** **Quelli di Faenza, il piatto piano e il piatto fondo.**
*kwehl*-lee dee fah-*ehn*-tsah eel *pyaht*-toh *pyah*-noh eh eel
*pyaht*-toh *fohn*-doh
*The ones made in Faenza, the dinner plates and the bowls.*

**Non dimenticare forchette, coltelli e cucchiai per il minestrone.**
nohn dee-mehn-tee-*kah*-reh fohr-*keht*-teh kohl-*tehl*-lee eh
koohk-*kyah*-ee pehr eel mee-neh-*stroh*-neh
*Don't forget forks, knives, and spoons for the minestrone soup.*

**Salvatore:** **Mamma, non bastano i bicchieri per l'acqua.**
*mahm*-mah nohn *bah*-stah-noh ee beek-*kyeh*-ree pehr
*lah*-kwah
*Mom, there aren't enough water glasses.*

**Mamma:** **Non importa, li ho qui nella lavastoviglie.**
nohn eem-*pohr*-tah lee oh kwee *nehl*-lah
lah-vah-stoh-*vee*-lyeh
*That's okay. I have them here in the dishwasher.*

**Aggiungiamo anche i bicchieri da vino. Grazie.**
aj-joohn-*jah*-moh *ahn*-keh ee beek-*kyeh*-ree dah *vee*-noh
*grah*-tsyeh
*Let's add wine glasses, too. Thanks.*

## WORDS TO KNOW

| | | |
|---|---|---|
| **apparecchiare** | ahp-pahr-ehk-*kyah*-reh | *to set the table* |
| **bicchiere [m]** | beek-*kyeh*-reh | *drinking glass (for water, wine, and so on)* |
| **coltello [m]** | kohl-*tehl*-loh | *knife* |
| **cucchiaio [m]** | koohk-*kyah*-yoh/ee | *spoon* |
| **forchetta [f]** | fohr-*keht*-tah | *fork* |
| **piatto [m]** | *pyaht*-toh | *dish* |
| **il piatto piano [m]** | eel *pyaht*-toh *pyah*-noh | *dinner plate* |
| **il piatto fondo [m]** | eel *pyaht*-toh *fohn*-doh | *bowl (for soup or pasta)* |
| **scopa [f]** | *skoh*-pah | *broom* |
| **sparecchiare** | spah-rehk-*kyah*-reh | *to clear the table* |
| **tazza [f]** | *taht*-tsah | *mug/cup* |
| **tovaglia [f]** | toh-*vah*-lyah | *tablecloth* |
| **tovagliolo [m]** | toh-vah-*lyoh*-loh | *napkin* |

**CULTURAL WISDOM**

Did you know that some of the most beautiful ceramics are produced throughout Italy? Many are hand-painted and are true works of art. Some towns well-known for their ceramics include Faenza (Emilia Romagna), Deruta and Orvieto (Umbria), Vietri (Amalfi Coast), and Caltagirone (Sicily). It might be hard to visit one of these towns and not buy some ceramics to bring back home.

# Cooking at Home

If you love to **cucinare** (kooh–chee–*nah*–reh) *(cook)*, you'll certainly have fun buying your ingredients in an Italian market or supermarket. Maybe you're enrolled in a cooking school in Tuscany this summer. But even if you're not in Italy and like to practice your Italian by listening to Italian cooking channels, you're going to need some essential kitchen vocabulary.

# Talkin' the Talk

Listen to the following recipe by Amedeo, chef for the **Italiani In Cucina** food network. This is only part of the recipe, but enough to get you started on some important kitchen terminology. (Track 10)

**Amedeo:** **Buongiorno e benvenuti a "Italiani in Cucina." Oggi prepariamo le penne all'arrabbiata per quattro persone.**

bwohn *johr*-noh eh behn-veh-*nooh*-tee a ee-tah-*lyah*-nee een kooh-*chee*-nah *ohj*-jee preh-pah-*ryah*-moh leh *pehn*-neh ahl-lahr-rahb-*byah*-tah pehr *kwaht*-troh pehr-*soh*-neh
*Hello, and welcome to "Italians in the Kitchen." Today we will be preparing penne all'arrabbiata for four people.*

**Gli ingredienti sono:**
lyee een-greh-*dyehn*-tee *soh*-noh
*The ingredients are:*

**500 grammi di pomodori**
*cheen*-kweh-*chehn*-toh *grahm*-mee dee poh-moh-*doh*-ree
*500 grams of tomatoes*

**Mezzo chilo di penne**
*mehd*-dzoh *kee*-loh dee *pehn*-neh
*Half a kilo of penne*

**Un cucchiaio di peperoncino**
oohn koohk-*kyah*-yoh dee peh-peh-rohn-*chee*-noh
*One tablespoon of hot pepper*

**Olio d'oliva extra vergine**
*Oh*-lyoh doh-*lee*-vah *ehk*-strah *vehr*-jee-neh
*Extra-virgin olive oil*

**Quattro spicchi di aglio**
*kwaht*-troh *speek*-kee dee *ah-l*yoh
*Four cloves of garlic*

**Un mazzetto di prezzemolo**
oohn maht-*tseht*-toh dee preht-*tseh-m*oh-loh
*A small bunch of parsley*

**Inoltre, avrete bisogno di:**
ee-*nohl*-treh ah-*vreh*-teh bee-*zoh*-nyoh dee
*Furthermore, you will need:*

**Una pentola grande per la pasta**
*ooh*-nah *pehn*-toh-lah *grahn*-deh pehr lah *pah*-stah
*A large pot for the pasta*

**Una padella grande per la salsa**
*ooh*-nah pah-*dehl*-lah pehr lah *sahl*-sah
*A large pan for the sauce*

**Sale e pepe**
*sah*-leh eh *peh*-peh
*Salt and pepper*

**Innanzitutto fate bollire una pentola grande di acqua per la pasta.**
een-nahn-tsee-*tooht*-toh *fah*-teh bohl-*lee*-reh *ooh*-nah *pehn*-toh-lah *grahn*-deh dee *ah-k*wah pehr lah *pah*-stah
*First of all, put a large pot of water on to boil for the pasta.*

# Doing Household Chores

Italians do like to keep a spic and span house. We don't know anyone who likes to clean house, but if you've found an Italian roommate and you're going to be dividing the chores, you may as well know how to say some of these things.

## Talkin' the Talk

Jenny and Lucia are two new roommates who have just moved in together while attending the University of Bologna. They're dividing the household chores, or **faccende domestiche** (fahch-*chehn*-deh doh-*meh*-stee-keh).

| Jenny: | **Allora, come vogliamo dividere le faccende di casa?** |
|---|---|
| | ahl-*loh*-rah *koh*-meh voh-*lyah*-moh dee-*vee*-deh-reh leh fach-*chehn*-deh dee *kah*-zah |
| | *So how should we divide the chores?* |

| Lucia: | **Facciamo a settimane alterne.** |
|---|---|
| | fah-*chah*-moh ah seht-tee-*mah*-neh ahl-tehr-*nah*-teh |
| | *Let's do alternating weeks.* |

| Jenny: | **Una buon'idea.** |
|---|---|
| | *ooh*-nah *bwohn*-ee-*deh*-ah |
| | *Good idea.* |

*(continued)*

*(continued)*

**Questa settimana io porto fuori la spazzatura e pulisco il bagno e la cucina.**
*kweh*-stah seht-tee-*mah*-nah *ee*-oh *pohr*-toh *fwoh*-ree lah spaht-tsah-*tooh*-rah eh pooh-*lee*-skoh eel *bah*-nyoh e lah kooh-*chee*-nah
*This week I'll take out the garbage and clean the bathroom and kitchen.*

Lucia: **Ed io passo l'aspirapolvere, spolvero tutta la casa e innaffio le piante.**
ehd *ee*-oh *pahs*-soh lah-*spee*-rah-*pohl*-veh-reh *spohl*-veh-roh *tooht*-tah lah *kah*-zah eh een-*nahf*-fyoh leh *pyahn*-teh
*And I'll vacuum, dust the whole house, and water the plants.*

## WORDS TO KNOW

| | | |
|---|---|---|
| **bucato** | booh-*kah*-to | *laundry* |
| **camera [f]** | *kah*-meh-rah | *room* |
| **fare il bucato** | *fah*-reh eel booh-*kah*-to | *to do laundy* |
| **fare il letto** | *fah*-reh eel leht-toh | *to make the bed* |
| **innaffiare** | een-nahf-*fyah*-reh | *to water* |
| **lavare i pavimenti [m]** | lah-*vah*-reh ee pah-vee-*mehn*-tee | *to wash the floors* |
| **lavare i piatti** | lah-*vah*-reh ee *pyaht*-tee | *to dishwash* |
| **mettere in ordine** | *meht*-teh-reh een *ohr*-dee-neh | *to straighten up* |
| **passare l'aspirapolvere** | pahs-*sah*-reh lah-spee-rah-*pohl*-veh-reh | *to vacuum* |
| **passare la scopa** | pahs-*sah*-reh lah *skoh*-pah | *to sweep* |
| **portare fuori la spazzatura** | pohr-*tah*-reh *fwoh*-ree lah spaht-tsah-*tooh*-rah | *to take out the garbage* |
| **pulire** | pooh-*lee*-reh | *to clean* |
| **spolverare** | spohl-veh-*rah*-reh | *to dust* |

# FUN & GAMES

This is an easy one! Identify the various rooms and items marked with a solid, numbered line with their Italian names. For extra credit, keep on naming as many items as you can! See Appendix C for the answer key.

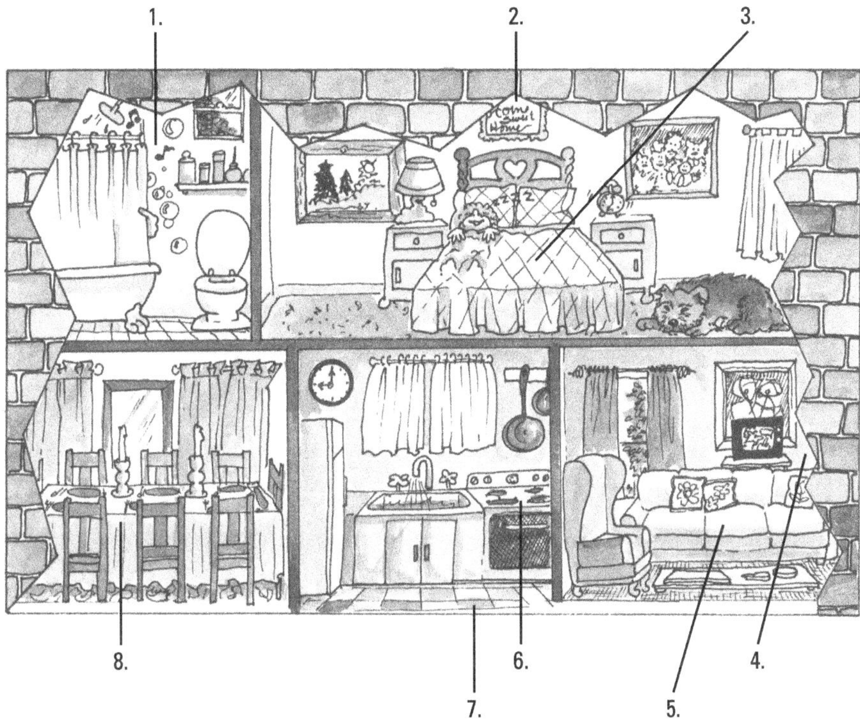

*Illustration by Liz Kurtzman*

# Chapter **6**

# Where Is the Colosseum? Asking Directions

Have you ever been lost in a foreign city or country? If so, you realize how helpful it is when you know enough of the native language to be able to ask for directions — and to make sense of the response. In this chapter, we give you some helpful conversational tips that make it easier to find your way around.

## Finding Your Way: Asking for Specific Places

When asking for directions, it's always polite to start your question with one of the following expressions. The first three are formal (use with strangers and older people):

» **Scusi.** (*skooh*-zee) (*Excuse me* — you singular)

» **Mi scusi.** (mee *skooh*-zee) (*Excuse me* — you singular)

» **Mi scusino.** (mee *skooh*-zee-noh) (*Excuse me* — you plural)

Here are some informal ways:

>> **Scusa.** (*skooh*-zah) *(Excuse me — you singular)*

>> **Scusate.** (skooh-zah-teh) *(Excuse me — you plural)*

Then you can continue with your questions and statements like the following:

>> **Dove siamo adesso?** (doh-veh *syah*-moh ah-dehs-soh) *(Where are we now?)*

>> **Mi sono perso. Dov'è il duomo?** (mee *soh*-noh *pehr*-soh doh-*veh* eel *dwoh*-moh) *(I'm lost. Where is the cathedral?)*

>> **Può indicarmi la strada per il centro?** (pwoh een-dee-*kahr*-mee lah *strah*-dah pehr eel *chehn*-troh) *(Can you show me the way downtown?)*

>> **Per la stazione?** (pehr lah stah-*tsyoh*-neh) *(How do I get to the station?)*

>> **Dov'è il Colosseo?** (doh-*veh* eel koh-lohs-*seh*-oh) *(Where is the Colosseum?)*

>> **Un'informazione, per favore!** (oohn-een-fohr-mah-*tsyoh*-neh pehr fah-*voh*-reh) *(I need some information, please!)*

>> **È questa via Garibaldi?** (eh *kweh*-stah *vee*-ah gah-ree-*bahl*-dee) *(Is this via Garibaldi?)*

Here are some possible answers, and not in any particular order (mix and match according to context!), to the preceding questions:

>> **Si è proprio qui vicino!** (see eh *proh*-pryoh kwee vee-*chee*-noh) *(Yes, it is very close!)*

>> **Segua la strada principale fino al centro.** (*seh*-gwah lah *strah*-dah preen-chee-*pah*-leh *fee*-noh ahl *chehn*-troh) *(Follow the main street to the city center.)*

>> **Vada sempre dritto.** (*vah*-dah *sehm*-preh *dreet*-toh) *(Go straight ahead.)*

>> **È in fondo a sinistra.** (eh een *fohn*-doh ah see-*nee*-strah) *(It's down at the end, on the left side.)*

>> **È la terza strada a sinistra.** (eh lah *tehr*-tsah *strah*-dah ah see-*nee*-strah) *(It's the third street on the left.)*

>> **È dopo il terzo semaforo a destra.** (eh *doh*-poh eel *tehr*-tsoh seh-*mah*-foh-roh ah *deh*-strah) *(It's after the third light, on the right.)*

>> **È vicino alla posta.** (eh vee-*chee*-noh *ahl*-lah *poh*-stah) *(It's near the post office.)*

>> **Attraversi il ponte, poi c'è una piazza e lì lo vede.** (aht-trah-*vehr*-see eel *pohn*-teh poi cheh *ooh*-nah *pyaht*-tsah eh lee loh *veh*-deh) *(Cross the bridge, then there's a square and there you see it.)*

>> **Ha sbagliato strada.** (ah zbah-*lyah*-toh *strah*-dah) *(You went the wrong way.)*

# Talkin' the Talk

Anna Maria and Robert are looking for the Trevi Fountain. They're on Rome's via del Corso and stop to ask a Carabiniere (a type of police officer) for directions. Note that here the Carabiniere uses the "you plural form" because he's speaking to two adults he doesn't know.

| | |
|---|---|
| **Anna Maria:** | **Scusi, è qui vicino la Fontana di Trevi?**<br>skooh-zee eh kwee vee-chee-noh lah fohn-tah-nah dee treh-vee<br>*Excuse me, is the Trevi Fountain nearby?* |
| **Carabiniere:** | **Sì, è proprio qui vicino! Girino a destra in Via delle Muratte e proseguano all'incirca 200 metri.**<br>see eh proh-*pryoh* kwee vee-*chee*-noh *jee*-ree-noh ah *deh*-strah een *vee*-ah *dehl*-leh mooh-*raht*-teh eh *proh*-seh-*gwah*-noh ahl-leen-*cheer*-cah *dooh*-eh *chehn*-toh *meh*-tree<br>*Yes, it's very close. Take a right on via delle Muratte and then keep going for about 200 meters.* |
| **Anna Maria:** | **Molte grazie.**<br>*mohl*-teh *grah*-tsyeh<br>*Many thanks.* |
| **Carabiniere:** | **Non c'è di che.**<br>nohn cheh dee keh<br>*Don't mention it.* |

# Knowing Where You Are and Following Directions

Four orientations you already know are the cardinal points of the compass: north, south, east, and west. The four directions are especially helpful to know when you use a map. The following are **i quattro punti cardinali** (ee *kwaht*-troh *poohn*-tee kahr-dee-*nah*-lee) *(the four cardinal points):*

>> **nord** (nohrd) *(north)*

>> **est** (ehst) *(east)*

>> **sud** (soohd) *(south)*

>> **ovest** (*oh*-vehst) *(west)*

You may hear the directions used in sentences like the following:

>> **Trieste è a nord-est.** (tree-*eh*-steh eh ah nohrd-*ehst*) *(Trieste is to the northeast.)*

>> **Napoli è a sud.** (*nah*-poh-lee eh ah soohd) *(Naples is to the south.)*

>> **Roma è a ovest.** (*roh*-mah eh ah *oh*-vehst) *(Rome is to the west.)*

>> **Bari è a sud-est.** (*bah*-ree eh ah soohd-*ehst*) *(Bari is to the southeast.)*

The following sections give you important vocabulary and phrases that can help you navigate where you're going.

## Identifying distances when walking

Some lovely city centers, such as the ones in Verona and Ravenna, are closed off to traffic, so you need to get around on foot. Knowing how to orient yourself in relation to people and buildings when following or giving directions is important. Italians also use meters to describe distances on foot:

>> **davanti a** (dah-*vahn*-tee ah) *(in front of)*

>> **dietro** (*dyeh*-troh ah) *(behind)*

>> **vicino a** (vee-*chee*-noh ah) *(near)*

>> **accanto a** (ahk-*kahn*-toh ah) *(next to)*

>> **di fronte a** (dee-*frohn*-teh ah) *(in front of; opposite)*

>> **dentro** (*dehn*-troh) *(inside)*

>> **fuori** (*fwoh*-ree) *(outside)*

>> **sotto** (*soht*-toh) *(under; below)*

>> **sopra** (*soh*-prah) *(above)*

## Recognizing where you're headed

You also need to know relationship between distance and the direction in which you're headed. By the way, the word for direction is **la direzione** (lah dee–reh–*tsyoh*–neh):

>> **dritto** (*dreet*-toh) *(straight)*

>> **sempre dritto** (*sehm*-preh *dreet*-toh) *(straight ahead)*

>> **fino a** (*fee*-noh ah) *(to; up to)*

>> **prima** (*pree*-mah) *(before)*

>> **dopo** (*doh*-poh) *(after)*

>> **a destra** (ah *deh*-strah) *(on/to the right)*

>> **a sinistra** (ah see-*nee*-strah) *(on/to the left)*

>> **dietro l'angolo** (*dyeh*-troh *lahn*-goh-loh) *(around the corner)*

>> **all'angolo** (ahl-*lahn*-goh-loh) *(at the corner)*

>> **all'incrocio** (ahl-leen-*kroh*-choh) *(at the intersection)*

## Giving and receiving directions

Here is some more helpful vocabulary you can use for giving and receiving directions:

>> **il marciapiede** (eel mahr-chah-*pyeh*-deh) *(sidewalk)*

>> **la piazza** (lah *pyaht*-tsah) *(square)*

>> **il largo** (eel *lahr*-goh) *(square)*

>> **la strada** (lah *strah*-dah) *(road; street)*

>> **la via** (lah *vee*-ah) *(road; street)*

>> **la via principale** (lah *vee*-ah preen-chee-*pah*-leh) *(main street)*

>> **il vicolo** (eel *vee*-koh-loh) *(alley; lane)*

>> **la calle** (lah *kahl*-leh) *(narrow Venetian street; term found only in Venice)*

>> **il viale/il corso** (eel *vyah*-leh/eel *kohr*-soh) *(avenue)*

>> **il ponte** (eel *pohn*-teh) *(bridge)*

>> **il sottopassaggio** (eel *soht*-toh-pahs-*sahj*-joh) *(underpass)*

# Talkin' the Talk

Laurie is visiting Florence from Oregon and has just finished a mid-morning coffee break in Piazza della Repubblica. She asks Enzo, who is standing near her, how to get to the post office.

**Laurie:**   **Scusi, dov'è l'ufficio postale?**
*skooh*-zee doh-*veh* loohf-*fee*-choh poh-*stah*-leh
*Excuse me, where is the post office?*

**Enzo:**   **È dietro l'angolo, là, sotto i portici. L'accompagno?**
eh *dyeh*-troh *lahn*-goh-loh lah *soht*-toh ee *pohr*-tee-chee lahk-kohm-*pah*-nyoh
*It's around the corner, over there, underneath the colonnade/covered walkway. Would you like me to go with you?*

**Laurie:**   **Grazie. No grazie, vado da sola.**
*grah*-tsyeh noh *grah*-tsyeh *vah*-doh dah *soh*-lah
*Thank you. No thank you, I'll go by myself.*

**TIP**

When Italians say or write an address, they include the type of street (via, viale, corso, piazza) followed by the name of the street and then the number: **Via Veneto** (*vee*–ah *veh*–neh–toh) 12:

>> **Abito in Via Merulana 7.** (*ah*-bee-toh een *vee*-ah meh-rooh-*lah*-nah *seht*-teh) *(I live in Via Merulana 7.)*

>> **Angela vive in Piazza Garibaldi 12.** (ahn-*jeh*-lah *vee*-veh een *pyat*-tsa gah-ree-*bahl*-dee doh-*dee*-chee) *(Angela lives in Garibaldi Square 12.)*

We thought you might want to know the translation and pronunciation of a famous Italian proverb you may have heard:

**Tutte le strade portano a Roma.** (*tooht*-teh leh *strah*-deh *pohr*-tah-noh ah *roh*-mah) *(All roads lead to Rome.)*

# Talkin' the Talk

PLAY THIS

Mary is in **Bologna** (boh-*loh*-nyah) for the first time. She has visited the city and walked a lot, and now she wants to go back to the train station. Because she can't remember the way, she asks an older gentleman. (Track 11)

| | |
|---|---|
| **Mary:** | **Scusi?**<br>*skooh*-zee<br>*Excuse me?* |
| **Man:** | **Sì?**<br>see<br>*Yes?* |
| **Mary:** | **Dov'è la stazione centrale?**<br>doh-*veh* lah stah-*tsyoh*-neh chehn-*trah*-leh<br>*Where is the central station?* |
| **Man:** | **Prenda la prima a destra.**<br>*prehn*-dah lah *pree*-mah ah *deh*-strah<br>*Take the first right.* |
| **Mary:** | **Poi?**<br>poi<br>*Then?* |
| **Man:** | **Poi la terza a sinistra.**<br>poi lah *tehr*-tsah ah see-*nee*-strah<br>*Then the third left.* |
| **Mary:** | **Sì?**<br>see<br>*Yes?* |

*(continued)*

(continued)

**Man:** **Poi la seconda, no la prima . . .**
poi lah seh-*kohn*-dah noh lah *pree*-mah
*Then the second, no the first . . .*

**Mary:** **Grazie . . . prendo un taxi!**
*grah*-tsyeh *prehn*-doh oohn *tah*-ksee
*Thank you . . . I'll take a taxi!*

## WORDS TO KNOW

| | | |
|---|---|---|
| **la strada principale [f]** | lah *strah*-dah preen-chee-*pah*-leh | *main street* |
| **il semaforo [m]** | eel seh-*mah*-foh-roh | *traffic light* |
| **il ponte [m]** | eel *pohn*-teh | *bridge* |
| **la piazza [f]** | lah *pyaht*-tsah | *square* |
| **il centro [m]** | eel *chehn*-troh | *downtown; city center* |
| **la stazione [f]** | lah stah-*tsyoh*-neh | *station* |
| **il duomo [m]** | eel *dwoh*-moh | *cathedral* |
| **l'ufficio postale [m]** | looh-*fee*-choh poh-*stah*-leh | *post office* |
| **la rotonda (f)** | lah roh-*tohn*-dah | *traffic circle* |

# Getting a Move on It: Verbs You Can Use

You need to know certain verbs when trying to understand directions. Here are some helpful verbs for finding your way:

>> **andare** (ahn-*dah*-reh) *(to go)*

>> **girare a destra/a sinistra** (jee-*rah*-reh ah *deh*-strah/ah see-*nee*-strah) *(to turn right/left)*

>> **prendere** (*prehn*-deh-reh) *(to take)*

>> **proseguire** (proh-seh-*gwee*-reh) *(to continue)*

>> **seguire** (seh-*gwee*-reh) *(to follow)*

>> **tornare indietro** (tohr-*nah*-reh een-*dyeh*-troh) *(to go back)*

Imperatives are useful verb forms to know in a variety of situations, including when you're trying to get around in unfamiliar territory. This list shows *you* (informal singular) with the verb form (**tu**), *you* (formal singular) with the verb form (**lei**), *you* (informal plural) with the verb form (**voi**), and *you* (formal plural) with the verb form (**loro**) which hasn't been introduced before but it is useful for giving commands. Check out Chapter 2 for help on deciding when to use formal or informal forms.

Appendix B provides you with the conjugations of some regular and irregular verbs.

>> **Va'/Vada/Andate/Vadano!** (vah/*vah*-dah/ahn-*dah*-teh/*vah*-dah-noh) *(Go!)*

>> **Gira/Giri/Girate/Girino!** (*jee*-rah/*jee*-ree/jee-*rah*-teh/*jee*-ree-noh) *(Turn!)*

>> **Prendi/Prenda/Prendete/Prendano!** (*prehn*-dee/*prehn*-dah/prehn-*deh*-teh/prehn-*dah*-noh) *(Take!)*

>> **Prosegui/Prosegua/Proseguite/Proseguano!** (proh-*seh*-gwee/proh-*seh*-gwah/proh-seh-*gwee*-teh/proh-*seh*-gwah-noh) *(Go on!)*

>> **Segui/Segua/Seguite/Seguano!** (*seh*-gwee/*seh*-gwah/seh-*gwee*-teh/*seh*-gwah-noh) *(Follow!)*

>> **Torna/Torni/Tornate/Tornino!** (*tohr*-nah/*tohr*-nee/tohr-*nan*-teh/*tohr*-nee-noh) *(Go back!)*

>> **Attraversa/Attraversi/Attraversate/Attraversino!** (aht-trah-*vehr*-sah/aht-trah-*vehr*-see/aht-trah-vehr-*sah*-teh/aht-trah-*vehr*-see-noh) *(Cross!)*

Notice that these verb endings vary, seemingly without any consistent pattern. This isn't a mistake — they depend on the verb's infinitive ending (**-are**, **-ere**, or **-ire**), and whether the verb is regular or irregular. The easiest approach is to trust us and to familiarize yourself with these verbs and their endings — you don't need to learn them all at once.

You may want to know how near or far you are from your destination. Here are some typical questions and responses:

>> **Quant'è lontano?** (kwahn-*teh* lohn-*tah*-noh) *(How far is it?)*

>> **È molto lontano?** (eh *mohl*-toh lohn-*tah*-noh) *(Is it very far?)*

>> **Quanto dista?** (*kwahn*-toh *dee*-stah) *(How far is it?)*

>> **Saranno cinque minuti.** (sah-*rahn*-noh *cheen*-kweh mee-*nooh*-tee) *(About five minutes.)*

>> **Circa un chilometro.** (*cheer*-kah oohn kee-*loh*-meh-troh) *(About one kilometer.)*

>> **Non saranno più di 150 metri.** (nohn sah-*rahn*-noh pyooh dee *chehn*-toh-cheen-*qwahn*-tah *meh*-tree) *(It's no more than 150 meters away.)*

>> **No, un paio di minuti.** (noh oohn *pah*-yoh dee mee-*nooh*-tee) *(No, a couple of minutes.)*

>> **Posso arrivarci a piedi?** (*pohs*-soh ahr-ree-*vahr*-chee ah *pyeh*-dee) *(Can I walk there?)*

>> **Certo, è molto vicino.** (*chehr*-toh eh *mohl*-toh vee-*chee*-noh) *(Sure, it's very close.)*

>> **È un po' lontano.** (eh oohn *poh* lohn-*tah*-noh) *(It's a bit far.)*

>> **È proprio a due passi.** (eh *proh*-pryoh ah *dooh*-eh *pahs*-see) *(It's very close. Literally: Just a couple of steps away.)*

>> **È all'incirca 20 metri di distanza.** (eh ahl-leen-*cheer*-kah *vehn*-tee *meh*-tree dee dee-*stahn*-tsah) *(It's about 20 meters away.)*

# Talkin' the Talk

Jenny and Lucy are visiting Rome and would like to walk to their favorite pizzeria in Trastevere from the converted monastery where they're staying, which is now a bed and breakfast. They ask the woman at the front desk how to get there.

**Jenny:** **Scusi, un'informazione, per favore.**
*skooh*-zee oohn-een-fohr-mah-*tsyoh*-neh pehr fah-*voh*-reh
*Excuse me, we'd like some information, please.*

**Woman:** **Prego!**
*preh*-goh
*How can I help you?*

**Jenny:** **Quanto dista la pizzeria Ai marmi?**
*kwahn*-toh *dee*-stah lah peet-tseh-*ree*-ah ahy *mahr*-mee
*How far is the pizzeria Ai marmi?*

**Woman:** **È vicino, potete andarci a piedi facilmente.**
eh vee-*chee*-noh poh-*teh*-teh ahn-*dahr*-chee ah *pyeh*-dee fah-cheel-*mehn*-teh
*It's close, you can get there easily on foot.*

| Woman: | **Quando uscite dal B&B girate a destra, e all'incrocio girate ancora a destra. Proseguite in Viale Trastevere all'incirca 100 metri e vedrete la pizzeria a sinistra.** |
|---|---|
| | *qwahn*-doh ooh-*shee*-teh dahl bee-ehn-bee jee-*rah*-teh ah *deh*-strah eh ahl-leen-*kroh*-choh jee-*rah*-teh ahn-*koh*-rah ah *deh*-strah proh-seh-*gwee*-teh in *vyah*-leh trah-*steh*-veh-reh ahl-leen-*cheer*-kah *chehn*-toh *meh*-tree eh veh-*dreh*-teh lah peet-tseh-*ree*-ah ah see-*nee*-strah |
| | *When you leave the B&B, take a right and then at the intersection take another right. Go down Viale Trastevere for about 100 meters and you'll see the pizzeria on the left.* |
| Lucy: | **Scusi, non ho capito, può ripetere più lentamente, per favore?** |
| | *skooh*-zee nohn oh kah-*pee*-toh pwoh ree-*peh*-teh-reh pyooh *lehn*-tah-mehn-teh pehr fah-*voh*-reh |
| | *I'm sorry, but I didn't understand. Would you please repeat a bit more slowly?* |
| Woman: | **Certo! Allora, esci dal B&B e gira a destra. Va bene?** |
| | *chehr*-toh ahl-*loh*-rah *eh*-shee dahl bee-ehn-bee eh *gee*-rah ah *deh*-strah vah *beh*-neh |
| | *Of course. You leave the B&B and turn right. Okay?* |

# When You Don't Understand: What to Say

Occasionally, maybe frequently, you may not understand the directions someone gives you. For those times, you need some useful polite expressions to ask the other person to repeat their directions.

>> **Come, scusi?** (*koh*-meh *skooh*-zee) *(Pardon/Sorry, what did you say?)* (formal)

>> **Come, scusa?** (*koh*-meh *skooh*-zah) *(Pardon/Sorry, what did you say?)* (informal)

>> **Mi scusi, non ho capito.** (mee *skooh*-zee nohn oh kah-*pee*-toh) *(I'm sorry, I didn't understand.)*

>> **Può ripetere più lentamente, per favore?** (pwoh ree-*peh*-teh-reh pyooh lehn-tah-*mehn*-teh pehr fah-*voh*-reh) *(Would you please repeat it more slowly?)*

When someone does you a favor — such as giving you directions — you want to thank them, and that's easy: **Mille grazie!** (*meel*-leh *grah*-tsyeh) *(Thank you very much!)*

<table>
<tr><td colspan="3" align="center">WORDS TO KNOW</td></tr>
<tr><td>numero [m]</td><td>nooh-meh-roh</td><td>number</td></tr>
<tr><td>minuto [m]</td><td>mee-nooh-toh</td><td>minute</td></tr>
<tr><td>lentamente</td><td>lehn-tah-mehn-teh</td><td>slowly</td></tr>
<tr><td>autobus [m]</td><td>ow-toh-boohs</td><td>bus</td></tr>
<tr><td>fermata [f]</td><td>fehr-mah-tah</td><td>bus stop</td></tr>
<tr><td>macchina [f]</td><td>mahk-kee-nah</td><td>car</td></tr>
</table>

# Looking For a Specific Location

When you're looking for a specific place, these sentences can help you ask the right questions:

» **Mi sa dire dov'è la stazione?** (mee sah *dee*-reh doh-*veh* lah stah-*tsyoh*-neh) (*Can you tell me where the station is?*)

» **Devo andare all'aeroporto. Qual è la strada da prendere?** (*deh*-voh ahn-*dah*-reh ahl-lah-eh-roh-*pohr*-toh kwah- *leh* lah *strah*-dah dah *prehn*-deh-reh) (*I have to go to the airport. What road should I take?*)

» **Sto cercando il teatro Valle.** (stoh chehr-*kahn*-doh eel teh-*ah*-troh *vahl*-leh) (*I'm looking for the Valle theater.*)

» **Dov'è il cinema Astoria, per favore?** (doh-*veh* eel *chee*-neh-mah ah-*stoh*-ryah pehr fah-*voh*-reh) (*Where is the Astoria cinema, please?*)

» **Come posso arrivare al Museo Etrusco?** (*koh*-meh *pohs*-soh ahr-ree-*vah*-reh ahl mooh-*zeh*-oh eh-*trooh*-skoh) (*How can I get to the Etruscan Museum?*)

» **La strada migliore per il centro, per favore?** (lah *strah*-dah mee-*lyoh*-reh pehr eel *chehn*-troh pehr fah-*voh*-reh) (*The best way downtown, please?*)

» **Che chiesa è questa?** (keh *kyeh*-zah eh *kweh*-stah) (*What church is this?*)

» **Quale autobus va all'ospedale?** (*kwah*-leh *ow*-toh-boohs vah ahl-loh-speh-*dah*-leh) (*Which bus goes to the hospital?*)

» **Come faccio ad arrivare all'università?** (*koh*-meh *fach*-choh ahd ahr-ree-*vah*-reh ahl-looh-nee-vehr-see-*tah*) (*How can I get to the university?*)

# Talkin' the Talk

Peter wants to meet with a friend at a restaurant on via Torino. After getting off the bus, he asks a girl for directions. (Track 12)

**Peter:**   **Scusa?**
*skooh*-zah
*Excuse me?*

**Girl:**   **Dimmi.**
*deem*-mee
*Can I help you.*

**Peter:**   **Sto cercando via Torino.**
stoh chehr-*kahn*-doh *vee*-ah toh-*ree*-noh
*I'm looking for via Torino.*

**Girl:**   **Via Torino?**
*vee*-ah toh-*ree*-noh
*Via Torino?*

**Peter:**   **È qui vicino, no?**
eh kwee vee-*chee*-noh noh
*It's close by, isn't it?*

**Girl:**   **No, è lontanissimo.**
noh eh lohn-tah-*nees*-see-moh
*No, it's very far away.*

**Peter:**   **Oddio, ho sbagliato strada!**
ohd-*dee*-oh oh sbah-*lyah*-toh *strah*-dah
*Oh my goodness, I went the wrong way!*

**Girl:**   **Devi prendere il 20 verso il centro.**
*deh*-vee *prehn*-deh-reh eel *vehn*-tee *vehr*-soh eel *chehn*-troh
*You have to take the [bus number] 20 to the city center.*

Amy Jo is spending her junior year abroad in Florence and living with a family near the Boboli Gardens. She is at the Piazza Duomo and has to meet her roommate Oona at the Uffizi Gallery, but she is a little disoriented. (See Figure 6-1.) She asks a young street musician how to get there.

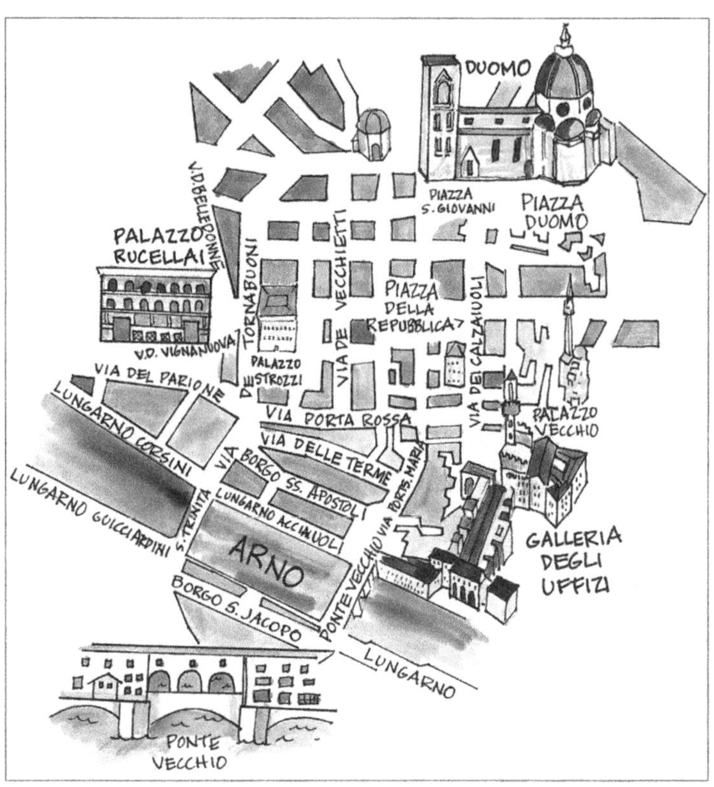


FIGURE 6-1: Map of the historic district of Florence, Italy.

*Illustration by Liz Kurtzman*

| | |
|---|---|
| **Amy Jo:** | **Scusa, un'informazione, per favore. Sono un po' persa.** <br> *skooh*-zah oohn-een -fohr-mah-*tsyoh*-neh perh fah-*voh*-reh *soh*-noh oohn poh *pehr*-sah <br> *Excuse me, I need some information please. I'm a little lost.* |
| **Musician:** | **Dimmi!** <br> *deem*-mee <br> *Shoot!* (Literally: *Tell me.*) |

**Amy Jo:** **Come posso arrivare alla Galleria degli Uffizi?**
*koh*-meh *pohs*-soh ahr-ree-*vah*-reh *ahl*-lah gahl-leh-*ree*-ah
*deh*-lyee ooh-*fee*-tsee
*How can I get to the Uffizi Gallery?*

**Musician:** **Non è lontano. Vai sempre dritto in Via dei Calzaiuoli finché arrivi a Piazza della Signoria. Guarda un po' in giro quando arrivi.**
nohn eh lohn-*tah*-noh vahy *sehm*-preh *dreet*-toh een *vee*-ah
dey *kahl*-tsah-*ywoh*-lee feen-*keh* ahr-*ree*-vee ah *pyaht*-tsah
*dehl*-lah see-nyoh-*ree*-ah *gwahr*-dah oohn poh in *gee*-roh
*qwahn*-doh ahr-*ree*-vee
*It's not far. Just go straight down Via dei Calzaiuoli until you get to Piazza della Signoria. Look around when you get there.*

**Amy Jo:** **Quanti minuti ci vogliono a piedi?**
*kwahn*-tee mee-*nooh*-tee chee *voh*-lyoh-noh ah *pyeh*-dee
*How many minutes away is it on foot?*

**Musician:** **Una decina.**
*oohn*-ah deh-*chee*-nah
*About 10.*

**Amy Jo:** **Grazie!**
*grah*-tsyeh
*Thank you!*

## WORDS TO KNOW

| | | |
|---|---|---|
| **a destra** | ah *deh*-strah | *to the right* |
| **a sinistra** | ah see-*nee*-strah | *to the left* |
| **stazione [f]** | stah-*tsyoh*-neh | *station* |
| **aeroporto [m]** | ah-eh-roh-*pohr*-toh | *airport* |
| **teatro [m]** | teh-*ah*-troh | *theater* |
| **cinema [m]** | *chee*-neh-mah | *cinema* |
| **chiesa [f]** | *kyeh*-zah | *church* |
| **ospedale [m]** | oh-speh-*dah*-leh | *hospital* |
| **ponte (m)** | *pohn*-teh | *bridge* |

# FUN & GAMES

Take a look at Figure 6-1, the map of Florence's city center and provide the following information. See Appendix C for the answer key.

1. Palazzo Rucellai is in via _________________.

2. Two bridges on this map are the _____________ and the _________________.

3. The river that runs through Florence is called the _______________.

4. A building that is attached to the Galleria degli Uffizi is the _________________.

5. The Duomo sits on what two piazzas? _____________________.

6. The roads running alongside the Arno have what word in common in their names? _________________________________

7. _________________ looks like the main piazza in Florence's center.

# Chapter **7**

# Food Glorious Food — and Don't Forget the Drinks

You're probably familiar with the names of many Italian foods, such as spaghetti, ravioli, espresso, pizza, and pasta. Italians have three main meals:

» **la (prima) colazione** (lah *pree*-mah koh-lah-*tsyoh*-neh) *(breakfast)*

» **il pranzo** (eel *prahn*-tsoh) *(lunch)*

» **la cena** (lah *cheh*-nah) *(dinner)*

**Uno spuntino** (*ooh*-noh spoohn-*tee*-noh) *(a snack)* is something you have when you're hungry between meals. **La merenda** (lah meh-*rehn*-dah) is a snack that most children enjoy daily mid-afternoon.

Reading the sections in this chapter, you can find a lot of information about food and drinks, going grocery shopping, and dining out. This chapter invites you to take a closer look at some of the variations that make Italian food so famous. **"Buon appetito!"** (bwohn ahp-peh-*tee*-toh)! *(Enjoy your meal!)*.

# Drinking Italian Style

Italians enjoy a wide range of beverages, from espresso to wine, beer, and beyond. While breakfast is often a private or family-centered matter, aperitivo is a social affair, with people gathering at bars across the city to enjoy it together. This section talks about many sorts of drinks, starting, obviously, with good Italian coffee, but covering also water, tea, and some spirits.

## Expressing your love for espresso

You may have to order an espresso at your favorite coffee emporium back home, but in Italy, you get the same drink by asking the **barista** (bah-*ree*-stah) *(barista/ bartender)* ot **il cameriere** (eel kah-meh-*ryeh*-reh) *(the waiter)* for just **un caffè** (oohn kahf-*feh*) *(a coffee)*.

## ITALY'S NATIONAL DRINK: ESPRESSO

Use the following terms exactly as you see them when ordering your coffee at the **bar** *(cafe),* and you will definitely be understood!

- **Un caffè** (kahf-*feh*): When you order **caffè**, you automatically get an espresso.

- **Un caffè decaffeinato/Un deca** (oohn kahf-*feh* deh-*kahf* -fay-nah-toh/oohn deh-*kaf):* Decaffeinated espresso.

- **Un caffè ristretto** (ree-*streht*-toh): Very strong and concentrated espresso.

- **Un caffè doppio** (*dohp*-pyoh): Double espresso.

- **Un caffè lungo** (*loohn*-goh): Espresso with more water to make it less concentrated.

- **Un caffè çorretto** (kohr-*reht*-toh): Espresso with a bit of cognac or other liquor.

- **Un cappuccino** (kahp-pooh-*chee*-noh): Espresso with frothed milk.

- **Un caffellatte** (kahf-fehl-*laht*-teh): Espresso with plenty of milk.

- **Un caffè macchiato** (mahk-*kyah*-toh): Espresso with a touch of milk.

- **Un latte macchiato** (*laht*-teh mahk-*kyah*-toh): Hot milk with just a touch of espresso.

- **Un caffè americano** (kahf-*feh* ah-meh-ree-*kah*-noh): Espresso topped off with hot water served in a larger cup.

- **Un caffè d'orzo** (kahf-*feh dohr*-zoh): A caffeine-free coffee substitute made from roasted barley, and can be ordered like you would regular coffee, with variations like **"caffè d'orzo macchiato."**

- **Un caffè freddo/shakerato** (kahf-*feh frehd*-doh/shah-keh-*rah*-toh): Iced espresso shaken like a martini with liquid cane sugar and ice.

And here are some tips when ordering your Italian coffee.

- Super-size coffee portions don't exist in Italy, and there is one size for a cappuccino and a caffellatte.

- The concept of coffee "to go" is primarily used by tourists. Italians generally have their coffee standing at the bar.

- Italians don't drink cappuccino after breakfast (11ish at the latest).

- And beware! **latte** means milk. If you're hankering for a glass of warm milk, say **Un bicchiere di latte caldo** (oohn beek-*kyeh*-reh dee *laht*-teh *kahl*-doh). If you want a latte, order **un caffellatte** (latte in English is short for caffellatte).

In addition to **caffè,** you can enjoy a nice cup of **cioccolata calda** (chohk-koh-*lah*-tah *kahl*-dah) (*hot cocoa;* cold chocolate milk doesn't exist in Italy); **tè** (teh) (*tea*) or **tè freddo** (teh *frehd*-doh) (*iced tea*); **una tisana** (*ooh*-nah tee-*zah*-nah) (*herbal tea*) like **camomilla** (kah-moh-*meel*-lah) (*chamomile tea*); **un succo di frutta** (oohn *soohk*-koh dee *frooht*-tah) (*fruit juice*); **una spremuta** (*ooh*-nah spreh-*mooh*-tah) (*fresh-squeezed fruit juice*).

CULTURAL WISDOM

Tap water is safe to drink in Italy, and you're encouraged to fill your water bottles at public fountains unless you see a sign that reads **acqua non potabile** (*ah*-kwah nohn poh-*tah*-bee-leh) (*nondrinkable* or *not potable water*). At a restaurants, when you ask for water, you'll be served bottled water, which you must pay for. You can choose from options like **acqua minerale** (*ah*-kwah mee-neh-*rah*-leh) (*mineral water*), which can be **acqua gassata/gasata** (*ah*-kwah gahs-*sah*-tah/gah-*zah*-tah) (*sparkling water*) also called **acqua frizzante** (ah-kwah freet-tsahn-teh), or **acqua liscia** or **naturale** (*ah*-kwah *lee*-shah or nah-tooh-*rah*-leh) (*still water*). In **estate** (eh-*stah*-teh) (*summer*), you may find yourself looking for **ghiaccio** (*gyahch*-choh) (*ice*), but most bars will serve only a small amount in drinks.

TIP

When you order a drink in Italy, you may need to specify how much you want, such as a whole bottle, a carafe, or just a glass. Use the following words:

>> **Una bottiglia di . . .** (*ooh*-nah boht-*tee*-lyah dee) (*A bottle of . . .*)

>> **Un bicchiere di . . .** (oohn beek-*kyeh*-reh dee) (*A glass of . . .*)

>> **Una caraffa di . . .** (*ooh*-nah kah-*rahf*-fah dee) *(A carafe/pitcher of . . .)*

>> **Un litro di . . .** (oohn *lee*-troh dee) *(A liter of . . . )*

>> **Mezzo litro di . . .** (*mehd*-dzoh *lee*-troh dee) *(Half a liter of . . . )*

>> **Un quartino di . . .** (oohn kwahr-*tee*-noh dee) *(A quarter of a liter of)*

When do you pay for your drinks in an Italian coffee bar? It depends. Normally, you have your coffee or whatever first and pay afterward. In little Italian bars, where just one or two people work behind the counter, you simply tell the cashier what you had and pay then. In bigger bars, and especially in large cities with many tourists, you first pay at the register, get a receipt called **scontrino** (skohn-*tree*-noh), take that receipt over to the barista who will fill your order.

## Enjoying beverages with more of a kick

Italy is also famous for its **vini** (*vee*-nee) *(wines)* and other fermented beverages, like the popular after-dinner drinks **limoncello** (lee-mohn-*chehl*-loh) and **grappa** (*grahp*-pah). Each region has its own varieties of wine and spirits, so make certain you try some of the wines and liquors of the regions you visit.

# Talkin' the Talk

Friends eating a casual meal in a **trattoria** (traht-toh-*ree*-ah) are ordering wine to have with their meal. They are in Tuscany and have ordered **pappa al pomodoro** (*pahp*-pah ahl poh-moh-*doh*-roh) (a Tuscan bread soup) and a **bistecca alla fiorentina** (bee-*stehk*-kah *ahl*-lah fyoh-rehn-*tee*-nah) (a large, thickly cut T-bone steak, grilled and often served rare).

Server: **Ecco la lista dei vini.**
    *ehk*-koh lah *lee*-stah dey *vee*-nee
    *Here's the wine list.*

Laura: **Che cosa ci consiglia?**
    keh *koh*-za chee kohn-*see*-lyah
    *What do you recommend?*

Server: **Abbiamo un ottimo Chianti della casa.**
    ahb-*byah*-moh oohn *oht*-tee-moh *kyahn*-tee *dehl*-lah *kah*-zah
    *We have an excellent house Chianti.*

| **Silvio:** | **Allora, prendiamo un po' di vino rosso con la bistecca.** |
| | Ahl-*loh*-rah prehn-*dyah*-moh oohn poh dee *vee*-noh *rohs*-soh kohn lah bee-*stehk*-kah |
| | *We'll have some red wine, then, with the steak.* |
| **Laura:** | **Sì. Quello della casa.** |
| | see *kwehl*-loh *dehl*-lah *kah*-zah |
| | *Yes. The house wine.* |
| **Silvio:** | **Perfetto!** |
| | pehr-*feht*-toh |
| | *Perfect!* |

In Italy, the **aperitivo** (ah-peh-ree-*tee*-voh) *(before-dinner drink)* is usually taken at the bar, either standing or seated at a **tavolino** (tah-voh-*lee*-noh) *(small table)*. **Campari** (kahm-*pah*-ree) *(Campari)*, **prosecco** (proh-*sehk*-koh) *(a dry sparkling wine)*, and **spritz** (spreetz), made with **Aperol** (*ah*-peh-rohl), prosecco, and a splash of soda, are popular **aperitivi** (ah-peh-ree-*tee*-vee), but you can also get alcohol-free aperitivi like **un Crodino** (oohn kroh-*dee*-noh) or **un Sanbitter** (oohn sahn-*beet*-tehr). The aperitivo is frequently served with an assortment of free snacks like olives and potato chips. Some bars may offer a buffet of snacks and finger foods enough that you might skip dinner altogether. This is called **apericena** (ah-peh-ree-*cheh*-nah) (Literally: aperitif with dinner), where you pay for your drinks, but the food is included.

# Talkin' the Talk

Teresa and Laura are meeting around 7:00 p.m. before going out to dinner. They are at a table outdoors.

| **Server (Remo):** | **Ditemi!** |
| | *dee*-teh-mee |
| | *How can I help you?* |
| **Teresa:** | **Io prendo un Bitter Campari con una fetta di arancia.** |
| | *ee*-oh *prehn*-doh oohn *beet*-tehr kahm-*pah*-ree kohn *ooh*-nah *feht*-tah dee ah-*rahn*-chah |
| | *I'll have a Campari with a slice of orange.* |

*(continued)*

*(continued)*

| | |
|---|---|
| **Laura:** | **Per me un prosecco, grazie.** |
| | pehr meh oohn proh-*sehk*-koh *grah*-tsyeh |
| | *For me a prosecco, thank you.* |
| **Remo:** | **Altro?** |
| | *ahl*-troh |
| | *Anything else?* |
| **Teresa:** | **Avete delle noccioline?** |
| | ah-*veh*-teh *dehl*-leh noch-choh-*lee*-neh |
| | *Do you have any peanuts?* |
| **Remo:** | **No, mi dispiace, sono finite.** |
| | noh mee dee-*spyah*-cheh *soh*-noh fee-*nee*-teh |
| | *I'm sorry, we're all out.* |

You may prefer to get a **birra** (*beer*-rah) (*beer*) **grande, media,** or **piccola** (*grahn*-deh, *meh*-dyah or *peek*-koh-lah) (*large, medium, or small*) **alla spina** (*ahl*-lah *spee*-nah) (*draft beer*), in a **bottiglia** (boht-*tee*-lyah) (*bottle*) or in a **lattina** (laht-*tee*-nah) (*can*).

# Dining Out: The Beginning and the Ending

One of the more enjoyable (if potentially fattening) ways to explore a new culture is through its cuisine. Those who love Italian food are lucky — Italian-style restaurants are plentiful in North America. And, if you're fortunate enough to travel to Italy, your taste buds are in for a real treat! Just be aware that some dishes you associate with Italy may not exist there, or they're often prepared differently than in the United States.

This section discusses the beginning and endings of meals — from making reservations to paying the tab.

## Making reservations

Unless you're going to a **pizzeria** (peet-tseh-*ree*-ah) (*pizza place*) or a **trattoria** (traht-toh-ree-ah) (*small restaurant*) down the street, you may need to reserve a table if you're planning on dining in a nice Italian restaurant. Consider making a reservation no earlier than 7 p.m. Italians, like most Europeans, eat dinner later and the farther south you go, the later people eat. Although having dinner in Milan at 8 p.m. is normal, if you get an invitation in Rome, expect to sit at the table around 9 p.m. or later.

# Talkin' the Talk

**PLAY THIS**

Mr. Di Leo calls for reservations at his favorite restaurant. (Track 13)

| | |
|---|---|
| **Waiter:** | **Pronto! Ristorante Roma.**<br>*prohn*-toh ree-stoh-*rahn*-teh *roh*-mah<br>*Hello! Roma Restaurant.* |
| **Sig. Di Leo:** | **Buonasera. Vorrei prenotare un tavolo.**<br>*bwoh*-nah-*seh*-rah vohr-*rey* preh-noh-*tah*-reh oohn *tah*-voh-loh<br>*Good evening! I would like to reserve a table.* |
| **Waiter:** | **Per stasera?**<br>pehr stah-*seh*-rah<br>*For this evening?* |
| **Sig. Di Leo:** | **No, per domani.**<br>noh pehr doh-*mah*-nee<br>*No, for tomorrow.* |
| **Waiter:** | **Per quante persone?**<br>pehr *kwahn*-teh pehr-*soh*-neh<br>*For how many people?* |
| **Sig. Di Leo:** | **Per due.**<br>pehr *dooh*-eh<br>*For two.* |
| **Waiter:** | **A che ora?**<br>ah keh *oh*-rah<br>*At what time?* |
| **Sig. Di Leo:** | **Alle nove.**<br>*ahl*-leh *noh*-veh<br>*At nine.* |
| **Waiter:** | **A che nome?**<br>ah keh *noh*-meh<br>*In whose name?* |
| **Sig. Di Leo:** | **Di Leo.**<br>dee *leh*-oh<br>*Di Leo.* |

## WORDS TO KNOW

| | | |
|---|---|---|
| **tavolo [m]** | *tah*-voh-loh | *table* |
| **cameriere [m]** | kah-meh-*ryeh*-reh | *waiter* |
| **domani** | doh-*mah*-nee | *tomorrow* |
| **prenotazione [f]** | preh-noh-tah-*tsyoh*-neh | *reservation* |
| **stasera** | stah-*seh*-rah | *this evening* |

# Paying for your meal

You don't need to use cash in restaurants. All of them, nowadays, accept credit card payments.

**TIP**

Tipping in Italy isn't obligatory, however, leaving a 10 to 15 percent gratuity is appreciated for good service. Often a **coperto** (koh–pehr-toh) *(cover charge)* is added to your bill just to sit down — this fee isn't a tip and covers linens, plates, silverware, and often bread; if **il servizio** (eel sehr–*vee*-tsyoh) *(service charge)* is included, additional tipping isn't necessary.

When you're ready for the bill, **il conto** (eel *kohn*-toh), you ask the server "to bring" it to you. The server will never bring it to you unless you ask for it. Use the verbs **portare** (pohr–*tah*–reh) or **fare** (*fah*–reh) and say:

> **Ci porta/fa il conto, per favore?** (chee *pohr*-tah/fah eel *kohn*-toh perh fah-*voh*-reh) *(Will you please bring us the bill?)* (formal)

> Or simply

> **Il conto, per favore!** (eel *kohn*-toh pehr fah-*voh*-reh) *(The bill, please.)*

## SAVE THAT RECEIPT

**CULTURAL WISDOM**

Be sure to hang on to **lo scontrino** (loh skohn-*tree*-noh) *(the receipt)* for a certain distance after leaving an Italian bar, shop, or restaurant where you've made a purchase. This is important in Italy because **la Guardia di Finanza** (lah *gwahr*-dyah dee fee-*nahn*-tsah) *(Financial Guard)* often checks if you have the receipt with you. If you leave without one and are caught, you and the owner of the establishment may have to pay a fine.

# Having Breakfast

Your first meal of the day is always **la prima colazione** (lah *pree*-mah koh-lah-*tsyoh*-neh) *(breakfast)*.

Some Italians begin the day with **un caffè** (oohn kahf-*feh*) *(espresso)* at home, but many stop for breakfast in **un bar** (oohn bahr) on their way to work. Breakfast consists of coffee and **una pasta** (*ooh*-nah *pah*-stah) *(a pastry)*, which can be **salata** (sah-*lah*-tah) *(savory)*, **semplice** (*sehm*-plee-cheh) *(plain)*, or filled with **marmellata** (mahr-mehl-*lah*-tah) *(jam)*, **crema** (*kreh*-mah) *(custard)*, or **cioccolato** (chohk-koh-*lah*-toh) *(chocolate)*.

## Talkin' the Talk

The person behind the counter in a coffee bar in Italy is called **il barista** (eel bah-*ree*-stah) *(the barista/bartender)*.

| | |
|---|---|
| **Barista:** | **Buongiorno!**<br>bwohn-*johr*-noh<br>*Good morning!* |
| **Sig. Zampieri:** | **Buongiorno! Un caffè e una pasta alla crema per favore.**<br>bwohn-*johr*-noh oohn kahf-*feh* eh *ooh*-nah *pah*-stah *ahl*-lah *kreh*-mah pehr fah-*voh*-reh<br>*Good morning! One espresso and a custard pastry please.* |
| **Barista:** | **Qualcos'altro?**<br>*qwahl*-kohz-*ahl*-troh<br>*Anything else?* |
| **Sig. Zampieri:** | **Una spremuta d'arancia, per favore.**<br>*ooh*-nah spreh-*mooh*-tah dah-*rahn*-chah pehr fah-*voh*-reh<br>*One fresh-squeezed orange juice, please.* |
| **Barista:** | **Ecco la spremuta.**<br>*ehk*-koh lah spreh-*mooh*-tah<br>*Here's your juice.* |

# Eating Lunch

Italians do **il pranzo** (eel *prahn*–tsoh) *(lunch)* differently from many other countries. The traditional courses are as follows:

>> **antipasto** (ahn-tee-*pah*-stoh) *(appetizer)*: Usually served hot and/or cold, and it can vary from region to region.

>> **primo piatto** (*pree*-moh *pyaht*-toh) *(first course)*: Although this comes after the antipasto, it's still called a first course. The **primo** consists of all kinds of **pasta** (*pah*-stah) *(pasta)*, **risotto** (ree-*zoht*-toh) *(risotto)*, or **minestra** (mee-*neh*-strah) *(soup)*.

>> **secondo** (seh-*kohn*-doh) *(second course)*: This generally consists of **carne** (*kahr*-neh) *(meat)* or **pesce** (*peh*-sheh) *(fish)*, prepared in a wide variety of ways.

>> **contorno** (kohn-*tohr*-noh) *(side dish)*: Usually vegetables that complement the **secondo** and may be ordered separately.

>> **dolce** (*dohl*-cheh) *(dessert)*: Last, but certainly not least, dessert may be **una fetta di torta** (*ooh*-nah *feht*-tah dee *tohr*-tah) *(a slice of cake)*, **frutta fresca** (*froot*-tah *freh*-skah) *(fresh fruit)*, or **una macedonia** (*ooh*-nah mah-cheh-*doh*-nyah) *(fruit salad)*.

Figure 7–1 shows a typical Italian lunch menu.

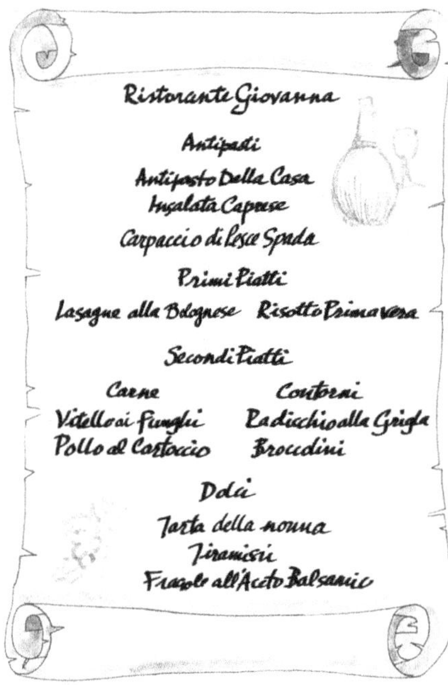


**FIGURE 7-1:**
A typical Italian lunch menu, from antipasti to il dolce.

*Illustration by Liz Kurtzman*

The verb **prendere** (*prehn*-deh-reh) (Literally: *to take,* but here, *to have*) is the verb to use when talking about having food and drinks.

| Conjugation | Pronunciation |
| --- | --- |
| **io prendo** | *ee*-oh *prehn*-doh |
| **tu prendi** | tooh *prehn*-dee |
| **lui/lei prende** | *looh*-ee/ley *prehn*-deh |
| **noi prendiamo** | noi prehn-*dyah*-moh |
| **voi prendete** | voi prehn-*deh*-teh |
| **loro prendono** | *loh*-roh *prehn*-doh-noh |

Pasta usually means durum wheat made with flour and water. Some different types include

>> **spaghetti** (spah-*geht*-tee) *(spaghetti)*

>> **bucatini** (booh-kah-*tee*-nee) *(thick, tube-like spaghetti)*

>> **penne** (*pehn*-neh) *(short, cylinder-shaped pasta shaped to a point at each end)*

>> **fusilli** (fooh-*zeel*-lee) *(spiral-shaped pasta)*

>> **rigatoni** (ree-gah-*toh*-nee) *(short, cylinder-shaped, and grooved pasta)*

On the other hand, **pasta all'uovo** (*pah*-stah ahl-*lwoh*-voh) *(egg pasta)* is made with eggs and flour. It includes **tagliatelle** (tah-lyah-*tehl*-leh) *(flat noodles),* **fettuccine** (feht-tooh-*chee*-neh) *(narrow, flat noodles),* and *tonnarelli* (tohn-nah-*rehl*-lee) *(tubular noodles),* to mention just a few. If you are invited over for dinner in Italy you may be lucky enough to be served **pasta fatta in casa** (*pah*-stah *faht*-tah een *kah*-zah) *(homemade pasta),* which today can also be bought in some delis.

Incidentally, when you have a bite of pasta, you should make sure that it's **al dente** (ahl *dehn*-teh) (Literally: *to the tooth*). It means that the pasta is a little hard so that you really need to use your teeth!

## THE MANY MEANINGS OF "PREGO"

**Prego** (*preh*-goh) has several meanings. When you say it in response to **grazie** (*grah*-tsyeh) *(thank you),* it means "you're welcome." But clerks and servers also use it to ask you what you would like or if they can help you. You often hear **prego** when you enter a public office or shop. You also use **prego** when you give something to someone. In this case, the word is translated as "here you are." Prego is also a formal answer when you ask for permission. Following are a few examples of how prego is used:

- **Grazie.** (*grah*-tsyeh) *(Thank you.)*

  **Prego.** (*preh*-goh) *(You're welcome.)*

- **Prego?** (*preh*-goh) *(Can I help you?)*

  **Posso entrare?** (*pohs*-soh ehn-*trah*-reh) *(May I come in?)*

  **Prego.** (*preh*-goh) *(Please.)*

- **Prego, signore.** (*preh*-goh see-*nyoh*-reh) *(Here you are, sir.)*

  **Grazie.** (*grah*-tsyeh) *(Thank you.)*

The following conjugation shows the conditional form of the verb **volere** (*voh-leh*–reh) *(to want)*, used to express a desire or to make a polite request.

| Conjugation | Pronunciation |
| --- | --- |
| **io vorrei** | *ee*-oh vohr-*rey* |
| **tu vorresti** | too vohr-*reh*-stee |
| **lui/lei vorrebbe** | *looh*-ee/ley vohr-*rehb*-beh |
| **noi vorremmo** | noi vohr-*rehm*-moh |
| **voi vorreste** | voi vohr-*reh*-steh |
| **loro vorrebbero** | *loh*-roh vohr-*rehb*-beh-roh |

# Enjoying Dinner

Italians often have **la cena** (lah *cheh*–nah) *(supper/dinner)* at home, but they also eat out. Here we discuss a few options you have for dinner. In the "Shopping for Food" section later in this chapter, we introduce to the different types of eateries available to you. Supper time varies throughout the peninsula; for example, restaurants in Venice stop serving dinner earlier than those in Rome, where you can go as late as 9 or 10 p.m.

# Talkin' the Talk

PLAY THIS

A group of friends gather at a local pizzeria for dinner. Their exchanges are quite informal. (Track 14)

**Sandra:** **Che cosa prendiamo?**
keh *koh*-zah prehn-*dyah*-moh
*What should we have?*

**Laura:** **Non lo so! Guardiamo il menù.**
nohn loh soh gwahr-*dyah*-moh eel meh-*nooh*
*I don't know! Let's look at the menu.*

**Silvio:** **Avete fame?**
ah-*veh*-teh *fah*-meh
*Are you hungry?*

**Laura:** **Ho fame; prendo una pizza margherita.**
oh *fah*-meh *prehn*-doh *ooh*-nah *peet*-tsah mahr-geh-*ree*-tah
*I'm hungry; I'm getting a pizza margherita.*

**Sandra:** **Io non tanto.**
*ee*-oh nohn *tahn*-toh
*I'm not so hungry.*

**Silvio:** **Allora cosa prendi Sandra?**
ahl-*loh*-rah *koh*-zah *prehn*-dee *sahn*-drah
*So what are you going to have, Sandra?*

**Sandra:** **Vorrei qualcosa di leggero.**
vohr-*rey* kwahl-*koh*-zah dee lehj-*jeh*-roh
*I'd like something light.*

**Un'insalatona.**
oohn-een-sah-*lah*-toh-nah
*A big salad.*

**Silvio:** **Poco originale . . .**
*pohk*-koh oh-ree-jee-*nah*-leh
*Kind of boring . . .*

Most Italian pizzerias have a wide range of pizzas. They're individual servings. You can also get pasta, a wide selection of entrees and salads there, and afterwards a dessert.

You have certainly heard of Italian **gelato** (jeh-*lah*-toh) *(ice cream)*. Go for the **gelato artigianale** (jeh-*lah*-toh ahr-tee-jah-*nah*-leh) *(artisanal ice cream — made in a* **gelateria** (jeh-lah-teh-*ree*-ah). You can have it in a **cono** (*koh*-noh) *(cone)* or a **coppetta** (kohp-*peht*-tah) *(cup).* You also have to decide on the **gusto** (*gooh*-stoh) *(flavor)* and size, which usually goes according to euros or according to **palline** (pahl-*lee*-neh) *(scoops).*

# Talkin' the Talk

Laura and Silvio stop for some ice cream. (Track 15)

**PLAY THIS**

| | | |
|---|---|---|
| **Server:** | **Prego?** | |

**Server:**    **Prego?**
*preh*-goh
*What would you like?*

**Laura:**    **Due coni, per favore.**
*dooh*-eh *koh*-nee pehr fah-*voh*-reh
*Two ice cream cones, please.*

**Server:**    **Da quanto?**
dah *kwahn*-toh
*What size?*

**Silvio:**    **Uno da due euro, e l'altro da 1 euro e 50.**
*ooh*-noh dah *dooh*-eh *eh*-ooh-roh eh *lahl*-troh dah
oohn *eh*-ooh-roh eh cheen-*qwahn*-tah
*One for two euros, and the other for one-fifty.*

**Server:**    **Che gusti?**
keh *gooh*-stee
*Which flavors?*

**Silvio:**    **Fragola e limone.**
*frah*-goh-lah eh lee-*moh*-neh
*Strawberry and lemon.*

**Server:**    **Prego. E Lei?**
*preh*-goh eh ley
*Here you are. And you?*

| Laura: | **Crema, cioccolato, cocco, e noce.** |
|---|---|
| | *kreh*-mah chohk-koh-*lah*-toh *kohk*-koh eh *noh*-cheh |
| | *Custard, chocolate, coconut, and walnut.* |
| Silvio: | **3 euro e 50.** |
| | treh *eh*-ooh-roh eh cheen-*qwahn*-tah |
| | *Three and a half euros.* |
| Server: | **Sì, grazie. Ecco lo scontrino.** |
| | See, *grah*-tsyeh *ehk*-koh loh *skohn*-tree-noh |
| | *Yes, thanks. Here's the receipt.* |

* * *

*Note* the word **euro** in the preceding dialogue. Euro is both singular and plural, so say, **1 euro** (oohn *eh*-ooh-roh) *(one euro)* or **3 euro e 50** *(three euros and 50 cents).*

In some **gelaterie,** you can also find **frullati** (froohl-*lah*-tee) *(smoothies),* **frappé** (frahp-*peh*) *(which can be a fruit milk shake or a frozen fruit shake),* and **yogurt** (yoh-goohrt) *(yogurt).*

# Shopping for Food

Many people do their grocery shopping in a **supermercato** (sooh-pehr-mehr-*kah*-toh) *(supermarket)* even if there are other places to get it. But most Italian cities have specialty shops, starting with the **alimentari** (ah-lee-mehn-*tah*-ree), where you can get many items — everything from **latte** (*laht*-teh) *(milk)* to **carta igienica** (*kahr*-tah ee-*jeh*-nee-kah) *(toilet paper).* These shops, with their specific selection of goods, provide the personal attention often lacking in supermarkets. The following sections identify some places people buy food.

## At the butcher shop

From the **macelleria** (mah-*chehl*-leh-ree-ah) *(butcher shop)* you can ask the **macellaio** (mah-chehl-*lah*-yoh *(butcher)* for items like the following:

>> **agnello** (ah-*nyehl*-loh) *(lamb)*

>> **bistecca** (bee-*stehk*-kah) *(steak)*

>> **coniglio** (koh-*nee*-lyoh) *(rabbit)*

>> **maiale** (mah-*yah*-leh) *(pork)*

>> **manzo** (*mahn*-dzoh) *(beef)*

>> **pollo** (*pohl*-loh) *(chicken)*

>> **vitello** (vee-*tehl*-loh) *(veal)*

## At the fish shop

In a **pescheria** (*peh*-skeh-ree-ah) (*fish shop*) you can ask the **pescivendolo** (peh-she-*vehn*-doh-loh) (*fishmonger*) for the **pesce** (*peh*-sheh) (*fish*) you like. Some common types of fish, depending on the region, include

>> **acciuga** (ahch-*chooh*-gah) *(anchovies)*

>> **branzino** (brahn-*zee*-noh) *(sea bass)*

>> **calamaro** (kah-lah-*mah*-roh) *(squid)*

>> **cozza** (*koht*-tsah) *(mussel)*

>> **frutti di mare** (*frooht*-tee dee *mah*-reh) *(shellfish)*

>> **gambero** (*gahm*-beh-roh) *(prawn)*

>> **gamberetto** (gahm-beh-*reht*-toh) *(small shrimp)*

>> **merluzzo** (mehr-*looht*-tsoh) *(cod)*

>> **orata** (oh-*rah*-tah) *(sea bream)*

>> **polpo/polipo** (*pohl*-poh *poh*-lee-poh) *(octopus)*

>> **pesce spada** (*peh*-sheh *spah*-dah) *(swordfish)*

>> **seppia** (*sehp*-pyah) *(cuttlefish)*

>> **sogliola** (*soh*-lyoh-lah) *(sole)*

>> **spigola** (*spee*-goh-lah) *(snapper)*

>> **tonno** (*tohn*-noh) *(tuna)*

>> **vongola** (*vohn*-goh-lah) *(clam)*

Common simple preparations are **al forno** (ahl-*for*-noh) *(baked)*, **alla griglia** (*ahl*-lah *gree*-lyah) *(grilled)*, and **in padella** (een pah-*dehl*-lah) *(in the skillet)*.

# At the bakery

In a **panetteria** (pah-neht-teh-*ree*-ah) *(bakery)*, you can try all sorts of different kinds of **pane** (*pah*-neh) *(bread)*, as well as some oven-baked **dolci** (*dohl*-chee) *(sweets)*.

In some Italian bakeries you can also find **pizza al taglio** (*peet*-tsah ahl *tah*-lyoh) *(slices of pizza)* and **focaccia** (foh-*kach*-chah) and pay according to weight.

## Talkin' the Talk

| | |
|---|---|
| **Sig.ra Belli:** | **Ha del pane biologico?**<br>ah dehl *pah*-neh byoh-*loh*-jee-koh<br>*Do you have any organic bread?* |
| **Baker:** | **Ho dei panini, o questo tipo Matera, tutti cotti nel forno a legna.**<br>oh dey pah-*nee*-nee oh *kweh*-stoh *tee*-poh mah-*teh*-rah *tooht*-tee *koht*-tee nehl *fohr*-noh ah *leh*-nyah<br>*I have these rolls or this Matera-style one, all baked in our wood-burning oven.* |
| **Aig.ra Belli** | **Mi dà quello rustico per favore.**<br>mee *dah kwehl*-loh *rooh*-stee-koh peh fah-*voh*-reh<br>*I'll take that hard-crust one please.* |
| | **Quant'è?**<br>kwahn-*teh*<br>*How much is it?* |
| **Baker:** | **3 euro e 50 centesimi.**<br>treh *eh*-ooh-roh eh cheen-*qwahn*-tah chehn-*teh*-zee-mee<br>*Three euros and 50 cents.* |
| **Sig.ra Belli** | **Grazie e arrivederci.**<br>*grah*-tsyeh-eh eh ahr-ree-veh-*dehr*-chee<br>*Thank you, and good-bye.* |
| **Baker:**<br>**to another**<br>**customer:** | **Desidera?**<br>deh-*zee*-deh-rah<br>*What would you like?* |

*(continued)*

(continued)

| Paolo: | **Un pezzo di pizza al pomodoro.** |
|---|---|
| | oohn *peht*-tsoh dee *peet*-tsah ahl poh-moh-*doh*-roh |
| | *A slice* (Literally: *a piece*) *of pizza with tomatoes.* |
| Baker: | **Così va bene?** |
| | koh-*zee* vah *beh*-neh |
| | *Is this okay?* |
| Paolo | **Un po' più grande, per favore.** |
| | oohn *poh* pyooh *grahn*-deh pehr fah-*voh*-reh |
| | *A little bigger please.* |
| Baker | **Così?** |
| | koh-*zee* |
| | *Like this?* |

# At the market

Italians buy **frutta** (*frooht*-tah) (*fruit*) and **verdura** (vehr-*dooh*-rah) (*vegetables*) primarily in **supermercati** (sooh-pehr-mehr-*kah*-tee) (*supermarkets*), **mercati all'aperto** (mehr-*kah*-tee ahl-lah-*pehr*-toh) (*open-air markets*), and **fruttivendoli** (frooht-tee-*vehn*-doh-lee) (*greengrocers*). Local markets and fruit and vegetable markets offer a more traditional and lively shopping experience with fresh, often locally sourced produce. Some markets, like the one in Milan, are very large and offer a wide variety of choices, sometimes at more affordable prices. In most cases, open-air markets are held once a week and are similar to the farmers' markets found in the United States.

**REMEMBER**

Items are priced according to weight, usually by the **chilo** (*kee*-loh) (*kilo*). You know that when you hear **un etto** (oohn *eht*-toh), it means 100 grams. **Mezz'etto** (mehdz-*zeht*-toh) is 50 grams, because **mezzo** (*mehdz*-zoh) means "half." Likewise, a **mezzo chilo** (*mehdz*-zoh *kee*-loh) is half a kilo. Meat, fish, fruits, cheese, cold cuts and vegetables are sold by weight. Refer to Chapter 4 for more information about the metric system.

Table 7-1 lists common fruits and vegetables that you might find at an open-air market.

**CULTURAL WISDOM**

Some Italian markets seem to be made exclusively for tourists, but Italians themselves shop there too. You may think that haggling and bargaining are common at Italian markets, but that isn't true. You can certainly try it with a leather jacket at the market in a big city like Florence, but it's better to leave it alone when buying food items.

## Fruits and Vegetables

| Italian/Plural | Pronunciation | Translation |
| --- | --- | --- |
| **albicocca/albicocche [f]** | ahl-bee-*kohk*-kah/keh | *apricot/s* |
| **ananas [m]** | *ah*-nah-nahs | *pineapple* |
| **arancia/arance [f]** | ah-*rahn*-chah/-cheh | *orange/s* |
| **asparago/i [m]** | ah-*spah*-rah-goh/-jee | *asparagus* |
| **banana/e [f]** | bah-*nah*-nah/-neh | *banana/s* |
| **broccoli [m/pl.]** | *brohk*-koh-lee | *broccoli* |
| **carota/e [f]** | kah-*roh*-tah/-teh | *carrot/s* |
| **cavolo/i [m]** | *kah*-voh-loh/-lee | *cabbage/s* |
| **ciliegia/e [f]** | chee-*lyeh*-jah/-jeh | *cherry/cherries* |
| **cocomero/i [m]**<br>**anguria/e [f]** | koh-*koh*-meh-roh/-ree<br>ahn-*goo*-ryah/ryeh | *watermelon/s* |
| **fico/fichi [m]** | *fee*-koh/-kee | *fig/s* |
| **fragola/e [f]** | *frah*-goh-lah/-leh | *strawberry/strawberries* |
| **fungo/funghi [m]** | *foohn*-goh/-gee | *mushroom/s* |
| **limone/i [m]** | lee-*moh*-neh/-nee | *lemon/s* |
| **mela/e [f]** | *meh*-lah/-leh | *apple/s* |
| **melanzana/e [f]** | meh-lahn-*dzah*-nah/-neh | *eggplant/s* |
| **melone/i [m]** | meh-*loh*-neh/-nee | *melon/s* |
| **peperone/i [m]** | peh-peh-*roh*-neh/-nee | *pepper/s* |
| **pera/e [f]** | *peh*-rah/-reh | *pear/s* |
| **pesca/pesche [f]** | *peh*-skah/-skeh | *peach/es* |
| **pomodoro/i [m]** | poh-moh-*doh*-roh/-ree | *tomato/es* |
| **pompelmo/i [m]** | pohm-*pehl*-moh/-mee | *grapefruit/s* |
| **prugna/e [f]** | *prooh*-nyah/-nyeh | *plum/s* |
| **spinaci [m/pl.]** | spee-*nah*-chee | *spinach* |
| **uva [f]** | *ooh*-vah | *grapes* |
| **zucchino/i [m]** | dzoohk-*kee*-noh/-nee | *zucchini* |

# FUN & GAMES

We talk a lot about food in this chapter. To reward ourselves at the end, we allow ourselves a really good fruit shake. Fill in the Italian for the following various fruits. See Appendix C for the answer key. Have fun!

1. pineapple _ _ _ _ _ _
2. cherry _ _ _ _ _ _ _ _
3. grape _ _ _
4. pear _ _ _ _
5. watermelon _ _ _ _ _ _ _ _ _
6. strawberry _ _ _ _ _ _

IN THIS CHAPTER

» **Shopping at department stores and boutiques**

» **Getting the right size**

» **Finding colors, fabrics, and accessories**

» **Trying on shoes**

# Chapter **8**

# Shopping Italian Style

taly is famous throughout the world for its fashion, **la moda** (lah *moh*-dah), as well as for its **stilisti** (stee-*lee*-stee) *(designers)* — such as **Armani** (ahr-*mah*-nee) and **Valentino** (vah-lehn-*tee*-noh). You might suddenly feel inspired to shop, and what better place to shop than in Italy! In Italian, a famous brand is called **la griffe** (lah greef) (a French word) or **la firma** (lah *feer*-mah) that means literally "the signature." So, if a product is "designer" or from a famous fashion house, Italians say that it is **griffato** (greef-*fah*-toh) or **firmato** (feer-*mah*-toh) — "signed."

## Figuring Out What to Shop

Shopping can be an informative and fun way to learn about a culture because of the ways that colors and fabrics differ. For example, you can always tell what color is in fashion and how careful Italians are about wearing ironed clothes just by walking down a city street. In Italy, you can explore lots of boutiques and designer shops, as well as numerous department stores. Here we explore where you can shop and how to find your way around.

# Deciding between department stores and boutiques

North Americans have access to huge **centri commerciali** (*chehn*-tree kohm-*mehr*-chah-lee) (*shopping malls*), where you really can find everything. In Italy, people shop in **grandi magazzini** (*grahn*-dee mah-gahd-*dzee*-nee) (*department stores*), which are smaller compared to American ones. The biggest Italian department stores are **Coin** (koh-*een*), **Upim** (*ooh*-peem), and **Rinascente** (ree-nah-*shehn*-teh). All three carry a variety of items; however, many Italians prefer to shop in smaller, privately owned stores where service is key.

What's shopping in Italian? Italians say **fare la spesa** (*fah*-reh lah *speh*-zah) for grocery shopping, while **fare spese** (*fah*-reh *speh*-zeh) or **fare (lo) shopping** (*fah*-reh loh *shohp*-peeng) for everything else. The good news is that you only have to conjugate the verb **fare**. (See Chapter 2 and Appendix B for this verb conjugated.)

In some places, you may notice signs — like the one over the door that reads **uscita di sicurezza** (ooh-*shee*-tah dee see-kooh-*reht*-tsah) (*emergency exit*) — that can be very useful. Some of these signs say the following:

>> **entrata** (ehn-*trah*-tah) (*entrance*)

>> **uscita** (ooh-*shee*-tah) (*exit*)

>> **spingere** (*speen*-jeh-reh) (*to push*)

>> **tirare** (tee-*rah*-reh) (*to pull*)

>> **orario di apertura** (oh-*rah*-ryoh dee ah-pehr-*tooh*-rah) (*business hours*)

>> **aperto** (ah-*pehr*-toh) (*open*)

>> **chiuso** (*kyooh*-zoh) (*closed*)

>> **la scala mobile** (lah *skah*-lah *moh*-bee-leh) (*escalator*)

>> **l'ascensore** (lah-shehn-*soh*-reh) (*elevator*)

>> **la cassa** (lah *kahs*-sah) (*cash register*)

# Finding your way around stores

Italian stores offer a wide variety of products while maintaining their Italian style. Prices are clearly labeled in euros. During **saldi** (*sahl*-dee) and **svendite** (*zvehn*-dee-teh) (*sales*), **il prezzo** (eel *preht*-tsoh) (the *price*) on the label is already discounted, but you may find tags reading **saldi alla cassa** (*sahl*-dee *ahl*-lah *kahs*-sah) (*discount taken at the cash register*) meaning the discount is applied at the register. A piece of good news! All prices include VAT (value added tax, the Italian equivalent of sales tax). That means that the price you see is the price you pay — no extra charges at checkout.

The following are some signs indicating various **reparti** (reh–*pahr*–tee) *(departments)* or the names of individual boutiques:

>> **abbigliamento da donna/da uomo** (ahb-bee-lyah-*mehn*-toh dah *dohn*-nah/ dah *woh*-moh) *(women's/men's wear)*

>> **accessori** (ahch-chehs-*soh*-ree) *(accessories)*

>> **biancheria per la casa** (byahn-keh-*ree*-ah pehr lah *kah*-zah) *(household linens and towels)*

>> **casalinghi** (kah-zah-*leen*-gee) *(housewares)*

>> **intimo donna** (*een*-tee-moh *dohn*-nah) *(ladies' intimate apparel)*

>> **intimo uomo** (*een*-tee-moh *woh*-moh) *(men's intimate apparel)*

>> **profumeria** (proh-fooh-meh-*ree*-ah) *(perfume shop;* here, beside perfume, you can buy shampoo, barrettes, creams, makeup, and other related items)

# Talkin' the Talk

Here are three separate dialogues where a salesperson directs customers to different departments.

| | |
|---|---|
| **Sig.ra Verdi:** | **Sto cercando l'abbigliamento da bambino.**<br>stoh chehr-*kahn*-doh lahb-bee-lyah-*mehn*-toh dah bahm-*bee*-noh<br>*I'm looking for children's wear.* |
| **Salesperson:** | **Al secondo piano.**<br>ahl seh-*kohn*-doh *pyah*-noh<br>*On the second floor.* |
| **Sig. Marchi:** | **Dove devo andare per ritirare un paio di pantaloni?**<br>*doh*-veh *deh*-voh ahn-*dah*-reh *pehr* ree-tee-*rah*-reh oohn *pah*-yoh dee pahn-tah-*loh*-nee<br>*Where should I go to pick up a pair of pants?* |

*(continued)*

(continued)

| Salesperson: | **Deve rivolgersi al commesso del reparto uomo.** |
|---|---|
| | *deh*-veh ree-*vohl*-jehr-see ahl kohm-*mehs*-soh dehl reh-*pahr*-toh *woh*-moh |
| | *You need to see the salesperson in the men's department.* |
| Anna: | **Dove sono i camerini, per favore?** |
| | *doh*-veh *soh*-noh ee kah-meh-*ree*-nee pehr fah-*voh*-reh |
| | *Where are the fitting rooms, please?* |
| Salesperson: | **Vede l'uscita di sicurezza? I camerini sono sulla sinistra.** |
| | *veh*-deh looh-*shee*-tah dee see-kooh-*reht*-tsah ee kah-meh-*ree*-nee *soh*-noh *soohl*-lah see-*nee*-strah |
| | *Do you see the emergency exit? The fitting rooms are to the left.* |

GRAMMATICALLY
SPEAKING

**Avere bisogno di** (ah-*veh*-reh bee-*zoh*-nyoh dee) *(to need)* is a common expression in Italian useful when shopping. See Chapter 2 and Appendix B for the conjugation of the verb **avere** *(to have)*. As the speaker you would say:

**Ho bisogno di . . .** (oh bee-*zoh*-nyoh dee) *(I need . . . )*

When you're in a store and have a question or need advice, you turn to **la commessa** [f] (lah kohm-*mehs*-sah) or **il commesso** [m] (eel kohm-*mehs*-soh) *(the salesperson)* and say, **"Mi può aiutare, per favore?"** (mee pwoh ah-yooh-*tah*-reh pehr fah-*voh*-reh) *(Can you help me, please?)*. Of course, if you're just looking and a salesperson asks, **"Desidera?"** (deh-*zee*-deh-rah) *(Can I help you?)*, you can answer, **"Posso dare un'occhiata?"** (*pohs*-soh *dah*-reh oohn-ohk-*kyah*-tah) *(Is it all right if I just look around?)*.

## WORDS TO KNOW

| vestiti [m/pl.] | veh-*stee*-tee | *clothes* |
|---|---|---|
| abito [m] | *ah*-bee-toh | *suit* |
| camicetta [f] | kah-mee-*cheht*-tah | *blouse* |
| camicia [f] | kah-*mee*-chah | *shirt* |

| | | |
|---|---|---|
| **cappotto [m]** | kahp-*poht*-toh | *coat* |
| **completo [m]** | kohm-*pleh*-toh | *outfit* |
| **costume da bagno [m]** | koh-*stooh*-meh dah *bah*-nyoh | *bathing suit* |
| **giacca [f]** | *jahk*-kah | *jacket; sports jacket* |
| **gonna [f]** | *gohn*-nah | *skirt* |
| **impermeabile [m]** | eem-pehr-meh-*ah*-bee-leh | *raincoat* |
| **jeans [m]** | jeenz | *jeans* |
| **maglia [f]** | *mah*-lyah | *sweater* |
| **maglietta [f]** | mah-*lyeht*-tah | *T-shirt* |
| **pantaloni [m/pl.]** | pahn-tah-*loh*-nee | *pants* |
| **tailleur [m]** | tah-*lyehr* | *woman's suit* |
| **vestito [m]** | veh-*stee*-toh | *man's suit* |
| **vestito [m]** | veh-*stee*-toh | *dress* |
| **piccolo** | *peek*-koh-loh | *small* |
| **grande** | *grahn*-deh | *large* |

# Knowing What You're Buying

When shopping, it's important to be able to easily point to the dress, shoes, or other item you want. Demonstrative adjectives and pronouns and knowing the name of **colori** (coh-*loh*-ree) *(colors)* in Italian can help you do this. After you identify what you want, familiarity with Italian **taglie** (*tah*-lyeh) *(sizes)* can also be a plus. In this section, we explore how to clearly distinguish between two or more items, how to convert sizes, and how to use colors in Italian.

# This one or that one? Demonstrative adjectives and pronouns

English uses the demonstrative adjectives and pronouns *this* and *these* to specify what you're referring to. In Italian, they agree in both gender and number with the noun they modify or replace. The demonstrative adjective **questo** (*kweh*-stoh) has four forms that agree with the noun that follows: **questo, questa, questi, queste** (*kweh*-stoh, *kweh*-stah, *kweh*-stee, *kweh*-steh). These forms can function as pronouns — standing alone and replacing a noun. Consider these examples:

>> **Questo cotone è ottimo!** (*kweh*-stoh *coh-toh-neh eh oht*-tee-moh) *(This cotton is great!)*

>> **Signora, sono questi i suoi pantaloni?** (see-*nyoh*-rah *soh*-noh *kweh*-stee ee *swoi* pahn-tah-*loh*-nee) *(Ma'am, are these yours pants?)*

In these examples, you can see the masculine forms for singular and plural: **questo** and **questi,** respectively. The following examples illustrate the feminine forms: **questa** (singular) and **queste** (plural).

>> **Questa è la sua giacca?** (*kweh*-stah eh lah *sooh*-ah *jahk*-kah) *(Is this your jacket?)*

>> **No, le mie sono queste.** (noh leh *mee*-eh *soh*-no *kweh*-steh) *(No, these are mine.)*

# Decoding Italian sizes

You know the problem — whenever you travel to another country, clothing sizes — called **taglie** (*tah*-lyeh) or **misure** (mee-*zooh*-reh) in Italy — change and you never know which one corresponds to yours. Table 8-1 helps you with this problem by giving you the most common sizes.

In Italy you won't have any difficulties with sizes like S, M, L, and XL because they are used the same way: S for small, M for medium, L for large, and XL for extra-large. Beware, though, that an Italian L seems to correspond to a North American S.

## Clothing Sizes

| Italian Size | American Size | Canadian Size |
| --- | --- | --- |
| *Women's dress sizes* | | |
| 40 | 4 | 6 |
| 42 | 6 | 8 |
| 44 | 8 | 10 |
| 46 | 10 | 12 |
| 48 | 12 | 14 |
| *Men's suit sizes* | | |
| 48 | 38 | 40 |
| 50 | 40 | 42 |
| 52 | 42 | 44 |
| 54 | 44 | 46 |
| 56 | 46 | 48 |

# Talkin' the Talk

**PLAY THIS**

Giovanna has found the skirt she's been looking for. She asks the saleswoman if she can try it on. (Track 16)

**Giovanna:** **Posso provare questa gonna?**
*pohs*-soh proh-*vah*-reh *kweh*-stah *gohn*-nah
*May I try on this skirt?*

**Saleswoman:** **Certo. Che taglia porta?**
*chehr*-toh keh *tah*-lyah *pohr*-tah
*Sure. What size do you wear?*

**Giovanna:** **La quarantadue.**
lah kwah-*rahn*-tah-*dooh*-eh
*42.*

**Saleswoman:** **Forse è un po' piccola.**
*fohr*-seh eh oohn poh *peek*-koh-lah
*Perhaps it's a little bit small.*

**Giovanna:** **Me la provo.**
meh lah *proh*-voh
*I'll try it on.*

*(continued)*

*(continued)*

Giovanna returns from the dressing room.

| | |
|---|---|
| **Saleswoman:** | **Va bene?**<br>vah *beh*-neh<br>*Does it fit?* |
| **Giovanna:** | **È troppo stretta. Ha una taglia più grande?**<br>eh *trohp*-poh *streht*-tah ah *ooh*-nah *tah*-lyah pyooh *grahn*-deh<br>*It's too tight. Do you have it in a larger size?* |
| **Saleswoman:** | **Nella sua taglia solo blu.**<br>*nehl*-lah *sooh*-ah *tah*-lyah *soh*-loh blooh<br>*In your size, only in blue.* |

## Focusing on colors

Of course, knowing some **colori** is important. To make life a little easier for you, we put the most common colors in the following table. Some colors agree in number and gender, some agree only in number, and some are invariable, that is, they never change! Table 8-2 is organized accordingly (with the first set agreeing in number and gender).

**TABLE 8-2**

### Colors

| Italian | Pronunciation | Translation |
|---|---|---|
| *Color adjectives that agree in number and gender (o/a/i/e)* | | |
| **rosso** | *rohs*-soh | *red* |
| **giallo** | *jahl*-loh | *yellow* |
| **azzurro** | ahd-*dzoohr*-roh | *sky blue* |
| **bianco** | *byahn*-koh | *white* |
| **grigio** | *gree*-joh | *gray* |
| **nero** | *neh*-roh | *black* |
| *Color adjectives that agree only in number (e/i)* | | |
| **verde** | *vehr*-deh | *green* |
| **marrone** | mahr-*roh*-neh | *brown* |

| Italian | Pronunciation | Translation |
| --- | --- | --- |
| ***Color adjectives that never change, invariable!*** | | |
| **rosa** | *roh*-zah | *pink* |
| **beige** | *behj* | *beige* |
| **blu** | blooh | *blue* |
| **arancione** | ah-rahn-*choh*-neh | *orange* |
| **viola** | *vyoh*-lah | *purple* |

# Talkin' the Talk

Matteo is looking for a new suit for the summer.

**Salesperson:**     **La posso aiutare?**
lah *pohs*-soh ah-yooh-*tah*-reh
*May I help you?*

**Matteo:**     **Sì. Cerco una giacca sportiva blu . . .**
see *chehr*-koh *ooh*-nah *jak*-kah spohr-*tee*-vah blooh
*Yes. I'm looking for a blue sports jacket . . .*

    **. . . con pantaloni bianchi di lino**
kohn pahn-tah-*loh*-nee *byahn*-kee dee *lee*-noh
*. . . to go with some white linen pants.*

**Salesperson:**     **Benissimo. Ecco . . . Provi questi**
beh-*nees*-see-moh *ehk*-koh *proh*-vee *kweh*-stee
*Very well. Here you go . . . Try these on.*

Matteo returns with a smile on his face.

**Salesperson:**     **Vanno bene?**
*Vahn*-noh *beh*-neh
*Okay?*

**Matteo:**     **Sì, mi vanno bene. Li prendo.**
see mee *vahn*-noh *beh*-neh lee *prehn*-doh
*Yes, they fit me well. I'll take them.*

<table>
<tr><th colspan="3">WORDS TO KNOW</th></tr>
<tr><td>camoscio [m]</td><td>kah-moh-shoh</td><td>suede</td></tr>
<tr><td>cotone [m]</td><td>koh-toh-neh</td><td>cotton</td></tr>
<tr><td>fodera [f]</td><td>foh-deh-rah</td><td>lining</td></tr>
<tr><td>lana [f]</td><td>lah-nah</td><td>wool</td></tr>
<tr><td>lino [m]</td><td>lee-noh</td><td>linen</td></tr>
<tr><td>pelle [f]</td><td>pehl-leh</td><td>leather</td></tr>
<tr><td>seta [f]</td><td>seh-tah</td><td>silk</td></tr>
<tr><td>velluto [m]</td><td>vehl-looh-toh</td><td>velvet</td></tr>
<tr><td>viscosa [f]</td><td>vee-skoh-zah</td><td>rayon</td></tr>
</table>

# Accessorizing

Of course, you want to complement your outfit with beautiful **accessori** (ahch-chehs–*soh*–ree) *(accessories)* to give it that final touch. We list some of them to give you a sense of the variety available:

- **anello** (ah-*nehl*-loh) *(ring)*
- **berretto** (behr-*reht*-toh) *(cap)*
- **borsa** (*bohr*-sah) *(handbag/bag)*
- **calze** (kahl-*tseh*) *(stockings)*
- **calzini** (kahl-*tseeh*-nee) *(socks)*
- **cappello** (kahp-*pehl*-loh) *(hat)*
- **cintura** (cheen-*tooh*-rah) *(belt)*
- **collana** (kohl-*lah*-na) *(necklace)*
- **collant** (kohl-*lahn*) *(tights/pantyhose)*
- **cravatta** (krah-*vaht*-tah) *(tie)*
- **gioielli** (joh-*yehl*-lee) *(jewelry)*
- **guanti** (*gwahn*-tee) *(gloves)*
- **ombrello** (ohm-*brehl*-loh/oh-rehk-*kee*-nee) *(umbrella)*
- **orecchini** (oh-rehk-*kee*-nee) *(earrings)*
- **sciarpa** (*shahr*-pah) *(scarf)*

Giovanni wants to buy a scarf for his wife. He asks the salesperson for help.

| | |
|---|---|
| **Giovanni:** | **Vorrei una sciarpa rossa.**<br>vohr-*rey ooh*-nah *shahr*-pah *rohs*-sah<br>*I'd like a red scarf.* |
| **Salesperson:** | **Ne abbiamo una bellissima, di cashmere.**<br>neh ahb-*byah*-moh *ooh*-nah behl-*lees*-see-mah dee *kahsh*-meer<br>*We have a very beautiful cashmere one.* |
| | **È in saldo.**<br>eh een *sahl*-doh<br>*It's on sale.* |
| **Giovanni:** | **Sono scontati questi guanti viola?**<br>*soh*-noh *skohn*-tah-tee *kweh*-stee *gwahn*-tee *vyoh*-lah<br>*Are these purple gloves on sale?* |
| **Salesperson:** | **Sì.**<br>see<br>*Yes.* |

## Stepping out in style

Oh yes, this is important stuff. You know that Italy is the leader in the shoe industry. You won't believe what good taste Italians have in **scarpe** (*skahr*-peh) *(shoes)*. You may just find the shoes of your dreams, whether they be a regular **paio di scarpe** (*pah*-yoh dee *skahr*-peh) *(pair of shoes)* **con o senza tacco** (kohn oh *sehn*-tsah *tahk*-koh) *(with or without heels)*, **pantofole** (pahn-*toh*-foh-leh) *(slippers)*, **sandali** (*sahn*-dah-lee) *(sandals)*, or **stivali** (stee-*vah*-lee) *(boots)*.

When you try on footwear, some words you may need to use are

- » **stretto/i/a/e** (*streht*-toh/tee/tah/teh) *(tight)*

- » **largo/ghi/ga/ghe** (*lahr*-goh/gee/gah/geh) *(loose/wide)*

- » **corto/i/a/e** (*kohr*-toh/tee/tah/teh) *(short)*

- » **lungo/ghi/ga/ghe** (*loohn*-goh/gee/gah/geh) *(long)*

You may notice that Italians use **numero** (*nooh*-meh-roh) *(number)* for shoe sizes, and **taglia** or **misura** *(size)* for clothing sizes.

Table 8-3 shows women's and men's shoe sizes and their conversions.

**TABLE 8-3**     **Shoe Sizes**

| Women's Shoe Sizes | | | Men's Shoe Sizes | | |
|---|---|---|---|---|---|
| U.S. and Canada | European | United Kingdom | U.S. and Canada | European | United Kingdom |
| 5 | 35 | 3 | 5.5 | 37.5 | 5 |
| 5.5 | 36 | 3.5 | 6 | 38 | 5.5 |
| 6 | 36.5 | 4 | 6.5 | 38.5 | 6 |
| 6.5 | 37 | 4.5 | 7 | 39 | 6.5 |
| 7 | 37.5 | 5 | 7.5 | 40 | 7 |
| 7.5 | 38 | 5.5 | 8 | 41 | 7.5 |
| 8 | 39 | 6 | 8.5 | 42 | 8 |
| 8.5 | 39.5 | 6.5 | 9 | 43 | 8.5 |
| 9 | 40 | 7 | 9.5 | 43.5 | 9 |
| 9.5 | 41 | 7.5 | 10 | 44 | 9.5 |
| 10 | 41.5 | 8 | 10.5 | 44.5 | 10 |
| 10.5 | 42 | 8,5 | 11 | 45 | 10.5 |
| 11 | 42.5 | 9 | 11.5 | 45.5 | 11 |
| 11.5 | 43 | 9.5 | 12 | 46 | 11.5 |

# Talkin' the Talk

If you see the pair of shoes of your dreams **in vetrina** (een veh-*tree*-nah) *(in the shop window)* and you'd like to try them on, you can follow Michela's example. (Track 17)

| | |
|---|---|
| **Michela:** | **Posso provare le scarpe esposte in vetrina?**<br>*pohs*-soh proh-*vah*-reh leh *skahr*-peh eh-*spoh*-steh een veh-*tree*-nah<br>*May I try on the pair of shoes in the window?* |
| **Salesperson:** | **Quali?**<br>*kwah*-lee<br>*Which ones?* |
| **Michela:** | **Quelle blu, a destra.**<br>*kwehl*-leh blooh ah *deh*-strah<br>*The blue ones, on the right.* |
| **Salesperson:** | **Che numero porta?**<br>keh *nooh*-meh-roh *pohr*-tah<br>*What size do you wear?* |
| **Michela:** | **Trentasette.**<br>*trehn*-tah-*seht*-teh<br>*37.* |
| **Salesperson:** | **Ecco qua. Un trentasette . . . sono strette?**<br>*ehk*-koh kwah oohn *trehn*-tah-*seht*-teh *soh*-noh *streht*-teh<br>*Here they are. A 37 . . . are they tight?* |
| **Michela:** | **No. Sono comodissime.**<br>noh *soh*-noh koh-moh-*dees*-see-meh<br>*No. They are very comfortable.* |
| | **Quanto vengono?**<br>*kwahn*-toh *vehn*-goh-noh<br>*How much do they cost?* |
| **Salesperson:** | **Novanta euro.**<br>noh-*vahn*-tah *eh*-ooh-roh<br>*90 euros.* |

# FUN & GAMES

We give you a lot of information and vocabulary about clothes shopping in this chapter. See how many articles of clothing you can identify on the following couple. See Appendix C for the answer key.

*Illustration by Liz Kurtzman*

# Chapter **9**

# Having Fun Out on the Town

Going out on the town is always fun. In general, Italians are sociable people who enjoy having a good time. You see them having espressos together **al bar** (ahl bahr) *(at a café)* or drinks at night **in piazza** (een *pyaht*-tsah) *(in the square)*. Most Italians love to go out in the evening, crowding the streets until late at night.

Italy is a popular vacation destination, and Italian cities offer a great variety of cultural events, from local fairs and **sagre** (*sah*-greh) *(town celebrations related to harvests)* to open-air festivals, music events, and city-wide celebrations. The variety is endless, and fun is guaranteed. Festivals relating to saints are held for the **santo patrono** (*sahn*-toh pah-*troh*-noh) *(patron saint)* and are religious in nature.

In this chapter, we give you information you need to take in cultural attractions and socialize.

# Diving Into the Culture

No matter where you live or where you travel, most major cities have a weekly **pubblicazione** (poohb–blee–kah–*tsyoh*–neh) *(publication)* listing information about upcoming events. These guides may include dates, descriptions, and times for theaters, exhibitions, festivals, films, and more. Many also provide tips for shopping and restaurants and are now frequently available online or in app form.

**CULTURAL WISDOM**

In smaller towns without weekly magazines, you may see events announced on posters. You can also find information in the local newspapers.

Of course, newspapers, websites, and apps aren't your only sources of information about things to do and see. Asking the following questions can help you get the answers you're looking for:

>> **Cosa c'è da fare di sera?** (*koh*-zah cheh dah *fah*-reh dee *seh*-rah) *(What is there to do in the evenings?)*

>> **Può suggerirmi qualcosa?** (pwoh soohj-jeh-*reer*-mee kwahl-*koh*-zah) *(Can you recommend something to me?)*

>> **C'è un concerto stasera?** (cheh oohn kohn-*chehr*-toh stah-*seh*-rah) *(Is there a concert tonight?)*

>> **Ci sono ancora posti?** (chee *soh*-noh ahn-*koh*-rah *poh*-stee) *(Are there any seats left?)*

>> **Dove si comprano i biglietti?** (*doh*-veh see *kohm*-prah-noh ee bee-*lyeht*-tee) *(Where can we get tickets?)*

>> **Quanto vengono i biglietti?** (*kwahn*-toh *vehn*-goh-noh ee bee-*lyeht*-tee) *(How much are the tickets?)*

>> **A che ora comincia lo spettacolo?** (ah keh *oh*-rah koh-*meen*-chah loh speht-*tahk*-koh-loh) *(What time does the show begin?)*

>> **Non c'è niente di più economico?** (nohn cheh *nyehn*-teh dee pyooh eh-koh-*noh*-mee-koh) *(Isn't there anything cheaper?)*

# Talkin' the Talk

Arturo works at a theater. He is bombarded with questions from patrons before the show.

**Sig. Paoli:** **Quando comincia lo spettacolo?**
*kwahn*-doh koh-*meen*-chah loh speht-*tah*-koh-loh
*When does the show start?*

**Arturo:** **Alle sette e mezza.**
*ahl*-leh *seht*-teh eh *mehdz*-dzah
*At half past seven.*

**Erika:** **A che ora finisce?**
ah keh *oh*-rah fee-*nee*-sheh
*What time is it over?*

**Arturo:** **Verso le dieci.**
*vehr*-soh leh *dyeh*-chee
*About 10 p.m.*

**Erika:** **C'è un intervallo?**
cheh oohn een-tehr-*vahl*-loh
*Is there an intermission?*

**Arturo:** **Sì, tra il secondo e il terzo atto.**
see trah eel seh-*kohn*-doh eh eel *tehr*-tsoh *aht*-toh
*Yes, between the second and third acts.*

## WORDS TO KNOW

| | | |
|---|---|---|
| **a che ora?** | ah keh *oh*-rah | *what time?* |
| **quando?** | *kwahn*-doh | *when?* |
| **dove?** | *doh*-veh | *where?* |
| **divertente** | dee-vehr-*tehn*-teh | *fun* |
| **biglietto [m]** | bee-*lyeht*-toh | *ticket* |
| **spettacolo [m]** | speht-*tah*-koh-loh | *show* |
| **cominciare** | koh-meen-*chah*-reh | *to start/begin* |
| **finire** | fee-*nee*-reh | *to finish/end* |

It's well known that Italy produces a great number of films, and there are many Italian directors who are famous throughout the world: Fellini, Rossellini, Bertolucci, De Sica, and Nanni Moretti, to name a few. Some of their works are considered classics of Italian culture, and we highly recommend them to you. Other contemporary directors to look for include Paolo Sorrentino, Gabriele Salvatores, Francesca Archibugi, Matteo Garrone, Ferzan Özpetek, and Emanuele Crialese.

**La dolce vita** and **La strada** are among Fellini's masterpieces. The dramatic and moving **Roma città aperta** (*Rome, Open City*) is one of Rossellini's most significant movies. To complete the image of the Italian cinema between 1945 and 1957, you need to include De Sica's **Ladri di biciclette** (*The Bicycle Thief*). Bertolucci belongs to a subsequent period and is known for his **Il conformista** (*The Conformist*) whereas Moretti's **Caro diario** (*Dear Diary*) made a big contribution to disseminate Italian culture abroad in the 1990s.

Then we have Roberto Benigni, who not only directed one of the most successful "foreign" films of modern times but won an Academy Award for acting in **La vita è bella** — *Life Is Beautiful.*

# Going to the movies

Going **al cinema** (ahl *chee*-neh-mah) (*to the movies*) is a popular activity almost everywhere. In Italy, American films usually are **doppiati** (dohp-*pyah*-tee) (*dubbed*) into Italian. On the other hand, why not go to an original Italian film? Doing so provides you with a good opportunity to polish your Italian.

Some questions for going to the movies include the following:

>> **Andiamo al cinema?** (ahn-*dyah*-moh ahl *chee*-neh-mah) (*Shall we go to the movies?/How about going to the movies?*)

>> **Cosa danno?** (*koh*-zah *dahn*-noh) (*What's playing?*)

>> **Dove lo danno?** (*doh*-veh loh *dahn*-noh) (*Where is [the movie] being shown?*)

>> **È in lingua/versione originale?** (eh in *leen*-gwah/vehr-*syoh*-neh oh-ree-jee-nah-leh) (*Is the film in the original language?*)

>> **Dov'è il cinema Trianon?** (doh-*veh* eel *chee*-neh-mah *tree*-ah-nohn) (*Where is the Trianon cinema?*)

Often saying the name of the movie theater is sufficient, for example, **Dov'è il Trianon?** (doh-*veh* eel *tree*-ah-nohn) (*Where is the Trianon?*).

# Talkin' the Talk

Ugo and Bianca are two Fellini fans. Ugo wants to go to the movies and asks his girlfriend Bianca if she feels like going with him. (Track 18)

**Ugo:** **Andiamo al cinema?**
ahn-*dyah*-moh ahl *chee*-neh-mah
*How about going to the movies?*

**Bianca:** **Che film vuoi vedere?**
keh feelm vwoi veh-*deh*-reh
*Which movie would you like to see?*

**Ugo:** **La dolce vita, naturalmente.**
lah *dohl*-cheh *vee*-tah *nah*-tooh-rahl-*mehn*-teh
*La dolce vita, of course.*

**Bianca:** **Oh, l'ho visto solo tre volte!**
oh loh *vee*-stoh *soh*-loh treh *vohl*-teh
*Oh, I've only seen it three times!*

**Dove lo danno?**
*doh*-veh loh *dahn*-noh
*Where is it being shown?*

**Ugo:** **Al Tiziano, qui vicino.**
ahl tee-*tsyah*-noh kwee vee-*chee*-noh
*At the Tiziano, nearby.*

**Bianca:** **A che ora comincia?**
ah keh *oh*-rah koh-*meen*-chah
*What time does it start?*

**Ugo:** **Esattamente fra cinque minuti!**
eh-zaht-tah-*mehn*-teh frah *cheen*-kweh mee-*nooh*-tee
*In exactly five minutes!*

**Bianca:** **Cosa aspettiamo?**
*koh*-zah ah-speht-*tyah*-moh
*What are we waiting for?*

Italian movie theaters used to be rather small, showing only one movie at a time. Today, virtually all large Italian cities have big **multisala** (moohl-tee-*sah*-lah) (*multiplex*).

# Talkin' the Talk

Films are an interesting topic of conversation. Here is a typical dialogue between two friends, Chiara and Alberto.

| | |
|---|---|
| **Chiara:** | **Hai visto l'ultimo film di Salvatores?** |
| | ahy *vee*-stoh *loohl*-tee-moh feelm dee sahl-vah-*toh*-rehs |
| | *Have you seen the new Salvatores movie?* |
| **Alberto:** | **Ancora no, e tu?** |
| | ahn-*koh*-rah noh eh tooh |
| | *Not yet, and you?* |
| **Chiara:** | **Sì, ieri sera.** |
| | see *yeh*-ree *seh*-rah |
| | *Yes, last night.* |
| **Alberto:** | **Com'è?** |
| | koh-*meh* |
| | *How is it?* |
| **Chiara:** | **L'attore principale è bravissimo!** |
| | laht-*toh*-reh preen-chee-*pah*-leh eh brah-*vees*-see-moh |
| | *The lead actor is really good!* |
| **Alberto:** | **Ma dai! Lo dici perché è bello!** |
| | mah dahy loh *dee*-chee pehr-*keh* eh *behl*-loh |
| | *Come on! You say that because he's good looking!* |
| **Chiara:** | **E allora? E il film è così divertente!** |
| | eh ahl-*loh*-rah eh eel feelm eh koh-*zee* dee-vehr-*tehn*-teh |
| | *So what? And the movie is so funny!* |
| **Alberto:** | **L'ultimo film di Salvatores era così serio.** |
| | *loohl*-tee-moh feelm dee sahl-vah-*toh*-rehs *eh*-rah koh-*zee seh*-ryoh |
| | *Salvatores' last film was so serious.* |

| | | |
|---|---|---|
| **Chi è il regista?** | kee eh eel reh-*jee*-stah | *Who is the director?* |
| **Chi sono gli attori?** | kee *soh*-noh lyee aht-*toh*-ree | *Who's starring?* |
| **attore [m]** | aht-*toh*-reh | *actor* |
| **attrice [f]** | aht-*tree*-cheh | *actress* |
| **trama [f]** | *trah*-mah | *plot* |
| **scena [f]** | *sheh*-nah | *scene* |

## Going to the theater

The language of the theater and the cinema is very similar. Of course, when you attend a play, opera, or symphony, you have a variety of seating options. For example, you can sit in **la platea** (lah plah-*teh*-ah) (*the orchestra*), **i palchi** (eeh *pahl*-kee) (*the box seats*), or **il loggione** (eel lohj-*joh*-neh) (*the gallery*), which used to be called **la piccionaia** (lah peech-choh-*nah*-yah) (Literally: *the pigeon loft*) because it's high up.

## Talkin' the Talk

Eugenio wants to find out whether seats are available for a performance of a play he wants to see. He's speaking on the phone with someone at the theater box office.

**Ticket Agent:** **Pronto?**
*prohn*-toh
*Hello?*

**Eugenio:** **Buongiorno. È il Teatro Valle?**
bwohn-*johr*-noh eh eel teh-*ah*-tro *vahl*-leh
*Good morning. Is this the Valle Theater?*

**Ticket Agent:** **Sì. Mi dica.**
see mee *dee*-kah
*Yes. May I help you?* (Literally: *Tell me.*)

*(continued)*

(continued)

| Eugenio: | **Vorrei prenotare dei posti.** |
| --- | --- |
| | vohr-*rey* preh-noh-*tah*-reh dey *poh*-stee |
| | *I'd like to reserve some seats.* |

| Ticket Agent: | **Per quale spettacolo?** |
| --- | --- |
| | pehr *kwah*-leh speht-*tah*-koh-loh |
| | *For which performance?* |

| Eugenio: | ***Aspettando Godot**, domani sera.* |
| --- | --- |
| | ah-speht-*tahn*-doh goh-*doh* doh-*mah*-nee *seh*-rah |
| | *Waiting for Godot, tomorrow evening.* |

| Ticket Agent: | **Mi dispiace. È tutto esaurito.** |
| --- | --- |
| | mee dee-*spyah*-cheh eh *tooht*-toh eh-zah-ooh-*ree*-toh |
| | *I'm sorry. It's sold out.* |

| Eugenio: | **Ci sono repliche?** |
| --- | --- |
| | chee *soh*-noh *reh*-plee-keh |
| | *Are there other performances?* |

| Ticket Agent: | **L'ultima è dopodomani.** |
| --- | --- |
| | *loohl*-tee-mah eh *doh*-poh-doh-*mah*-nee |
| | *The last one is the day after tomorrow.* |

**GRAMMATICALLY SPEAKING**

Did you notice that the title of the play, *Waiting for Godot* has no preposition in Italian? In English, you wait for someone, but in Italian, it's "waiting someone" — **aspettare qualcuno** (ah-speht-*tah*-reh kwahl-*kooh*-noh). You may also hear **ti aspetto** (tee ah-*speht*-toh) (*I'm waiting for you*).

# Talkin' the Talk

Eugenio talks with his friends about the play and then calls the box office again.

| Voice: | **Pronto?** |
| --- | --- |
| | *prohn*-toh |
| | *Hello?* |

| Eugenio: | **Ho telefonato due minuti fa.** |
| --- | --- |
| | oh teh-leh-foh-*nah*-toh *dooh*-eh mee-*nooh*-tee fah |
| | *I called two minutes ago.* |

| | |
|---|---|
| **Voice:** | **Sì, mi dica!**<br>See mee *dee*-kah<br>*Yes, how can I help you?* |
| **Eugenio:** | **Sì, vorrei prenotare tre posti per dopodomani**<br>see vohr-*rey* preh-noh-*tah*-reh treh *poh*-stee pehr *doh*-poh-doh-*mah*-nee<br>*Yes, I'd like to reserve three seats for day after tomorrow.* |
| **Voice:** | **Che posti desidera?**<br>keh *poh*-stee deh-*zee*-deh-rah<br>*Which seats would you like?* |
| **Eugenio:** | **Non troppo cari.**<br>nohn *trohp*-poh *kah*-ree<br>*Not too expensive.* |
| **Voice:** | **La platea costa trentadue euro.**<br>lah plah-*teh*-ah *koh*-stah *trehn*-tah-*dooh*-eh *eh*-ooh-roh<br>*The orchestra is 32 euros.* |
| **Eugenio:** | **Ci sono tre posti centrali?**<br>chee *soh*-noh treh *poh*-stee chehn-*trah*-lee<br>*Are there three middle seats?* |
| **Voice:** | **Un momento . . . sì, tre posti nella quindicesima fila**.<br>oohn moh-*mehn*-toh see treh *poh*-stee *nehl*-lah kween-dee-*cheh*-zee-mah *fee*-lah<br>*Just a moment . . . yes, three seats in row 15.* |
| | **Paga con Bancomat o con carta di credito?**<br>*pah*-gah kohn *bahn*-koh-maht oh kohn *kahr*-tah dee *kreh*-dee-toh<br>*Will you pay with an debit card or a credit card?* |
| **Eugenio:** | **Bancomat, per favore.**<br>*bahn*-koh-maht pehr fah-*voh*-reh<br>*Debit card, thank you (Literally: please).* |

If you come to Italy, you can catch an opera by Verdi, Puccini, or Rossini in renowned theaters such as Milan's **La Scala** (lah *skah*–lah), Naples's **San Carlo** (sahn *kahr*–loh), or the opera houses of Florence and Palermo. In the summer months, be sure to explore theater and music festivals — which offer a wide variety of repertoires at different venues throughout the cities — such as the famous *Ravenna Festival* or the *Verdi Festival* in Parma and Busseto. You can also see outdoor operas in Verona, performed at the old Roman **Arena** (ah–*reh*–nah).

Following are some useful phrases related to performances:

>> **la danza classica/moderna/contemporanea** (lah *dahn*-tsah *klahs*-see-kah/moh-*dehr*-nah/kohn-tehm-poh-*rah*-neh-ah) (*classical/modern/contemporary dance*)

>> **lo spettacolo** (loh speht-*tah*-koh-loh) (*the show; the performance*)

>> **la prova generale pubblica** (lah *proh*-vah jeh-neh-*rah*-leh *poohb*-blee-kah) (*public dress rehearsal*)

>> **la replica** (lah *reh*-plee-kah) (*repeat performance*)

>> **la matinée** (eel mah-tee-*neh*) (*matinee*)

>> **lo spettacolo pomeridiano** (loh speht-*tah*-koh-loh poh-meh-ree-*dyah*-noh) (*afternoon performance*)

**CULTURAL WISDOM**

You can usually purchase tickets through the theater's website or through dedicated apps, such as *VivaTicket* and *TicketOne*. Alternatively, you can purchase tickets **al botteghino** (ahl boht-teh-*gee*-noh) (*at the theater box office*) at specific times, posted on signs outside the theater. At the box office you can pay for the tickets and either pick them up immediately or before the performance begins.

# Going to a museum

Here are some of the most visited museums with the richest collections: the **Uffizi** (oohf-*fee*-tsee) Gallery in Florence; the **Galleria Borghese** (gahl-leh-*ree*-ah bohr-*geh*-zeh) and the **Musei Vaticani** (mooh-*zeh*-ee vah-tee-*kah*-nee) in Rome; the **Peggy Guggenheim Collection** in Venice; and the **Museo della Scienza e della Tecnica Leonardo da Vinci** (mooh-*zeh*-oh *dehl*-lah *shehn*-tsah eh *dehl*-lah *tehk*-nee-kah leh-oh-*nahr*-doh dah *veen*-chee) in Milan. Every two years Venice also hosts the **Biennale** (by-ehn-*nah*-leh), where you can view the work of many well-known and emerging contemporary international artists.

## Talkin' the Talk

Here two friends are about to go **al museo** (ahl mooh-*zeh*-oh) (*to the museum*).

Luisa:    **Ciao, Flavia, dove vai?**
chow *flah*-vyah *doh*-veh vahy
*Hello, Flavia, where are you going?*

| Flavia: | **Ciao! Alla mostra di Caravaggio.** |
| | chow *ahl*-lah *moh*-strah dee kah-rah-*vaj*-joh |
| | *Hello! To the Caravaggio exhibit.* |

| Luisa: | **Ma dai! ci vado anch'io!** |
| | mah dahy chee *vah*-doh ahn-*kee*-oh |
| | *You don't say! I'm going there too!* |

| Flavia: | **Allora andiamo insieme!** |
| | ahl-*loh*-rah ahn-*dyah*-moh een-*syeh*-meh |
| | *In that case, let's go together!* |

| Luisa: | **Certo! Viene anche Janet.** |
| | *chehr*-toh *vyeh*-neh *ahn*-keh jah-*neht* |
| | *Sure! Janet is coming too.* |

| Flavia: | **La conosco?** |
| | lah koh-*noh*-skoh |
| | *Do I know her?* |

| Luisa: | **Sì, la mia amica americana**. |
| | see lah *mee*-ah ah-*mee*-kah ah-meh-ree-*kah*-nah |
| | *Yes, my American friend.* |

| Flavia: | **Dove avete appuntamento?** |
| | *doh*-veh ah-*veh*-teh ahp-poohn-tah-*mehn*-toh |
| | *Where are you meeting?* |

| Luisa: | **Davanti al museo.** |
| | dah-*vahn*-tee ahl mooh-*zeh*-oh |
| | *In front of the museum.* |

# Going to a local festival

In this chapter's introduction we refer to the local **sagra** (*sah–greh*) (*village fairs*) and festivals you can find throughout Italy especially during the spring, summer, and fall. The themes of these events vary widely — from those with political origins such as **La festa dell'Unità** (lah *feh*–stah dehl-looh-nee-*tah*) (originally associated with the left-leaning newspaper l'Unità and now linked to the Democratic party), to those celebrating nature and cuisine. Capalbio's **Sagra del Cinghiale** (*sah*–grah dehl cheen-*gyah*-leh) (*Wild-Boar Festival*) and Cesenatico's **Sagra del Pesce Azzurro** (*sah*–grah dehl *peh*–sheh ahd–*dzooh*–roh) (*Blue Fish Festival*) are two that come to mind. If you happen upon a local **sagra,** be sure to drop in; these festivals are often the perfect venues for experiencing local culture and homemade food.

Paola tries to convince Martino to go to the Sagra dell'Uva in Bertinoro.

| | |
|---|---|
| **Paola:** | **Lo sai che oggi c'è la Sagra dell'uva a Bertinoro?** |
| | loh sahy keh *oj*-jee cheh lah *sah*-grah dehl-*looh*-vah ah behr-tee-*noh*-roh |
| | *Did you know that today there is the grape festival in Bertinoro?* |
| **Martino:** | **Divertente! Facciamoci un salto!** |
| | dee-vehr-*tehn*-teh fahch-*chah*-moh-chee oohn *sahl*-toh |
| | *(Sounds like) fun! Let's swing by!* |
| **Paola:** | **Partiamo subito?** |
| | pahr-*tyah*-moh *sooh*-bee-toh |
| | *Do you want to leave right away?* |
| **Martino:** | **Sì, perché no?** |
| | see pehr-*keh* noh |
| | *Yes, why not?* |
| **Paola:** | **In quel paese fanno anche degli ottimi cappelletti!** |
| | in kwehl pah-*eh*-zeh *fahn*-noh *deh*-lyee *oht*-tee-mee kahp-pehl-*leht*-tee |
| | *They make great cappelletti in that town.* |
| **Martino:** | **Ottimo, così ci fermiamo a cena.** |
| | *oht*-tee-moh *koh*-zee chee fehr-*myah*-moh ah *cheh*-nah |
| | *Great! This way we can stay for supper.* |

## Going to a concert

If you're interested in music, you can certainly find plenty to enjoy — from the **Umbria Jazz Festival** (*oohm*-bryah jehts *feh*-stee-vahl) to the **Festival dei Due Mondi** (*feh*-stee-vahl dey *dooh*-eh *mohn*-dee) in Spoleto, to performances by your favorite Italian **cantautore** (kahn-tah-ooh-*toh*-reh) (*singer–songwriter*).

Italy is full of old and beautiful churches and cathedrals, where **musicisti** (mooh-zee-*chee*-stee) (*musicians*) often perform classical music concerts. You can also hear concerts in other venues — sometimes right in the heart of a city, in a piazza.

# Talkin' the Talk

La signora and il signor Tiberi are reading the morning paper. Suddenly, Mrs. Tiberi cries out:

| | |
|---|---|
| **Sig.ra Tiberi:** | **Guarda qui!** <br> *gwahr-dah kwee* <br> *Look here!* |
| **Sig. Tiberi:** | **Che c'è?** <br> *keh cheh* <br> *What's up?* |
| **Sig.ra Tiberi:** | **Martedì c'è Allevi a Roma!** <br> *mahr-teh-dee cheh ahl-leh-vee ah roh-mah* <br> *Allevi is in Rome on Tuesday!* |
| **Sig. Tiberi:** | **Dà un concerto?** <br> *dah oohn kohn-chehr-toh* <br> *Is he going to give a concert?* |
| **Sig.ra Tiberi:** | **Sì, al Conservatorio.** <br> *see ahl kohn-sehr-vah-toh-ryoh* <br> *Yes, at the Conservatory.* |
| **Sig. Tiberi:** | **Sarà tutto esaurito?** <br> *sah-rah tooht-toh eh-zow-ree-toh* <br> *Will it already be sold out?* |
| **Sig.ra Tiberi:** | **Forse no!** <br> *fohr-seh noh* <br> *Maybe not!* |
| **Sig. Tiberi:** | **Vai al botteghino?** <br> *vahy ahl boht-teh-gee-noh* <br> *Are you going to the box office?* |
| **Sig.ra Tiberi:** | **Prima telefono.** <br> *pree-mah teh-leh-foh-noh* <br> *I'm going to call first.* |

**CULTURAL WISDOM**

Giovanni Allevi is an internationally famous Italian pianist. We do hope that signor and signora Tiberi find two tickets for this event. **Buona fortuna!** (*bwoh*-nah fohr-*tooh*-nah) (*Good luck!*)

<table>
<tr><td colspan="3">WORDS TO KNOW</td></tr>
<tr><td>musica [f]</td><td>mooh-zee-kah</td><td>music</td></tr>
<tr><td>concerto [m]</td><td>kohn-chehr-toh</td><td>concert</td></tr>
<tr><td>esaurito</td><td>eh-zah-ooh-ree-toh</td><td>sold out</td></tr>
<tr><td>piano(forte) [m]</td><td>pyah-noh(fohr-teh)</td><td>piano</td></tr>
<tr><td>museo [m]</td><td>mooh-zeh-oh</td><td>museum</td></tr>
<tr><td>insieme</td><td>een-syeh-meh</td><td>together</td></tr>
</table>

Maybe you know a musician or someone who plays an instrument in their leisure time. You're probably curious about some things, such as:

>> **Che strumento suoni?** (keh strooh-*mehn*-toh *swoh*-nee) *(Which instrument do you play?)*

  **Suono il violino.** (*swoh*-noh eel vyoh-*lee*-noh) *(I play the violin.)*

>> **Dove suonate stasera?** (*doh*-veh swoh-*nah*-teh stah-*seh*-rah) *(Where are you playing tonight?)*

  **Suoniamo al Blu Notte.** (swoh-*nyah*-moh ahl blooh *noht*-teh) *(We're playing at the Blu Notte.)*

>> **Chi suona in famiglia?** (kee *swoh*-nah in fah-*mee*-lyah) *(Who in your family plays an instrument?)*

# Going to a party or other event

Getting or giving **un invito** (oohn een-*vee*-toh) *(an invitation)* is always a pleasurable experience. **Una festa** (*ooh*-nah *feh*-stah) *(a party)* is a great opportunity to meet new people. In Italian, the verb **invitare** (een-vee-*tah*-reh) often means to treat someone to something. For example, if someone says, **"Posso invitarti a teatro?"** (*pohs*-soh een-vee-*tahr*-tee ah teh-ah-troh) *(May I invite you to the theater?)*, it means that the person is going to make the arrangements and cover the cost for you.

The following expressions are other ways to suggest an activity:

>> **Che ne pensi di andare a Roma?** (keh neh *pehn*-see dee ahn-*dah*-reh ah *roh*-mah) *(What do you think about going to Rome?)*

>> **Che ne dici di uscire stasera?** (keh neh *dee*-chee dee ooh-*shee*-reh stah-*seh*-rah) *(What do you think* [Literally: say] *about going out tonight?)*

>> **Andiamo in piscina!** (ahn-*dyah*-moh in pee-*shee*-nah) *(Let's go to the swimming pool!)*

>> **Mangiamo una pizza!** (mahn-*jah*-moh *ooh*-nah *peet*-tsah) *(Let's have pizza!)*

>> **Perché non andiamo a teatro?** (pehr-*keh* nohn ahn-*dyah*-moh ah teh-*ah*-troh) *(Why don't we go to the theater?)*

The word **perché** is special. In this chapter, we use it to ask the question *why.* However, it also means *because.* A dialogue might go like this:

**Perché non mangi?** (pehr-*keh* nohn *mahn*-jee) *(Why aren't you eating?)*

**Perché non ho fame.** (pehr-*keh* nohn oh *fah*-meh) *(Because I'm not hungry.)*

# Talkin' the Talk

Guido has a new job. He's very happy and wants to share his excitement with a couple of friends. He decides to **dare una festa** (*dah*-reh *ooh*-nah *feh*-stah) *(throw a party)* and tells his friend Caterina about it.

| | |
|---|---|
| **Guido:** | **Ho deciso!**<br>oh deh-*chee*-zoh<br>*I've decided!* |
| **Caterina:** | **Cosa?**<br>*koh*-zah<br>*What?* |
| **Guido:** | **Faccio una festa!**<br>*fahch*-choh *ooh*-nah *feh*-stah<br>*I'm throwing a party!* |
| **Caterina:** | **Perchè? Quando?**<br>pehr-*keh kwahn*-doh<br>*Why? When?* |
| **Guido:** | **Per il mio nuovo lavoro. Sabato sera.**<br>pehr il *mee*-oh *nwoh*-voh lah-*voh*-roh *sah*-bah-toh *seh*-rah<br>*For my new job. Saturday night.* |
| **Caterina:** | **Una festa con musica, balli, birra?**<br>*ooh*-nah *feh*-stah kohn *mooh*-zee-kah *bahl*-lee *beer*-rah<br>*A party with music, dancing, and beer?* |

*(continued)*

*(continued)*

| Guido: | **Certo. Mi aiuti?** |
|---|---|
| | *chehr*-toh mee ah-*yooh*-tee |
| | *Certainly. Will you help me?* |
| Caterina: | **Come no!** |
| | *koh*-meh noh |
| | *Of course!* |

**CULTURAL WISDOM**

Nowadays, you can send and receive invitations in many different ways. You might receive an invitation by phone, via email, through messaging apps like WhatsApp, or you may be invited by your host face to face.

# Talkin' the Talk

**PLAY THIS**

Guido will have a party at his house next Saturday. He calls Sara to invite her. (Track 19)

| Sara: | **Ciao Guido, come va?** |
|---|---|
| | chow *gwee*-doh *koh*-meh vah |
| | *Hi Guido, how are you?* |
| Guido: | **Molto bene! Sei libera sabato sera?** |
| | *mohl*-toh *beh*-neh sey *lee*-beh-rah *sah*-bah-toh *seh*-rah |
| | *Very well. Are you free Saturday night?* |
| Sara: | **È un invito?** |
| | eh oohn een-*vee*-toh |
| | *Is this an invitation?* |
| Guido: | **Sì, alla mia festa.** |
| | see *ahl*-lah *mee*-ah *feh*-stah |
| | *Yes, to my party.* |
| Sara: | **Fantastico! A che ora?** |
| | fahn-*tah*-stee-koh ah keh *oh*-rah |
| | *Great! What time?* |
| Guido: | **Verso le nove.** |
| | *vehr*-soh leh *noh*-veh |
| | *About nine.* |
| Sara: | **Cosa posso portare? Il gelato va bene?** |
| | *koh*-zah *pohs*-soh pohr-*tahr*-eh eel jeh-*lah*-toh vah *beh*-neh |
| | *What can I bring? Is ice cream okay?* |

**Guido:** **Ottimo. Quello piace a tutti.**
*oht*-tee-moh *qwehl*-loh *pyah*-cheh ah *tooht*-tee
*Great. Everyone likes ice cream.*

**Sara:** **Allora, d'accordo. Grazie!**
ahl-*loh*-rah dahk-*kohr*-doh *grah*-tsyeh
*Okay then. Thanks!*

Figure 9-1 shows the invitation Guido sent to friends he couldn't reach by phone (note, the stressed syllables in the translations are underlined).

**FIGURE 9-1:**
A casual invitation, suitable for WhatsApp, email, or print.

*Illustration by Liz Kurtzman*

# Talkin' the Talk

Both Franco and Emma have received Guido's invitation. They're now talking about whether or not they'll go to the party.

**Franco:** **Vieni alla festa di Guido?**
*vyeh*-nee *ahl*-lah *feh*-stah dee *gwee*-doh
*Are you going to Guido's party?*

**Emma:** **No, mi annoio alle feste.**
noh mee ahn-*noh*-yoh *ahl*-leh *feh*-steh
*No, I get bored at parties.*

**Franco:** **Ti annoi?**
tee ahn-*noy*
*You get bored?*

**Emma:** **Sì, non ballo e non bevo.**
see nohn *bahl*-loh eh nohn *beh*-voh
*Yes, I don't dance and don't drink.*

**Non mi diverto**
nohn mee dee-*vehr*-toh
*I don't have fun.*

**Franco:** **Ma ti piace chiacchierare.**
Mah tee *pyah*-che *kyahk*-kyeh-rah-reh
*But you like to chat!*

**Emma:** **Sì, ma senza musica di sottofondo.**
see mah *sehn*-tsah *mooh*-zee-kah dee *soht*-toh-*fohn*-doh
*Yes, but without background music.*

Sometimes you may get invited to a more formal event, **un evento di gala** (oohn eh-*vehn*-toh dee *gah*-lah) (*a gala event*) or **un evento in abito da sera** (oohn eh-*vehn*-toh een *ah*-bee-toh dah seh-rah) (*a black tie event*) where the language may be quite different. Figure 9-2 is an example of a formal invitation to the opening of an exhibition by artist Elisa Catalini (note, the stressed syllables in the translations are underlined).

FIGURE 9-2:
The classic formal, engraved invitation.

*Illustration by Liz Kurtzman*

## WORDS TO KNOW

| | | |
|---|---|---|
| **invito [m]** | een-*vee*-toh | *invitation* |
| **festa [f]** | *feh*-stah | *party* |
| **suonare** | swoh-*nah*-reh | *to play (a musical instrument)* |
| **perché** | pehr-*keh* | *why/because* |
| **bere** | *beh*-reh | *to drink* |
| **ballare** | bahl-*lah*-reh | *to dance* |

Now it's your turn to invite an Italian friend to your party. Use the following words to fill in the blanks in this invitation. See Appendix C for the answer key.

aspetto, dove, festa, invitato, ora, perché, sabato, verso

**C'è una** (1) ______ **e tu sei** (2) _______. (There's a party and you're invited.)

**Quando?** (3) ______ **24 luglio** (When? Saturday, July 24.)

**A che** (4) ______? (5) ______ **le 9.** (What time? About 9 o'clock.)

(6) ______? **A casa mia**. (Where? At my place.)

(7) ______? **Per festeggiare insieme!** (Why? To celebrate together!)

**Ti** (8) ______. (I'll be waiting for you.)

Buon divertimento! (Have a nice time!)

Chapter **10**

# From Ring to Ping: Phones, Texts, Emails, & More

n this chapter, you encounter expressions and phrases about telephones and telecommunication — for example, what to say when someone calls you and how to leave a message. We show you some examples of common phone dialogues as well as some common phrases and practices to consider when emailing and texting.

## Communicating Made Simple

**Pronto!** (*prohn*-toh) (*Hello!*) is the first thing you hear when you talk to an Italian on the phone. In most languages, people answer the phone with the same word they use for saying hello in person, but in Italian, you use **pronto** to say hello only on the phone.

You can answer the phone and say, **"Pronto. Chi parla?"** (*prohn*-toh kee *pahr*-lah) (*Hello, who's speaking?*)

And a typical response might be **"Sono Sabrina. C'è Stefano?"** (*soh*-noh sah-*bree*-nah cheh *steh*-fah-noh) *(This is Sabrina. Is Stefano there?)*

You can also say, **"Casa Ferrari? Sono Susanna. Posso parlare con Michele per favore?"** (*kah*-zah fehr-*rah*-ree *soh*-noh sooh-*zahn*-nah *pohs*-soh pahr-*lah*-reh kohn mee-*keh*-leh pehr fah-*voh*-reh) *(Is this the Ferraris? This is Susan. May I please speak with Michael?)*

The following sections discuss how Italians connect and communicate through mobile devices using cellphones, text messaging, and the super popular messaging app WhatsApp.

## Connecting via cellphones, texts, and WhatsApp

Italians love their **cellulari** (*chehl*-looh-*lah*-ree) *(cellular phones)*, there's no doubt about that. They were one of the first cultures to fully embrace the **telefonino** (teh-leh-foh-*nee*-noh) *(cellphone)* back in the 1980s, when they adopted this useful accessory as a fashion statement.

As you read the following sections about common ways to communicate today in Italy, keep these useful phone phrases in mind:

>> **Avete un telefono?** (ah-*veh*-teh oohn teh-*leh*-foh-noh) *(Is there/Do you have a [public] telephone?)*

>> **Hai WhatsApp?** (ahy *uohts*-ahp) *(Do you have WhatsApp?)*

>> **Ha un recapito telefonico?** (ah oohn reh-*kah*-pee-toh teh-leh-*foh*-nee-koh) *(Do you have a contact phone number?)* (You might hear this when you go to change money at the bank.)

>> **Qual è il suo/tuo numero di telefono?** (kwah-*leh* eel *sooh*-oh *nooh*-meh-roh dee teh-*leh*-foh-noh) *(What is your phone number?)* (formal/informal)

### Cellphones

When you're in Italy you need to have your own cellphone because public phones are nearly impossible to find, and hotel phones are very expensive to use. If you take your phone with you from the United States or Canada, make sure that it will work in Italy and that calls won't cost you a mint. Of course, you can buy a phone when you get to Italy or, better yet, a sim card, to insert in yours. If you buy a new phone or a new sim card, you can purchase phone time and data allotment at the local **tabaccheria** (tah-bahk-*keh*-ree-ah) *(tobacconist)* or via the phone company website. You can do the same thing at any branch of the phone store where you bought your cellphone.

## Text messaging

Because most people including Italians tend to text more frequently than make phone calls these days (because it is much cheaper and trendier), you should know how to say a couple of important things, such as **messaggino** (mehs-sahj-*jee*-noh) or **sms** (*ehs*-seh-*ehm*-meh-*ehs*-seh) *(text message)*, and **"mandami un messaggino"** (*mahn*-dah-mee oohn mehs-sahj-*jee*-noh) *(Text me.* Literally: *"Send me a text message.")*.

## WhatsApp

These days, just about everyone in Italy uses WhatsApp to stay in touch. It's free, easy to use, and works over Wi-Fi or data, so you don't have to worry about call or text charges. Whether you're making plans with friends, sending photos to family, or sharing your location, WhatsApp is the go-to app. If you're traveling in Italy, make sure to download it — it's how most people communicate.

# Talkin' the Talk

**PLAY THIS**

Giorgio is back in Naples again and decides to give an old friend a call. (Track 20)

| Simona: | **Pronto!** |
| | *prohn*-toh |
| | *Hello!* |

| Giorgio: | **Pronto, Simona?** |
| | *prohn*-toh see-*moh*-nah |
| | *Hello, Simona?* |

| Simona: | **Sì, chi parla?** |
| | see kee *pahr*-lah |
| | *Yes, who's speaking?* |

| Giorgio: | **Sono Giorgio.** |
| | *soh*-noh *johr*-joh |
| | *It's Giorgio.* |

| Simona: | **Che bella sorpresa!** |
| | keh *behl*-lah sohr-*preh*-zah |
| | *What a nice surprise!* |

*(continued)*

(continued)

| | |
|---|---|
| | **Sei di nuovo a Napoli?** |
| | sey dee *nwoh*-voh ah *nah*-poh-lee |
| | *Are you in Naples again?* |
| **Giorgio:** | **Sì, sono arrivato stamattina.** |
| | see *soh*-noh ahr-ree-*vah*-toh stah-maht-*tee*-nah |
| | *Yes, I arrived this morning.* |
| **Simona:** | **Ci vediamo stasera?** |
| | chee veh-*dyah*-moh stah-*seh*-rah |
| | *Are we going to meet tonight?* |
| **Giorgio:** | **Ti chiamo per questo!** |
| | tee *kyah*-moh pehr *kweh*-stoh |
| | *That's why I'm calling!* |

## Calling for business or pleasure

Whether you want to find out what time a show starts, make a dental appointment, or just chat with a friend, the easiest way to accomplish any of these tasks is usually to use your cellphone or send a text message. This section takes you through the nuts and bolts of talking on the phone.

# Talkin' the Talk

The following is a formal dialogue between two **signori** (see-*nyoh*-ree) *(gentlemen)* who met only once.

| | |
|---|---|
| **Sig. Palladino:** | **Pronto?** |
| | *prohn*-toh |
| | *Hello?* |
| **Sig. Nieddu:** | **Pronto, il signor Palladino?** |
| | *prohn*-toh eel see-*nyohr* pahl-lah-*dee*-noh |
| | *Hello, Mr. Palladino?* |
| **Sig. Palladino:** | **Sì. Con chi parlo?** |
| | see kohn kee *pahr*-loh |
| | *Yes. Who am I speaking to?* |
| **Sig. Nieddu:** | **Sono Carlo Nieddu.** |
| | *soh*-noh *kahr*-loh *nyehd*-dooh |
| | *This is Carlo Nieddu.* |

**Si ricorda di me?**
see ree-*kohr*-dah dee meh
*Do you remember me?*

Sig. Palladino: **No, mi dispiace.**
noh mee dee-*spyah*-cheh
*I don't, I'm sorry.*

Sig. Nieddu: **Il cugino di Enza.**
eel kooh-*jee*-noh dee *ehn*-tsah
*Enza's cousin.*

Sig. Palladino: **Ma certo, mi scusi tanto!**
mah *chehr*-toh mee *skooh*-zee *tahn*-toh
*But, of course, excuse me!*

Sometimes you call just to **fare due chiacchiere al telefono** (*fah*–reh *dooh*–eh *kyahk*–kyeh–reh ahl teh–*leh*–foh–noh) *(to chat on the phone)*, but the person on the other end of the line may not be prepared for a lengthy chat.

When you are really busy and don't have time to speak, you may need the following phrases. The first is informal, and the second is one you might use at work:

**Ti posso richiamare più tardi?** (tee *pohs*-soh ree-kyah-*mah*-reh pyooh *tahr*-dee) *(Can I call you back later?)*

or

**La posso richiamare fra mezz'ora?** (lah *pohs*-soh ree-kyah-*mah*-reh frah mehd-*dzoh*-rah) *(Can I call you back in half an hour?)*

# Talkin' the Talk

On other occasions your call may be quite welcome, as is Monica's:

Monica: **Ciao, mamma, ti disturbo?**
chow *mahm*-mah tee dee-*stoohr*-boh
*Hello, Mom. Is it a good time?*

Lucia: **No, assolutamente.**
noh ahs-soh-looh-tah-*mehn*-teh
*Not at all.*

*(continued)*

(continued)

| Monica: | **Volevo sentire cosa fate per Pasqua.** |
|---|---|
| | voh-*leh*-voh sehn-*tee*-reh *koh*-zah *fah*-teh pehr *pah*-skwah |
| | *I wanted to hear what you were doing for Easter.* |
| Lucia: | **Andiamo tutti dalla nonna.** |
| | ahn-*dyah*-moh *tooht*-tee *dahl*-lah *nohn*-nah |
| | *We're all going to Grandma's.* |
| Monica: | **Ottimo! Buon'idea.** |
| | *oht*-tee-moh bwohn-ee-*deh*-ah |
| | *Great! Good idea!* |

## WORDS TO KNOW

| | | |
|---|---|---|
| **cellulare [m]** | chehl-looh-*lah*-reh | *cellular phone* |
| **compagnia telefonica [f]** | cohm-pah-*nyee*-ah teh-leh-*foh*-nee-kah | *phone company* |
| **telefonino [m]** | teh-leh-foh-*nee*-noh | *me cellphone* |
| **ricarica [f]** | ree-*kah*-ree-kah | *top-up* |
| **carta SIM [f]** | *kahr*-tah seem | *sim card* |
| **messaggino [m]** | mehs-sahj-*jee*-noh | *text message* |

# Making Arrangements over the Phone

Reserving a table at a restaurant, making an appointment, and ordering tickets for a concert are all activities you usually do by phone. In this section we introduce you to the Italian way of handling these matters.

The expression **a domani** (ah doh-*mah*-nee) (*see you tomorrow*) is a bit different in Italian because it doesn't have a verb. In English, *see you tomorrow* includes the verb "to see" to indicate that you will see the other person the day after. Italian is more concise; **a domani** — literally means, "until tomorrow."

**PLAY THIS**

Mrs. Elmi calls her doctor's office to make an appointment. She is speaking with the doctor's nurse. (Track 21)

**Sig.ra Elmi:** **Buongiorno, sono la signora Elmi. Vorrei prendere un appuntamento.**
bwohn-*johr*-noh *soh*-noh lah see-*nyoh*-rah *ehl*-mee vohr-*rey* prehn-deh-reh oohn ahp-poon-tah-*mehn*-toh
*Good morning, this is Ms. Elmi. I'd like to make an appointment.*

**Nurse:** **È urgente?**
eh oohr-*jehn*-teh
*Is it urgent?*

**Sig.ra Elmi:** **Purtroppo sì.**
poohr-*trohp*-poh see
*Unfortunately, it is.*

**Nurse:** **Va bene alle quattro e mezza?**
vah *beh*-neh *ahl*-leh *kwaht*-troh eh *mehd*-dzah
*Today at 4:30?*

**Sig.ra Elmi:** **Va benissimo, grazie.**
vah beh-*nees*-see-moh *grah*-tsyeh
*That's great, thank you.*

**Nurse:** **Prego. Ci vediamo più tardi.**
*preh*-goh chee veh-*dyah*-moh pyooh *tahr*-dee
*You're welcome. See you later.*

# Handling Missed Calls and Messages

This section offers useful terminology about asking to speak to people and leaving messages. Today, this may happen in a hotel — the person you're calling is unavailable, so you need to be comfortable with leaving a message.

You're familiar with the situation: You're waiting for a call, but you need to go out. When you get back, you want to know whether anyone called for you. You can ask that question at the lobby in several ways:

>> **Ha chiamato qualcuno per me?** (ah kyah-*mah*-toh kwahl-*kooh*-noh pehr meh) *(Has anybody called for me?)*

>> **Mi ha chiamato qualcuno?** (mee ah kyah-*mah*-toh kwahl-*kooh*-noh) *(Did anybody call for me?)*

>> **Mi ha cercato nessuno?** (mee ah chehr-*kah*-toh nehs-*sooh*-noh) *(Has anybody called for me?)*

# Talkin' the Talk

Leo wants to give Camilla a call, but she's not home, so he leaves a message for her.

| | |
|---|---|
| **Leo:** | **Buongiorno, sono Leo.**<br>bwohn-*johr*-noh *soh*-noh *leh*-oh<br>*Good morning, this is Leo.* |
| **Voice:** | **Ciao Leo.**<br>chow *leh*-oh<br>*Hello, Leo.* |
| **Leo:** | **C'è Camilla?**<br>cheh kah-*meel*-lah<br>*Is Camilla in?* |
| **Voice:** | **No, è appena uscita.**<br>noh eh ahp-*peh*-nah ooh-*shee*-tah<br>*No, she's just gone out.* |
| **Leo:** | **Quando la trovo?**<br>*kwahn*-doh lah *troh*-voh<br>*When can I reach her?* |
| **Voice:** | **Verso le nove.**<br>*vehr*-soh leh *noh*-veh<br>*Around 9.* |

<table>
<tr><td>Leo:</td><td>Le posso lasciare un messaggio?<br>leh pohs-soh lah-shah-reh oohn mehs-sahj-joh<br>Can I leave her a message?</td></tr>
<tr><td>Voice:</td><td>Come no, dimmi.<br>koh-meh noh deem-mee<br>Of course, go ahead.</td></tr>
</table>

As you can see, there are different ways to ask to speak to someone, say that they're not available, and ask to leave a message. This informal dialogue shows one way of expressing these ideas, and the dialogue that follows presents another situation in a formal exchange.

# Talkin' the Talk

PLAY THIS

Mr. Marchi calls Mr. Trevi's office to talk about an upcoming meeting. Mr. Trevi's secretary picks up the phone. (Track 22)

<table>
<tr><td>Secretary:</td><td>Pronto?<br>prohn-toh<br>Hello?</td></tr>
<tr><td>Sig. Marchi:</td><td>Buongiorno, sono Ennio Marchi.<br>bwohn-johr-noh soh-noh ehn-nyoh mahr-kee<br>Good morning, this is Ennio Marchi.</td></tr>
<tr><td>Secretary:</td><td>Buongiorno, dica.<br>bwohn-johr-noh dee-kah<br>Good morning, can I help you?</td></tr>
<tr><td>Sig. Marchi:</td><td>Potrei parlare con il signor Trevi?<br>poh-trey pahr-lah-reh kohn eel see-nyohr treh-vee<br>Can I speak to Mr. Trevi?</td></tr>
<tr><td>Secretary:</td><td>Mi dispiace, è in riunione.<br>mee dee-spyah-cheh eh een ree-ooh-nyoh-neh<br>I'm sorry, he's in a meeting.</td></tr>
<tr><td>Sig. Marchi:</td><td>Posso lasciare un messaggio?<br>poh-trey lah-shahr-lyee oohn mehs-sahj-joh<br>May I leave a message?</td></tr>
<tr><td>Secretary:</td><td>Certo. Prego.<br>chehr-toh preh-goh<br>Of course. Go ahead . . .</td></tr>
</table>

Sometimes you don't understand the name of the person you're talking to and need to ask for the spelling. In Italian there is no actual verb for *to spell*, so you ask: **Come si scrive?** (*koh*-meh-see *skree*-veh) (*How do you spell it?* Literally: *How do you write it?*)

Don't worry too much about this; as long as you know the basic Italian alphabet in Chapter 1, you can spell someone's name!

## WORDS TO KNOW

| | | |
|---|---|---|
| **pronto** | *prohn*-toh | *hello* |
| **chiacchierare** | kyahk-kyeh-*rah*-reh | *to chat* |
| **Attenda in linea!** | aht-*tehn*-dah een *lee*-neh-ah | *Please hold!* |
| **chiamare** | kyah-*mah*-reh | *to call* |
| **chiamata [f]** | kyah-*mah*-tah | *call* |
| **informazione [f]** | een-fohr-mah-*tsyoh*-neh | *information* |
| **sorpresa [f]** | sohr-*preh*-zah | *surprise* |

# What Did You Do Last Weekend? — Talking about the Past

Not all phone calls have to do with leaving messages, of course. One age-old reason for a phone conversation is so friends can catch up on each other's lives. Imagine you had such a great time at the beach last weekend that you can't wait to call and tell your best friend all about it. But to be able to communicate what you did, who you saw, and where you went, you first need to understand the Italian equivalent of the present perfect and the simple past.

When you speak about something that happened in the past — that is when you say *I spoke* or *I have spoken* — you use the **passato prossimo** (pahs-*sah*-toh prohs-see-moh) in Italian, which corresponds to the present perfect in English. The **passato prossimo** is a compound tense: It consists of more than one word, as in "I have heard." Take a look at how it works in these examples:

» **Ho ascoltato una canzone.** (oh ah-skohl-*tah*-toh *ooh*-nah kahn-*tsoh*-neh)
*(I listened/I have listened to a song.)*

» **Sono andato alla spiaggia.** (*soh*-noh ahn-*dah*-toh *ahl*-lah *spyahj*-jah)
*(I went/I have gone to the beach.)*

The structure of the **passato prossimo** is similar to the present perfect. It's composed of the present tense of either the verb **avere** (ah-*veh*-reh) *(to have)* or **essere** (*ehs*-ser-reh) *(to be)* plus the past participle of the verb. In the preceding examples, **ascoltato** (ah-skohl-*tah*-toh) *(listened)* is the past participle of **ascoltare** (ah-skohl-*tah*-reh) *(to listen to)*, and **andato** (ahn-*dah*-toh) *(gone)* is the past participle of **andare** (ahn-*dah*-reh) *(to go)*.

Just remember this formula to make the **passato prossimo:**

Present tense of the helping verb (**essere** or **avere**) + the past participle of the verb, generally ending in **–ato** (*ah*-toh) for **–are** verbs, **–uto** (*ooh*-toh) for **–ere** verbs, and **–ito** (*ee*-toh) for **–ire** verbs.

**Lei** (ley) is the formal way of saying *you.* Use **lei** to address someone you don't know well or with whom you need to be polite.

So how do you know when to use **essere** or **avere** as your helping verb in the **passato prossimo?** *Transitive verbs* (those that take a direct object), take **avere** and *intransitive verbs* (those that don't take a direct object) use **essere.** Usage is your guide as the following sections explain.

## Using avere

In Table 10-1 you can see how to conjugate a verb (an **–are** verb in this case) with **avere** in the **passato prossimo** as the helping verb.

Some past participles are irregular. They follow no rule and simply must be memorized. See Appendix B for examples. Table 10-2 provides you with some common regular past participles and some very common irregular past participles of verbs that are conjugated with **avere.**

## Passato Prossimo with Avere

| Avere + Past Participle | Translation |
| --- | --- |
| **ho chiamato** (oh kyah-*mah-toh*) | *I called/have called/I did call* |
| **hai chiamato** (ahy kyah-*mah-toh*) | *you called/have called/you did call* |
| **ha chiamato** (ah kyah-*mah-toh*) | *he/she called/has called you (formal) called/have called* |
| **abbiamo chiamato** (ahb-*byah*-moh kyah-*mah-toh*) | *we called /have called* |
| **avete chiamato** (ah-*veh*-teh kyah-*mah-toh*) | *you (pl.) called/have called* |
| **hanno chiamato** (*ahn*-noh kyah-*mah-toh*) | *they called/have called* |



## Past Participles Using Avere

| Infinitive | Past Participle |
| --- | --- |
| **ascoltare** (ah-skohl-*tah*-reh) (*to listen*) | **ascoltato** (ahs-kohl-*tah*-toh) (*listened*) |
| **comprare** (kohm-*prah*-reh) (*to buy*) | **comprato** (kohm-*prah*-toh) (*bought*) |
| **telefonare** (teh-leh-foh-*nah*-reh) (*to phone*) | **telefonato** (teh-leh-foh-*nah*-toh) (*phoned/called*) |
| **conoscere** (koh-*noh*-sheh-reh) (*to know, to meet*) | **conosciuto** (koh-noh-*shooh*-toh) (*known/met*) |
| **ricevere** (ree-*cheh*-veh-reh) (*to receive*) | **ricevuto** (ree-cheh-*vooh*-toh) (*received*) |
| **dire** (*dee*-reh) (*to say*) | **detto** (*deht*-toh) (*said*) |
| **fare** (*fah*-reh) (*to do, to make*) | **fatto** (*faht*-toh) (*done/made*) |
| **leggere** (*lehj*-jeh-reh) (*to read*) | **letto** (*leht*-toh) (*read*) |
| **scrivere** (*skree*-veh-reh) (*to write*) | **scritto** (*skreet*-toh) (*written*) |
| **vedere** (veh-*deh*-reh) (*to see*) | **visto** (*vee*-stoh) (*seen*) |

Asking about last weekend is always a reason to call your friend to hear what they did.

Rosa calls her best friend Tiziana to catch up on her weekend.

| | |
|---|---|
| **Rosa:** | **Che cosa hai fatto questo fine settimana?**<br>keh *koh*-zah ahy *faht*-toh *kweh*-stoh *fee*-neh<br>seht-tee-*mah*-nah<br>*What did you do last weekend?* |
| **Tiziana:** | **Ho conosciuto un uomo meraviglioso!**<br>oh koh-noh-*shooh*-toh oohn *woh*-moh meh-rah-vee-*lyoh*-zoh<br>*I met a wonderful man!* |
| **Rosa:** | **Racconta tutto!**<br>rahk-*kohn*-tah *tooht*-toh<br>*Tell me everything!* |
| **Tiziana:** | **Sabato sono andata al mare.**<br>*sah*-bah-toh *soh*-noh ahn-*dah*-tah ahl *mah*-reh<br>*Saturday I went to the beach.* |
| **Rosa:** | **Da sola?**<br>dah *soh*-lah<br>*Alone?* |
| **Tiziana:** | **Sì, e lì ho incontrato Enrico.**<br>see eh lee oh een-kohn-*trah*-toh ehn-*ree*-koh<br>*Yes, and I met Enrico there.* |
| **Rosa:** | **Per caso?**<br>pehr *kah*-zoh<br>*By chance?* |
| **Tiziana:** | **No, me l'ha presentato Davide.**<br>noh meh lah preh-zehn-*tah*-toh *dah*-vee-deh<br>*No, David introduced me to him.* |

## Using essere

When the **passato prossimo** is formed with the present tense of **essere** *(to be)*, the past participle ends according to the subject: masculine singular **-o**, feminine singular **-a**, masculine plural **-i**, or feminine plural **-e.** Note the endings of the past participles in Table 10-3.

## Passato Prossimo with Essere

| Essere + Past participle | | Translation |
| --- | --- | --- |
| **io sono uscito/a** | (*ee*-oh *soh*-noh ooh-*shee*-toh/ah) | *I went out* |
| **tu sei uscito/a** | (tooh sey ooh-*shee*-toh/ah) | *You went out* |
| **lui/lei è uscito/a** | (*looh*-ee/ley eh ooh-*shee*-toh/ah) | *He/she went out* |
| **Lei è uscito/a** | (ley eh ooh-*shee*-toh/ah) | *You (formal) went out* |
| **noi siamo usciti/e** | (noi *syah*-moh ooh-*shee*-tee/eh) | *We went out* |
| **voi siete usciti/e** | (voi *syeh*-teh ooh-*shee*-tee/eh) | *You out* |
| **loro sono usciti/e** | (*loh*-roh *soh*-noh ooh-*shee*-tee/eh) | *They went out* |

Note the endings of the past participles in Table 10-4 of the most common verbs that take **essere** as the helping verb. Keep in mind that these verbs are conjugated with **essere,** not only in the present perfect tense, but also in any other compound tense.



## Past Participles Using Essere

| Infinitive | Past Participle | Translation |
| --- | --- | --- |
| **andare** (ahn-*dah*-reh) (*to go*) | **andato/-a/-i/-e** (ahn-*dah*-toh/tah/tee/teh) | *gone* |
| **arrivare** (ahr-ree-*vah*-reh) (*to arrive*) | **arrivato/-a/-i/-e** (ahr-ree-*vah*-toh/tah/tee/teh) | *arrived* |
| **entrare** (ehn-*trah*-reh) (*to enter*) | **entrato/-a/-i/-e** (ehn-*trah*-toh/tah/tee/teh) | *entered* |
| **stare** (*stah*-reh) (to stay) | **stato/-a/-i/-e** (*stah*-toh/tah/tee/teh) | *been* |
| **partire** (pahr-*tee*-reh) (*to leave*) | **partito/-a/-i/-e** (pahr-*tee*-toh/tah/tee/teh) | *left* |
| **venire** (veh-*nee*-reh) (*to come*) | **venuto/-a/-i/-e** (veh-*nooh*-toh/tah/tee/teh) | *came* |
| **tornare** (tohr-*nah*-reh) (*to return*) | **tornato/-a/-i/-e** (tohr-*nah*-toh/tah/tee/teh) | *returned* |
| **nascere** (nah-*sheh*-reh) | **nato/-a/-i/-e** (*nah*-toh/tah/tee/teh) | *to be born* |
| **morire** (moh-*ree*-reh) | **morto/-a/-i/-e** *mohr*-toh/tah/tee/teh) | *to die* |

# Discussing Your Job

The world is getting smaller, and business contact with people in other countries is common. Whether by phone, chat, or email, it's becoming more and more important to know how to communicate with business colleagues around the world. If you happen to have business contacts with Italian companies, knowing some basic Italian business vocabulary may be useful.

Italian has at least four words for "company" — **la compagnia** (lah kohm-pah-*nyee*-ah), **la ditta** (lah *deet*-tah) (which also means *the firm*), **l'azienda** (lah-*dzyehn*-dah), and *la società* (lah soh-cheh-*tah*). These words are virtually interchangeable.

**L'ufficio** (loohf-*fee*-choh) is Italian for *office.* The following sentences give you a taste of the phrases you hear in **uffici** (oohf-*fee*-chee) *(offices)* everywhere:

>> **La mia scrivania è troppo piccola.** (lah *mee*-ah skree-vah-*nee*-ah eh *trohp*-poh *peek*-koh-lah) *(My desk is too small.)*

>> **È una grande società?** (eh *ooh*-nah *grahn*-deh soh-cheh-*tah*) *(Is it a big company?)*

>> **Lavora per una piccola agenzia.** (lah-*voh*-rah pehr *ooh*-nah *peek*-koh-lah ah-jehn-*tsee*-ah) *(He works for a small agency.)*

>> **Amo il mio lavoro.** (*ah*-moh eel *mee*-oh lah-*voh*-roh) *(I love my job.)*

The following sections look at two important aspects of business life — the people and the equipment.

## The human element

Even if you are a **libero professionista** (*lee*-beh-roh proh-fehs-syoh-*nee*-stah) *(self-employed professional)*, chances are that your **lavoro** (lah-*voh*-roh) *(job)* puts you in contact with other people. All those people have titles and names, as the following short exchanges show:

>> **Il mio capo è una donna.** (eel *mee*-oh *kah*-poh eh *ooh*-nah *dohn*-nah) *(My boss is a woman.)*

>> **Hai un assistente personale?** (ahy ooh-nahs-see-*stehn*-teh pehr-soh-*nah*-leh) *(Do you have a personal assistant?)*

>> **No, il nostro team ha un segretario.** (noh eel *noh*-stroh team ah oohn seh-greh-*tah*-ryoh) *(No, our team has a secretary.)*

Chapter 17 discusses names of professions — something you may share during small talk.

## Office equipment

Even the smallest offices today utilize a wide variety of equipment. Many of these "technology" words are the same in Italian as they are in English: computer, fax, and email are used and pronounced as they are in English, and the Italian for "photocopy" and "photocopier" are fairly intuitive — **fotocopia** (foh-toh–*koh*–pyah) and **fotocopiatrice** (foh–toh–koh–pyah–*tree*–cheh), respectively.

The following sentences help you develop a solid foundation in Italian office vocabulary.

» **Posso usare la stampante, per favore?** (*pohs*-soh ooh-*zah*-reh lah stahm-*pahn*-teh pehr fah-*voh*-reh) *(May I use the printer, please?)*

» **Il lavoro non va bene.** (eel lah-*voh*-roh nohn vah *beh*-neh) *(Work isn't going well.)*

» **Il fax è arrivato.** (eel *fahks* eh ahr-ree-*vah*-toh) *(The fax arrived.)*

» **Quando ha spedito l'e-mail?** (*kwahn*-doh ah speh-*dee*-toh lee-*meyl*) *(When did you send the e-mail?)*

## Talkin' the Talk

Mr. Miller, an American businessman, has been trying unsuccessfully to send his Italian associate, il signor Tosi, some important information.

**Mr. Miller:** **Ha ricevuto la mia raccomandata?**
*ah* ree-cheh-*vooh*-toh lah *mee*-ah rahk-koh-mahn-*dah*-tah
*Have you received the express letter I sent?*

**Sig. Tosi:** **No, oggi non è arrivato niente.**
noh *ohj*-jee nohn eh ahr-ree-*vah*-toh *nyehn*-teh
*No, nothing has arrived yet today.*

| Mr. Miller: | **Le invio un'email con il documento in allegato.** |
|---|---|
| | leh een-*vee*-oh oohn ee-*meyl* kohn eel doh-kooh-*mehn*-toh een ahl-leh-*gah*-toh |
| | *I'll send you an email with the document as an attachment.* |
| Sig. Tosi: | **Va benissimo. Oggi lavoro fino a tardi.** |
| | vah beh-*nees*-see-moh *ohj*-jee lah-*voh*-roh *fee*-noh ah *tahr*-dee |
| | *That's great. I'm working late today.* |

## WORDS TO KNOW

| allegato [m] | ahl-leh-*gah*-toh | *attachment* |
|---|---|---|
| messaggio [m] | mehs-*sahj*-joh | *message* |
| lavoro [m] | lah-*voh*-roh | *work* |
| è rotto | eh *roht*-toh | *it's broken* |
| macchina [f] | *mahk*-kee-nah | *machine* |
| tempo [m] | *tehm*-poh | *time* |
| tardi | *tahr*-dee | *late* |

**TIP**

In Italy, want ads often request information on an applicant's personality. Also, job advertisements don't usually contain mailing addresses. Instead, ads list fax or email addresses. You send your **domanda d'assunzione** (doh-*mahn*-dah dahs-soohn-*tsyoh*-neh) (*job application*) and/or your curriculum vitae or resume via fax, post, or email.

## WORDS TO KNOW

| colloquio [m] | kohl-*loh*-kwee-oh | *interview* |
|---|---|---|
| curriculum vitae [m] | koohr-ree-*kooh*-loohm *vee*-teh | *resume* |
| assistente [m/f] | ahs-see-*stehn*-teh | *assistant* |
| annuncio [m] | ahn-*noohn*-choh | *advertisement* |
| responsabile [m/f] | reh-spohn-*sah*-bee-leh | *responsible* |
| affidabile | ahf-fee-*dah*-bee-leh | *dependable* |

You're Mario's guest, but he's gone out for a moment. The telephone rings and you have to answer it. Fill the gaps in this incomplete phone conversation. See Appendix C for the answer key.

| | |
|---|---|
| You: | (1) ______! (Hello!) |
| Caller: | Ciao, sono Chiara. Con chi (2) ______? (Hello, I'm Chiara. With whom am I speaking?) |
| You: | Sono un (3) ______ di Mario. (I'm a friend of Mario's.) |
| Caller: | (4) ______ Mario? (Is Mario in?) |
| You: | No, è (5) ______ uscito. (No, he's just gone out.) |
| Caller: | Gli posso (6) ______? (Can I leave him a message?) |
| You: | Certo (7) ______. (Of course. Please.) |

Mario returns and asks:

| | |
|---|---|
| Mario: | Ha (8) ______ qualcuno per me? (Has anybody called for me?) |

# Chapter **11**

# Recreation and the Outdoors

n this chapter, we talk about the fun stuff — playing sports, pastimes, and generally enjoying yourself. Plus, we throw in a section about reflexive verbs so that you can talk about enjoying yourself — correctly.

Maybe you use your **fine settimana** (*fee*-neh *seht-tee-mah*-nah) (*weekends*) as a chance to play sports like **calcio** (*kahl*-choh) (*soccer*), **tennis** (*tehn*-nees) (*tennis*), **padel** (*pah*-dehl) (*padel*), or **pallavolo** (*pahl*-lah-*voh*-loh) (*volleyball*). Or perhaps you park yourself in front of the TV to watch **pallacanestro** (*pahl*-lah-kah-*neh*-stroh) (*basketball*). In any case, being able to talk about sports and other recreational activities is a plus in any language.

## Enjoying the Great Outdoors

Who doesn't love getting outside when in Italy? Whether you're strolling through a neighborhood park, heading to the mountains for fresh air, or planning a picnic by a lake or river, there's no shortage of ways to soak up the beauty of the Italian outdoors.

The following sentences describe activities you do outdoors. Notice that the Italians have appropriated a few English words — picnic and jogging:

>> **Mi piace camminare nel verde.** (mee *pyah*-cheh kahm-*mee*-nah-reh nehl *vehr*-deh) *(I like to walk in nature.)*

>> **Facciamo un picnic. C'è un bel prato qui vicino?** (fahch-*chah*-moh oohn peek-neek cheh oohn behl *prah*-toh kwee vee-*chee*-noh) *(Let's have a picnic. Is there a nice lawn/meadow nearby?)*

>> **Mi piace andare in bicicletta.** (mee *pyah*-cheh ahn-*dah*-reh een bee-chee-*kleht*-tah) *(I like to go biking.)*

>> **Faccio jogging nel parco.** (*fahch*-choh *johg*-geen nehl *pahr*-koh) *(I go jogging in the park.)*

Maybe you like to go up into the mountains to be close to nature. Even when enjoying Mother Nature on your own, you may still want to know some vocabulary to express the wonders you see, such as **"Che bel panorama!"** (keh behl pah–noh–rah–mah) *(What a great view!).* Here are some words for things you might spot while wandering through a forest:

>> **l'alba** (*lahl*-bah) *(sunrise)*

>> **l'albero** (*lahl*-beh-roh) *(tree)*

>> **il bosco** (eel *boh*-skoh) *(woods)*

>> **il fiore** (eel *fyoh*-reh) *(flower)*

>> **il panorama** (eel pah-noh-*rah*-mah) *(view)*

>> **la pianta** (lah *pyahn*-tah) *(plant)*

>> **il pino** (eel *pee*-noh) *(pine)*

>> **il prato** (eel *prah*-toh) *(meadow; lawn)*

>> **la quercia** (lah *kwehr*-chah) *(oak)*

>> **il tramonto** (eel trah-*mohn*-toh) *(sunset)*

# Talkin' the Talk

Enzo is talking to Cristina about their vacation for the summer. He has it all figured out already, but Cristina is skeptical. (Track 23)

**PLAY THIS**

| | |
|---|---|
| **Enzo:** | **Quest'anno andiamo in montagna!**<br>*kweh*-stahn-noh ahn-*dyah*-moh een mohn-*tah*-nyah<br>*This year we're going to the mountains!* |
| **Cristina:** | **Stai scherzando?**<br>stahy skehr-*tsahn*-doh<br>*Are you kidding?* |
| **Enzo:** | **È rilassante: boschi, aria fresca . . .**<br>eh ree-lahs-*sahn*-teh *boh*-skee *ah*-ryah *freh*-skah<br>*It's relaxing: woods, fresh air . . .* |
| **Cristina:** | **È noioso! E non si può nuotare!**<br>eh noh-*yoh*-zoh eh nohn see *pwoh* nwoh-*tah*-reh<br>*It's boring. And you can't swim!* |
| **Enzo:** | **Ci sono le piscine, i laghi e i fiumi!**<br>chee *soh*-noh leh pee-*shee*-neh ee *lah*-gee eh ee *fyooh*-mee<br>*There are swimming pools, lakes, and rivers!* |
| **Cristina:** | **Ma dai, pensa al mare, al sole . . .**<br>mah dahy *pehn*-sah ahl *mah*-reh ahl *soh*-leh<br>*Come on, think of the sea, the sun . . .* |
| **Enzo:** | **Facciamo passeggiate, visitiamo i rifugi, mangiamo quel buon cibo di montagna.**<br>fach-*chah*-moh pahs-sehj-*jaht*-teh vee-zee-*tyah*-moh ee ree-*fooh*-jee mahn-*jah*-moh kwel bwohn *chee*-boh dee mohn-*tah*-nyah<br>*We can go hiking, visit some rifugi, and eat that good mountain food.* |
| **Cristina:** | **Oh no. Io rimango a casa!**<br>oh noh *ee*-oh ree-*mahn*-goh ah *kah*-zah<br>*Oh no. I'll stay home!* |

**CULTURAL WISDOM**

The Alps and Dolomites offer marvelous terrain for hiking and skiing. A **rifugio** (ree–*fooh*–joh) is a rustic mountain lodge that people hike or ski to. You can enjoy a warm, home-cooked meal there and even spend the night in some.

WORDS TO KNOW

| | | |
|---|---|---|
| **campagna [f]** | kahm-*pah*-nyah | *countryside* |
| **gita [f]** | *jee*-tah | *excursion/tour* |
| **fiume [m]** | *fyooh*-meh | *river* |
| **guida [f]** | *gwee*-dah | *guide* |
| **lago [m]** | *lah*-goh | *lake* |
| **mare [m]** | *mah*-reh | *sea* |
| **montagna [f]** | mohn-*tah*-nyah | *mountain* |

# Talkin' the Talk

Animals are always an interesting topic, and knowing the names of some of them in another language can be helpful.

**Carla:** **Ti piacciono gli animali?**
tee *pyach*-choh-noh lyee ah-nee-*mah*-lee
*Do you like animals?*

**Alessandra:** **Sì, ho una piccola fattoria.**
see oh *ooh*-nah *peek*-koh-lah faht-toh-*ree*-ah
*Yes, I have a small farm.*

**Carla:** **Davvero?**
dahv-*veh*-roh
*Really?*

**Alessandra:** **Ho un cane, due gatti e una capretta.**
oh oohn *kah*-neh *dooh*-eh *gaht*-tee eh ooh-nah
kah-*preht*-tah
*I have a dog, two cats, and a little goat.*

**Carla:** **Ti piacciono i cavalli?**
tee *pyahch*-choh-noh ee kah-*vahl*-lee
*Do you like horses?*

**Alessandra:** **Sì, mi piacciono.**
see mee *pyach*-choh-noh
*Yes, I like them.*

<table>
<tr><td colspan="3"><h1>WORDS TO KNOW</h1></td></tr>
<tr><td>cane [m]</td><td>kah-neh</td><td>dog</td></tr>
<tr><td>cavallo [m]</td><td>kah-vahl-loh</td><td>horse</td></tr>
<tr><td>capra [f]</td><td>kah-prah</td><td>goat</td></tr>
<tr><td>gallo [m]</td><td>gahl-loh</td><td>rooster</td></tr>
<tr><td>gatto [m]</td><td>gaht-toh</td><td>cat</td></tr>
<tr><td>gallina [f]</td><td>gahl-lee-nah</td><td>chicken</td></tr>
<tr><td>maiale [m]</td><td>mah-yah-leh</td><td>pig</td></tr>
<tr><td>mucca [f]</td><td>moohk-kah</td><td>cow</td></tr>
<tr><td>uccello [m]</td><td>oohch-chehl-loh</td><td>bird</td></tr>
<tr><td>lupo [m]</td><td>looh-poh</td><td>wolf</td></tr>
<tr><td>pecora [f]</td><td>peh-koh-rah</td><td>sheep</td></tr>
<tr><td>tacchino [m]</td><td>tahk-kee-noh</td><td>turkey</td></tr>
</table>

# Speaking Reflexively

GRAMMATICALLY
SPEAKING

One of the first verbs you may encounter is a reflexive verb. **Mi chiamo Alice** (mee *kyah*-moh ah-*lee*-cheh) — literally *I call myself Alice* — uses the reflexive verb **chiamarsi** (kyah-*mahr*-see) *(to call oneself)*. **Lavarsi** (lah-*vahr*-see) *(to wash oneself)* and **divertirsi** (dee-vehr-*teer*-see) *(to enjoy oneself, to have a good time, to have fun)* are two more examples of reflexive verbs. But not all Italian reflexive verbs are reflexive in English, and vice versa. Some verbs like **svegliarsi** (zveh-*lyahr*-see) *(to wake up)* aren't reflexive in English, although they are in Italian.

In Italian, you can recognize a reflexive verb by its infinitive form ending in **-si** (see), which means *oneself.* To conjugate a reflexive verb, first remove the **-si** ending, and conjugate it just like any other **–are, –ere,** and **–ire** verb. The only difference is that you need to add a reflexive pronoun, which agrees with the subject, before the verb. Notice how **divertirsi** becomes a regular present tense **–ire** verb, except that a reflexive pronoun is added.

| Conjugation | Pronunciation | Translation |
|---|---|---|
| **mi diverto** | mee dee-*vehr*-toh | *I'm enjoying myself* |
| **ti diverti** | tee dee-*vehr*-tee | *you're enjoying yourself* |
| **si diverte** | see dee-*vehr*-teh | *he/she is enjoying him/herself. you are enjoying yourself (formal)* |
| **ci divertiamo** | chee dee-vehr-*tyah*-moh | *we're enjoying ourselves* |
| **vi divertite** | vee dee-vehr-*tee*-teh | *you (pl.) are enjoying yourself* |
| **si divertono** | see dee-*vehr*-toh-noh | *they are enjoying themselves* |

Here are some more examples:

>> **annoiarsi** (ahn-noh-*yahr*-see) *(to be bored)*: **Vi annoiate in campagna?** (vee ahn-noh-*yah*-teh een kahm-*pah*-nyah) *(Do you get bored in the countryside?)*

>> **svegliarsi** (zveh-*lyahr*-see) *(to wake up)*: **A che ora ti svegli?** (ah keh oh-rah tee zveh-lyee) *(What time do you wake up?)*

Table 11-1 shows a list of some common everyday reflexive verbs.

**TABLE 11-1**

## Reflexive Verbs

| Verb | Pronunciation | Meaning |
|---|---|---|
| **accomodarsi** | ahk-koh-moh-*dahr*-see | *to make oneself at home, to get comfortable* |
| **alzarsi** | ahl-*tsahr*-see | *to get up* |
| **arrabbiarsi** | ahr-rahb-*byahr*-see | *to be (get) angry* |
| **innamorarsi** | een-nah-moh-*rahr*-see | *to fall in love* |
| **farsi la barba** | *fahr*-see lah *bahr*-bah | *to shave (for a man)* |
| **fermarsi** | fehr-*mahr*-see | *to stop (oneself)* |
| **laurearsi** | lah-ooh-reh-*ahr*-see | *to graduate from a university* |
| **lavarsi** | lah-*vahr*-see | *to wash (oneself)* |
| **mettersi** | *meht*-tehr-see | *to put on (clothes, contact lenses, glasses)* |
| **pettinarsi** | peht-tee-*nahr*-see | *to comb one's hair* |

| Verb | Pronunciation | Meaning |
| --- | --- | --- |
| **sedersi** | seh-*dehr*-see | *to sit down* |
| **svegliarsi** | zveh-*lyahr*-see | *to wake up* |
| **trasferirsi** | trah-sfeh-*reer*-see | *to move form from one city to another* |
| **vestirsi** | veh-*steer*-see | *to get dressed* |

# Talkin' the Talk

Maria Pia and Mauro are discussing what they enjoy doing on their weekends. (Track 24)

**Maria Pia:** **Cosa fai durante i fine settimana?**
*koh*-zah fahy dooh-*rahn*-teh ee *fee*-neh seht-tee-*mah*-nah
*How do you spend your weekends?*

**Mauro:** **Faccio sport, leggo, incontro amici.**
*fahch*-choh spohrt *lehg*-goh een-*kohn*-troh ah-*mee*-chee
*I play sports, I read, I meet friends.*

**Ti piace leggere?**
tee *pyah*-cheh *lehj*-jeh-reh
*Do you like to read?*

**Maria Pia:** **È la mia passione!**
eh lah *mee*-ah pahs-*syoh*-neh
*It's my passion!*

**Che cosa leggi?**
keh *koh*-zah *lehj*-jee
*What do you read?*

**Mauro:** **Soprattutto letteratura contemporanea.**
soh-praht-*tooht*-toh leht-teh-rah-*tooh*-rah
kohn-tehm-poh-*rah*-neh-ah
*Mostly contemporary literature.*

# Playing Sports

**Fare sport** (*fah*-reh spohrt) (*to play a sport*) and talking about sports is a favorite pastime for people all over the world. And whether you travel to Italy or just want to invite your Italian neighbor to play tennis, knowing sports terms is always helpful.

In Italian some sports you "do" so you pair them with **fare** (*fah*-reh) (*to do*). With other sports instead you use **giocare a** (joh-*kah*-reh ah) (*to play*) or **andare a/in** (ahn-*dah*-reh ah/een) (*to go*). Then there are sports that use the verb that describes the sport itself, like **pattinare** (paht-tee-*nah*-reh) (*to skate*). Table 11-2 is divided into sports/activities that are paired with **fare, giocare a,** and **andare a/in.** Despite the fact that **giocare a** is mostly used with team sports and **fare** with individual sports, there isn't a rule to clearly differentiate these two verbs, and we suggest that you memorize at least how to form the sports that you practice and/or that you like the most.

**TABLE 11-2**  **Sports Verbs**

| Italian | Pronunciation | Translation |
|---|---|---|
| **fare** *fah*-reh *(to do)* | | |
| **atletica leggera** | aht-leh-*tee*-kah lehj-*jeh*-rah | *track* |
| **canotaggio** | kah-noh-*taj*-joh | *crew/rowing* |
| **ciclismo** | chee-*klee*-zmoh | *cycling* |
| **danza** | *dahn*-tsah | *dance* |
| **equitazione** | eh-kwee-tah-*tsyoh*-neh | *riding* |
| **ginnastica artistica** | geen-*nah*-stee-kah ahr-*tee*-stee-kah | *gymnastics* |
| **jogging** | *johg*-geen | *jogging* |
| **lotta** | *loht*-tah | *wrestling* |
| **nuoto** | *nwoh*-toh | *swimming* |
| **palestra** | pah-*leh*-strah | *to go to the gym* |
| **scherma** | *skehr*-mah | *fencing* |
| **sci** | shee | *skiing* |
| **sci nautico** | shee *nah*-ooh-koh | *water skiing* |

| Italian | Pronunciation | Translation |
| --- | --- | --- |
| **sollevamento pesi** | sohl-leh-vah-*mehn*-toh *peh*-zee | *weightlifting* |
| **snowboard** | snoh-*bohrd* | *snowboarding* |
| **giocare a** joh-*kah*-reh ah *(to play)* | | |
| **calcio** | *kahl*-choh | *soccer* |
| **padel** | *pah*-dehl | *padel* |
| **pallacanestro** | *pahl*-lah-kah-*neh*-stroh | *basketball* |
| **pallavolo** | *pahl*-lah-*voh*-loh | *volleyball* |
| **ping pong** | peeng-pohng | *ping-pong* |
| **rugby** | *rahg*-bee | *rugby* |
| **tennis** | *tehn*-nees | *tennis* |
| **golf** | gohlf | *golf* |
| **andare** (ahn-*dah*-reh) *(to go)* | | |
| **a cavallo** | ah kah-*vahl*-loh | *riding (a horse)* |
| **in bicicletta** | een bee-chee-*kleht*-tah | *biking* |

The following conjugations are for these three important sports verbs: **fare**, **andare**, and **giocare**.

| Conjugation | Pronunciation |
| --- | --- |
| **io faccio** | *ee*-oh *fahch*-choh |
| **tu fai** | tooh fahy |
| **lui/lei fa** | *looh*-ee/ley fah |
| **noi facciamo** | noi fahch-*chah*-moh |
| **voi fate** | voi *fah*-teh |
| **loro fanno** | *loh*-roh *fahn*-noh |
| **io vado** | *ee*-oh *vah*-doh |
| **tu vai** | tooh vahy |
| **lui/lei va** | *looh*-ee/ley vah |

| noi andiamo | noi ahn-*dyah*-moh |
| voi andate | voi ahn-*dah*-teh |
| loro vanno | *loh*-roh *vahn*-noh |
| io gioco | *ee*-oh *joh*-koh |
| tu giochi | tooh *joh*-kee |
| lui/lei gioca | *looh*-ee/ley *joh*-kah |
| noi giochiamo | noi joh-*kyah*-moh |
| voi giocate | voi joh-*kah*-teh |
| loro giocano | *loh*-roh *joh*-kah-noh |

Italians love to follow sports on TV; ranked by their popularity they include the following:

» **calcio** (*kahl*-choh) *(soccer)*

» **Formula 1** (*fohr*-mooh-lah *ooh*-noh) *(Formula One car racing)*

» **ciclismo** (*chee*-klee-zmoh) *(cycling)*

» **moto GP** (*moh*-toh gee pee) *(motorcycle racing)*

» **rugby** (*rahg*-bee) *(rugby)*

» **pallavolo** (*pahl*-lah-*voh*-loh) *(volleyball)*

» **pallacanestro/basket** (*pahl*-lah-kah-*neh*-stroh/*bah*-skeht) *(basketball)*

» **sci alpino** (shee ahl-*pee*-noh) *(downhill ski racing)*

Many people play **calcio** and **calcetto** (kahl–*cheht*–toh), also called calcio a **cinque** (*kahl*–choh ah *cheen*–kweh), which is five–against–five soccer, often played indoors on a smaller field.

Then there is **bocce** (*bohch*–cheh) *(lawn bowling)*. Many towns offer small **bocce** courts where older men usually play.

# Talkin' the Talk

Giulia and Stefano have just met at the university and found out that they live in the same neighborhood. On the way to the bus stop Stefano strikes up a conversation about his favorite topic, sports. (Track 25)

**Stefano:** **Fai qualche sport?**
fahy *kwahl*-keh spohrt
*What sports do you play?*

**Giulia:** **Faccio nuoto e vado a cavallo.**
fahch-choh nwoh-toh eh vah-doh ah kah-vahl-loh
*I swim and go horse back riding.*

**Stefano:** **Equitazione?**
eh-kwee-tah-tsyoh-neh
*Riding?*

**Giulia:** **È il mio sport preferito! Giochi a tennis?**
eh eel mee-oh spohrt preh-feh-ree-toh joh-kee ah tehn-nees
*It's my favorite sport! Do you play tennis?*

**Stefano:** **No, faccio palestra.**
noh *fahch*-choh pah-*leh*-strah
*No, I go to the gym.*

**Giulia:** **Body building?**
*boh*-dee *beel*-deeng
*Body building?*

**Stefano:** **Faccio il tapis roulant in inverno e corro in pineta in estate.**
*fahch*-choh eh eel tah-*pee*-rooh-*lahn* een een-*vehr*-noh eh *kohr*-roh een pee-*neh*-tah een eh-*stah*-teh
*I use the treadmill in the winter, and I run in the pine forest in the summer.*

Italians use the French word **tapis roulant** for treadmill.

# Talking about Hobbies and Interests

You can certainly do a lot of other things in your leisure time without getting worn out playing sports. Here you familiarize with a variety of them in Italian.

>> Some typical questions (and varied responses) to ask about **il tempo libero** (eel *tehm*-poh *lee*-beh-roh) *(free time)* include the following:

>> **Che cosa ti piace fare nel tempo libero?** (keh *koh*-zah tee *pyah*-che *fah*-reh nehl *tehm*-poh *lee*-beh-roh) *(What do you like to do in your free time?)*

**Mi piace cucinare e fare l'uncinetto.** (mee *pyah*-cheh kooh-chee-*nah*-reh eh *fah*-reh loohn-chee-*neht*-toh) *(I look to cook and crochet.)*

>> **Qual è il tuo passatempo preferito? (**kwah-*leh* eel *tooh*-oh pahs-sah-*tehm*-poh preh-feh-*ree*-toh) *(What is your favorite pastime?)*

**Il mio passatempo preferito è . . . /i miei passatempi preferiti sono . . .** (eel *mee*-oh pahs-sah-*tehm*-poh preh-feh-*ree*-toh eh/ee *myey* pahs-sah-*tehm*-pee preh-feh-*ree*-tee *soh*-noh) *(My favorite pastime is . . . /My favorite pastimes are . . .)*

    **fare i giochi da tavolo e giocare a scacchi.** (*fah*-reh ee *joh*-kee dah *tah*-voh-loh eh joh-*kahr*-reh ah *skahk*-kee) *(playing board games and chess.)*

    **stare con gli amici. (***stah*-reh kohn lyee ah-*mee*-chee) *(hanging out with friends.)*

>> **Quali sport fai?** (*kwah*-lee spohrt fahy) *(What sports do you play?)*

**Faccio lo sci e gioco a tennis.** (*fahch*-cho loh shee eh *joh*-koh ah *tehn*-nees) *(I ski and play tennis.)*

## LIKING THINGS

You spend your free time doing recreational things that you like. To say you like something or that you like to do something you use the verb **piacere** (pyah-*cheh*-reh) *(to like;* Literally: *to be pleasing to)* This verb is a bit weird because you usually use it only in the third person singular or the third person plural of any verb tense.

*Third person singular:* if what you like is singular or an infinitive.

| | | |
|---|---|---|
| **Mi piace correre.** | mee *pyah*-cheh *kohr*-reh-reh | *I like to run.* |
| **Mi piace il mare.** | mee *pyah*-cheh eel *mah*-reh | *I like the sea.* |

*Third person plural:* if what you like is plural.

| | | |
|---|---|---|
| **Mi piacciono gli sport invernali**. | mee *pyach*-choh-noh lyee spohrt een-vehr-*nah*-lee | *I like winter sports.* |

Only your pronouns change, which are indirect object pronouns and literally mean "such and such a thing is pleasing to 'someone'." These are **mi, ti, gli, le, ci, vi, gli/ loro** (mee, tee, lyee, leh, chee, vee, lyee /*loh*-roh) [*to me, to you, to him, to her, to us, to you (pl.), to them*]. You don't use the personal pronouns (**io, tu, lui, lei,** and so on) with **piacere**.

# Talkin' the Talk

Have a look at what Serena and Nicoletta are talking about. Nicoletta apparently prefers peaceful and calm activities, whereas Serena likes to participate in sports that make her sweat.

**Serena:**     **Cosa fai questo fine settimana?**
*koh*-zah fahy *kweh*-stoh *fee*-neh seht-tee-*mah*-nah
*What are you going to do this weekend?*

**Nicoletta:**     **Vado in campagna.**
*vah*-doh een kahm-*pah*-nyah
*I'm going to the countryside.*

**Serena:**     **È un'idea fantastica!**
eh oohn-ee-*deh*-ah fahn-*tah*-stee-kah
*That's a great idea!*

**Nicoletta:**     **Ho una casetta vicino al lago.**
oh *ooh*-nah kah-*zeht*-tah vee-*chee*-noh ahl *lah*-goh
*I have a small house close to the lake.*

**Serena:**     **Ideale per riposarsi.**
ee-deh-*ah*-leh pehr ree-poh-*zahr*-see
*Ideal for relaxing.*

**Nicoletta:**     **Sì, leggo, scrivo, passeggio lungo il lago.**
see *lehg*-goh *skree*-voh pahs-*sehj*-joh *loohn*-goh eel *lah*-goh
*Yes, I read, I write, I take walks around the lake.*

*(continued)*

*(continued)*

| | |
|---|---|
| **Serena:** | **Non fai sport?** |
| | nohn fahy spohrt |
| | *Don't you play any sports?* |
| **Nicoletta:** | **Vado in bicicletta.** |
| | *vah*-doh een bee-chee-*kleht*-tah |
| | *I ride my bike.* |

Participating in sports isn't the only hobby you can have. Some hobbies are more sedentary, like reading, sewing, or playing musical instruments.

# Talkin' the Talk

**PLAY THIS**

Ernesto and Tommaso are discovering that not all sports are physical. (Track 26)

| | |
|---|---|
| **Ernesto:** | **Non ti annoi mai?** |
| | nohn tee ahn-*noy* mahy |
| | *Don't you ever get bored?* |
| **Tommaso:** | **No, ho molti interessi.** |
| | noh oh *mohl*-tee een-teh-*rehs*-see |
| | *No, I have many interests.* |
| **Ernesto:** | **Per esempio?** |
| | pehr eh-*zehm*-pyoh |
| | *For example?* |
| **Tommaso:** | **Amo leggere e andare al cinema.** |
| | *ah*-moh *lehj*-jeh-reh eh ahn-*dah*-reh ahl *chee*-neh-mah |
| | *I love to to read and go to the movies.* |
| **Ernesto:** | **Non fai sport?** |
| | nohn fahy sport |
| | *Don't you play any sports?* |
| **Tommaso:** | **Faccio yoga e meditazione.** |
| | *fach*-choh *yoh*-gah eh meh-dee-tah-*tsyoh*-neh |
| | *I do yoga and meditate.* |

Many people love music, whether they like to **ascoltare la musica** (ah-skohl-*tah*-reh lah *mooh*-zee-kah) *(listen to music)* or **suonare uno strumento** (swoh-*nah*-reh *ooh*-noh strooh-*mehn*-toh) *(play an instrument)*. Of course, there are all kinds of music, from classica (*klahs*-see-kah) *(classical)* to **jazz** (jehts) to **rock** (rohk).

# Talkin' the Talk

Emilia and Isabel are two classmates getting to know each other a little better.

**Emilia:** **Mi piace molto ascoltare la musica. E a te?**
mee *pyah*-cheh *mohl*-toh ah-skohl-*tah*-reh lah *mooh*-zee-kah eh ah teh
*I like to listen to music a lot. And you?*

**Isabel:** **Ho molta musica sul mio i-Phone.**
oh *mohl*-tah *mooh*-zee-kah soohl *mee*-oh ahy-fohn
*I have a lot of music on my iPhone.*

**Emilia:** **Tu suoni uno strumento?**
tooh *swoh*-nee *ooh*-noh strooh-*mehn*-toh
*Do you play an instrument?*

**Isabel:** **Suono il violoncello e il pianoforte.**
*swoh*-noh eel vee-oh-lohn-*chehl*-loh eh eel *pyah*-noh-*fohr*-teh
*I play the cello and the piano.*

**Emilia:** **Sei brava?**
sey *brah*-vah
*Are you good?*

**Isabel:** **Si, mi piace molto suonare. E tu?**
see mee *pyah*-cheh *mohl*-toh swoh-*nah*-reh eh tooh
*I guess so. I really like to play music. And you?*

**Emilia:** **Suono il flauto, ma preferisco cantare in un coro.**
*swoh*-noh eel *flah*-oh-toh mah preh-feh-*ree*-skoh kahn-*tah*-reh een oohn *koh*-roh
*I play the flute, but I prefer to sing in the choir.*

## WORDS TO KNOW

| | | |
|---|---|---|
| **ascoltare** | ah-skohl-*tah*-reh | *to listen to* |
| **batteria [f]** | baht-teh-*ree*-ah | *drums* |
| **chitarra [f]** | kee-*tahr*-rah | *guitar* |
| **clarinetto [m]** | klah-ree-*neht*-toh | *clarinet* |
| **coro [m]** | *koh*-roh | *choir* |
| **flauto [m]** | *flah*-oh-toh | *flute* |
| **giocare a** | joh-*kah*-reh ah | *to play a sport, cards, game* |
| **piano(forte) [m]** | pyah-noh-*fohr*-teh | *piano* |
| **sassofono [m]** | sahs-*soh*-foh-noh | *saxophone* |
| **suonare** | swoh-*nah*-reh | *to play an instrument* |
| **tromba [f]** | *trohm*-bah | *trumpet* |
| **violoncello [m]** | vee-oh-lohn-*chehl*-loh | *cello* |
| **violino [m]** | vee-oh-*lee*-noh | *violin* |
| **voce [f]** | *voh*-cheh | *voice* |

Now it's time for you to have some fun! In the following box, try to find the names of some plants and animals I introduced in this chapter. I provide the English, but you have to find the Italian.

Find the Italian for these words: horse, flower, bird, cat, wolf, oak, pine, cow, sheep, tree. See Appendix C for the answer key.

### Word Seek

| A | J | A | R | O | C | E | P | O | S |
|---|---|---|---|---|---|---|---|---|---|
| U | I | V | S | W | S | O | P | A | B |
| A | H | C | E | M | L | U | Y | O | A |
| C | I | K | R | L | L | U | V | G | D |
| C | G | B | A | E | F | O | L | E | D |
| U | N | V | M | Z | U | I | N | S | D |
| M | A | R | X | J | C | Q | O | I | Y |
| C | G | A | T | T | O | E | I | R | P |
| A | L | B | E | R | O | P | S | T | E |
| F | R | H | O | L | L | E | C | C | U |

*© John Wiley & Sons, Inc.*

# 3
# Italian on the Go

IN THIS CHAPTER

» **Making travel plans**

» **Coming and going: arrivare and partire**

» **Taking a tour**

» **Going to the beach**

» **Looking forward to your trip: the simple future**

# Chapter **12**
# Planning a Trip

Everybody likes to get away from the daily grind and check out new environments and activities during their free time. Tourists and Italians alike flock to **la spiaggia** (lah *spyahj*-jah) *(to the beach)*, head **in montagna** (een mohn-*tah*-nyah) *(to the mountains)*, or **in campagna** (een kahm-*pah*-nyah) *(to the countryside)*. Some Italians take long trips outside of Italy. Whatever you do, this chapter can give you some important vocabulary and terms. **Buon viaggio!** (bwohn *vyahj*-joh) *(have a nice trip!)* or **buone vacanze!** (*bwoh*-neh vah-*kahn*-tseh) *(have a nice vacation!).*

## Deciding When and Where to Go

Deciding when to take a trip can be just as important as choosing your destination. You probably don't want to visit Washington, D.C. in August when the weather can be unbearably hot and humid. Italy also has many cities that really heat up in the summer. In fact, many Italians living in those cities escape for most of August to cooler places, such as the beaches of Sardegna or the cool Dolomites. On the other hand, the summer months are also **l'alta stagione** (*lahl*-tah stah-*joh*-neh) *(high season)* for tourists, which means popular destinations can be crowded and expensive.

# Taking a Tour

Whether you're in a city or rural area, you can usually find fun and interesting sights to see. Bus tours are for the most part organized in great detail, and the price generally includes the cost of the bus, lunch, dinner, and the services of a tour guide. A guided tour, or day trip, **una gita organizzata** (*ooh*-nah *jee*-tah ohr-gah-need-*dzah*-tah) *(an organized tour),* may be the most efficient, cost-effective, and informative way to check out nearby attractions. Here are some useful questions to know:

>> **Ci sono gite organizzate?** (chee *soh*-noh *jee*-teh ohr-gah-need-*dzah*-teh) *(Are there any organized tours?)*

>> **Quanto costa la gita?** (*kwahn*-toh *koh*-stah lah *jee*-tah) *(How much does the tour cost?)*

>> **C'è una guida che parla inglese?** (cheh *ooh*-nah *gwee*-dah keh *pahr*-lah een-*gleh*-zeh) *(Is there an English-speaking guide?)*

>> **Dove si comprano i biglietti?** (*doh*-veh see *kohm*-prah-noh ee bee-*lyeht*-tee) *(Where do you buy tickets?)*

# Talkin' the Talk

Lucia and Renzo are in a tour office, talking to a tour agent and deciding which trip to go on the next day.

| | |
|---|---|
| Lucia: | **C'è una bella gita sul lago di Como domani.**<br>cheh *ooh*-nah *behl*-lah *gee*-tah soohl *lah*-goh dee *koh*-moh doh-*mah*-nee<br>*There's a nice trip to Lake Como tomorrow.* |
| Renzo: | **Vuoi andare, vero?**<br>vwoi ahn-*dah*-reh *veh*-roh<br>*You want to go, don't you?* |
| Lucia: | **Sarebbe carino. E tu?**<br>sah-*rehb*-beh kah-*ree*-noh eh tooh<br>*It would be nice. What about you?* |
| Renzo: | **Non amo le gite in autobus.**<br>nohn *ah*-moh leh *gee*-teh een *ah*-ooh-toh-boohs<br>*I don't like bus trips.* |

| Lucia: | **Ma è una gita a piedi!** |
| --- | --- |
| | mah eh *ooh*-nah *jee*-tah ah *pyeh*-dee |
| | *But it's a walking tour!* |
| | |
| Renzo: | **Ottimo! A che ora inizia la gita?** |
| | *oht*-tee-moh ah keh *oh*-rah ee-*nee-tsyah* lah *jee*-tah |
| | *Great! What time does the trip start?* |
| | |
| Agent: | **Alle sette e trenta.** |
| | *ahl*-leh *seht*-teh eh *trehn*-tah |
| | *At 7:30 a.m.* |
| | |
| Renzo: | **Quanto dura?** |
| | *kwahn*-toh *dooh*-rah |
| | *How long is it going to last?* |
| | |
| Agent: | **Circa cinque ore.** |
| | *cheer*-kah *cheen*-kweh *oh*-reh |
| | *About five hours.* |

# Booking a Trip/Traveling to a Foreign Country

You never know — you just might want to book a trip to another country while you're in Italy. When you're ready to book your flight or hotel, you may want to consider using **un'agenzia viaggi** (ooh-nah-jehn-*tsee*-ah vyahj-jee) *(a travel agency)*. There, you can get plane tickets, hotel reservations, or complete tour packages.

As you walk by the travel agency, your eye will undoubtedly be drawn to special all-inclusive package deals to Malta, Tunisia, and the Canary Islands — to name a few.

**INCREDIBILI OFFERTE!! Gran Canaria, La Palma. Euro 616 a persona. Comprende: volo + hotel + tasse e commissioni. Colazione a buffet.** (een-kreh-*dee*-bee-lee ohf-*fehr*-teh grahn kah-*nah*-ryah lah *pahl*-mah *eh*-ooh-roh sehy-*chehn*-toh-*seh*-dee-chee ah pehr-*soh*-nah kohm-*prehn*-deh *voh*-loh oh-*tehl tahs*-seh eh kom-mees-*syoh*-nee koh-lah-*tsyoh*-neh ah booh-*feh*)

*(Incredible deals!! Gran Canaria. La Palma. 616 euros per person. Includes flight, hotel, departure fees, and buffet breakfast.)*

# Talkin' the Talk

Alessandro has just seen this sign for the Canary Islands. He's talking to Giorgio the travel agent.

**Giorgio:** **Buongiorno, mi dica.**
bwohn-*johr*-noh mee *dee*-kah
*Good morning, can I help you? (Literally: Tell me.)*

**Alessandro:** **Vorrei fare un viaggio alle Isole Canarie.**
vohr-*rey fah*-reh oohn *vyahj*-joh *ahl*-leh *ee*-zoh-leh kah-*nah*-ryeh
*I'd like to take a trip to the Canary Islands.*

**Giorgio:** **Dove, esattamente?**
*doh*-veh eh-zaht-tah-*mehn*-teh
*Where exactly?*

**Alessandro:** **Tenerife o La Palma.**
teh-neh-*ree*-feh oh lah *pahl*-mah
*Tenerife or La Palma.*

**Giorgio:** **Un viaggio organizzato?**
oohn *vyahj*-joh ohr-gah-need-*dzah*-toh
*An organized trip?*

**Alessandro:** **No, vorrei soltanto prenotare il volo.**
noh vohr-*rey* sohl-*tahn*-toh preh-noh-*tah*-reh eel *voh*-loh
*No, I'd like to book just the flight.*

**Giorgio:** **E per gli spostamenti interni?**
eh pehr lyee *spoh*-stah-*mehn*-tee een-*tehr*-nee
*And what about moving around between islands?*

**Alessandro:** **Mi sposterò in autobus e traghetto.**
mee spoh-steh-*roh* een *ah*-ooh-toh-boohs eh trah-*geht*-toh
*I'll get around by bus and ferry.*

**Giorgio:** **Quando vuole partire?**
*kwahn*-doh *vwoh*-leh pahr-*tee*-reh
*When do you want to leave?*

**Alessandro:**      **La prima settimana di febbraio.**
lah *pree*-mah seht-tee-*mah*-nah dee fehb-*brah*-yoh
*The first week of February.*

**Giorgio:**      **E il ritorno?**
eh eel ree-*tohr*-noh
*And return?*

**Alessandro:**      **La terza settimana di febbraio.**
*lah* tehr-tsah seht-tee-*mah*-nah dee fehb-*brah*-yoh
*The third week of February.*

- - -

**CULTURAL WISDOM**

Several years ago, a new vacation concept became popular in Italy: **l'agriturismo** (lah-gree-tooh-*ree*-zmoh) *(the farm stay)*. During these types of vacations, people travel to the countryside or the mountains, where they stay in farmhouses. These accommodations range from spartan to luxurious and romantic, and most are good options for families. Guests can help out on the farm, ride horses, and swim at some. This type of lodging also allows you to eat traditional regional food and puts you miles away from formal, impersonal hotels.

Another popular type of lodging is the **bed and breakfast**, which you can find throughout the Italian peninsula.

You can easily find an abundance of both online as you research for your trip.

## VISAS AND PASSPORTS

All you need is a passport (**un passaporto**) (pahs-sah-*pohr*-toh) to visit Italy if you're going for less than three months. If you stay longer, you'll need **un visto** (oohn *vee*-stoh) *(a visa)*. However, starting in late 2026, you'll need to obtain a travel authorization called ETIAS (European Travel Information and Authorization System).

If you fly to Italy, the main airports are **Malpensa** (mahl-*pehn*-sah) in Milan and **Leonardo da Vinci** (leh-oh-*nahr*-doh dah *veen*-chee) in Rome, but you can also fly into Venice, Bologna, Palermo, and Naples — other popular (and less hectic) airports.

# Arriving and Leaving: The Verbs "Arrivare" and "Partire"

To help you understand the verbs **arrivare** (ahr-ree-*vah*-reh) *(to arrive)* and **partire** (pahr-*tee*-reh) *(to leave)*, we include some simple sentences here. As you see, when these verbs are used in connection with a specific place (like a city) **arrivare** is always followed by the preposition **a** (ah) *(at/to/in).* When referring to arrival in a country, you use the preposition **in** (een) *(in).* **Partire** is always followed by the preposition **da** (dah) *(from)* when leaving from a place, and by **per** (pehr) *(for)* when you're heading to a destination:

>> **Luca parte da Torino alle cinque.** (*looh*-kah *pahr*-teh dah toh-*ree*-noh *ahl*-leh *cheen*-kweh) *(Luca leaves from Turin at five o'clock.)*

>> **Arrivo a Taormina nel pomeriggio.** (ahr-*ree*-voh ah tah-ohr-*mee*-nah nehl poh-meh-*reej*-joh) *(I'm arriving in Taormina in the afternoon.)*

**Arrivare** and **partire** are conjugated like other regular **-are** and **-ire** verbs, which you can check out in Chapter 2 or in Appendix B.

# Talkin' the Talk

Filippo and Marzia are spending some time together before Filippo has to catch a plane. (Track 27)

**Marzia:** **A che ora parte l'aereo?**
ah keh *oh*-rah *pahr*-teh lah-*eh*-reh-oh
*What time does the plane leave?*

**Filippo:** **Alle nove di mattina.**
*ahl*-leh *noh*-veh dee maht-*tee*-nah
*At 9 a.m.*

**Marzia:** **A che ora arrivi a Los Angeles?**
ah keh *oh*-rah ahr-*ree*-vee ah loh *zahn*-jeh-lehs
*What time do you arrive in Los Angeles?*

**Filippo:** **Alle undici di notte.**
*ahl*-leh *oohn*-dee-chee dee *noht*-teh
*At 11 p.m.*

## Going to the Beach or to the Spa

Italy has roughly 4,400 miles of coastline, so it's no surprise that Italians and tourists alike flock to Italy's famous beaches, which can be either sandy (**sabbiose,** sahb-*byoh*-seh) or pebble (**con ciottoli,** kohn *choht*-toh-lee), each with its own unique advantages (and clientele). Most beaches feature one of the most beloved Italian institutions: **lo stabilimento balneare** (loh stah-bee-lee-*mehn*-toh bahl-neh-*ah*-reh), or more simply, **il bagno** (eel *bah*-nyoh), a combination bar, beach club, and restaurant where you can rent **un ombrellone** (oohn ohm-brehl-*loh*-neh) *(a beach umbrella)* and **un lettino** (oohn leht-*tee*-noh) *(a lounge chair)* for the day, week, or even the entire season. Here, you and the children can also play **beach volley** *(beach volleyball)* or **racchettoni** (rahk-keht-*toh*-nee) *(beach tennis)* or rent a **pedalò** (peh-dah-*loh*) *(paddle boat)*.

Don't worry, though — paying isn't the only way to enjoy the sea. Many Italian beaches also have **spiagge libere** (*spyahj*-jeh *lee*-beh-reh) *(free public beaches)* where you can bring your own beach towel and umbrella and enjoy the sun and waves without spending a thing. These areas are sometimes smaller and less equipped but offer a relaxed, no-frills way to soak up the seaside.

Italy also boasts many wonderful, natural hot springs and spas, known as **terme** (*tehr*-meh). Some are full-service wellness centers offering treatments and services for a fee — like those in Chianciano, Montecatini, or Fiuggi. Others are more rustic and open-air: in places like Vulcano, some **sorgenti termali** (sohr-*jehn*-tee tehr-*mah*-lee) (*hot springs*) require a small fee; in Calabria, you can find both free and paid options; and in Ischia, many of the springs are free and open to the public.

# Using the Simple Future Tense

Sometimes you need a verb form that indicates that something will happen in the near future. In Italian, this tense is called **futuro semplice** (fooh-*tooh*-roh *sehm*-plee-cheh) (*simple future*). However, using the present tense when referring to a future event is also common. The following sentences use the simple future tense:

>> **Andrò in Italia.** (ahn-*droh* een ee-*tah*-lyah) *(I will go to Italy.)*

>> **Quando arriverai a Palermo?** (*kwahn*-doh ahr-ree-veh-*rahy* ah pah-*lehr*-moh) *(When will you arrive in Palermo?)*

>> **Non torneremo troppo tardi.** (nohn tohr-neh-*reh*-moh *trohp*-poh *tahr*-dee) *(We won't be back too late.)*

To form the simple future tense of regular verbs, start with the infinitive, remove the final **-e**, and add the future endings **-ò, -ai, -à, -emo, -ete, -anno.** For **-are** verbs you also need to change the **-a** in the infinitive to an **-e** before adding the endings. Note the stem change in Table 12-1.

## SENDING LETTERS AND POSTCARDS

So if you're one of those people who still enjoys sending **cartoline** (kahr-toh-*lee*-neh) *(postcards)* and **lettere** (*leht*-teh-reh) *(letters)* while traveling, you're going to need to find an **ufficio postale** (oohf-*fee*-choh poh-*stah*-leh) *(post office)* or **tabaccaio** (tah-bahk-*kah*-yoh) *(tobacconist)* where you can purchase **francobolli** (frahn-koh-*bohl*-lee) *(stamps)* and **buste** (*booh*-steh) *(envelopes)*.

## Simple Future

| Parlare = PARLER- | Prendere= PRENDER | Partire= PARTIR | Translation |
|---|---|---|---|
| parler**ò** | prender**ò** | partir**ò** | *I will talk/speak, take/have, leave* |
| parler**ai** | prender**ai** | partir**ai** | *you will talk/speak, take/have, leave* |
| parler**à** | prender**à** | partir**à** | *he/she/you* [formal] *will talk/speak, take/have, leave* |
| parler**emo** | prender**emo** | partir**emo** | *we will talk/speak, take/have, leave* |
| parler**ete** | prender**ete** | partir**ete** | *you will talk/speak, take/have, leave* |
| parler**anno** | prender**anno** | partir**anno** | *they will talk/speak, take/have, leave* |

# FUN & GAMES

Fill in the missing words with one of three possible answers under each sentence. See Appendix C for the answer key.

1. **Quest'anno andiamo in _____.** *(This year we're going to the mountains.)*

   **a.** albergo

   **b.** montagna

   **c.** aereo

2. **Il volo parte _____ Palermo alle tre.** *(The flight leaves from Palermo at three o'clock.)*

   **a.** da

   **b.** su

   **c.** a

3. **Passo le vacanze in _____.** *(I spend my vacation in the countryside.)*

   **a.** mare

   **b.** campagna

   **c.** montagna

4. **Dov'è la mia _____?** *(Where is my suitcase?)*

   **a.** stanza

   **b.** piscina

   **c.** valigia

5. **È un _____ organizzato.** *(It's an organized trip.)*

   **a.** viaggio

   **b.** treno

   **c.** volo

# Chapter **13**
# Money, Money, Money

On the one hand, you can never have enough of it; on the other hand, money can cause trouble. This is especially true for situations abroad or when you're dealing with foreign money in general. This chapter doesn't cover only currency — you know how tiresome converting foreign currencies can be — but all the terms you need to know about money.

## Going to the Bank

Dealing with banks isn't always fun, but sometimes you can't avoid them. In this section, we give you some banking terms that can help you manage a conversation at the bank.

You may need to go to the bank for several reasons. For example, you may want to **cambiare valuta** (kahm-*byah*-reh *vah*-looh-tah) *(to change money)*, **prelevare contanti** (preh-leh-*vah*-reh kohn-*tahn*-tee) *(to withdraw money)*, or **versare soldi sul tuo conto** (vehr-*sah*-reh *sohl*-dee soohl *tooh*-oh *kohn*-toh) *(to deposit money into your account)*. Other reasons could be **aprire un conto** (ah-*pree*-reh oohn *kohn*-toh) *(to open an account)* or **riscuotere un assegno** (ree-*skwoh*-teh-reh oohn ahs-*seh*-nyoh) *(to cash a check)*.

Other phrases you may find helpful include

>> **Mi dispiace, il suo conto è scoperto.** (mee dee-*spyah*-cheh eel *sooh*-oh *kohn*-toh eh skoh-*pehr*-toh) *(I'm sorry, your account is overdrawn.)*

>> **Può girare l'assegno per favore?** (*pwoh* jee-*rah*-reh lahs-*seh*-nyoh pehr fah-*voh*-reh) *(Could you endorse the check, please?)*

>> **Quant'è il tasso d'interesse?** (kwant-*eh* eel *tahs*-soh deen-teh-*rehs*-seh) *(What is the interest rate?)*

**CULTURAL WISDOM**

To make life easier for you — and to help you avoid standing in front of closed doors — we include the typical hours of Italian banks: They're open Monday through Friday, generally from 8:30 a.m. to 1:00 p.m., and then again from 2:00 to 3:30 p.m. These are general guidelines; hours can vary from city to city.

# Talkin' the Talk

Il signor Blasio asks for a statement of his account. He talks to **un'impiegata** (oohn-eem-pyeh-*gah*-tah) *(a female employee).*

**Sig. Blasio:** **Vorrei riscuotere un assegno.**
vohr-*rey* ree-*skwoh*-teh-reh oohn ahs-*seh*-nyoh
*I'd like to cash a check.*

**Clerk:** **Un documento, per favore. Firmi questa ricevuta, per favore.**
oohn doh-kooh-*mehn*-toh pehr fah-*voh*-reh *feer*-mee *kweh*-stah ree-cheh-*vooh*-tah pehr fah-*voh*-reh
*Some ID please. Please sign this receipt.*

**Sig. Blasio:** **Vorrei anche il mio estratto conto.**
vohr-*rey ahn*-keh eel *mee*-oh eh-*straht*-toh *kohn*-toh
*I'd like to get my bank statement too.*

**Clerk:** **Il suo numero di conto?**
eel *sooh*-oh *nooh*-meh-roh dee *kohn*-toh
*Your account number?*

**Sig. Blasio:** **Sette zero cinque nove.**
*seht*-teh *dzeh*-roh *cheen*-kweh *noh*-veh
*Seven zero five nine.*

**Clerk:** **Grazie. Attenda un momento . . .**
*grah*-tsyeh aht-*tehn*-dah oohn moh-*mehn*-toh
*Thank you. Wait one moment . . .*

**Ecco a lei!**
*ehk*-koh ah ley
*Here you are!*

| Sig. Blasio: | **Grazie mille, arrivederci!** |
|---|---|

*grah*-tsyeh *meel*-leh ahr-ree-veh-*dehr*-chee
*Thanks so much, good-bye!*

## WORDS TO KNOW

| conto corrente [m] | *kohn*-toh kohr-*rehn*-teh | *checking account* |
|---|---|---|
| estratto conto [m] | eh-*straht*-toh *kohn*-toh | *bank statement* |
| tasso d'interesse [m] | *tahs*-soh deen-teh-*rehs*-seh | *interest rate* |
| libretto degli assegni [m] | lee-*breht*-toh *deh*-lyee ahs-*seh*-nyee | *checkbook* |
| carta di credito [f] | *kahr*-tah dee *kreh*-dee-toh | *credit card* |
| ricevuta [f] | ree-cheh-*vooh*-tah | *receipt* |
| girare | jee-*rah*-reh | *to endorse* |
| riscuotere | ree-*skwoh*-teh-reh | *to cash* |

# Changing Money

You're more likely to need to change money when you're abroad. If you're in Italy and want to exchange dollars for **euro** (*eh*-ooh-roh) *(euros)*, you would go either to a **banca** (*bahn*-kah) *(bank)* or an **ufficio di cambio** (oohf-*fee*-choh dee *kahm*-byoh) *(exchange office)*. Better yet, go to a **bancomat** (*bahn*-koh-maht) *(ATM)* to withdraw euros. Some places definitely offer better exchange rates, so shop around if you have time.

Because Italy is frequented by tourists from all over the world, clerks in exchange offices usually have experience dealing with English-speaking people. Still, you just might want to complete a transaction in Italian while at an exchange office.

# Talkin' the Talk

Liza Campbell, an American tourist, needs to change some dollars for euros. She goes to a bank and talks to the teller. (Track 28)

**Ms. Campbell:** **Buongiorno, vorrei cambiare alcuni dollari in euro.**
bwohn-*johr*-noh vohr-*rey* kahm-*byah*-reh ahl-*kooh*-nee *dohl*-lah-ree een *eh*-ooh-roh
*Hello, I'd like to change some dollars into euros.*

**Teller:** **Benissimo. Quanti dollari?**
beh-*nees*-see-moh *kwahn*-tee *dohl*-lah-ree
*Very well. How many dollars?*

**Ms. Campbell:** **Duecento. Quant'è il cambio?**
*dooh*-eh-*chehn*-toh kwahn-*teh* eel *kahm*-byoh
*Two hundred. What's the exchange?*

**Teller:** **Oggi un euro vale un dollaro e venti. Ci sono poi cinque euro di commissione.**
*oj*-jee oohn *eh*-ooh-roh *vah*-leh oohn *dohl*-lah-roh eh *vehn*-tee chee *soh*-noh poi *cheen*-kweh *eh*-ooh-roh dee kohm-mees-*syoh*-neh
*Today the euro is worth a $1.20. There is also a five-euro commission.*

**Ms. Campbell:** **Va bene.**
vah *beh*-neh
*Okay.*

**Teller:** **Mi serve un documento.**
mee *sehr*-veh oohn doh-kooh-*mehn*-toh
*I need some ID.*

**Ms. Campbell:** **Ecco.**
*ehk*-koh
*Here.*

**Teller:** **Sono 166 Euro meno i 5 euro di commissione.**
*soh*-noh chehn-toh-sehs-*sahn*-tah-sey *eh*-ooh-roh *meh*-noh ee *cheen*-kweh *eh*-ooh roh dee kohm-mee-*syoh*-neh
*It comes to 166 euros less the 5 euro exchange fee.*

**Ms. Campbell:** **Grazie mille!**
*grah*-tsyeh *meel*-leh
*Thanks a million!*

Nowadays, exchanging money isn't the most efficient way to get the local currency. In Italy, as in most Western countries, you can find a **bancomat** (*bahn-koh-maht*) *(ATM)* almost anywhere. And, depending on where you shop or eat, you can often pay with a **carta di credito** (*kahr*-tah dee *kreh*-dee-toh) *(credit card)*. The following phrases can help you find the cash you need — or at least the nearest ATM:

>> **Dov'è il bancomat più vicino?** (doh-*veh* eel *bahn*-koh-maht pyooh vee-*chee*-noh) *(Where is the nearest ATM?)*

>> **Mi scusi, potrebbe cambiarmi una banconota da 100 euro?** (mee *skooh*-zee poh-*trehb*-beh kahm-*byahr*-mee *ooh*-nah bahn-koh-*noh*-tah da *chehn*-toh *eh*-ooh-roh) *(Excuse me, would you be able to change a 100 euro bill?)*

>> **Mi dispiace, non ho spiccioli.** (mee dee-*spyah*-cheh nohn oh *speech*-choh-lee) *(I'm sorry, I haven't any small change.)*

## WORDS TO KNOW

| | | |
|---|---|---|
| **in contanti** | een kohn-*tahn*-tee | *in cash* |
| **versare** | vehr-*sah*-reh | *to deposit* |
| **accettare** | ahch-cheht-*tah*-reh | *to accept* |
| **bancomat [m]** | *bahn*-koh-maht | *ATM* |
| **cambiare** | kahm-*byah*-reh | *to change* |
| **spiccioli [m/pl.]** | *speech*-choh-lee | *small change* |

# Using Credit Cards

In Canada and the United States, you can take care of almost all your financial needs without ever handling cash. You can pay for nearly everything with your debit or credit card, and you can even use your credit card to get cash at ATMs or in some banks — though remember that, whether in the United States or in Italy, getting cash with a credit card is generally more expensive than using a **bancomat** *(debit card)*. (Note that the word **bancomat** in Italian refers to both the debit card and the ATM machine itself.) This is the same in Italy, although cash is still the customary form of payment in many places, especially in smaller towns or for smaller purchases.

Since 2022, Italian businesses have been legally obligated to accept electronic payments. However, some smaller shops or cafés may still discourage card use for very small purchases — like a single espresso — and you might even get a disapproving look for trying to use your card. In these situation paying in cash for small purchases remains a common and culturally welcomed practice. These are some phrases you may find useful:

- » **Posso pagare con il bancomat?** (*pohs*-soh pah-*gah*-reh kohn eel *bahn*-koh -maht?) *(Can I pay with my debit card?)*

- » **Posso pagare con la carta di credito?** (*pohs*-soh pah-*gah*-reh kohn lah *kahr*-tah dee *kreh*-dee-toh) *(May I pay with my credit card?)*

- » **Mi dispiace, non accettiamo carte di credito.** (mee dee-*spyah*-cheh nohn ahch-cheht-*tyah*-moh *kahr*-teh dee *kreh*-dee-toh) *(I'm sorry, we don't accept credit cards.)*

# Talkin' the Talk

Ms. Johnson wants to withdraw some euros with her credit card but discovers that the ATM is out of order. She enters the bank and asks the cashier what's up.

| | |
|---|---|
| **Ms. Johnson:** | **Scusi, il bancomat non funziona.** <br> *skooh*-zee eel *bahn*-koh-maht nohn foohn-*tsyoh*-nah <br> *Excuse me, the ATM isn't working.* |
| **Cashier:** | **Lo so, signora, mi dispiace!** <br> loh soh see-*nyoh*-rah mee dee-*spyah*-cheh <br> *I know, madam, I'm sorry!* |
| **Ms. Johnson:** | **Ma ho bisogno di contanti.** <br> mah oh bee-*zoh*-nyoh dee kohn-*tahn*-tee <br> *But I need cash.* |
| **Cashier:** | **Può prelevare qui alla cassa.** <br> pwoh preh-leh-*vah*-reh kwee *ahl*-lah *kahs*-sah <br> *You can make a withdrawal here at the counter.* |
| **Ms. Johnson:** | **D'accordo, grazie.** <br> dak-*kohr*-doh *grah*-tsyeh <br> *Okay, thanks.* |

Normally, things go easily and you don't have any problems using credit cards. But you may be asked to show your identification for security purposes. The following phrases can help you be prepared for this situation:

>> **Potrei vedere un documento per favore?** (poh-*trey* veh-*deh*-reh oohn doh-kooh-*mehn*-toh pehr fah-*voh*-reh) *(May I please see your identification?)*

>> **Potrebbe darmi il suo passaporto, per favore?** (poh-*trehb*-beh *dahr*-mee eel *sooh*-oh pahs-sah-*pohr*-toh pehr fah-*voh*-reh) *(Would you please give me your passport?)*

>> **Il suo indirizzo?** (eel *sooh*-oh een-dee-*reet*-tsoh) *(What is your address?)*

The following sentence shows you how this rather formal verb — **attendere** (aht–*tehn*–deh–reh) *(to wait)* — is used:

**Attenda, per favore** (aht-*tehn*-dah pehr fah-*voh*-reh) *(Please wait.)*

# Talkin' the Talk

While Ms. Johnson explores her options with the cashier, another person enters the bank and starts to complain:

| | |
|---|---|
| **Signora Gradi:** | **Il bancomat ha mangiato la mia carta.**<br>eel *bahn*-koh-maht ah mahn-*jah*-toh lah *mee*-ah *kahr*-tah<br>*The ATM machine ate my card.* |
| **Teller:** | **Ha digitato il numero giusto?**<br>ah dee-jee-*tah*-toh eel *nooh*-meh-roh *jooh*-stoh<br>*Did you enter the right number?* |
| **Signora Gradi:** | **Certo! Che domanda!**<br>*chehr*-toh keh doh-*mahn*-dah<br>*Of course! What a question!* |
| **Teller:** | **Mi scusi, a volte capita.**<br>mee *skooh*-zee ah *vohl*-teh *kah*-pee-tah<br>*Excuse me, but it can happen.* |
| **Signora Gradi:** | **Cosa posso fare?**<br>*koh*-zah *pohs*-soh *fah*-reh<br>*What can I do?* |
| **Teller:** | **Attenda un momento . . .**<br>aht-*tehn*-dah oohn moh-*mehn*-toh<br>*Wait a moment . . .* |

<table>
<tr><th colspan="3" style="text-align:center">WORDS TO KNOW</th></tr>
<tr><td>Certo!</td><td>chehr-toh</td><td>Of course!</td></tr>
<tr><td>bancomat [m]</td><td>eel bahn-koh-maht</td><td>ATM/debit card</td></tr>
<tr><td>digitare</td><td>dee-jee-tah-reh</td><td>to enter</td></tr>
<tr><td>prelevare</td><td>preh-leh-vah-reh</td><td>to withdraw</td></tr>
<tr><td>funzionare</td><td>foohn-tsyoh-nah-reh</td><td>to work; to function</td></tr>
<tr><td>contanti [m/pl.]</td><td>kohn-tahn-tee</td><td>cash</td></tr>
<tr><td>Che domanda!</td><td>keh doh-mahn-dah</td><td>What a question!</td></tr>
</table>

# Looking at Various Currencies

Along with many other European countries, the Italian monetary unit is the **euro** (*eh*-ooh-roh). There are 1 euro coins and 2 euro coins, and then larger bills (5, 10, 20, 50, 100, and so on). The plural form is **euro** (*eh*-ooh-roh), and the abbreviation is €. That's right, the singular and the plural forms are exactly the same in spelling and pronunciation. Smaller denominations are in **centesimi** (chehn-*teh*-zee-mee) (*cents*) and are coins. (You can check out Chapter 4 for numbers.)

## Talkin' the Talk

Patrizia is planning her vacation to Albania. She is planning on taking the **aliscafo** (ah-leeh-*skah*-foh) *(high-speed ferry)* from Ancona tomorrow. She talks to her friend, Milena, about exchanging her money.

**Patrizia:** **Sai qual è il cambio euro in lek albanesi?**
sahy kwah-*leh* eel *kahm*-byoh *eh*-ooh-roh een lehk ahl-bah-*neh*-zee
*Do you know the exchange rate for euros to Albanian lek?*

**Milena:** **Non ne ho idea!**
nohn neh oh ee-*deh*-ah
*I have no idea!*

<table>
<tr><td>Patrizia:</td><td>Domani parto per Borsh per un mese. . .<br>doh-mah-nee pahr-toh pehr bohr-sh perh oohn meh-zeh<br>Tomorrow I'm leaving for Borsh for a month.</td></tr>
<tr><td>Milena:</td><td>. . . e non hai ancora cambiato!<br>eh nohn ahy ahn-koh-rah kahm-byah-toh<br>. . . and you haven't changed your money yet!</td></tr>
<tr><td>Patrizia:</td><td>Posso farlo al porto.<br>pohs-soh fahr-loh ahl pohr-toh<br>I can do it at the port.</td></tr>
<tr><td>Milena:</td><td>Ma no, è più caro!<br>mah noh eh pyooh kah-roh<br>No, that's more expensive!</td></tr>
<tr><td>Patrizia:</td><td>Oh, buono a sapersi! Mi accompagni in banca, per favore?<br>Oh bwoh-noh ah sah-pehr-see mee ahk-kohm-pah-nyee een bahn-kah pehr fah-voh-reh<br>Oh, good to know! Will you come with me to the bank, please?</td></tr>
</table>

**CULTURAL WISDOM**

The **euro** is legal tender in 20 of the 27 countries that belong to the European Union (EU). So, if you travel among EU countries after you have euros in your possession, you don't have to change money in every country you visit.

Table 13–1 shows the currencies of various countries.



## Currencies

| Italian | Pronunciation | English single/plural | Where used |
|---|---|---|---|
| **dollaro/dollari** | *dohl*-lah-roh/<br>*dohl*-lah-ree | *dollar/dollars* | Canada, United States; Australia, New Zealand |
| **sterlina/e** | stehr-*lee*-nah/<br>stehr-*lee*-neh | *pound/pounds* | United Kingdom |
| **peseta/pesetas** | peh-*zeh*-tah/<br>peh-*zeh*-tahs | *pesetas/pesetas* | Mexico |

Cristina is at the bank. **Allo sportello** (*ahl*-loh spohr-*tehl*-loh) (*at the counter*), she talks with her high school buddy Paolo who is now the bank teller.

| | |
|---|---|
| **Patrizia:** | **Ciao Paolo. Vorrei cambiare cinquecento euro in sterline.** |
| | chow *pah*-oh-loh vohr-*rey* kahm-*byah*-reh *cheen*-kweh-*chehn*-toh *eh*-oohr-roh een stehr-*lee*-neh |
| | *Hi Paolo. I'd like to change 500 euros into British pounds.* |
| **Teller:** | **Vai in Inghilterra?** |
| | vahy een een-geehl-*tehr*-rah |
| | *Are you going to England?* |
| **Patrizia:** | **Sì.** |
| | see |
| | *Yes.* |
| **Teller:** | **Sai che puoi usare il bancomat ed è anche più sicuro?** |
| | sahy keh pwoi ooh-*zah*-reh eel *bahn*-koh-maht ehd eh *ahn*-keh pyooh see-*kooh*-roh |
| | *Do you know that you can use the ATM machine and that it's even safer?* |
| **Patrizia:** | **Hai ragione, allora cambio solo duecento euro.** |
| | ahy rah-*joh*-neh ahl-*loh*-rah *kahm*-byoh *soh*-loh *dooh*-eh-*chehn*-toh *eh*-ooh-roh |
| | *You're right, I'm just going to change 200 euros.* |
| **Teller:** | **Ecco le tue sterline, fai buon viaggio!** |
| | *ehk*-koh leh *tooh*-eh stehr-*lee*-neh fahy bwon *vyahj*-joh |
| | *Here are your pounds, have a good trip!* |

## WORDS TO KNOW

| | | |
|---|---|---|
| **prendere** | *prehn*-deh-reh | *to take* |
| **viaggio [m]** | *vyahj*-joh | *trip* |
| **aeroporto [m]** | ah-eh-roh-*pohr*-toh | *airport* |
| **cambiare** | kahm-*byah*-reh | *to exchange* |
| **domani** | doh-*mah*-nee | *tomorrow* |

# FUN & GAMES

Here's a little game for you. First define each word from this chapter and then find them in the word search puzzle. See Appendix C for the answer key.

```
C A R T A D I C R E D I T O D
S O K S Z N B O Y D O Y Y D O
E R R Y P A Z G E C L S A M C
T R J U N O G P S D L P N F U
A X A C E B R P Q Z A K U L M
M G A I A M I T Q S R X K J E
O L W A B C T O E Y O R J I N
C H L N C M E N I L R E T S T
N C K I E B A I N V L N L H O
A J O A S S A C K R A O Z P H
B L T R I C E V U T A A S E K
I E H T W N L C N X M K Q G V
Q J A U Y C V O Q A G M N A Q
Q L N Q E K C Y P D F Q L V W
Z Q X X B E J M W F Y Y L E K
```



Banca ______________________________

Bancomat ______________________________

Cambiare ______________________________

Carta di credito ______________________________

Cassa ______________________________

Contanti ______________________________

Documento ______________________________

Dollaro _______________________________

Euro _______________________________

Lek _______________________________

Ricevuta _______________________________

Spiccioli _______________________________

Sportello _______________________________

Sterline _______________________________

# Chapter **14**

# Getting Around: Planes, Trains, Taxis, & Buses

Whether you're visiting Italy, or you just need to explain to an Italian-speaking friend how to get across town, transportation vocabulary really comes in handy. This chapter helps you navigate the airport and secure transportation to get where you're going after you're on the ground — whether by taxi, bus, car, or train. You can also figure out what to do at customs, how to find missing luggage, and how to rent a car. **Andiamo** (ahn-*dyah*-moh) — **Let's go!**

## Getting through the Airport

You're in luck — it's very likely that you can get by with English when you're at an Italian airport. Both Italian and English are usually spoken there. Still, you might find yourself in a situation where the person next to you in an airport only knows Italian. Just in case, we provide you with some useful navigational material. Besides, you'll probably want a chance to practice the language you'll be immersed in as soon as you step outside the airport.

# Checking in

The counter where you finally hand off your luggage is called check-in — in Italian **accettazione** (ahch-cheht-tah-*tsyoh*-neh). In fact, people often use "check-in" in Italian, too. You also pick up your boarding pass at the check-in counter, so conversation is usually inevitable.

## ............ Talkin' the Talk ............

Ms. Adami is checking in. She shows her ticket and passport to the agent and leaves her suitcases at the counter.

| | |
|---|---|
| **Agent:** | **Il suo biglietto, per favore.**<br>eel *sooh*-oh bee-*lyeht*-toh pehr fah-*voh*-reh<br>*Your ticket, please.* |
| **Sig.ra Adami:** | **Ecco.**<br>*ehk*-koh<br>*Here it is.* |
| **Agent:** | **Passaporto?**<br>pahs-sah-*pohr*-toh<br>*Passport?* |
| **Sig.ra Adami:** | **Prego.**<br>*preh*-goh<br>*Here you are.* |
| **Agent:** | **Quanti bagagli ha?**<br>*kwahn*-tee bah-*gah*-lyee ah<br>*How many suitcases do you have?* |
| **Sig.ra Adami:** | **Due valigie e un bagaglio a mano.**<br>*dooh*-eh vah-*lee*-jeh eh oohn bah-*gah*-lyoh ah *mah*-noh<br>*Two suitcases and one piece of carry-on luggage.* |
| **Agent:** | **Qual è la sua destinazione?**<br>qwahl-*eh* lah *sooh*-ah deh-stee-nah-*tsyoh*-neh<br>*What is your destination?* |
| **Sig.ra Adami:** | **New York.**<br>nooh yohrk<br>*New York.* |
| **Agent:** | **Ha fatto Lei le proprie valigie?**<br>ah *faht*-toh ley leh *proh*-pryeh vah-*lee*-jeh<br>*Did you pack you own bags?* |

| **Sig.ra Adami:** | **Sì.** |
| --- | --- |
| | see |
| | *Yes.* |

| **Agent:** | **Le ha sempre avute sottomano da quando le ha chiuse?** |
| --- | --- |
| | leh ah *sehm*-preh ah-*vooh*-teh *soht*-toh *mah*-noh dah *qwahn*-doh leh ah *kyooh*-zeh |
| | *Have they been with you the whole time since you closed them?* |

| **Sig. ra Adami:** | **Sí. Posso avere un posto vicino al finestrino, per favore?** |
| --- | --- |
| | see *pohs*-soh ah-*veh*-reh oohn *poh*-stoh vee-*chee*-noh ahl fee-neh-*stree*-noh pehr fah-*voh*-reh |
| | *Yes. May I please have a window seat?* |

| **Agent:** | **Un attimo. Ora controllo: sì, il 16A. Ecco la sua carta d'imbarco.** |
| --- | --- |
| | oohn *aht*-tee-moh *oh*-rah kohn-*trohl*-loh see eel *seh*-dee-chee ah *ehk*-koh lah *sooh*-ah *kahr*-tah deem-*bahr*-koh |
| | *One second, I'm going to check now. Yes, 16A. Here is your boarding pass.* |

| | **L'imbarco è alle nove e quindici, uscita tre. Prosegua per il controllo di sicurezza.** |
| --- | --- |
| | leem-*bahr*-koh eh *ahl*-leh *noh*-veh eh *kween*-dee-chee ooh-*shee*-tah treh proh-*seh*-gwah ahl kohn-*trohl*-loh dee see-kooh-*reht*-tsah |
| | *Boarding is at 9:15, gate 3. You can move on to security now.* |

# WORDS TO KNOW

| | | |
| --- | --- | --- |
| **imbarco [m]** | eem-*bahr*-koh | *boarding* |
| **valigia [f]** | vah-*lee*-jah | *suitcase* |
| **uscita [f]** | ooh-*shee*-tah | *gate* |
| **bagaglio a mano [m]** | bah-*gah*-lyoh ah *mah*-noh | *carry-on luggage* |
| **passaporto [m]** | pahs-sah-*pohr*-toh | *passport* |
| **bagaglio [m]** | bah-*gah*-lyoh | *baggage* |

# Dealing with excess baggage

Sometimes you take so much with you and your suitcases are so heavy that the airline charges an extra fee to transport your luggage. You don't have much say: You simply have to pay. These phrases can help:

>> **Questa valigia eccede il limite.** (*qweh*-stah vah-*lee*-jah ehch-*cheh*-deh eel *lee*-mee-teh) *(This bag is over the weight limit.)*

>> **Ha un eccesso di bagaglio.** (ah oohn ehch-*chehs*-soh dee bah-*gah*-lyoh) *(You have excess luggage.)*

>> **Deve pagare un supplemento.** (*deh*-veh pah-*gah*-reh oohn soohp-pleh-*mehn*-toh) *(You have to pay a surcharge.)*

>> **Questo bagaglio a mano eccede le misure.** (*kweh*-stoh bah-*gah*-lyoh ah *mah*-noh ehch-*cheh*-deh leh mee-*zoo*-reh) *(This carry-on bag exceeds the size limit.)*

Before you go to the airport, always check the weight limit of your bags and how much an extra suitcase will cost. That way you can plan ahead — even buy an extra suitcase if necessary and avoid having to throw out items at check-in.

# Waiting to board the plane

Before boarding, you may encounter unforeseen situations, such as delays or even cancellations. If that happens, you'll probably want to ask some questions.

## Talkin' the Talk

Mr. Campo is in the boarding area. He asks the agent if his flight is on time. Always be prepared for cryptic answers.

| | |
|---|---|
| **Sig. Campo:** | **Il volo è in orario?**<br>eel *voh*-loh eh een oh-*rah*-ryoh<br>*Is the flight on time?* |
| **Agent:** | **No, è in ritardo.**<br>noh eh een ree-*tahr*-doh<br>*No, there has been a delay.* |

| Sig. Campo: | **Di quanto?** |
| | dee *kwahn*-toh |
| | *How long?* |
| Agent: | **Per ora trenta minuti.** |
| | pehr oh-rah *trehn*-tah mee-*nooh*-tee |
| | *Thirty minutes for now.* |

## WORDS TO KNOW

| | | |
|---|---|---|
| **supplemento [m]** | soohp-pleh-*mehn*-toh | *supplement* |
| **circa** | *cheer*-kah | *about* |
| **in ritardo** | een ree-*tahr*-doh | *late; delayed* |
| **volo [m]** | *voh*-loh | *flight* |
| **in orario** | een oh-*rah*-ryoh | *on time* |
| **cancellato** | cahn-chehl-*lah*-toh | *cancelled* |

# Going through customs

After you exit a plane in Italy, you're immediately hit by voices speaking a foreign language. You have to take care of necessities, such as finding a bathroom, changing money, and looking for a taxi.

Visitors from countries in the European Union need only **la carta d'identità** (lah *kahr*-tah dee-dehn-*tee*-tah) (*the identity card*) to enter Italy. Nationals of all other countries need a valid **passaporto** (pahs-sah-*pohr*-toh) (*passport*), and sometimes also a visa. Usually, at **controllo passaporti** (kohn-*trohl*-loh pahs-sah-*pohr*-tee) (*passport control*), you don't exchange many words, and the ones you do exchange are usually routine.

If you have something to declare, you do so **alla dogana** (*ahl*-lah doh-*gah*-nah) (*at customs*). The examples that follow should help ease any concerns you might have. Generally, you can just walk through the line that says **"Niente da dichiarare,"** (*nyehn*-teh dah dee-kyah-*rah*-reh) (*nothing to declare*) and no one will say anything to you. But occasionally you may be stopped for a random check:

**Niente da dichiarare?** (*nyehn*-teh dah dee-kyah-*rah*-reh) (*Anything to declare?*)

**No, niente.** (noh *nyehn*-teh) (*No, nothing.*)

**Per favore, apra questa valigia.** (pehr fah-*voh*-reh *ah*-prah *kweh*-stah vah-*lee*-jah) (*Please, open this suitcase.*)

**È nuovo il computer?** (eh *nwoh*-voh eel kohm-*pyooh*-tehr) (*Is this computer new?*)

**Sì, ma è per uso personale.** (see mah eh pehr *ooh*-zoh pehr-soh-*nah*-leh) (*Yes, but it's for personal use.*)

**Per questo deve pagare il dazio.** (pehr *kweh*-stoh *deh*-veh pah-*gah*-reh eel *dah*-tsyoh) (*You have to pay duty on this.*)

When you pass through customs, you may have to declare any goods that you purchased, if over a certain dollar/euro amount. You may need to say:

**Ho questa cosa/queste cose/da dichiarare.** (oh *kweh*-stah *koh*-zah/*kweh*-steh *koh*-zeh/dah dee-kyah-*rah*-reh) (*I have this thing/these things/to declare.*)

# Talkin' the Talk

Mrs. Johnson asks a woman passing by where she can find a luggage cart.

| | |
|---|---|
| **Mrs. Johnson:** | **Scusi, dove sono i carrelli?** <br> *skooh*-zee *doh*-veh *soh*-noh ee kahr-*rehl*-lee <br> *Excuse me. Where are the luggage carts?* |
| **Woman:** | **Al ritiro bagagli.** <br> ahl ree-*tee*-roh bah-*gah*-lyee <br> *At the baggage claim.* |
| **Mrs. Johnson:** | **Servono monete?** <br> *sehr*-voh-noh moh-*neh*-teh <br> *Do I need coins/change?* |
| **Woman:** | **Sì, da un euro.** <br> see dah oohn *eh*-ooh-roh <br> *Yes, 1 euro coin.* |

# Dealing With Lost Luggage

Losing luggage is always a possibility when flying to Italy, especially if you're changing planes, but don't despair: 80 percent of misplaced luggage turns up within 24 hours, and most of the rest within three days. The airline will deliver your bags to your hotel or apartment, or you can return to the airport for them if you need them sooner.

## Talkin' the Talk

Giancarlo, Teresa, and Emilia have just arrived at the Bologna airport via Amsterdam, but their bags are not on the baggage claim belt.

| | |
|---|---|
| **Giancarlo:** | **Ci sono altre valige dal volo da Amsterdam?**<br>chee *soh*-noh *ahl*-treh vah-*lee*-jeh dahl *voh*-loh dah *ahm*-stehr-dahm<br>*Are there other bags from the Amsterdam flight?* |
| **Facchino (Porter):** | **Non ce ne sono altre.**<br>nohn cheh neh *soh*-noh *ahl*-treh<br>*No, there are no more.* |
| **Giancarlo:** | **Le nostre mancano.**<br>leh *noh*-streh *mahn*-kah-noh.<br>*Ours are missing.* |
| | **Cosa dobbiamo fare?**<br>*koh*-zah dohb-*byah*-moh *fah*-reh<br>*What should we do?* |
| **Facchino:** | **Si rivolga all' Ufficio Assistenza Bagagli.**<br>see ree-*vohl*-gah ahl-loohf-*fee*-choh ahs-see-*stehn*-tsah *bah-gah-lyee*<br>*Go to the the Missing Baggage Office.* |

At the Missing Baggage Office.

| | |
|---|---|
| **Impiegato (Employee):** | **Dica pure.**<br>*dee*-kah *pooh*-reh<br>*How can I help you?* |

*(continued)*

(continued)

| | |
|---|---|
| **Giancarlo:** | **Non sono arrivati i nostri bagagli da Amsterdam.**<br>nohn *soh*-noh ahr-ree-*vah*-tee ee *noh*-stree bah-*gah*-lyee dah *ahm*-stehr-dahm<br>*Our bags from Amsterdam didn't arrive.* |
| **Impiegato:** | **Avete le ricevute dei bagagli?**<br>ah-*veh*-teh leh ree-cheh-*vooh*-teh dey bah-gah-lyee<br>*Do you have the baggage receipts?* |
| **Giancarlo:** | **Eccole qui.**<br>*ehk*-koh-leh qwee<br>*Here they are.* |
| **Impiegato:** | **Bisogna riempire questo modulo con il vostro recapito, numero di telefono, e descrizione dei bagagli.**<br>bee-*zoh*-nyah ree-ehm-*pee*-reh *qweh*-stoh *moh*-dooh-loh kohn eel *voh*-stroh reh-*kah*-pee-toh *nooh*-meh-roh dee teh-*leh*-foh-noh eh deh-skree-*tsyoh*-neh dey bah-*gah*-lyee<br>*You need to fill out this form with your address, phone number, and description of the bags.* |
| | **Vi telefoneremo appena arriveranno.**<br>Vee teh-leh-foh-neh-*reh*-moh ahp-*peh*-nah ahr-ree-veh-*rahn*-noh<br>*We'll call you as soon as they arrive.* |

## WORDS TO KNOW

| | | |
|---|---|---|
| **dogana [f]** | doh-*gah*-nah | *customs* |
| **dichiarare** | dee-kyah-*rah*-reh | *to declare* |
| **niente** | *nyehn*-teh | *nothing* |
| **pagare** | pah-*gah*-reh | *to pay* |
| **uso personale [m]** | *ooh*-zoh pehr-soh-*nah*-leh | *personal use* |
| **modulo [m]** | *moh*-dooh-loh | *form* |
| **ricevuta [f]** | ree-cheh-*vooh*-tah | *receipt* |

# Talkin' the Talk

Mrs. Johnson just passed customs and she wants to withdraw money to pay for a taxi and to hold her over for the first few days. She asks a porter where she can do so.

| | |
|---|---|
| **Mrs. Johnson:** | **Mi scusi?** <br> mee *skooh*-zee <br> *Excuse me?* |
| **Porter:** | **Prego!** <br> *preh*-goh <br> *Yes, how can I help you?* |
| **Mrs. Johnson:** | **Dov'è un bancomat?** <br> doh-*veh* oohn *bahn*-koh-maht <br> *Where is an ATM?* |
| **Porter:** | **In fondo al corridoio vicino all'ufficio cambio, signora.** <br> een *fohn*-doh ahl kohr-ree-*doh*-yoh vee-*chee*-noh ahl-loohf-*fee*-choh *kahm*-byoh see-*nyoh*-rah <br> *At the end of the corridor near the money exchange office, Ma'am.* |
| **Mrs. Johnson:** | **C'è anche una banca?** <br> cheh *ahn*-keh *ooh*-nah *bahn*-kah <br> *Is there also a bank?* |
| **Passerby:** | **No, c'è soltanto uno sportello di cambio.** <br> noh cheh sohl-*tahn*-toh *ooh*-noh spohr-*tehl*-loh dee *kahm*-byoh <br> *No, there is only a window to change money.* |
| **Mrs. Johnson:** | **Benissimo. Grazie mille.** <br> beh-*nees*-see-moh *grah*-tsyeh *meel*-leh <br> *Thank you very much.* |

| arrivo [m] | ahr-*ree*-voh | *arrival* |
| --- | --- | --- |
| partenza [f] | pahr-*tehn*-tsah | *departure* |
| vacanza [f] | vah-*kahn*-tsah | *vacation* |
| ritiro bagagli [m] | ree-*tee*-roh bah-*gah*-lyee | *baggage claim* |
| cambio [m] | *kahm*-byoh | *exchange* |
| destinazione [f] | deh-stee-nah-*tsyoh*-neh | *destination* |
| entrata [f] | ehn-*trah*-tah | *entrance* |

# Renting a Car

Italy is a beautiful country, and while you're visiting, you may want to consider taking tours of both the cities and the countryside. If you don't have a car, renting one is a great way to explore different areas. That said, Italian traffic can sometimes feel overwhelming. For instance, Italians start to honk even before the traffic light turns green, in anticipation of the change and to urge drivers to get moving. Parking can also test your patience, especially in town centers, some of which don't even allow cars. Even medium-sized cars can struggle to fit through narrow streets or make turns where cars are allowed. We don't want to scare you, though — just enjoy the adventure!

CULTURAL WISDOM

To drive a car or motorcycle in Italy, you must be at least 18 years old and have a valid **patente** (pah-*tehn*-teh) (*driver's license*). Renting a car is easy and can be done at any airport.

Whether you reserve by phone, online, or in person, the process is the same: Just let the company know what kind of car you want and the terms of the rental. If possible, research your options before getting to Italy — this way, you'll have a car waiting for you when you arrive.

# Talkin' the Talk

Mr. Brown is staying in Italy for two weeks and wants to rent a car to visit different cities. He goes to the rental service booth at the airport and talks to **l'impiegato** (leem-pyeh-*gah*-toh) *(the agent)*.

**Mr. Brown:** **Vorrei noleggiare una macchina.**
vohr-*rey* noh-lehj-*jah*-reh *ooh*-nah *mahk*-kee-nah
*I would like to rent a car.*

**Agent** **Che tipo?**
keh *tee*-poh
*What kind?*

**Mr. Brown:** **Di media cilindrata col cambio automatico.**
dee *meh*-dyah chee-leen-*drah*-tah kohl *kahm*-byoh
ow-toh-*mah*-tee-koh
*A mid-size with an automatic transmission.*

**Agent:** **Per quanto tempo?**
pehr *kwahn*-toh *tehm*-poh
*For how long?*

**Mr. Brown:** **Una settimana.**
*ooh*-nah seht-tee-*mah*-nah
*One week.*

**Quanto è per la settimana?**
*kwahn*-toh eh pehr lah seht-tee-*mah*-nah
*What does it cost for a week?*

**Agent:** **C'è un'offerta questa settimana: 18 euro al giorno.**
cheh oohn-ohf-*fehr*-tah *qweh*-stah seht-tee-*mah*-nah
dee-*choht*-toh *eh*-ooh-roh ahl *johr*-noh
*There is a special this week: 18 euros per day.*

**Mr. Brown:** **L'assicurazione è inclusa?**
lahs-see-kooh-rah-*tsyoh*-neh eh een-*klooh*-zah
*Is insurance included?*

**Agent:** **Sì, con la polizza kasko.**
see kohn lah *poh*-leet-tsah *kah*-skoh
*Yes, it includes a comprehensive policy.*

Other words and expressions that you may need when renting a car or getting fuel at a gas station include the following:

>> **l'aria condizionata/il climatizzatore** (*lah*-ryah kohn-dee-tsyoh-*nah*-tah /eel klee-mah-*teed*-dzah-toh-reh) *(air conditioning)*

>> **il cabriolet/la decappottabile** (eel *kah*-bryoh-leh/lah deh-kahp-*poht*-tah-bee-leh) *(convertible)*

>> **fare benzina** (*fah*-reh behn-*dzee*-nah) *(to get gas)*

>> **Faccia il pieno.** (*fahch*-chah eel *pyeh*-noh) *(Fill it up.)*

>> **la benzina senza piombo** (lah behn-*dzee*-nah *sehn*-tsah *pyohm*-boh) *(unleaded fuel)*

>> **la benzina super** (lah behn-*dzee*-nah *sooh*-pehr) *(premium fuel)*

>> **Controlli l'olio.** (kohn-*trohl*-lee *loh*-lyoh) *(Check the oil.)*

A car with an automatic transmission could cost you significantly more because they aren't as common in Italy; most people drive a car with a manual transmission.

# Navigating Public Transportation

If you'd prefer not to drive, you can get around quite comfortably using public transportation; taxis, trains, and buses are reliable options. The following sections show you how to navigate them in Italian.

## Calling a taxi

Haling a taxi in Italy won't get you far, because taxi drivers typically wait at designated taxi stands or respond to phone calls. The good news is that Italians use the same word, **taxi** (*tah*–ksee), which has become part of the Italian language. You can usually get a taxi number from hotel staff, restaurant employees, signs at taxi stands, or tourist information offices. Here are some helpful phrases to get you on your way:

>> **Può chiamarmi un taxi?** (pwoh kyah-*mahr*-mee oohn *tah*-ksee) *(Can you call me a taxi?)*

>> **Vorrei un taxi, per favore.** (vohr-*rey* oohn *tah*-ksee pehr fah-*voh*-reh) *(I'd like a taxi, please.)*

In case you are asked **per quando?** (pehr *kwahn*-doh) *(for when?)*, you need to be ready with an answer. The following are some common responses:

>> **subito** (*sooh*-bee-toh) *(right now)*

>> **fra un'ora** (frah oohn-*oh*-rah) *(in one hour)*

>> **alle due del pomeriggio** (*ahl*-leh *dooh*-eh dehl poh-meh-*reej*-joh) *(at 2 p.m.)*

>> **domani mattina alle 5 e mezzo** (doh-*mah*-nee maht-*tee*-nah *ahl*-leh *cheen*-qweh eh *mehd*-dzoh) *(tomorrow morning at 5:30 a.m.)*

After you get in the taxi, the driver will ask where to take you. Here are some potential destinations:

>> **Alla stazione, per favore.** (*ahl*-lah stah-*tsyoh*-neh pehr fah-*voh*-reh) *(To the train station, please.)*

>> **All'areoporto.** (*ahl*-lah-eh-roh-*pohr*-toh) *(To the airport.)*

>> **In via Veneto.** (een *vee*-ah *veh*-neh-toh) *(To via Veneto.)*

>> **A questo indirizzo: via Leopardi, numero 3.** (ah *kweh*-stoh een-dee-*reet*-tsoh *vee*-ah leh-oh-*pahr*-dee *nooh*-meh-roh treh) *(To this address: via Leopardi, number 3.)*

Finally, you have to pay. Simply ask the driver **Quant'è?** (kwahn-*teh*) *(How much is it?)*. Even though Italian law requires taxis to accept credit cards, some drivers may prefer cash, so it's a good idea to ask before getting in.

If you prefer to pay digitally or track your taxi location, you can use one of the several apps available in Italy for taxis: Some of the most widely used are FreeNow, itTaxi, and WeTaxi.

In Italy, Uber works a bit differently than in the United States — you won't find everyday drivers picking you up. Instead, most rides are through Uber Black, a premium service that uses licensed professional drivers and high-end vehicles, and it's mainly available in big cities like Rome and Milan.

CULTURAL
WISDOM

# Moving by train

You can still buy a train ticket **alla stazione** (*ahl*-lah stah-*tsyoh*-neh) (at the station) or at **un'agenzia di viaggi** (*ooh*-nah-jehn-*tsee*-ah dee *vyahj*-jee) (*a travel agency*), but nowadays purchasing your ticket online is the best way to go. Just visit the Italian national rail website at `www.trenitalia.com`, which provides information about travel time and prices.

If you want to take a faster train that stops only at the main stations, like an **Inter City (IC)** (*een*-tehr *see*-tee) or **Euro City (EC)** (*eh*-ooh-roh *see*-tee), you'll need to pay a **supplemento** (soohp-pleh-*mehn*-toh) *(surcharge)*. You can travel in either first class or second class. On some trains, it's a good idea to reserve your seat; on others, a reservation is absolutely required. The faster trains in Italy called **Freccia** (*frech-chah*) — **Frecciarossa** (*frech*-chah-ros-sah), **Frecciaargento** (*frech*-chah-ahr-*jehn*-toh), and **Frecciabianca** (*frech*-chah-*byahn*-kah) — can reach 300+ kilometers per hour). **Italo** (*ee*-tah-loh), is a privately owned company, in contrast to the state-owned Trenitalia, offering services on the high-speed train network. You can buy tickets for **Italo** at their booth inside train stations or at their website (www.italotreno.com/en).

Keep in mind that in Italy, if you have a paper ticket you have to validate it *before* entering **il binario** (eel bee-*nah*-ryoh) *(the platform; the track)*. To make this easy, train stations have validation boxes near the entrance to the platforms. If you purchased your ticket online, make sure to read the instructions on how to validate your electronic ticket on your phone.

# Talkin' the Talk

**PLAY THIS**

Bianca is at the train station in Rome. She goes to an information counter (**ufficio informazioni**) (oohf-*fee*-choh een-fohr-mah-*tsyoh*-nee) to ask about a connection to Perugia. (Track 29)

**Bianca:**    **Ci sono treni diretti per Perugia?**
chee *soh*-noh *treh*-nee dee-*reht*-tee pehr peh-*rooh*-jah
*Are there direct trains to Perugia?*

**Agent:**    **No, deve prendere un treno per Terni.**
noh *deh*-veh *prehn*-deh-reh oohn *treh*-noh pehr *tehr*-nee
*No, you have to take a train to Terni.*

**Bianca:**    **E poi devo cambiare?**
eh poi *deh*-voh kahm-*byah*-reh
*And then do I have to change [trains]?*

**Agent:**    **Sì, prende un locale per Perugia.**
see *prehn*-deh oohn loh-*kah*-leh pehr peh-*rooh*-jah
*Yes, you take a local (slow) train for Perugia.*

**Bianca:**    **A che ora parte il prossimo treno?**
ah keh *oh*-rah *pahr*-teh eel *prohs*-see-moh *treh*-noh
*What time does the next train leave?*

| Agent: | **Alle diciotto e arriva a Terni alle diciannove.** |
| --- | --- |
| | *ahl*-leh dee-*choht*-toh eh ahr-*ree*-vah ah *tehr*-nee *ahl*-leh dee-chahn-*noh*-veh |
| | *At 6 p.m. It arrives in Terni at 7 p.m.* |

| Bianca: | **E per Perugia?** |
| --- | --- |
| | eh pehr peh-*rooh*-jah |
| | *And to Perugia?* |

| Agent: | **C'è subito la coincidenza.** |
| --- | --- |
| | cheh *sooh*-bee-toh lah koh-een-chee-*dehn*-tsah |
| | *There's an immediate connection.* |

After exploring your options, you have to decide and buy a ticket. In the following dialogue, Bianca does just that.

# Talkin' the Talk

**PLAY THIS**

Bianca goes to the ticket counter and buys her ticket. (Track 30)

| Bianca: | **Un biglietto per Perugia, per favore.** |
| --- | --- |
| | oohn bee-*lyeht*-toh pehr peh-*rooh*-jah pehr fah-*voh*-reh |
| | *One ticket to Perugia, please.* |

| Agent: | **Andata e ritorno?** |
| --- | --- |
| | ahn-*dah*-tah eh ree-*tohr*-noh |
| | *Round trip?* |

| Bianca: | **Solo andata. Quanto viene?** |
| --- | --- |
| | *soh*-loh ahn-*dah*-tah *kwahn*-toh *vyeh*-neh |
| | *One-way. How much is it?* |

| Agent: | **In prima classe 30 euro.** |
| --- | --- |
| | een *pree*-mah *klahs*-seh *trehn*-tah *eh*-ooh-roh |
| | *First class is 30 euros.* |

| Bianca: | **E in seconda?** |
| --- | --- |
| | eh een seh-*kohn*-dah |
| | *And second [class]?* |

| Agent: | **Diciotto.** |
| --- | --- |
| | dee-*choht*-toh |
| | *18.* |

*(continued)*

(continued)

| | |
|---|---|
| **Bianca:** | **Seconda classe, per favore.** |
| | seh-*kohn*-dah *klahs*-seh pehr fah-*voh*-reh |
| | *Second class, please.* |
| | |
| | **Da che binario parte?** |
| | dah keh bee-*nah*-ryoh *pahr*-teh |
| | *From which track does it leave?* |
| **Agent:** | **Binario tre.** |
| | bee-*nah*-ryoh treh |
| | *Track 3.* |

## WORDS TO KNOW

| binario [m] | bee-*nah*-ryoh | *platform; track* |
|---|---|---|
| biglietto [m] | bee-*lyeht*-toh | *ticket* |
| andata [f] | ahn-*dah*-tah | *one way* |
| ritorno [m] | ree-*tohr*-noh | *return trip* |
| supplemento [m] | soohp-pleh-*mehn*-toh | *surcharge* |

# Going by bus, tram, or subway

If you don't have a car, the most common ways to get from point A to point B are walking, taking the bus, or — especially in larger cities — riding a bus, tram, or subway. Here we give you the essential Italian vocabulary for these situations.

Some Italian cities have streetcars, or trams, and most have buses. Interestingly, in Italian, the word for tram is **il tram** (eel trahm). The word for bus is **l'autobus** (*lah*-ooh-toh-boohs), or **il bus** (eel boohs). Large buses that travel from one city to another are called **il pullman** (eel *poohl*-mahn) or **la corriera** (lah kohr-*ryeh*-rah).

You can buy bus or tram tickets in Italian bars, **dal giornalaio** (dahl johr-nah-*lah*-yoh) *(at newspaper stands)*, or **dal tabaccaio** (dahl tah-bahk-*kah*-yoh) *(tobacco shop)*. The latter are little shops where you can purchase cigarettes, stamps, and newspapers. You can find them on virtually every street corner in Italy, and they're recognizable by either a black-and-white sign or a blue-and-white sign with a big T on it.

Nowadays many cities and regions also have their own dedicated apps for public transport, where you can find routes and purchase your ticket.

# Talkin' the Talk

Gerardo wants to get to the train station. He's standing at a bus stop but is a little unsure about which bus to take. He asks a man who is also waiting.

| | |
|---|---|
| **Gerardo:** | **Mi scusi.**<br>mee *skooh*-zee<br>*Excuse me.* |
| **Man:** | **Prego?**<br>*preh*-goh<br>*Yes?* |
| **Gerardo:** | **Quest'autobus va alla stazione?**<br>kweh-stah-ooh-toh-boohs vah *ahl*-lah stah-*tsyoh*-neh<br>*Does this bus go to the station?* |
| **Man:** | **Sì.**<br>see<br>*Yes.* |
| **Gerardo:** | **Dove si comprano i biglietti?**<br>*doh*-veh see *kohm*-prah-noh ee bee-*lyeht*-tee<br>*Where can I buy tickets?* |
| **Man:** | **In questo bar.**<br>een *kweh*-stoh bahr<br>*In this bar.* |

You probably want to take the most convenient and fastest means of transportation to reach your final destination. To choose the best option, it helps to know what is available — and sometimes, you can find a kind person to help you out.

# Talkin' the Talk

**PLAY THIS**

Tom, a Canadian tourist, wants to visit the cathedral downtown. He asks about the bus, but a woman advises him to take the subway instead because it takes less time. (There are subways in Turin, Brescia, Milan, Genoa, Rome, Naples, and Catania.) (Track 31)

| | |
|---|---|
| **Tom:** | **Scusi, quale autobus va al Duomo?** |
| | *skooh*-zee *kwah*-leh ah-ooh-*toh*-boohs vah ahl *dwoh*-moh |
| | *Excuse me, which bus goes to the Cathedral?* |
| **Woman:** | **Perché non prende la metropolitana?** |
| | pehr-*keh* nohn *prehn*-deh lah meh-troh-poh-lee-*tah*-nah |
| | *Why don't you take the subway?* |
| **Tom:** | **È meglio?** |
| | eh *meh*-lyoh |
| | *Is it better?* |
| **Woman:** | **Sì, ci mette cinque minuti!** |
| | see chee *meht*-teh *cheen*-kweh mee-*nooh*-tee |
| | *Yes, it takes five minutes!* |
| **Tom:** | **Dov'è la fermata della metropolitana?** |
| | doh-*veh* lah fehr-*mah*-tah *dehl*-lah meh-troh-poh-lee-*tah*-nah |
| | *Where is the subway station?* |
| **Woman:** | **Dietro l'angolo.** |
| | *dyeh*-troh *lahn*-goh-loh |
| | *Around the corner.* |

On the subway, Tom asks a student where he should disembark. Note that he uses the **tu** informal form.

| | |
|---|---|
| **Tom:** | **Scusa, sai qual è la fermata per il Duomo?** |
| | *skooh*-zah sahy kwahl-*eh* lah fehr-*mah*-tah pehr eel *dwoh*-moh |
| | *Excuse me, do you know which is the stop for the Cathedral?* |
| **Student:** | **La prossima fermata.** |
| | lah *pros*-see-mah fehr-*mah*-tah |
| | *The next stop.* |
| **Tom:** | **Grazie!** |
| | *grah*-tsyeh |
| | *Thanks!* |
| **Student:** | **Prego.** |
| | *preh*-goh |
| | *You're welcome.* |

## Reading maps and schedules

You don't need to know much to read a map — just a bit of vocabulary on it. Reading a schedule can be more challenging for travelers because they're written only in Italian. On schedules, you often come across the following words:

- **l'orario** (loh-*rah*-ryoh) *(the timetable)*
- **partenze** (pahr-*tehn*-tseh) *(departures)*
- **arrivi** (ahr-*ree*-vee) *(arrivals)*
- **giorni feriali** (*johr*-nee feh-*ryah*-lee) *(weekdays)*
- **giorni festivi** (*johr*-nee feh-*stee*-vee) *(Sundays and holidays)*
- **il binario** (eel bee-*nah*-ryoh) *(the track; the platform)*

The schedule in Figure 14-1 shows train names, trip duration, and price differences between first and second class.

| DEPARTURE STATION: BOLOGNA (TUTTE LE STAZIONI) | ARRIVAL STATION: ROMA (TUTTE LE STAZIONI) | | | | | | DATE: 19/1/2011 |
|---|---|---|---|---|---|---|---|
| DEPARTURE | ARRIVAL | LENGTH OF JOURNEY | TRAIN NO. | TRAIN CATEGORY | 1ST CLASS* | 2ND CLASS* | SELECT |
| 10:53 BOLOGNA | 13:13 ROMA TE | 02:20 | 9413 FRECCIARGENTO | | 80,00€ | 58,00€ | ● |
| 10:23 BOLOGNA | 12:45 ROMA TE | 02:22 | 9519 FRECCIAROSSA | | 80,00€ | 58,00€ | ● |
| 10:38 BOLOGNA | 12:55 ROMA TE | 02:17 | 9415 FRECCIARGENTO | | 80,00€ | 58,00€ | ● |
| 11:18 BOLOGNA | 15:24 ROMA TE | 04:06 | 589 | IC | 52,00€ | 38,50€ | ● |
| 13:00 BOLOGNA | 15:22 ROMA TE | 02:22 | 9521 FRECCIAROSSA | | 80,00€ | 58,00€ | ● |

**FIGURE 14-1:** Typical Italian train schedule.

Train schedules in Italy list the departure time, train number, and final destination of each train. Under the destination, you'll often see a list of **fermate** (fehr-mah-teh) *(major intermediate stops)* the train makes along the way. This helps you confirm that your stop is on the route.

On arrival boards, the final destination is shown, but the most recent last stop (where the train came from) may also appear to help you identify the incoming train. Keep in mind that arrival and departure **binari** (bee-nah-ree) *(platforms)* are subject to change — so keep an eye on the station's electronic displays or listen for announcements. Finally, don't forget that Europeans don't use a.m. or p.m.; instead, they use a 24-hour clock, also known as military time. That means that 1.00 is the hour after midnight and 13.00 is 1 p.m.

# Leaving Early or Arriving Late

Travel doesn't always go as planned — you might arrive late or early, or you may need to apologize for a delay. The following list includes useful terms to help you communicate in these situations:

>> **essere in anticipo** (*ehs*-seh-reh een ahn-*tee*-chee-poh) *(to be early)*

   **Probabilmente sarò in anticipo.** (proh-bah-beel-*mehn*-teh sah-*roh* een ahn-*tee*-chee-poh) *(I'll probably be early.)*

>> **essere puntuale** (*ehs*-seh-reh poohn-tooh-*ah*-leh) *(to be on time)*

   **L'autobus non è mai puntuale.** (*lah*-ooh-toh-boohs nohn eh mahy poohn-tooh-*ah*-leh) *(The bus is never on time.)*

>> **essere in ritardo** (*ehs*-seh-reh een ree-*tahr*-doh) *(to be late)*

   **L'aereo è in ritardo.** (lah-*eh*-reh-oh eh een ree-*tahr*-doh) *(The plane is late.)*

When talking about being late, you can use the verb **aspettare** (ah-speht-*tah*-reh) *(to wait)*. Here are a few examples of how to use this verb:

>> **Aspetto l'autobus da un'ora.** (ah-*speht*-toh *lah*-ooh-toh-boohs dah oohn-*oh*-rah) *(I've been waiting for the bus for an hour.)*

>> **Aspetta anche lei il ventitré?** (ah-*speht*-tah *ahn*-keh ley eel vehn-tee-*treh*) *(Are you also waiting for the number 23 bus?)*

Note that the verb **aspettare** doesn't require a preposition, unlike the English phrase to wait for. In Italian, to wait for someone, is simply **aspettare qualcuno: Beppe aspetta Tom** (*behp*-peh ah-*speht*-tah Tohm) *(Beppe is waiting for Tom.)*

# FUN & GAMES

What a mess! This schedule is really jumbled. The Italian words for **train, bus stop, train station, track, ticket, one way, return trip,** and **surcharge** are hidden in the following puzzle. If you want to get to your train on time, you have to solve it. Hurry up!! See Appendix C for the answer key.

## Word Seek

| B | S | M | T | A | T | A | M | R | E | F | O |
|---|---|---|---|---|---|---|---|---|---|---|---|
| I | T | U | D | H | G | L | T | X | L | N | C |
| N | S | Y | P | V | X | L | A | B | E | D | G |
| A | P | J | Y | P | B | E | I | R | S | H | D |
| R | K | D | A | J | L | G | T | X | F | X | V |
| I | V | D | U | Y | L | E | M | R | C | D | Q |
| O | I | D | Y | I | K | A | M | G | G | D | R |
| R | Z | J | E | L | X | S | T | E | E | L | K |
| B | C | T | C | P | M | D | Q | A | N | C | I |
| B | T | H | P | R | S | P | U | F | D | T | K |
| O | R | I | T | O | R | N | O | S | O | N | O |
| S | T | A | Z | I | O | N | E | Z | A | G | A |

# Chapter **15**
# Finding a Place to Stay

To really get to know Italians, the Italian language, and to enjoy the Italian lifestyle, you need to travel to Italy. If you're not lucky enough to have Italian friends who can offer you a place to stay, you need to find a hotel — and there are many creative options to choose from. This chapter shows you what to say when asking for a room or checking into a hotel. It also includes a crash course on possessive pronouns and adjectives as well as the imperative (or command) verb tense.

## Choosing a Place to Stay

Do some research about the different places you can stay while you're in Italy and try to find those with an authentic flair to them. There is a broad range of options to suit everyone. You can find conventional three-to-five-star **alberghi** (ahl-*behr*-gee) (*hotels*) and **villaggi turistici** (veel-*laj*-jee tooh-*ree*-stee-chee) (*resorts*) that offer either **mezza pensione** (*mehd*-dzah pehn-*syoh*-neh) (*breakfast plus one other meal*) or **pensione completa** (pehn-*syoh*-neh kohm-*pleh*-tah) (*breakfast, lunch, and dinner included in the price*). Then there are smaller, more personal lodgings, including family-run **bed and breakfasts** (pronounced just the same as in English, but with the rolled **r**), and **pensioni** (pehn-*syoh*-nee) (*small hotels or parts of someone's house where breakfast is usually served*) to mountain **rifugi** (ree-*fooh*-jee) (*mountain lodges that range from spartan to spa quality*), and the increasingly popular **agriturismo** (ah-gree-tooh-*ree*-zmoh) (*farm stay*). You can naturally find a variety of choices — from a single room in an apartment to a villa or even a castle — on sites like Airbnb. And if you're looking for cheaper options, you can always look for an **ostello della gioventù** (oh-*stehl*-loh *dehl*-lah joh-vehn-*too*) (*youth hostel*), but don't forget all of those former monasteries and convents!

# Reserving a Room

When you reserve a room in a hotel, you use the same terms as you do in a restaurant: **prenotare/fare una prenotazione** (preh-noh-*tah*-reh/fah-reh *ooh*-nah preh-noh-tah-*tsyoh*-neh) (*to make a reservation*). You can use either of the synonyms **la camera** (lah *kah*-meh-rah) or **la stanza** (lah *stahn*-tsah) (*the room*). Italian hotel terms may differ from those you're used to, so take a moment to see how to ask for what you need — in Italian.

**La camera singola** (lah *kah*-meh-rah *seen*-goh-lah) is a room with one twin bed, intended for one person. **La camera doppia** (lah *kah*-meh-rah *dohp*-pyah) is a room with two twin beds for two people, and **la camera matrimoniale** (lah *kah*-meh-rah *mah*-tree-moh-*nyah*-leh) has one large bed (usually a queen or king size) for two people.

In Italy, people commonly refer to rooms simply as **una singola, una doppia,** or **una matrimoniale** — everyone understands that you're talking about hotel rooms. Breakfast is generally included in most hotels but ask just to be sure. It's always a good idea to make reservations in advance, especially during **l'alta stagione** (*lahl*-tah stah-*joh*-neh) (*peak season*) — which in Italy typically means the summer months.

**PLAY THIS**

When you're making reservations or staying at a hotel, you may have a few questions about the room and available amenities. You'll likely encounter and use some of these common Italian sentences and phrases. (You can hear these common Italian when planning a trip on Track 33 of the audio files.)

>> **La stanza è con bagno?** (lah *stahn*-tsah eh kohn *bah*-nyoh) (*Does the room have a bathroom?*)

(Even fabulous five-star hotels may have some single rooms without bathrooms, so, ask this question only if you're in a nice hotel if you're asking for a less expensive single.)

>> **Posso avere una stanza con doccia?** (*pohs*-soh ah-*veh*-reh *ooh*-nah *stahn*-tsah kohn *dohch*-chah) (*May I have a room with a shower?*)

>> **Non avete stanze con la vasca?** (nohn ah-*veh*-teh *stahn*-tseh kohn lah *vah*-skah) *(Don't you have rooms with bathtubs?)*

>> **Avete una doppia al primo piano?** (ah-*veh*-teh *ooh*-nah *dohp*-pyah ahl *pree*-moh *pyah*-noh) *(Do you have a double room on the first floor?)*

(Note that this would be the second floor for Americans: Chapter 5 goes into the different floors of a building.)

>> **È una stanza tranquillissima e dà sul giardino.** (eh *ooh*-nah *stahn*-tsah trahn-kweel-*lees*-see-mah eh dah soohl jahr-*dee*-noh) *(The room is very quiet and looks out onto the garden.)*

>> **La doppia viene duecento euro a notte.** (lah *dohp*-pyah *vyeh*-neh *dooh*-eh-*chehn*-toh *eh*-ooh-roh ah *noht*-teh) *(A double room is 200 euros per night.)*

>> **La colazione è compresa?** (lah koh-lah-*tsyoh*-neh eh kohm-*preh*-zah) *(Is breakfast included?)*

>> **Può darmi una camera con aria condizionata?** (pwoh *dahr*-mee *ooh*-nah *kah*-meh-rah kohn *ah*-ryah kohn-dee-tsyoh-*nah*-tah) *(Can you give me a room with air conditioning?)*

>> **Dove sono i suoi bagagli?** (*doh*-veh *soh*-noh ee swoi bah-*gah*-lyee) *(Where is your baggage?)*

>> **Può far portare le mie valigie in camera, per favore?** (pwoh fahr pohr-*tah*-reh leh *mee*-eh vah-*lee*-jeh *een kah*-meh-rah pehr fah-*voh*-reh) *(Would you please have my bags brought to my room?)*

# Talkin' the Talk

Donatella is making reservations for five people. The receptionist tells her that only two double rooms are available, so Donatella has to figure out how to accommodate all five guests.

| | |
|---|---|
| **Donatella:** | **Buonasera.**<br>*bwoh*-nah-*seh*-rah<br>*Good evening.* |
| **Receptionist:** | **Buonasera, prego.**<br>*bwoh*-nah-seh-*rah preh*-goh<br>*Good evening, can I help you?* |
| **Donatella:** | **Avete stanze libere?**<br>ah-*veh*-teh *stahn*-tseh *lee*-beh-reh<br>*Do you have any rooms available?* |

*(continued)*

*(continued)*

| | | |
|---|---|---|
| **Receptionist:** | **Non ha la prenotazione?** | |
| | nohn ah lah preh-noh-tah-*tsyoh*-neh | |
| | *You don't have a reservation?* | |
| **Donatella:** | **Eh, no. . .** | |
| | eh noh | |
| | *No. . .* | |
| **Receptionist:** | **Abbiamo soltanto due doppie.** | |
| | ahb-*byah*-moh sohl-*tahn*-toh *dooh*-eh *dohp*-pyeh | |
| | *We have just two double rooms.* | |
| **Donatella:** | **Non c'è una stanza con tre letti?** | |
| | nohn cheh *ooh*-nah *stahn*-tsah kohn treh *leht*-tee | |
| | *Isn't there a room with three beds?* | |
| **Receptionist:** | **Possiamo aggiungere un letto.** | |
| | pohs-*syah*-moh ahj-*joohn*-jeh-reh oohn *leht*-toh | |
| | *We can add a bed.* | |
| **Donatella:** | **Benissimo, grazie.** | |
| | beh-*nees*-see-moh *grah*-tsyeh | |
| | *Very well, thank you.* | |

# WORDS TO KNOW

| | | |
|---|---|---|
| **aria condizionata [f]** | *ah*-ryah kohn-dee-tsyoh-*nah*-tah | *air conditioning/ conditioner* |
| **camera [f]/stanza [f]** | *kah*-meh-rah/*stahn*-tsah | *room* |
| **camera singola [f]** | *kah*-meh-rah *seen*-goh-lah | *single room* |
| **camera doppia [f]** | *kah*-meh-rah *dohp*-pyah | *room with two twin beds* |
| **camera matrimoniale [f]** | *kah*-meh-rah mah-tree-moh-*nyah*-leh | *room with a queen/ king size bed* |
| **colazione [f]** | koh-lah-*tsyoh*-neh | *breakfast* |
| **culla [f]** | *koohl*-lah | *crib* |
| **letto supplementare [m]** | *leht*-toh soohp-pleh-mehn-*tah*-reh | *extra bed* |

| servizio in camera [m] | sehr-*vee*-tsyoh een *kah*-meh-rah | *room service* |
|---|---|---|
| mezza pensione [f] | *mehd*-dzah pehn-*syoh*-neh | *half board* |
| pensione completa [f] | pehn-*syoh*-neh kohm-*pleh*-tah | *full board* |
| servizio sveglia [m] | sehr-*vee*-tsyoh *zveh*-lyah | *wake–up call* |

# Checking In

Registering at an Italian hotel isn't as difficult as you might imagine. However, you should expect the person at the front desk to ask for **un documento** (oohn doh-kooh-*mehn*-toh), such as a passport. They might even want to hang on to it for a few hours — but don't worry, you'll get it back!

## Settling in for your hotel stay

Many rooms come with items like **una cassaforte** (*ooh*-nah *kahs*-sah-*fohr*-teh) (*a safe*) for your valuables and **un frigorifero** (oohn free-goh-*ree*-feh-roh) (*a refrigerator*). You might also need **un fon** (oohn fohn) (*a blow dryer*). In these instances, you can ask **l'addetto alla reception** (lahd-*deht*-toh *ahl*-lah reception) (*the receptionist*), **il portiere** (eel pohr-*tyeh*-reh) (*the door attendant*), or the **servizio di pulizia** (sehr-*vee*-tsyoh dee poo-*lee*-tsyah) (*housekeeping*) for what you need. The following phrases can help you make those requests:

>> **Non trovo l'asciugacapelli/il fon.** (nohn *troh*-voh lah-shooh-gah-kah-*pehl*-lee/eel fohn) (*I can't find the hair dryer.*)

>> **Manca la carta igenica.** (*mahn*-kah lah *kahr*-tah ee-*jeh*-nee-kah) (*There is no toilet paper.*)

>> **È ancora aperto il bar?** (eh ahn-*koh*-rah ah-*pehr*-toh eel bahr) (*Is the bar still open?*)

>> **Vorrei un'altra coperta per favore.** (vohr-*rey* oohn-*ahl*-trah koh-*pehr*-tah pehr fah-*voh*-reh) (*I'd like one more blanket please.*)

>> **Dov'è la farmacia più vicina?** (doh-*veh* lah fahr-mah-*chee*-ah pyooh vee-*chee*-nah) (*Where is the closest pharmacy?*)

>> **Vorrei la sveglia domattina.** (vohr-*rey* lah *zveh*-lyah doh-maht-*tee*-nah) *(I'd like to get a wake-up call tomorrow morning.)*

>> **C'è un telefono nella mia stanza?** (cheh oohn teh-*leh*-foh-noh *nehl*-lah *mee*-ah *stahn*-tsah) *(Is there a telephone in my room?)*

Don't forget to say **scusi** (*skooh*–zee) *(excuse me)* and **per favore** (pehr–fah–*voh*–reh) *(please)!*

REMEMBER

## Requesting something during your stay

GRAMMATICALLY
SPEAKING

If you want another of something, notice that you write the feminine form **un'altra** (oohn–*ahl*–trah) differently than the masculine **un altro** (oohn *ahl*-troh). For feminine words that begin with a vowel, the indefinite article **un** requires an apostrophe; masculine words don't. Again, this rule applies to all feminine words that begin with a vowel after the indefinite article **un** (*a/an* in English). Masculine words do not take the apostrophe, even if they begin with a vowel.

The following list contains more words you may find useful during a hotel stay:

>> **fazzolettino di carta** (faht-tsoh-leht-*tee*-noh dee *kahr*-tah) *(tissue)*

>> **lettino** (leht-*tee*-noh) *(cot)*

>> **negozio di articoli da regalo** (neh-*goh*-tsyoh dee ahr-*tee*-koh-lee dah reh-*gah*-loh) *(gift shop)*

>> **parrucchiere** (pahr-roohk-*kyeh*-reh) *(hairdresser)*

>> **portacenere** (pohr-tah-*cheh*-neh-reh) *(ashtray)*

>> **piscina** (pee-*shee*-nah) *(swimming pool)*

## Talkin' the Talk

PLAY THIS

Mr. Baricco arrives at the hotel where he made reservations two weeks ago. He walks up to the receptionist. (Track 32)

Sig. Baricco: **Buonasera, ho una stanza prenotata.**
*bwoh*-nah-*seh*-rah oh *ooh*-nah *stahn*-tsah preh-noh-*tah*-tah
*Good evening, I have a reservation.*

Receptionist: **Il suo nome, prego?**
eel *sooh*-oh *noh*-meh *preh*-goh
*Your name, please?*

*(continued)*

| **Sig. Baricco:** | **Baricco.** |
| | bah-*reek*-koh |
| | *Baricco.* |

**Sig. Baricco:** **Baricco.**
bah-*reek*-koh
*Baricco.*

**Receptionist:** **Sì, una singola per due notti.**
see *ooh*-nah *seen*-goh-lah pehr *dooh*-eh *noht*-tee
*Yes, a single (room) for two nights.*

**Receptionist:** **Mi può dare per favore il passaporto e la carta di credito per le spese accessorie?**
mee pwoh *dah*-re pehr fah-*voh*-reh eel pahs-sah-*pohr*-toh eh lah *kahr*-tah dee *kreh*-dee-toh pehr leh *speh*-zeh ach-ches-*soh*-ryeh
*May I please have your passport and credit card for incidental charges?*

**Sig. Baricco:** **Certo.**
*chehr*-toh
*Sure.*

**Receptionist:** **Grazie. Bene . . . la sua chiave. È la stanza numero quarantadue al quarto piano.**
*grah*-tsyeh *beh*-neh lah *sooh*-ah *kyah*-veh eh lah *stahn*-tsah *nooh*-meh-roh kwah-*rahn*-tah-*dooh*-eh ahl *kwahr*-toh *pyah*-noh
*Thank you. Very good . . . here is your key. It's room number forty-two, fourth floor.*

**Sig. Baricco:** **Grazie. A che ora è la colazione?**
*grah*-tsyeh ah keh *oh*-rah eh lah koh-lah-*tsyoh*-neh
*Thank you. What time is breakfast?*

**Receptionist:** **Dalle sette alle nove.**
*dahl*-leh *seht*-teh *ahl*-leh *noh*-veh
*From seven till nine.*

**Sig. Baricco:** **Grazie. Buonanotte.**
*grah*-tsyeh *bwoh*-nah-*noht*-teh
*Thank you. Good-night.*

**Receptionist:** **Buonanotte.**
*bwoh*-nah-*noht*-teh
*Good-night.*

<table>
<tr><td colspan="3"><h2>WORDS TO KNOW</h2></td></tr>
<tr><td>avete</td><td>ah-veh-teh</td><td>do you (pl) have</td></tr>
<tr><td>dov'è</td><td>doh-veh</td><td>where is</td></tr>
<tr><td>dove sono</td><td>doh-veh soh-noh</td><td>where are</td></tr>
<tr><td>Può ripetere per favore?</td><td>pwoh ree-peh-teh-reh pehr fah-voh-reh</td><td>Could you repeat that please?</td></tr>
<tr><td>saldare il conto</td><td>sahl-dah-reh eel kohn-toh</td><td>to check out</td></tr>
<tr><td>indirizzo [m]</td><td>een-dee-reet-tsoh</td><td>address</td></tr>
</table>

Table 15-1 shows the singular and plural form of several hotel–related words along with their proper articles. For more on singular and plural articles and nouns, see Chapter 2.

**TABLE 15-1**   **Making Plurals**

| Singular Plural | Pronunciation | Translation |
| --- | --- | --- |
| **la cameriera/le cameriere** | lah kah-meh-ryeh-rah leh kah-meh-ryeh-reh | *chambermaid, chambermaids/ waitress, waitresses* |
| **il bagno/i bagni** | eel bah-nyoh ee bah-nyee | *bathroom/bathrooms* |
| **la chiave/le chiavi** | lah kyah-veh leh kyah-vee | *key/keys* |
| **il cameriere/i camerieri** | eel kah-meh-ryeh-reh ee kah-meh-ryeh-ree | *waiter/waiters* |
| **lo specchio/gli specchi** | loh spehk-kyoh lyee spehk-kyee | *mirror/mirrors* |
| **l'albergo/gli alberghi** | lahl-behr-goh lyee ahl-behr-gee | *hotel/hotels* |
| **la stanza/le stanze** | lah stahn-tsah leh stahn-tseh | *room/rooms* |
| **la camera/le camere** | lah kah-meh-rah leh kah-meh-reh | *room/rooms* |
| **la persona/le persone** | lah pehr-soh-nah leh pehr-soh-neh | *person/persons* |
| **il letto/i letti** | eel leht-toh ee leht-tee | *bed/beds* |
| **la notte/le notti** | lah noht-teh leh noht-tee | *night/nights* |
| **l'entrata/le entrate** | lehn-trah-tah leh ehn-trah-teh | *entrance/entrances, lobby* |

As we discuss in Chapter 2, a pronoun is a word that takes the place of a noun. For example, when you say *"Marco goes home,"* you can replace the name Marco with the personal or subject pronoun "he." Sometimes, a pronoun doesn't just replace a noun — it also shows ownership. For instance, in the sentence *"My bag is red and yours is black,"* the word yours is a possessive pronoun. It stands in for *"your bag"* and tells you who the bag belongs to.

# Yours, Mine, and Ours: Possessive Adjectives and Pronouns

Possessive pronouns (such as mine, yours, his) show ownership of something — usually a noun. In Italian, pronouns change based on the gender and number of the thing that is owned. The possessive pronoun must agree with the item it refers to, not with the owner. Unlike in English, Italian almost always uses the definite article in front of the possessive. These articles are **il, la, i,** and **le.**

Table 15-2 lists possessive adjectives and pronouns with their articles.

**TABLE 15-2**    **Possessive Adjectives and Pronouns**

| Possessive Pronoun | Masculine Singular | Feminine Singular | Masculine Plural | Feminine Plural | Pronunciation |
|---|---|---|---|---|---|
| my/mine | **il mio** | **la mia** | **i miei** | **le mie** | eel *mee*-oh/lah *mee*-ah/ee *myay*/leh *mee*-eh |
| your/yours | **il tuo** | **la tua** | **i tuoi** | **le tue** | eel *tooh*-oh/lah *tooh*-ah/ee *twohy*/leh *tooh*-eh |
| his/her/hers | **il suo** | **la sua** | **i suoi** | **le sue** | eel *sooh*-oh/lah *sooh*-ah/ee *swohy*/le *sooh*-eh |
| your/yours (formal) | **il suo** | **la sua** | **i suoi** | **le sue** | eel *sooh*-oh/lah *sooh*-ah/ee *swohy*/le *sooh*-eh |
| our/ours | **il nostro** | **la nostra** | **i nostri** | **le nostre** | eel *noh*-stroh/lah *noh*-strah/ee *noh*-stree/leh *noh*-streh |
| your/yours | **il vostro** | **la vostra** | **i vostri** | **le vostre** | eel *voh*-stroh/lah *voh*-strah/ee *voh*-stree/leh *voh*-streh |
| their/theirs | **il loro** | **la loro** | **i loro** | **le loro** | eel/lah/ee/leh *loh*-roh |

Following are some practical examples using possessive adjectives and pronouns:

>> **È grande la vostra stanza?** (eh *grahn*-deh lah *voh*-strah *stahn*-tsah) *(Is your room big?* — speaking to more than one person)

>> **Dov'è il tuo albergo?** (doh-*veh* eel *tooh*-oh ahl-*behr*-goh) *(Where is your hotel?)*

>> **Ecco i vostri documenti.** (*ehk*-koh ee *voh*-stree doh-kooh-*mehn*-tee) *(Here are your documents* — plural)

>> **Questa è la sua chiave.** (*kweh*-stah eh lah *sooh*-ah *kyah*-veh) *(This is your [formal] key.)* and also *(This is his/her key.)*

>> **La mia camera è molto tranquilla.** (lah *mee*-ah *kah*-meh-rah eh *mohl*-toh trahn-*kweel*-lah) *(My room is very quiet.)*

>> **Anche la nostra. E la tua?** (*ahn*-keh lah *noh*-strah eh lah *tooh*-ah) *(Ours, too. And yours?* [speaking to one person])

# Talkin' the Talk

You use possessive adjectives and pronouns all the time, so you need to know how to use them. In the following dialogue, family members are trying to sort out whose luggage is whose.

| Mamma: | **Dove sono i vostri bagagli?** |
| | *doh*-veh *soh*-noh ee *voh*-stree bah-*gah*-lyee |
| | *Where are your bags?* |

| Michela: | **Il mio è questo.** |
| | eel *mee*-oh eh *kweh*-stoh |
| | *Mine is this one.* |

| Mamma: | **E il tuo, Carla?** |
| | eh eel *tooh*-oh *kahr*-lah |
| | *And yours, Carla?* |

| Carla: | **Lo porta Giulio.** |
| | loh *pohr*-tah *jooh*-lyoh |
| | *Giulio is carrying it.* |

*(continued)*

|  |  |
|---|---|
| **Mamma:** | **No, Giulio porta il suo.**<br>noh *jooh*-lyoh *pohr*-tah eel *sooh*-oh<br>*No, Giulio is carrying his.* |
| **Carla:** | **Giulio, hai il mio bagaglio?**<br>*jooh*-lyoh ahy eel *mee*-oh bah-*gah*-lyoh<br>*Giulio, do you have my bag?* |
| **Giulio:** | **No, questi sono i miei!**<br>noh *kweh*-stee *soh*-noh ee myay<br>*No, these are mine!* |
| **Carla:** | **Sei sicuro?**<br>say see-*kooh*-roh<br>*Are you sure?* |
| **Giulio:** | **Com'è la tua valigia?**<br>koh-*meh* lah *tooh*-ah vah-*lee*-jah<br>*What does your suitcase look like?* |
| **Carla:** | **È rossa.**<br>eh *rohs*-sah<br>*It's red.* |

## WORDS TO KNOW

| | | |
|---|---|---|
| **bagaglio [m]** | bah-*gah*-lyoh | *baggage* |
| **cameriera [f]** | kah-meh-*ryeh*-rah | *chambermaid, waitress* |
| **garage [m]** | gah-*rahj* | *car park, garage* |
| **messaggio [m]** | mehs-*sahj*-joh | *message* |
| **portiere [m]** | pohr-*tyeh*-reh | *doorman* |
| **valigia [f]** | vah-*lee*-jah | *suitcase* |

# Speaking with Authority: The Imperative

When your boss says, **Venga nel mio ufficio!** (*vehn*-gah nehl *mee*-oh oohf-*fee*-choh) (*Come into my office!*) or you say to your children, **Mettete in ordine le vostre camere!** (meht-*teh*-teh een *ohr*-dee-neh leh *voh*-streh *kah*-meh-reh) (*Clean up your rooms!*), you're using an imperative — a request, a demand, or an invitation for someone to do something. This is how it works:

» **Singular informal:** You give a command or speak informally to one person — for example, a friend or a family member. In Italian, if a verb ends in **-are,** as in **mandare** (mahn-*dah*-reh) *(to send),* the informal imperative ends in **-a,** as in **Manda!** (*mahn*-dah) *(Send!).* If a verb ends in **-ere** or **-ire,** as in **prendere** (*prehn*-deh-reh) *(to take),* **aprire** (ah-*pree*-reh) *(to open),* and **finire** (fee-*nee*-reh) *(to finish),* the informal imperative ends in **-i,** as in **Prendi!** (*prehn*-dee) *(Take!),* **Apri!** (ah-*pree*) *(Open!),* and **Finisci!** (fee-*nee*-shee) *(Finish!).*

» **Singular formal:** You give a command or speak formally to one person — for example, someone you don't know well or in a formal situation. If the verb ends in **-are,** as in **mandare,** the formal imperative form ends in **-i,** as in **Mandi!** (*mahn*-dee) *(Send!).* If the verb ends in **-ere** or **-ire,** as in **prendere, aprire,** and **finire,** the formal imperative ends in **-a,** as in **Prenda!** (*prehn*-dah) *(Take!),* **Apra!** *(Open!),* and **Finisca!** (fee-*nee*-skah) *(Finish!).* As you can see, the informal and formal endings are essentially reversed.

» **Plural informal:** You use this form for two or more people. Verbs that end in **-are,** like **mandare,** have the plural imperative ending **-ate,** as in **Mandate!** (mahn-*dah*-teh) *(Send!).* Verbs that end in **-ere** change their endings to **-ete,** as in **Prendete!** (*prehn*-deh-teh) *(Take!).* Verbs that end in **-ire** change their endings to **-ite,** as in **Finite!** (fee-*nee*-teh) *(Finish!).*

» **Plural formal:** You use this form when speaking to two or more people in a formal situation. Verbs that end in **-are,** like **mandare,** have the plural formal imperative ending **-ino,** as in **Mandino!** (mahn-*dee*-noh) *(Send!).* Verbs that end in **-ere** or **-ire** change their endings to **-ano,** as in **Prendano!** (*prehn*-dah-noh) *(Take!),* **Partano!** (pahr-*tah*-noh) *(Leave!),* and **Finiscano!** (fee-*nee*-skah-noh) *(Finish!).*

» **Plural, including yourself:** You include yourself in the command by saying, for example, "Let's go!"

Good news! All verbs — including our examples **mandare, prendere,** and **finire** — change their endings to the imperative ending **-iamo** — namely, **Mandiamo!** (mahn-*dyah*-moh) *(Let's send!),* **Prendiamo!** (prehn-*dyah*-moh) *(Let's take/have!),* and **Finiamo!** (fee-*nyah*-moh) *(Let's finish!).* That's pretty easy, isn't it?

In case you're still struggling to grasp the pattern, Table 15-3 gives a quick overview.

**TABLE 15-3**     ## Imperative Verb Endings

| Form | -are verbs as in mandare *(to send)* | -ere verbs as in prendere *(to take)* | -ire verbs as in aprire *(to open)* | -ire (-isc) verbs as in finire *(to finish)* |
|---|---|---|---|---|
| Informal "you sing." | mand-**a** (send) | prend-**i** (take) | apr-**i** (open) | fin-**isci** (finish) |
| Formal "you sing." | mand-**i** (send) | prend-**a** (take) | apr-**a** (open) | fin-**isca** (finish) |
| Informal "you pl." | mand-**ate** (send) | prend-**ete** (take) | apr-**ite** (open) | fin-**ite** (finish) |
| Formal "you pl." | mand-**ino** (send) | prend-**ano** (take) | apr-**ano** (open) | fin-**iscano** (finish) |
| "We as in Let's. . ." | mand-**iamo** (let's send) | prend-**iamo** (let's take) | apr-**iamo** (let's open) | fin-**iamo** (let's finish) |

We can't let you get away without looking at some common exceptions to the preceding rules. Table 15-4 highlights a few verbs that don't follow the regular pattern.

**TABLE 15-4**     ## Exceptional Imperatives

| Informal Singular | Formal Singular | Translation |
|---|---|---|
| **Abbi pazienza!** (*ahb*-bee pah-*tsyehn*-tsah) | **Abbia pazienza!** (*ahb*-byah pah-*tsyehn*-tsah) | *Be patient!* (Literally, have patience) |
| **Da'!** (dah) | **Dia!** (*dee*-ah) | *Give!* |
| **Di' qualcosa!** (dee kwahl-*koh*-zah) | **Dica qualcosa!** (*dee*-kah kwahl-*koh*-zah) | *Say something!* |
| **Fa' qualcosa!** (fah kwahl-*koh*-zah) | **Faccia qualcosa!** (*fahch*-chah kwahl-*koh*-zah) | *Do something!* |
| **Sii buono!** (see *bwoh*-noh) | **Sia buono!** (*see*-ah *bwoh*-noh) | *Be good!* |
| **Sta' fermo!** (stah *fehr*-moh) | **Stia fermo!** (*stee*-ah *fehr*-moh) | *Be still!* |
| **Stai tranquillo!** (stai trahn-*kweel*-loh) | **Stia tranquillo** (*stee*-ah trahn-*kweel*-loh) | *Be calm! Don't worry!* |
| **Va via!** (vah *vee*-ah) | **Vada via!** (*vah*-dah *vee*-ah) | *Go away!* |
| **Vieni qua!** (*vyeh*-nee kwah) | **Venga qua!** (*vehn*-gah kwah) | *Come here!* |

We haven't even gotten to negative commands yet (and if you want more on commands, see *Italian Verbs For Dummies* by Teresa [John Wiley & Sons, Inc.]), but here are two phrases you may hear in Italy:

>> **Non ti preoccupare!** (nohn tee preh-ohk-kooh-*pah*-reh) *(Don't worry!)* (informal)

>> **Non si preoccupi!** (nohn see preh-*ohk*-kooh-pee) *(Don't worry!)* (formal)

# FUN & GAMES

Unscramble the following words below and then match them with their definitions in the following column. See Appendix C for the answer key.

| | |
|---|---|
| gorblea | bed |
| oinpnsee | hotel |
| rcaaem | luggage |
| asznat | suitcases |
| gilevia | room |
| aneoepozirtn | bathroom |
| tnloaireimma | room |
| lcaul | small hotel |
| cniapsi | crib |
| aehicv | pool |
| ttelo | key |
| ricmeeaer | room with a large bed |
| bgoan | reservation |
| ggbalaoi | waiter |

# Chapter **16**
# Handling Emergencies

Asking for help is never fun — after all you only need help when you're in a tough spot. This chapter helps you think about the kinds of unfortunate situations you might face or could encounter. Some may be minor inconveniences, and others could be far more serious. What follows are the language tools you need to communicate your troubles to those who can assist you.

## Asking for Help: A Quick Overview

Here is a general sampling of asking-for-help sentences. The first three are good for any kind of emergencies:

» **Aiuto!** (ah-*yooh*-toh) *(Help!)*

» **Aiutami!** (ah-*yooh*-tah-mee) *(Help me!)* (Informal)

» **Mi aiuti, per favore.** (mee ah-*yooh*-tee pehr fah-*voh*-reh) *(Help me, please.)* (Formal)

» **Chiamate la polizia!** (kyah-*mah*-teh lah poh-lee-*tsee*-ah) *(Call the police!)*

» **Ho bisogno di un medico.** (oh bee-*zoh*-nyoh dee oohn *meh*-dee-koh) *(I need a doctor.)*

>> **Dov'è il pronto soccorso?** (doh-*veh* eel *prohn*-toh *sohk*-kohr-*soh*) *(Where's the emergency room?)*

>> **Chiamate un'ambulanza!** (kyah-*mah*-teh ooh-nahm-booh-*lahn*-tsah) *(Call an ambulance!)*

**REMEMBER**

As you may have noticed, sentences directed at a group of people are conjugated using the voi form — for example, **chiamate** *(you call)*. In an emergency situation, you can use this form with anyone who may be listening to you.

In some situations, you may need to ask for a competent authority who speaks English. You can do so by saying:

>> **Mi scusi, parla inglese?** (mee *skooh*-zee *pahr*-lah een-*gleh*-zeh) *(Excuse me, do you speak English?)*

>> **C'è un medico che parli inglese?** (cheh oohn *meh*-dee-koh keh *pahr*-lee een-*gleh*-zeh) *(Is there a doctor who speaks English?)*

>> **Dove posso trovare un avvocato che parli inglese?** (*doh*-veh *pohs*-soh troh-*vah*-reh oohn ahv-voh-*kah*-toh keh *pahr*-lee een-*gleh*-zeh) *(Where can I find a lawyer who speaks English?)*

If you can't find a professional who speaks English, you may be able to find **un interprete** (oohn een-*tehr*-preh-teh) *(an interpreter)* to help you.

# Talking to Doctors

When you're in **l'ospedale** (loh-speh-*dah*-leh) *(the hospital)* or at **il medico** (eel *meh*-dee-koh) *(the doctor)*, you need to explain where it hurts or what the problem is. Doing so isn't always easy, because simply pointing to a spot may not be enough. But don't worry, we won't leave you in the lurch. This section shows you, among other things, how to refer to body parts in Italian (in Table 16-1) and what to say in a medical emergency.

**TABLE 16-1**

**Basic Body Parts**

| Italian | Pronunciation | Translation |
| --- | --- | --- |
| **il braccio** | eel *brahch*-choh | *the arm* |
| **il collo** | eel *kohl*-loh | *the neck* |
| **la gamba** | lah *gahm*-bah | *the leg* |

| Italian | Pronunciation | Translation |
| --- | --- | --- |
| **la mano** | lah *mah*-noh | *the hand* |
| **l'occhio** | *lohk*-kyoh | *the eye* |
| **la pancia** | lah *pahn*-chah | *the belly* |
| **il petto** | eel *peht*-toh | *the chest* |
| **il piede** | eel *pyeh*-deh | *the foot* |
| **lo stomaco** | loh *stoh*-mah-koh | *the stomach* |
| **la testa** | lah *teh*-stah | *the head* |

# Describing what ails you

The following phrases show how to say that something hurts. There are two ways to say this. The first uses the construction **fare male** (*fah*–reh *mah*–leh) *(to hurt)*. Use **fa** (fah) when referring to a singular body part that hurts:

>> **Mi fa male la gamba.** (mee fah *mah*-leh lah *gahm*-bah) *(My leg hurts.)*

>> **Mi fa male lo stomaco.** (mee fah *mah*-leh loh *stoh*-mah-koh) *(My stomach hurts.)*

>> **Mi fa male tutto il corpo.** (mee fah *mah*-leh *tooht*-toh eel *kohr*-poh) *(My whole body aches.)*

**TIP**

Use **fanno** (*fahn*–noh) when referring to more than one body part that hurts:

**Mi fanno male gli occhi.** (mee *fahn*-noh *mah*-leh lyee *ohk*-kee) *(My eyes hurt.)*

The other way to say that something hurts is with **avere mal di . . .** (ah–*veh*–reh mahl dee) followed by the body part; remember to conjugate the verb **avere** (ah–*veh*–reh) *(to have)* according to who is experiencing the pain. Here are some examples:

>> **Ho mal di schiena.** (oh mahl dee *skyeh*-nah) *(I have a backache.)*

>> **Ho mal di testa.** (oh mahl dee *teh*-stah) *(I have a headache.)*

>> **Mia figlia ha mal di denti.** (*mee*-ah *feel*-yah ah mahl dee *dehn*-tee) *(My daughter has a toothache.)*

There are still other ways to describe what ails you and explain your symptoms:

>> **Mi sono rotto/a una gamba.** (mee *soh*-noh *roht*-toh/ah *ooh*-nah *gahm*-bah) *(I broke my leg.)* (Use the feminine participle ending in **-a** if you're a woman.)

>> **Ho mal di gola.** (oh mahl dee *goh*-lah) *(I have a sore throat.)*

>> **Ho la pelle irritata.** (oh lah *pehl*-leh ee-ree-*tah*-tah) *(My skin is irritated.)*

>> **Mi sono storto/a il piede/la caviglia.** (mee *soh*-noh *stohr*-toh/ah eel *pyeh*-deh/lah kah-*vee*-lyah) *(I sprained my foot/ankle.)*

>> **Ho disturbi al cuore.** (oh dee-*stoohr*-bee ahl *kwoh*-reh) *(I have heart problems.)*

>> **Mi bruciano gli occhi.** (mee *brooh*-chah-noh lyee *ohk*-kee) *(My eyes burn.)*

>> **Mi sono slogato/a la spalla.** (mee *soh*-noh zloh-*gah*-toh/ah lah *spahl*-lah) *(I dislocated my shoulder.)*

>> **Mi sono fatto/a male alla mano.** (mee *soh*-noh *faht*-toh/ah *mah*-leh *ahl*-lah *mah*-noh). *(I hurt my hand.)*

>> **Sono caduto/a.** (*soh*-noh kah-*dooh*-toh/ah) *(I fell.)*

>> **Mia figlia ha questo brutto sfogo.** (*mee*-ah *fee*-lyah ah *qweh*-stoh *brooht*-toh *sfoh*-goh) *(My daughter has this terrible rash.)*

>> **Mio figlio ha la febbre a 40 C°.** (*mee*-oh *fee*-lyoh ah lah *fehb*-breh ah kwah-*rahn*-tah) *(My son has a temperature of 104 degrees.)*

REMEMBER

When you want to indicate a left or right body part, you need to know the gender of that body part. For a masculine nouns, use **destro** (*deh*–stroh) for right and **sinistro** (see–*nee*–stroh) for left. For a feminine noun you change the ending to **destra** (*deh*–strah) and **sinistra** (see–*nee*–strah).

GRAMMATICALLY
SPEAKING

Another small hurdle is that many body parts have irregular plural forms. Table 16-2 shows you some of the most common irregular plural forms.

**TABLE 16-2**

## Body Parts Plurals

| Singular (Pronunciation) | Plural (Pronunciation) | Translation |
| --- | --- | --- |
| **il braccio** (eel *brahch*-choh) | **le braccia** (leh *brahch*-chah) | *arm(s)* |
| **il dito** (eel *dee*-toh) | **le dita** (leh *dee*-tah) | *finger(s)* |
| **il dito del piede** (eel *dee*-toh dehl *pyeh*-deh) | **le dita del piede** (leh *dee*-tah dehl *pyeh*-deh) | *toe(s)* |

| Singular (Pronunciation) | Plural (Pronunciation) | Translation |
| --- | --- | --- |
| **il labbro** (eel *lahb*-broh) | **le labbra** (leh *lahb*-brah) | *lip(s)* |
| **il ginocchio** (eel jee-*nohk*-kyoh) | **le ginocchia** (leh jee-*nohk*-kyah) | *knee(s)* |
| **la mano** (lah *mah*-noh) | **le mani** (leh *mah*-nee) | *hand(s)* |
| **l'orecchio** (loh-*rehk*-kyoh) | **le orecchie** (leh oh-*rehk*-kyeh) | *ear(s)* |
| **l'osso** (*lohs*-soh) | **le ossa** (leh *ohs*-sah) | *bone(s)* |

Generally speaking, if you need to tell someone that you're not feeling well, you can always say **mi sento male** (mee *sehn*-toh *mah*-leh) (*I feel sick*), which comes from the expression **sentirsi male** (sehn-*teer*-see *mah*-leh) (*to feel sick*). You can also say **non mi sento bene** (nohn mee *sehn*-toh *beh*-neh) (*I don't feel well*), which comes from **non sentirsi bene** (nohn sehn-*teer*-see *beh*-neh) (*to not feel well*). The following shows you the conjugation of this common reflexive verb. For more on reflexive verbs, see Chapter 11.

| Conjugation | Pronunciation | English |
| --- | --- | --- |
| **mi sento male** | mee *sehn*-toh *mah*-leh | *I feel sick* |
| **ti senti male** | tee *sehn*-tee *mah*-leh | *you feel sick* |
| **si sente male** | see *sehn*-teh *mah*-leh | *he/she feels sick, you feel sick* [formal] |
| **ci sentiamo male** | chee sehn-*tyah*-moh *mah*-leh | *we feel sick* |
| **vi sentite male** | vee sehn-*tee*-teh *mah*-leh | *you feel sick* |
| **si sentono male** | see *sehn*-toh-noh *mah*-leh | *they feel sick* |

You may have noticed that **fa male** is preceded by **mi** (mee) (*me*). This word changes according to the speaker and the person who feels the pain. A doctor may ask you **Cosa le fa male?** (*koh*-zah leh fah *mah*-leh) (*What hurts you?*). **Le** is the indirect object pronoun for the formal "you."

Gloria goes to the doctor because her leg is swollen. However, without further examination, the doctor can't determine the cause of the problem. (Track 33)

| | | |
|---|---|---|
| **Gloria:** | **Mi fa molto male questa gamba.** | |
| | mee fah *mohl*-toh *mah*-leh *kweh*-stah *gahm*-bah | |
| | *My leg really hurts.* | |
| **Doctor:** | **Vedo che è gonfia.** | |
| | *veh*-doh keh eh *gohn*-fyah | |
| | *I can see that it's swollen.* | |
| **Gloria:** | **Devo andare all'ospedale?** | |
| | *deh*-voh ahn-*dah*-reh ahl-loh-speh-*dah*-leh | |
| | *Do I need to go to the hospital?* | |
| **Doctor:** | **Sì, bisogna fare le lastre.** | |
| | see bee-*zoh*-nyah *fah*-reh le *lah*-streh | |
| | *Yes, you'll need to have some X-rays.* | |

## WORDS TO KNOW

| | | |
|---|---|---|
| **aiuto [m]** | ah-*yooh*-toh | *help* |
| **pronto soccorso [m]** | *prohn*-toh sohk-*kohr*-soh | *emergency room* |
| **un'ambulanza [f]** | oohn-ahm-booh-*lahn*-tsah | *an ambulance* |
| **chiamate** | kyah-*mah*-teh | *call (you, pl. informal)* |
| **fare male** | *fah*-reh *mah*-leh | *to hurt* |
| **ospedale [m]** | oh-speh-*dah*-leh | *hospital* |
| **lastre [f/pl.]** | *lah*-streh | *X-rays* |
| **sinistro** | see-*nee*-strah/troh | *left* |
| **destro** | *deh*-stroh | *right* |
| **gonfio** | *gohn*-fyah/oh | *swollen* |
| **muscolo [m]** | *mooh*-skoh-loh | *muscle* |
| **tendine [m]** | *tehn*-dee-neh | *tendon* |

| mi gira la testa | mee *jee*-rah lah *teh*-stah | *I'm dizzy* |
|---|---|---|
| mi sento svenire | *mee*-sehn-toh zveh-*nee*-reh | *I'm about to faint* |
| avere mal di . . . | ah-*veh*-reh mahl dee | *to have a ___ache* |
| stomaco [m] | *stoh*-mah-koh | *stomach* |
| febbre [f] | *fehb*-breh | *fever* |

# Understanding professional medical vocabulary

Various professional people — not all of them doctors — can offer you medical assistance. They include

- » **il medico** (eel *meh*-dee-koh) *(doctor, both male and female)*
- » **il dottore** (eel doht-*toh*-reh) *(doctor, both female and male)*

  The feminine form of this noun is **la dottoressa** (lah doht-toh-*rehs*-sah).

  You can use either of these words for "doctor."
- » **lo/la specialista [m/f]** (loh/lah speh-chah-*lee*-stah) *(specialist)*
- » **il/la dentista [m/f]** (eel/lah dehn-*tee*-stah) *(dentist)*
- » **il chirurgo [m/f]** (eel kee-*roohr*-goh) *(the surgeon)*
- » **l'infermiere** (leen-fehr-*myeh*-reh) *(male nurse)*
- » **l'infermiera** (leen-fehr-*myeh*-rah) *(female nurse)*

Here's a question that you might need to ask at a doctor's office, along with some typical replies:

- » **Devo prendere qualcosa?** (*deh*-voh *prehn*-deh-reh kwahl-*koh*-zah) *(Do I have to take anything?)*
- » **No, si riposi e beva molta acqua.** (noh see ree-*poh*-zee eh *beh*-vah *mohl*-tah *ah*-kwah) *(No, rest and drink a lot of water.)*
- » **Ecco la ricetta.** (*ehk*-koh lah ree-*cheht*-tah) *(Here is your prescription.)*

# Getting what you need at the pharmacy

If you need **una medicina** (*ooh*-nah meh-dee-*chee*-nah) *(a medicine)*, you'll probably look for the nearest **farmacia** (fahr-mah-*chee*-ah) *(pharmacy)*. Typical pharmacy hours are from 8:30 a.m. to 8 p.m., usually with a lunch break from 1 to 4 p.m. But don't worry, there's always a pharmacy open in case of an emergency! You can find the address and phone number of the open pharmacy (**farmacia di turno**) (fahr-mah-*chee*-ah dee *toohr*-noh) posted on all pharmacy doors. You can also do a search online for **farmacie di turno** + your city.

Italy is one of those places where pharmacists still offer medical advice. These are true pharmacies — not the kind you find in the United States that also sell everything from canned food to beach chairs. In Italy, you generally don't walk in, browse, and help yourself, even to simple items like aspirin. This approach is common in many other types of Italian shops such as **la profumeria** (lah proh-fooh-meh-*ree*-ah) *(the perfume and makeup shop)*, shoe stores, and clothing boutiques. Many items are kept behind the counter. So, if you or a loved one has a minor ailment and it's not an emergency, you can go to the pharmacy for assistance.

# Talkin' the Talk

Anna has just walked into the **farmacia** with her six-year-old daughter, Maria, who was stung by about 100 mosquitoes the night before.

| | |
|---|---|
| **Farmacista:** | **Prego. Mi dica.**<br>*preh*-goh mee *dee*-kah<br>*Hello. How can I help you?* |
| **Anna:** | **Mia figlia è stata punta dalle zanzare ieri notte.**<br>*mee*-ah *fee*-lyah eh *stah*-tah *poohn*-tah *dahl*-leh dzahn-*dzah*-reh *yeh*-ree *noht*-teh<br>*My daughter was stung by mosquitoes last night.* |
| **Farmacista:** | **Vedo.**<br>*veh*-doh<br>*I can see.* |
| | **Le do una pomata contro il prurito.**<br>leh doh *ooh*-nah *poh*-mah-tah *kohn*-troh eel prooh-*ree*-toh<br>*I'll give you an anti-itch cream.* |

| Anna: | **Ha un prodotto anti-zanzara per i bambini?**
| | ah oohn proh-*doht*-toh *ahn*-tee-dzahn-*dzah*-rah pehr ee bahm-*bee*-nee
| | *Do you have something for children to keep mosquitoes away?*
| Farmacista: | **Si, ecco uno spray anti-zanzara molto sicuro per i bambini.**
| | see *ehk*-koh *ooh*-noh sprahy *ahn*-tee-dzahn-*dzah*-rah *mol*-toh see-*kooh*-roh pehr ee bahm-*bee*-nee
| | *Yes. Here's a mosquito repellant that's very safe for children.*

## Braving the dentist

Of course, you might find yourself in need of emergency dental work while in Italy. The first person to ask is the concierge at your hotel, the pharmacist, or even the friendly **barista** who's been serving you breakfast every morning. Try saying: **"Scusi, mi può consigliare un dentista di fiducia?"** (*skooh*–zee mee pwoh *kohn*-see–*lyah*–reh oohn dehn–*tee*–stah dee fee–*dooh*–chah) (*Excuse me, can you please recommend a good dentist?*).

# Talkin' the Talk

Giancarlo is at the dentist's with a terrible toothache.

| Giancarlo: | **Dottore, ho un terribile dolore al molare.**
| | doht-*toh*-reh oh oohn tehr-*ree*-bee-leh doh-*loh*-reh ahl moh-*lah*-reh
| | *Doctor, my molar really hurts.*
| Dentist: | **Vediamo. Purtroppo c'è un'infezione.**
| | veh-*dyah*-moh poohr-*trohp*-poh cheh oohn-een-feh-*tsyoh*-neh
| | *Let's see. Unfortunately, there's an infection.*
| | **Non posso fare altro che darle un antibiotico.**
| | nohn *pohs*-soh *fah*-reh *ahl*-troh keh *dahr*-leh oohn *ahn*-tee-*byoh*-tee-koh
| | *I can't do anything for you but give you an antibiotic.*
| | **Lo prenda due volte al giorno.**
| | loh *prehn*-dah *dooh*-eh *vohl*-teh ahl *johr*-noh
| | *Take it twice a day.*

# Reporting an Accident to the Police

There are other types of emergencies besides medical ones. For example, you might need to call the police to report something you've witnessed.

## Talkin' the Talk

Elena has just witnessed an elderly woman on a bicycle get hit by a scooter. She calls the police. (Track 34)

**PLAY THIS**

**Officer:** **Polizia.**
poh-lee-*tsee*-ah
*Police.*

**Elena:** **C'è stato un incidente.**
cheh *stah*-toh oohn een-chee-*dehn*-teh
*There's been an accident!*

**Officer:** **Dove?**
*doh*-veh
*Where?*

**Elena:** **Piazza Mattei.**
*pyaht*-tsah maht-*tey*
*Piazza Mattei.*

**Officer:** **Ci sono feriti?**
chee *soh*-noh fe-*ree*-tee
*Is anyone injured?*

**Elena:** **C'è una persona priva di sensi.**
cheh *ooh*-na pehr-*soh*-nah *pree*-vah dee *sehn*-see
*There's an unconscious person.*

**Officer:** **Mandiamo subito un'ambulanza.**
mahn-*dyah*-moh *sooh*-bee-toh oohn-ahm-booh-*lahn*-tsah
*We'll send an ambulance right away.*

If you're in Italy and you have an emergency, call 113 — the Italian national police number. They can also dispatch an ambulance if needed. This number is valid throughout Italy.

**CULTURAL WISDOM**

## WORDS TO KNOW

| | | |
|---|---|---|
| **ambulanza [f]** | ahm-booh-*lahn*-tsah | *ambulance* |
| **Che è successo?** | keh eh soohch-*chehs*-soh | *What happened?* |
| **emergenza [f]** | eh-mehr-*jehn*-tsah | *emergency* |
| **incidente [m]** | in-chee-*dehn*-teh | *accident* |
| **le lenti a contatto [f/pl.]** | leh *lenhn*-tee ah kohn-*taht*-toh | *contact lenses* |
| **soluzione [f]** | soh-looh-*tsyoh*-neh | *solution* |
| **ferito [m]** | feh-*ree*-toh | *injured (person)* |
| **pomata [f]** | poh-*mah*-tah | *cream* |
| **ricetta [f]** | ree-*cheht*-tah | *prescription* |

# I've Been Robbed! Knowing What to Do and Say When the Police Arrive

We hope you're never the target of a robbery. But if you are, we want you to be prepared with these key phrases when the police arrive:

» **Sono stato/a derubato/a.** (*soh*-noh *stah*-toh/tah deh-rooh-*bah*-toh/ah) *(I've been robbed.)*

» **C'è stato un furto nel mio appartamento.** (cheh *stah*-toh oohn *foohr*-toh nehl *mee*-oh ahp-pahr-tah-*mehn*-toh) *(There was a burglary in my apartment.)*

» **Sono entrati dei ladri in casa nostra.** (*soh*-noh ehn-*trah*-tee dey *lah*-dree een *kah*-zah *noh*-strah) *(Thieves broke into our house.)*

» **Mi hanno rubato la macchina.** (mee *ahn*-noh rooh-*bah*-toh lah *mahk*-kee-nah) *(My car has been stolen.)*

» **Mi hanno scippato/a.** (mee *ahn*-noh sheep-*pah*-toh/ah) *(My bag was snatched.)*

# Talkin' the Talk

A moped driver just stole Anna's **borsa** (*bohr*-sah) *(bag)*. Distraught, she calls 113 to **denunciare** (deh-noohn-*chah*-reh) *(to report)* **il furto** (eel *foohr*-toh) *(the theft)* to the police.

| | |
|---|---|
| **Officer:** | **Polizia.**<br>poh-lee-*tsee*-ah<br>*Police.* |
| **Anna:** | **Mi hanno appena scippata!**<br>mee *ahn*-noh ahp-*peh*-nah sheep-*pah*-tah<br>*Someone just snatched my bag!* |
| **Officer:** | **Si calmi e venga in questura.**<br>see *kahl*-mee eh *vehn*-gah een kweh-*stooh*-rah<br>*Calm down and come to police headquarters.* |
| **Anna:** | **È stato un uomo in motorino.**<br>eh *stah*-toh oohn *woh*-moh een moh-toh-*ree*-noh<br>*It was a man on a moped.* |
| **Officer:** | **Ho capito, ma deve venire qui.**<br>oh kah-*pee*-toh mah *deh*-veh veh-*nee*-reh kwee<br>*I got it, but you have to come here.* |
| **Anna:** | **Dov'è la questura?**<br>doh-*veh* lah kweh-*stooh*-rah<br>*Where are police headquarters?* |
| **Officer:** | **Dietro la posta centrale.**<br>*dyeh*-troh lah *poh*-stah chehn-*trah*-leh<br>*Behind the main post office.* |
| **Anna:** | **Vengo subito.**<br>*vehn*-goh *sooh*-bee-toh<br>*I'm coming at once.* |

## WORDS TO KNOW

| borsa [f] | *bohr*-sah | *bag* |
|---|---|---|
| furto [m] | *foohr*-toh | *theft* |
| denunciare | deh-noohn-*chah*-reh | *to report* |

| motorino [m] | moh-toh-*ree*-noh | *moped/scooter* |
|---|---|---|
| questura [f] | kweh-*stooh*-rah | *police headquarters* |
| scippare | sheep-*pah*-reh | *to snatch a bag* |
| scippo [m] | *sheep*-poh | *theft of a bag* |

When you need to report someone and describe a thief, knowing some essential words like hair color, height, and more is important. Many of these adjectives are also useful for describing other people such as friends, family members, classmates — not just thieves! You can form descriptive sentences like this:

**La persona era . . .** (lah pehr–*soh*–nah *eh*–rah) (*The person was . . .*):

>> **alta** (*ahl*-tah) *(tall)*

>> **bassa** (*bahs*-sah) *(short)*

>> **di media statura** (dee *meh*-dyah stah-*tooh*-rah) *(of medium height)*

>> **grassa** (*grahs*-sah) *(fat)*

>> **magra** (*mah*-grah) *(thin)*

Note: The preceding adjectives end in **-a** because they modify the noun **la persona,** which is feminine.

**I capelli erano . . .** (ee kah–*pehl*–lee *eh*–rah–noh) (*The hair was . . .*)

>> **castani** (kah-*stah*-nee) *(brown)*

>> **biondi** (*byohn*-dee) *(blond)*

>> **neri** (*neh*-ree) *(black)*

>> **rossi** (*rohs*-see) *(red)*

>> **scuri** (*skooh*-ree) *(dark)*

>> **chiari** (*kyah*-ree) *(fair)*

>> **lisci** (*lee*-shee) *(straight)*

>> **ondulati** (ohn-dooh-*lah*-tee) *(wavy)*

>> **ricci** (*reech*-chee) *(curly)*

>> **corti** (*kohr*-tee) *(short)*

>> **lunghi** (*loohn*-gee) *(long)*

**Aveva gli occhi . . .** (ah-*veh*-vah lyee *ohk*-kee) *(His/Her eyes were . . . )*

>> **azzurri** (ahd-*dzoohr*-ree) *(blue)*

>> **grigi** (*gree*-jee) *(gray)*

>> **marroni** (mahr-*roh*-nee) *(brown)*

>> **color nocciola** (*coh*-lohr noch-*chyoh*-lah) *(hazel)*

>> **verdi** (*vehr*-dee) *(green)*

**Era . . .** (*eh*-rah) *(He/she was . . .)*

>> **calvo/a** (*kahl*-voh) *(bald)*

>> **rasato/a** (rah-*zah*-toh) *(clean-shaven)*

**Aveva . . .** (ah-*veh*-vah) *(He/She had . . .)*

>> **la barba** (lah *bahr*-bah) *(a beard)*

>> **i baffi** (ee *bahf*-fee) *(a moustache)*

>> **la bocca larga** (lah *bohk*-kah *lahr*-gah) *(a wide mouth)*

>> **la bocca stretta** (lah *bohk*-kah *streht*-tah) *(a narrow mouth)*

>> **la bocca carnosa** (lah *bohk*-kah kahr-*noh*-zah) *(a plump mouth)*

>> **il naso lungo** (eel *nah*-zoh *loohn*-go) *(a long nose)*

>> **il naso corto** (eel *nah*-zoh *kohr*-toh) *(a short nose)*

# Dealing with Car Trouble

You don't have to be in a car crash to run into car trouble. Sometimes a mechanical problem can cause your car to break down. In situations like these, you need to call a mechanic who can help get you back on the road.

# Talkin' the Talk

Raffaella's car has broken down. She calls roadside assistance from her cell phone.

| | |
|---|---|
| **Mechanic:** | **Pronto.**<br>*prohn*-toh<br>*Hello.* |
| **Raffaella:** | **Pronto, ho bisogno d'aiuto!**<br>*prohn*-toh oh bee-*zoh*-nyoh dah-*yooh*-toh<br>*Hello, I need help!* |
| **Mechanic:** | **Che succede?**<br>keh soohch-*cheh*-deh<br>*What's wrong?* |
| **Raffaella:** | **Mi si è fermata la macchina.**<br>mee see eh fehr-*mah*-tah lah *mahk*-kee-nah<br>*My car broke down.* |
| **Mechanic:** | **Dove si trova?**<br>*doh*-veh see *troh*-vah<br>*Where are you?* |
| **Raffaella:** | **Sull'autostrada A1 prima dell'uscita Firenze Nord.**<br>soohl-lah-ooh-toh-*strah*-dah ah *ooh*-noh *pree*-mah dehl-looh-*shee*-tah fee-*rehn*-tseh nohrd<br>*On the A1 highway before the Florence North exit.* |
| **Mechanic:** | **Bene. Mando un carro attrezzi.**<br>*beh*-neh *mahn*-doh oohn *cahr*-roh aht-*treht*-tsee<br>*Okay. I'll send a tow truck.* |
| **Raffaella:** | **Ci vorrà molto?**<br>chee vohr-*rah mohl*-toh<br>*Will it take a long time?* |
| **Mechanic:** | **Dipende dal traffico. Al massimo mezz'ora.**<br>dee-*pehn*-deh dahl *trahf*-fee-koh ahl *mahs*-see-moh mehd-*dzoh*-rah<br>*It depends on the traffic. Half hour at the most.* |
| **Raffaella:** | **Venite il più presto possibile per favore!**<br>veh-*nee*-teh eel pyooh *preh*-stoh pohs-*see*-bee-leh pehr fah-*voh*-reh<br>*Come as soon as possible please!* |

# When You Need a Lawyer: Protecting Your Rights

Many of life's unpleasant moments require the help of an authorized professional. Often, that person is a lawyer who can assist you in complex situations. Therefore, knowing how to contact a lawyer is important. The following general questions and phrases can help you request legal assistance in Italian:

>> **Mi serve l'aiuto di un avvocato.** (mee *sehr*-veh lah-*yooh*-toh dee oohn ahv-voh-*kah*-toh) *(I need the help of a lawyer.)*

>> **Ho bisogno di assistenza legale.** (oh bee-*zoh*-nyoh dee ahs-see-*stehn*-tsah leh-*gah*-leh) *(I need legal assistance.)*

>> **Vorrei consultare il mio avvocato.** (vohr-*rey* kohn-soohl-*tah*-reh eel *mee*-oh ahv-voh-*kah*-toh) *(I'd like to consult my lawyer.)*

>> **Chiamate il mio avvocato, per favore.** (kyah-*mah*-teh eel *mee*-oh ahv-voh-*kah*-toh pehr fah-*voh*-reh) *(Call my lawyer, please.)*

After you find a lawyer, you can speak to them about your situation. Here are some examples of what you may need to say:

>> **Sono stato truffato/a.** (*soh*-noh *stah*-toh troohf-*fah*-toh/ah) *(I was cheated.)*

>> **Devo stipulare un contratto.** (*deh*-voh stee-pooh-*lah*-reh oohn kohn-*traht*-toh) *(I have to negotiate a contract.)*

>> **Ho avuto un incidente stradale.** (oh ah-*vooh*-toh oohn een-chee-*dehn*-teh strah-*dah*-leh) *(I've had a traffic accident.)*

>> **Voglio che mi vengano risarciti i danni.** (*voh*-lyoh keh mee *vehn*-gah-noh ree-sahr-*chee*-tee ee *dahn*-nee) *(I want to be compensated for the damages.)*

>> **Sono stato/a arrestato/a.** (*soh*-noh *stah*-toh/ah ahr-reh-*stah*-toh/ah) *(I've been arrested.)*

| WORDS TO KNOW | | |
| --- | --- | --- |
| **danno [m]** | *dahn*-noh | *damage* |
| **denunciare** | deh-noohn-*chah*-reh | *to report* |
| **denuncia [f]** | deh-*noohn*-chah | *report* |
| **incidente stradale [m]** | een-chee-*dehn*-teh strah-*dah*-leh | *traffic accident* |
| **macchina [f]** | *mahk*-kee-nah | *car* |
| **targa [f]** | *tahr*-gah | *license plate* |
| **patente [f]** | pah-*tehn*-teh | *license* |
| **libretto [m]** | lee-*breht*-toh | *registration* |
| **assicurazione [f]** | ahs-see-kooh-rah-*tsyoh*-neh | *insurance* |

# Reporting a Lost or Stolen Passport

Imagine you lose your passport — or it gets stolen while you're snoozing on the train. These things happen!

# Talkin' the Talk

When Diane gets off the train in Florence, she realizes that she no longer has her passport. She goes immediately to the police station.

| | | |
|---|---|---|
| **Diane:** | **Ho perso il passaporto! Non so cosa fare!** | |

Diane: **Ho perso il passaporto! Non so cosa fare!**
oh *pehr*-soh eel pahs-sah-*pohr*-toh nohn soh *koh*-zah *fah*-reh
*I've lost my passport! I don't know what to do!*

Police: **Sa dirmi dove, come, quando?**
sah *deer*-mee *doh*-veh *koh*-meh *kwahn*-doh
*Can you tell me where, when, and how?*

Diane: **Penso di averlo perso in treno.**
*pehn*-soh dee ah-*vehr*-loh *pehr*-soh een *treh*-noh
*I think I lost it on the train.*

Police: **Ora facciamo la denuncia.**
*oh*-rah fach-*chah*-moh lah deh-*noohn*-chah
*We'll file a report now.*

**Con questa denuncia, deve rivolgersi alla sua ambasciata o consolato.**
kohn *kweh*-stah deh-*noohn*-chah *deh*-veh ree-*vohl*-jehr-see *ahl*-lah *sooh*-ah ahm-bah-*shah*-tah oh kohn-soh-*lah*-toh
*You're going to need this report when you go to your Embassy or Consulate to apply for a new one.*

Diane: **Grazie.**
*grah*-tsyeh
*Thank you.*


(at the Embassy or Consulate)

Agent: **Dica?**
*dee*-kah
*How can I help you?*

Diane: (agitated) **Mi serve un nuovo passaporto! Subito!**
mee *sehr*-veh oohn *nwoh*-voh -pahs-sah-*pohr*-toh
*I need a new passport. Right away!*

Agent: **Si calmi. Servono due foto tessera . . .**
see *kahl*-mee *sehr* -voh-noh *dooh*-eh *foh*-toh *tehs*-seh-rah
*Calm down. You're going to need two ID-size photos . . .*

**. . . la denuncia della polizia, una copia del passaporto originale . . .**
lah deh-*noohn*-chah *dehl*-lah poh-lee-*tsee*-ah *ooh*-nah *koh*-pyah dehl pahs-sah-*pohr*-toh oh-ree-jee-*nah*-leh
*. . . the official police report, a copy of your original passport . . . (your hotel should have a copy of this)*

**. . . e un altro documento.**
eh oohn *ahl*-troh doh-kooh-*mehn*-toh
*. . . and another form of ID.*

# FUN & GAMES

See how many body parts you can remember by labeling as many of them as you can on the following picture. See Appendix C for the answer key.

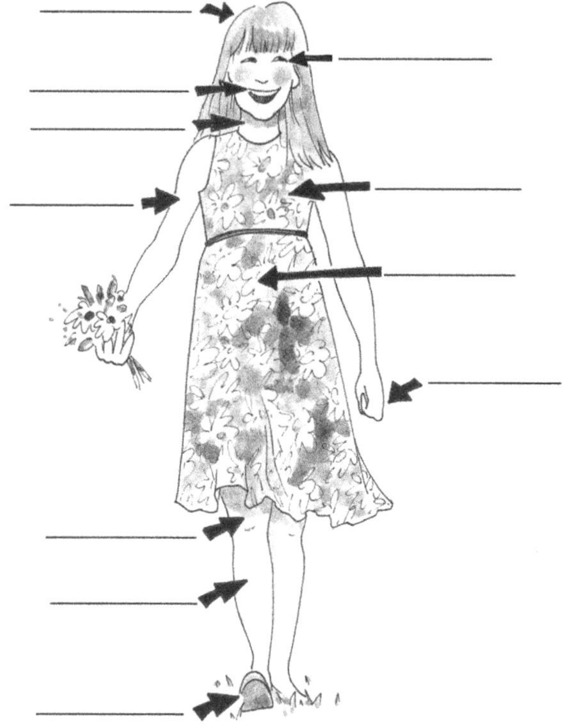

*Illustration by Liz Kurtzman*

IN THIS CHAPTER

» **Discovering interrogative pronouns**

» **Asking simple questions**

» **Taking care of basic needs**

» **Talking about yourself and your family**

» **Talking shop**

» **Talking about how things used to be — the imperfect**

» **Sending postcards, buying stamps**

# Chapter **17**
# Making Small Talk

This chapter presents you with some of the basic essentials that are sprinkled throughout the book, but that deserve a spotlight of their own. You probably have figured out how to form questions, but here's a handy reference for quick review. At the end of this chapter, we give you a crash course on the imperfect tense that will make your Italian perfect.

## Discovering Interrogative Pronouns

In Italian at least one thing is easier than in English: forming questions. In English, in most cases, you need a form of "to do," "to be," or "to have" to form a question. You also (mostly) have to invert part of the sentence construction. For example, "He goes to the movies" becomes "Does he go to the movies?" In Italian you simply ask, **"Lui va al cinema?"** (*looh*-ee vah ahl *chee*-neh-mah) (*Does he go to the movies?*). Just as there's no word for *does* in the previous sentence, there's no word for *are* in the following one: **Vai alla partita?** (vahy *ahl*-lah pahr-*tee*-tah) (*Are you going to the game?*)

In Italian, forming questions is very easy: A question has the same structure as an affirmative statement. You recognize a question only by the intonation of your voice and the use of a question mark in writing. For example:

| Luca va a scuola. | Luca va a scuola? |
| --- | --- |
| *looh*-kah vah ah *skwoh*-lah | *looh*-kah vah ah *skwoh*-lah |
| Luca goes to school. | Luca goes to school? or Does Luca go to school? |
| **Mangi la carne.** | **Mangi la carne?** |
| *mahn*-jee lah *kahr*-neh | *mahn*-jee lah *kahr*-neh |
| You eat/You're eating meat. | Do you eat/Are you eating meat? |

## Using interrogative pronouns

Italian also uses interrogative pronouns (when, where, what, and so on) to begin a question. Use the following pronouns:

>> **Chi?** (kee) *(Who?)*

>> **Che?** (keh) *(What?)*

>> **Che cosa?** (kee *koh*-zah) *(What?)*

>> **Cosa?** (*koh*-zah) *(What?)*

>> **Quando?** (*kwahn*-doh) *(When?)*

>> **Quanto/a?** (*kwahn*-toh/ah) *(How much?)*

>> **Quanti/e?** (*kwahn*-tee/eh) *(How many?)* (m/f)

>> **Quale/i?** (*kwah*-leh/ee) *(Which, what?)* (sing./pl.)

>> **Dove?** (*doh*-veh) *(Where?)*

>> **Perché?** (pehr-*keh*) *(Why?)*

>> **Come?** (*koh*-meh) *(How?)*

**Che, cosa,** and **che cosa** are often used interchangeably.

Some sample questions using these interrogative pronouns include

>> **Chi è?** (kee eh) *(Who is it/this?)*

>> **Cosa stai facendo?** (*koh*-zah stahy fah-*chehn*-doh) *(What are you doing?)*

>> **Quando arrivi?** (*kwahn*-doh ahr-*ree*-vee) *(When do you arrive?)*

>> **Dov'è la stazione?** (doh-*veh* lah stah-*tsyoh*-neh) *(Where is the station?)*

>> **Perché non sei venuto?** (pehr-*keh* nohn sey veh-*nooh*-toh) *(Why didn't you come?)*

>> **Come stai?** (*koh*-meh stahy) *(How are you?)*

>> **Come si dice "rain" in italiano?** (*koh*-meh see *dee*-cheh . . . in ee-tah-*lyah*-noh) *(How do you say "rain" in Italian?)*

## Asking simple questions

When you ask a question with an interrogative pronoun, like in English, you don't need the pronoun in the response. For example:

**Dov'è la Cappella Sistina?** (doh-*veh* lah kahp-*pehl*-lah see-*stee*-nah) *(Where is the Sistine Chapel?)*

**La Cappella Sistina è a Roma.** (lah kahp-*pehl*-lah see-*stee*-nah eh ah *roh*-mah) *(The Sistine Chapel is in Rome.)*

**Quante regioni ci sono in Italia?** (*kwahn*-teh reh-*joh*-nee chee *soh*-noh in ee-*tah*-lyah) *(How many regions are there in Italy?)*

**Ci sono 20 regioni.** (chee *soh*-noh *vehn*-tee reh-*joh*-nee) *(There are 20 regions.)*

TIP

The interrogatives **dove** (*doh*–veh) and **come** (*koh*–meh) can be contracted with the verb **essere** (*ehs*–sehr–reh) *(to be)* in the third person singular. Note that both the pronunciation and stress change in the contracted form. Take a look at these interrogatives with third person singular and third person plural verbs:

**Dov'è Mario?** (doh-*veh mah*-ryoh) *(Where's Mario?)*

**Dove sono i ragazzi?** (*doh*-veh *soh*-noh ee rah-*gaht*-tsee) *(Where are the boys?)*

**Com'è quel ristorante?** (koh-*meh* kwehl ree-stoh-*rahn*-teh) *(How is that restaurant? or What's that restaurant like?)*

**Come sono gli gnocchi?** (*koh*-meh *soh*-noh lyee *nyohk*-kee) *(How are the gnocchi?)*

TIP

Use **quale** (*kwah*-leh) in the singular, **quali** (*kwah*-lee) in the plural, but **qual è** (kwah-*leh*) when combined with the third person singular of **essere:**

**Quale** (*kwah*-leh): **Quale film vuoi vedere?** (*kwah*-leh feelm vwoi veh-*deh*-reh) *(What/which film do you want to see?)*

**Qual è** (kwah-*leh*): **Qual è il mare più profondo d'Italia?** (kwah-*leh* il mah-reh pyooh proh-*fohn*-doh dee-*tah*-lyah) *(What is the deepest sea in Italy?)*

**Quali vini preferisci?** (*kwah*-lee *vee*-nee preh-feh *ree*-shee) *(Which wines do you prefer?)*

Although they may seem insignificant, you really can't get around in Italian without the essential terms **c'è** (cheh) *(there is)* and **ci sono** (chee *soh*-noh) *(there are)*. These expressions are useful for both asking and answering questions. Just remember that both start with a "ch" sound, such as the following:

**Cosa c'è nel frigo?** (*koh*-zah cheh nehl *free*-goh) *(What's in the fridge?)*

**C'è un bar qui vicino?** (cheh oohn bahr kwee vee-*chee*-noh) *(Is there an bar nearby?)*

**Si, c'è il Bar Duomo.** (see cheh eel bahr *dwoh*-moh) *(Yes, there's the Bar Duomo.)*

**Ci sono ancora dei ravioli?** (chee *soh*-noh ahn-*koh*-rah dey rah-*vyoh*-lee) *(Are there any ravioli left?)*

**Si, ci sono**. (see chee *soh*-noh) *(Yes, there are.)*

# Taking Care of Basic Needs

Sometimes you just need to ask for something simple but essential. Here are a few phrases that will take you far:

**Scusi, dov'è il bagno per favore?** (*skooh*-zee doh-*veh* il bah-*nyoh* pehr fah-*voh*-reh) *(Excuse me, where is the bathroom please?)* Some people get fancy and ask for **la toilette** with a Frenchified accent; however, **bagno** gets you where you need to go (no pun intended).

**Scusi, dov'è la farmacia più vicina?** (*skooh*-zee doh-*veh* lah fahr-mah-*chee*-ah pyooh vee-*chee*-nah) *(Excuse me, where's the nearest pharmacy?)*

**Scusi, dov'è una banca?** (*skooh*-zee doh-*veh* ooh-nah *bahn*-kah) *(Excuse me, where is a bank?)*

**Ho bisogno di/Mi serve** (sing.)/**Mi servono**(pl.) (oh bee-*zoh*-nyoh dee/mee sehr-*veh*/mee *sehr*-voh-noh) *(I need . . . )*

**un parrucchiere** (oohn pah-rooh-*kyeh*-reh) *(a hairdresser)*

**un'estetista (per fare la ceretta)** (oohn-eh-steh-*tee*-stah) (pehr *fah*-reh lah cheh-*reht*-tah) *(an esthetician)* (for waxing)

**Sto cercando** (stoh chehr-*kahn*-doh) *(I'm looking for . . .)*

**il dentifricio** (eel dehn-tee-*free*-choh) *(toothpaste)*

**la crema solare** (lah *kreh*-mah soh-*lah*-reh) *(sunscreen)*

**i tamponi/gli assorbenti interni** (ee tahm-*poh*-nee/lyee ahs-sohr-*behn*-tee een-*tehr*-nee) *(tampons)*

**la carta igienica** (lah *kar*-tah ee-*jeh*-nee-kah) *(toilet paper)*

**qualcosa per le zanzare** (kwahl-*koh*-zah pehr leh dzahn-*dzah*-reh) *(something for mosquitoes)*

**qualcosa per il mal di testa** (kwahl-*koh*-zah pehr eel mahl dee *teh*-stah) *(something for a headache)*

**Vorrei** (vohr-*rey*) *(I'd like . . .)*

**Mi può/potrebbe consigliare . . . ?** (mee pwoh/poh-*trehb*-beh kohn-see-*lyah*-reh) *(Would you be able to recommend . . . ?)*

**Può ripetere lentamente, per favore?** (pwoh ree-*peh*-teh-reh lehn-tah-*mehn*-teh pehr fah-*voh*-reh) *(Would you repeat slowly, please?)*

**Non capisco.** (nohn kah-*pee*-skoh) *(I don't understand.)*

**Non lo so.** (nohn loh soh) *(I don't know.)*

# Talkin' the Talk

Massimo and Isa, two colleagues at work, are getting to know each other over a morning cappuccino, and naturally they end up using many of the interrogative pronouns in this chapter. (Track 35)

| | |
|---|---|
| **Massimo:** | **Cosa prendi?**<br>*koh*-zah *prehn*-dee<br>*What are you having?* |
| **Isa:** | **Un cappuccio e una pasta.**<br>oohn kahp-*pooh*-choh eh *ooh*-nah *pah*-stah<br>*A cappuccino and a pastry.* |
| **Massimo:** | **Quando hai cominciato il lavoro qui?**<br>*qwahn*-doh ahy koh-meen-*chah*-toh il lah-*voh*-roh kwee<br>*When did you start working here?* |
| **Isa:** | **Due mesi fa.**<br>*dooh*-eh *meh*-zee fah<br>*Two months ago.* |

*(continued)*

*(continued)*

| | |
|---|---|
| **Massimo:** | **Dov'eri prima?**<br>dohv-*eh*-ree *pree*-mah<br>*Where were you before?* |
| **Isa:** | **Lavoravo per la succursale veneta.**<br>lah-voh-*rah*-voh pehr lah soohk-koohr-*sah*-leh *veh*-neh-tah<br>*I was working for the branch in the Veneto region.* |
| **Massimo:** | **Come ti trovi?**<br>*koh*-meh tee *troh*-vee<br>*How do you like it so far?* |
| **Isa:** | **Mi piace abbastanza.**<br>mee *pyach*-cheh ahb-bah-*stahn*-tsah<br>*I like it well enough.* |
| | **E tu, da quanto tempo lavori per la compagnia?**<br>eh tooh dah *kwahn*-toh *tehm*-poh lah-*voh*-ree pehr lah kohm-pah-*nyee*-ah<br>*And how long have you been working for the company?* |
| **Massimo:** | **Da sei anni.**<br>dah sey *ahn*-nee<br>*For six years.* |
| | **Da quando mi sono laureato.**<br>dah *kwahn*-doh mee *soh*-noh lah-ooh-reh-*ah*-toh<br>*Since I graduated.* |
| | **Dove hai studiato?**<br>*doh*-veh ahy stooh-*dyah*-toh<br>*Where did you study?* |
| **Isa:** | **All'Università di Urbino. E tu?**<br>ahl-looh-nee-vehr-see-*tah* dee oohr-*bee*-noh eh tooh<br>*The University of Urbino. And you?* |
| **Massimo:** | **Bologna.**<br>boh-*loh*-nyah<br>*Bologna.* |
| **Isa:** | **Vuoi tornare a Bologna?**<br>vwoi tohr-*nah*-reh ah boh-*loh*-nyah<br>*Do you want to go back to Bologna?* |
| **Massimo:** | **Sì, un giorno vorrei tornarci.**<br>see oohn *johr*-noh vohr-*rey* tohr-*nahr*-chee<br>*Yes, some day I'd like to go back there.* |

**Pronto** (*prohn*-toh) means more than just "hello" when you answer the phone. It often means "ready," in which case it functions as an adjective and changes to match the noun it modifies. In other words, when the noun is masculine, the adjective ends in **-o — pronto.** If the noun is feminine, it ends in **-a — pronta** (*prohn*-tah). When modifying plural nouns, it ends in **i** (*ee*) (masculine plural) and **e** (*eh*) (feminine plural). Consider these examples:

>> **Ragazzi, siete pronti?** (rah-*gaht*-tsee see-*eh*-teh *prohn*-tee) *(Guys/kids, are you ready?)*

>> **La cena è pronta.** (lah *cheh*-nah eh *prohn*-tah) *(Dinner is ready.)*

Another use of **pronto** that you should know is the phrase **pronto soccorso** (*prohn*-toh sohk-*kohr*-soh) *(first aid; emergency room)*. In this context, **pronto** means "rapid."

**Presto** (*preh*-stoh), on the other hand, means either early or soon, and as an adverb, it's invariable — ending always in **-o.** For example: Siamo arrivati presto. (*syah*-moh ahr-ree-*vah*-tee *preh*-stoh) *(We arrived early.)*

## WORDS TO KNOW

| | | |
|---|---|---|
| **consigliare** | kohn-see-*lyah*-reh | *to recommend* |
| **pronto** | *prohn*-toh | *ready, hello (phone)* |
| **presto** | *preh*-stoh | *early, soon* |
| **non lo so** | nohn loh soh | *I don't know* |
| **da quanto tempo?** | dah *kwahn*-toh *tehm*-poh | *How long?* |
| **gemello/a [m/f]** | jeh-*mehl*-loh/ah | *twin* |
| **ditta [f]** | *deet*-tah | *company, firm* |
| **come ti trovi?** | *koh*-meh tee *troh*-vee | *How do you like it? (used only in new situations, like a job or a new place)* |
| **abbastanza** | ahb-bah-*stahn*-tsah | *enough* |
| **il bagno [m]** | il *bah*-nyoh | *bathroom* |
| **partita [f]** | pahr-*tee*-tah | *game* |
| **vorrei** | *vohr*-rey | *I would like* |

# Talking about Yourself and Your Family — More about Possessives

Chapter 15 explains how possessive adjectives and pronouns work, but the story doesn't end there.

There are specific rules for using possessive adjectives with family members. For singular family members the article is omitted; however, for plural family members the article is included:

**Mia sorella** (no definite article) (*mee*-ah soh-*rehl*-lah) (*my sister*) — **Le mie sorelle** (with definite article) (leh *mee*-eh soh-*rehl*-leh (*my sisters*)

Table 17-1 shows some other family members.



## Relatives

| Relative | Pronunciation | Definition |
|---|---|---|
| **marito** | mah-*ree*-toh | *husband* |
| **moglie** | *moh*-lyeh | *wife* |
| **figlio** | *fee*-lyoh | *son* |
| **figlia/e** | *fee*-lyah | *daughter/s* |
| **figli** | *fee*-lyee | *children/sons* |
| **nipote** | nee-*poh*-teh | *niece, nephew, granddaughter, grandson* |
| **nipoti** | nee-*poh*-tee | *nephews, nieces, grandsons, granddaughters, grandchildren* |
| **suocero/a** | *swoh*-cheh-roh/ah | *father-in-law/mother-in-law* |
| **nuora** | *nwoh*-rah | *daughter-in-law* |
| **genero** | *geh*-neh-roh | *son-in-law* |
| **zia/e** | *dzee*-ah/eh | *aunt/s* |
| **zio/i** | *dzee*-oh/ee | *uncle/s* |
| **cugino/a/i/e** | kooh-*jee*-noh/ah/ee/eh | *cousin* (m.)/*cousin* (f.)/*cousins* |
| **nonno/a/i/e** | *nohn*-noh/ah/ee/eh | *grandfather/grandmother/grandparents* |
| **madre** | *mah*-dreh | *mother* |
| **padre** | *pah*-dreh | *father* |
| **genitori** | geh-nee-*toh*-ree | *parents* |

# Talkin' the Talk

Teresa and Amy are two old friends catching up about their families after not having spoken for about 15 years. Notice how they use definite articles before plural family relatives, but omit the article before singular ones.

| | |
|---|---|
| **Teresa:** | **Ciao Amy. Sono Teresa.**<br>chow *ey*-mee *soh*-noh teh-*reh*-sah<br>*Hi Amy. It's Teresa.* |
| **Amy:** | **Da quanto tempo non ti sento!**<br>dah *kwahn*-toh *tehm*-poh nohn tee *sehn*-toh<br>*What a long time it's been!* |
| **Teresa:** | **Come stai?**<br>*koh*-meh stahy<br>*How are you?* |
| **Amy:** | **Sto bene!**<br>stoh *beh*-neh<br>*I'm well!* |
| | **Raccontami di te!**<br>rahk-*kohn*-tah-mee dee teh<br>*Tell me about you (yourself)!* |
| **Teresa:** | **Mi sono sposata undici anni fa.**<br>mee *soh*-noh spoh-*zah*-tah *oohn*-dee-chee *ahn*-nee fah<br>*I got married 11 years ago.* |
| | **Ho due figli.**<br>oh *dooh*-eh *fee*-lyee<br>*I have two children.* |
| | **Abito a Ravenna.**<br>*ah*-bee-toh ah rah-*vehn*-nah<br>*I live in Ravenna.* |
| **Amy:** | **Quanti anni hanno i tuoi figli?**<br>*kwahn*-tee *ahn*-nee *ahn*-noh ee twohy *fee*-lyee<br>*How old are your children?* |
| **Teresa:** | **Mia figlia Emilia Rosa ha dieci anni.**<br>*Mee*-ah *fee*-lyah eh-*mee*-lyah *roh*-zah ah *dyeh*-chee *ahn*-nee<br>*My daughter Emilia Rosa is ten years old.* |

*(continued)*

*(continued)*

> **E mio figlio Pietro ne ha otto.**
> eh *mee*-oh *fee*-lyoh *pyeh*-troh neh ah *oht*-toh
> *And my son Pietro is eight.*
>
> **Come sta la tua famiglia?**
> *koh*-meh stah lah *tooh*-ah fah-*mee*-lyah
> *How's your family doing?*

**Amy:** **Mio marito Sandro è sempre in giro per il mondo.**
*mee*-oh mah-*ree*-toh *sahn*-droh eh *sehm*-preh in *jee*-roh pehr il *mohn*-doh
*My husband Sandro is always traveling all over the world.*

> **Mia figlia Tania adesso ha diciotto anni e frequenta l'università.**
> *mee*-ah *fee*-lyah *tahn*-yah ah-*dehs*-soh ah dee-*choht*-toh *ahn*-nee eh freh-*kwehn*-tah looh-nee-vehr-see-*tah*
> *My daughter Tania is 18 years old and goes to college.*
>
> **E mio figlio Luca ne ha ventidue.**
> eh *mee*-oh *fee*-lyoh *looh*-kah neh ah *vehn*-tee-*dooh*-eh
> *And my son Luca is 22.*

**Teresa:** **Come passano gli anni.**
*koh*-meh *pahs*-sahn-oh lyee *ahn*-nee
*Time really flies.*

**Amy:** **Eh sì. Come stanno i tuoi genitori?**
eh see *koh*-meh *stahn*-noh ee twohy jeh-nee-*toh*-ree
*You bet. How are your parents?*

**Teresa:** **Stanno bene grazie.**
*stahn*-noh *beh*-neh *grah*-tsyeh
*They're well, thanks.*

> **Mio padre è in pensione finalmente.**
> *mee*-oh *pah*-dreh eh in pehn-*syoh*-neh fee-nahl-*mehn*-teh
> *My dad finally retired.*
>
> **E tua sorella? Dove abita?**
> eh *tooh*-ah soh-*rehl*-lah *doh*-veh *ah*-bee-tah
> *And your sister? Where does she live?*

**Amy:** **Mia sorella sta benone.**
*mee*-ah sohr-*ehl*-lah stah beh-*noh*-neh
*My sister's doing quite well.*

**Fa l'oculista nello studio di mio padre.**
fah loh-kooh-*lee*-stah *nehl*-loh *stooh*-dyoh dee *mee*-oh
*pah*-dreh
*She's an eye doctor in my dad's practice.*

**Abita vicino a me.**
*ah*-bee-tah vee-*chee*-noh ah meh
*She lives near me.*

Teresa:    **Allora, quando possiamo vederci?**
ahl-*loh*-rah *kwahn*-doh pohs-*syah*-moh veh-*dehr*-chee
*So, when can we see each other?*

Amy:    **Molto presto, spero.**
*mohl*-toh *preh*-stoh *speh*-roh
*Very soon, I hope.*

TIP

There's an exception to the rule about singular family members. Although most don't take the definite article like **mia madre** (*mee*-ah *mah*-dreh) and **mio padre** (*mee*-oh *pah*-dreh) — some shorter terms of endearment do. For example, **la mia mamma** (lah *mee*-ah mahm-mah) (*my mom*) and **il mio babbo/il mio papà** (eel *mee*-oh *bahb*-boh/eel *mee*-oh pah-*pah*) (*my dad*).

# Speaking Perfectly about the Past with the Imperfect

When you're making small talk, you'll often want to describe how things used to be — your old job, where you used to live, daily routines, or things you used to enjoy. That's where the **imperfetto** (eem-pehrf-*feht*-toh) (imperfect) comes in handy: It's used to describe past habits, repeated actions, and background information — the sort of things people often bring up when getting to know each other or catching up after not seeing each other for a while. Consider these examples:

>> **Lavoravo per la succursale veneta.** (lah-voh-*rah*-voh pehr lah soohk-koohr-*sah*-leh *veh*-neh-tah) (*I used to work for the branch in the Veneto region.*)

>> **Abitavo a Firenze quando ci siamo visti l'ultima volta.** (ah-bee-*tah*-voh ah fee-*rehn*-tseh *qwahn*-doh chee *syah*-moh *vee*-stee loohl-*tee*-mah *vohl*-tah) (*I was living in Florence the last time we saw each other.*)

As you can see in here, verbs in the imperfect often translate as *was/were* or *used to.* For example: **Lavoravo** (la-voh-*rah*-voh) *(I used to work/I was working).* To form the imperfect of regular **-are, -ere,** and **-ire** verbs, remove the final **-re** from the infinitive and add these endings: **-vo, -vi, -va, -vamo, -vate, -vano.** I continue to use **lavorare** as an example.

| Conjugation | Pronunciation | Translation |
| --- | --- | --- |
| **lavoravo** | lah-voh-*rah*-voh | *I used to work/I was working* |
| **lavoravi** | lah-voh-*rah*-vee | *you used to work/you were working* |
| **lavorava** | lah-voh-*rah*-vah | *he/she used to work/he/she was working* |
| **lavoravamo** | lah-voh-rah-*vah*-moh | *we used to work/we were working* |
| **lavoravate** | lah-voh-rah-*vah*-teh | *you used to work/you were working* |
| **lavoravano** | lah-voh-*rah*-vah-noh | *they used to work/they were working* |

There are very few irregular verbs in the imperfect like **dire** (*dee*-reh) *(to say/to tell),* **fare** (*fah*-reh) *(to do/to make),* and **bere** (*beh*-reh) *(to drink).* These verbs have the following irregular roots (but they have the same regular endings: **-vo, -vi, -va, vamo, -vate -vano**):

>> **dire** → dice- (*dee*-cheh)

>> **fare** → face- (*fah*-cheh)

>> **bere** → beve- (*beh*-veh)

Here are a couple examples:

>> **Bevevo sempre un caffè al bar.** (beh-*veh*-voh *sehm*-preh oon *kah*-feh ahl bahr) *(I used to drink a coffee at the café every day.)*

>> **Facevamo colazione alle otto.** (fah-cheh-*vah*-moh koh-lah-*tsyo*-neh *ahl*-leh *oht*-toh) *(We used to have breakfast at eight.)*

You need to memorize the irregular imperfect form of **essere** (*ehs*-seh-reh) *(to be)*:

| Conjugation | Pronunciation | Translation |
| --- | --- | --- |
| **ero** | *eh*-roh | *I was* |
| **eri** | *eh*-ree | *you were* |

| Conjugation | Pronunciation | Translation |
|---|---|---|
| **era** | *eh*-rah | *he/she/it was* |
| **eravamo** | eh-rah-*vah*-mo | *we were* |
| **eravate** | eh-rah-*vah*-teh | you (pl.) were |
| **erano** | *eh*-rah-noh | *they were* |

By the way, the imperfect is also used when talking about past weather — another classic small topic. Check out these examples:

>> **Com'era il tempo in montagna?** (koh-*meh*-rah eel *tehm*-poh een mohn-*tah*-nyah) *(What was the weather like in the mountains?)*

>> **C'era il sole! Faceva freddo, ma non nevicava.** (*che*-rah eel *soh*-leh fah-*cheh*-vah *frehd*-doh mah nohn neh-vee-*kah*-vah) *(It was sunny! It was cold, but it wasn't snowing.)*

# Talking Shop

Work is such a big part of so many people's lives that it's something you might want to be able to talk about when you're in Italy and striking up a conversation with someone you've just met.

So, the verb **lavorare** will be useful with a few other key terms:

>> **Che lavoro fa/fai?** (keh lah-*voh*-roh fah/fahy) *[What's your job/What do you do (for a living)?]* (formal/informal)

>> **Che mestiere fa/fai?** (keh meh-*styeh*-reh fah/fahy) *(What work do you do?)* (formal/informal)

You can generally answer this question in two ways. Pay attention to the verbs used and note the definite article in the first example:

>> **Faccio il/la dentista.** (*fach*-choh il/lah dehn-*tee*-stah) *(I'm a dentist.)* (m/f)

>> **Sono dentista.** (*soh*-noh dehn-*tee*-stah) *(I'm a dentist.)*

Italian has at least three words for "company" — **la compagnia** (lah kohm-pah-*nyee*-ah), **la ditta** (lah *deet*-tah) (which also means "the firm"), and **la società** (lah soh-cheh-*tah*). These words are virtually interchangeable.

**L'ufficio** (loohf-*fee*-choh) is Italian for "office." The following sentences give you a taste of phrases commonly heard in **uffici** (oohf-*fee*-chee) (*offices*) everywhere:

>> **È una grande società?** (eh *ooh*-nah *grahn*-deh soh-cheh-*tah*) *(Is it a big company?)*

>> **Non proprio, diciamo media.** (nohn *proh*-pryoh dee-*chah*-moh *meh*-dyah) *(Not really, let's say medium-sized.)*

>> **Lavoro per una piccola ditta.** (lah-*voh*-roh pehr *ooh*-nah *peek*-koh-lah *deet*-tah) *(I work for a small company.)*

>> **Mi piace il mio lavoro.** (mee *pyah*-cheh eel *mee*-oh lah-*voh*-roh) *(I like my job.)*

Table 17-3 shows some of the professions in the masculine form as well as careers with which you might be familiar.

**TABLE 17-3**

## Professions/Jobs

| Profession | Pronunciation | Meaning |
| --- | --- | --- |
| **archeologo** | ahr-keh-*oh*-loh-goh | *archeologist* |
| **architetto** | ahr-kee-*teht*-toh | *architect* |
| **avvocato** | ahv-voh-*kah*-toh | *lawyer* |
| **chirurgo** | kee-*roohr*-goh | *surgeon* |
| **commesso** | kohm-*mehs*-soh | *salesperson* |
| **dentista (m/f)** | dehn-*tee*-stah | *dentist* |
| **falegname** | fah-leh-*nyah*-meh | *carpenter* |
| **giornalista (m/f)** | johr-nah-*lee*-stah | *journalist* |
| **impiegato** | eehm-pyeh-*gah*-toh | *clerk/employee* |
| **ingegnere (m/f)** | een-geh-*nyeh*-reh | *engineer* |
| **insegnante (m/f)** | een-seh-*nyahn*-teh | *teacher* |
| **meccanico** | mehk-*kah*-nee-koh | *mechanic* |

| Profession | Pronunciation | Meaning |
| --- | --- | --- |
| **medico** | *meh*-dee-koh | *doctor* |
| **operaio** | oh-peh-*rah*-yoh | *factory worker* |
| **pasticciere** | pah-steech-*cheh*-reh | *baker* |
| **psicologo** | psee-*koh*-loh-goh | *psychologist* |
| **professore** | proh-fehs-*soh*-reh | *professor (grades 9-university)* |
| **segretario** | seh-greh-*tah*-ryoh | *secretary* |
| **stilista (m/f)** | stee-*lee*-stah | *designer* |

You might need some of the following as well when talking about jobs:

| Profession | Pronunciation | Translation |
| --- | --- | --- |
| **fabbrica** | *fahb*-bree-kah | *factory* |
| **capo** | *kah*-poh | *head, boss* |
| **padrone** | pah-*droh*-neh | *boss, owner* |
| **direttore** | dee-reht-*toh*-reh | *manager, director* |
| **sciopero** | *shoh*-peh-roh | *strike* |
| **stipendio** | stee-*pehn*-dyoh | *salary* |

Here are a couple questions you may ask a child:

>> **Che lavoro vuoi fare da grande?** (keh lah-*voh*-roh vwoi *fah*-reh dah *grahn*-deh) *(What work would you like to do when you grow up/are older?)*

>> **Cosa vuoi diventare?** (*koh*-zah vwoi dee-vehn-*tah*-reh) *(What do you want to be?)*

The word **sciopero** (*shoh*–peh–roh) *(strike)* is an important one to know in Italy, where strikes happen frequently.

# Talkin' the Talk

Lucia, a high-school teacher, is asking her young second-year Italian students what they want to be when they grow up.

| | |
|---|---|
| **Lucia:** | **Giovanna, che lavoro vuoi fare da grande?**<br>joh-*vahn*-nah keh lah-*voh*-roh vwoi *fah*-reh dah *grahn*-deh<br>*Giovanna, what do you want to do when you grow up?* |
| **Giovanna:** | **Voglio fare la veterinaria.**<br>*voh*-lyoh *fah*-reh lah veh-teh-ree-*nah*-ryah<br>*I want to be a veterinarian.* |
| **Lucia:** | **Perché?**<br>pehr-*keh*<br>*Why?* |
| **Giovanna:** | **Perché amo gli animali.**<br>pehr-*keh ah*-moh lyee ah-nee-*mah*-lee<br>*Because I love animals.* |
| **Lucia:** | **Riccardo, e tu?**<br>reek-*kahr*-doh eh tooh<br>*And you, Richard?* |
| **Riccardo:** | **Voglio fare il medico come il mio babbo.**<br>*voh*-lyoh *fah*-reh il *meh*-dee-koh *koh*-meh eel *mee*-oh *bahb*-boh<br>*I want to be a doctor like my dad.* |
| **Lucia:** | **Emilia, che lavoro ti interessa?**<br>eh-*mee*-lyah keh lah-*voh*-roh tee in-teh-*rehs*-sah<br>*Emilia, what kind of work are you interested in?* |
| **Emilia:** | **Vorrei fare l'insegnante delle elementari.**<br>vohr-*rey fah*-reh leen-seh-*nyahn*-teh *dehl*-leh eh-leh-mehn-*tah*-ree<br>*I'd like to be an elementary school teacher.* |
| **Lucia:** | **Bravi, ragazzi!**<br>*brah*-vee rah-*gaht*-tsee<br>*Good job, class!* |

| | | |
|---|---|---|
| **lavoro [m]** | lah-*voh*-roh | *work, job* |
| **insegnante [m/f]** | een-seh-*nyahn*-teh | *teacher* |
| **babbo [m]** | *bahb*-boh | *dad* |
| **medico [m/f]** | *meh*-dee-koh | *doctor* |
| **direttore [m]** | dee-reht-*toh*-reh | *director, manager* |
| **fabbrica [f]** | *fahb*-bree-kah | *factory* |
| **sciopero [m]** | *shoh*-peh-roh | *strike* |
| **stipendio [m]** | stee-*pehn*-dyoh | *salary* |
| **ti interessa/mi interessa** | tee een-teh-*rehs*-sah/ mee een-teh-*rehs*-sah | *you're interested in/ I'm interested in* |
| **tasse [f/pl.]** | *tahs*-seh | *taxes, tuition* |

# FUN & GAMES

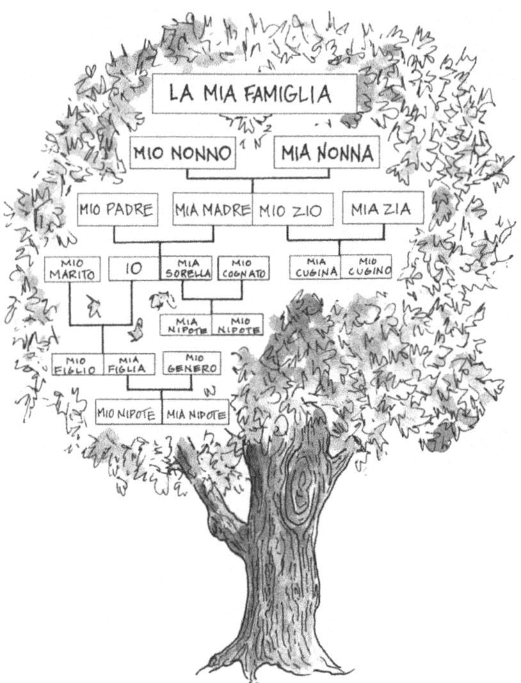


*Illustration by Liz Kurtzman*

Here are ten fill-in-the-blank questions. Pick words and terms from the family tree to complete each statement. You may need the plural for some of the possessive adjectives and relatives. See Appendix C for the answer key.

1. I miei genitori sono ____________ e _____________.

2. Il figlio di mia madre è _______________.

3. I figli di mio fratello sono ____________.

4. La madre della mia mamma è __________.

5. La sorella di mia madre è__________.

6. Il marito di mia sorella è ____________.

7. La moglie di mio figlio è ____________.

8. La sorella di mio figlio è ____________.

9. I figli di mia zia sono _____________.

10. La mamma di mio marito è _______________.

# The Part of Tens

# Chapter **18**
# Ten Ways to Pick Up Italian Quickly

Of course, you've already chosen one of the quickest ways to learn Italian — you picked up this book! For smaller bites of Italian, nibble on one or all of the suggestions in this chapter. Above all, practice, practice, practice!

## Read Italian Food Labels

These days, finding Italian-made food is easy in most countries. If you buy Italian food, read the original label a couple of times before you throw the package away. Usually, you can find an English translation alongside the Italian. In a few weeks, you won't need to read the English part anymore.

## Ask for Food in Italian

If you go to an Italian restaurant or pizzeria, don't be shy! Order your favorite dishes by using their original names and Italian pronunciations. (Don't forget that **bruschetta** is pronounced brooh-*skeht*-tah, with the **k** sound, just like

**porchetta** (pohr-*keht*-tah)!) Chapter 7 discusses important phrases and vocabulary to know when ordering food.

## Listen to Italian Music and Podcasts

You can easily pick up Italian words and pronunciation by listening to Italian music and singing along **una canzone** (ooh-nah kahn-*tsoh*-neh) (*a song*). You have access to scores of Italian singers through the internet (especially on YouTube). You can easily find the lyrics either by searching for them separately, or by modifying your YouTube search by adding the word "karaoke." Put as many songs as you can on your phone or MP3 player, and listen and sing along whenever you can. You could also spend some time listening to an Italian podcast.

## Read Italian Publications

Trying to read a newspaper in a foreign language can be very frustrating. Don't worry — experts say that journalistic language is the most difficult to understand. Culture, gossip, crime, and weather articles are undoubtedly the easiest to understand, and many online newspapers also offer small video clips. Most Italian newspapers are available online. By the way, Italians call the newspaper **il giornale** (eel johr-*nah*-leh).

## Watch Italian Movies and TV Programs with Italian Subtitles

We hope you like movies or more simply watching TV. Watching a movie or TV series in the original language is a great way to pick up words, expressions, and names, and you can even discover something about the country where the story takes place. You can find several Italian movies with English subtitles, from classic **neorealismo** (neh-oh-reh-ah-*leez*-moh) (*neorealism*) to the most recent releases. Many streaming services offer original Italian series with English or Italian subtitles, and you can even come across old familiar cartoons online, dubbed into Italian. You won't need subtitles for these.

# Switch Your Apps and Phone to Italian

Because you probably already spend a lot of time on your phone, you may want to switch the language on your apps and your phone to Italian. This way you also can discover some basic Italian technology language.

# Follow Italian Social Media Accounts

Following social media accounts can significantly boost your Italian language skills by listening and connecting to native-speakers often in a casual, engaging format. Don't limit yourself to just one platform, like Instagram. Go all in — explore different options, find what you enjoy, and discover what makes you feel comfortable in an Italian setting.

# Share Your Interest

Learning a language with other people is much more pleasant (and easier!) than doing it on your own. Having company while you broaden your knowledge of Italian is helpful not only because language is primarily a means of communicating with others, but also because fun is a vital element in every learning process. Put an ad up on the local library bulletin board or post on social media to start an Italian conversation group — you never know what doors this will open for you!

# Surf the Net

Nothing is easier than looking for information on the internet. To find information about Italy, type the name of a famous city or monument in Italian, such as **Venezia** (veh-*neh*-tysah) (Venice) or **Colosseo** (koh-lohs-*seh*-oh) (the Colesseum), to mention just two. Each city and region has its own official website filled with all sorts of useful information. The best place to start is www.google.it, the Italian Google.

# Cook like an Italian

One of our favorite sites is Giallo Zafferano (`www.giallozafferano.it`). Not only will you find great recipes, but you'll also discover cooking videos in Italian that you can watch again and again as you cook alongside the chefs. After a while, you'll have mastered the whole kitchen and cooking vocabulary.

# Chapter **19**

# Ten Things to Know When Traveling to Italy

We hope the title of this chapter isn't too dramatic. Remember that you should always approach the learning process as fun. So, to avoid some cultural *faux pas* that could potentially be embarrassing, we want to give you some advice to help you deal with such situations: some, rather general, about greeting someone in Italy, some about dressing properly, and finally some, more specific, about shopping in a supermarket, and dining out.

## Ciao Isn't for Everyone

**REMEMBER**

**Ciao** (chow) is a common way to say *hello* and *good-bye* that even people who don't speak Italian are familiar with. However, Italians use it only with persons they address with the informal **tu** (tooh) *(you)* — see Chapter 2 for an explanation of the use of **tu.** Many nonspeakers of Italian use the formal **lei** (ley) when talking to someone but still say **ciao.** For instance, don't use ciao when saying hello to the employee behind the counter. This misstep is no big deal but when you're addressing someone formally, it's more authentically Italian to say **buongiorno** (bwohn-*johr*-noh) *(good morning)* or **buonasera** (bwoh-nah-*seh*-rah) *(good evening)* when meeting someone or **arrivederci** (ahr-ree-veh-*dehr*-chee) *(good-bye)* when you're about to leave.

# Modesty Sometimes Matters . . .

In Italy there's a dress code to visit churches and cathedrals. Entering religious sites wearing shorts, skirts, and sleeveless tops isn't allowed: Your **spalle** (*spahl*-leh) (*shoulders*) and **ginocchia** (gee-*nohk*-kyah) (*knees*) must be covered (and yes, this applies to everyone). Especially in large cathedrals, you'll find people at the door who won't let you in if you aren't properly dressed. You often wait in line for hours, only to realize there's a dress code sign just before you're about to enter the church. Don't waste your money on an overpriced shawl that street vendors sell outside major churches to cover up.

# Weigh Your Fruit and Vegetables While Wearing Gloves

At the supermarket in Italy, the matter of kilos versus pounds isn't the only problem. You also have to be aware of certain habits. When weighing **frutta e verdura** (*frooht*-tah eh vehr-*dooh*-rah) (*fruits and vegetables*), you have to wear gloves that you can find near the produce bags in order to touch and pick up your selection. You also don't want to get to the **cassa** (*kahs*-sah) (*cash register*), perhaps after standing in a long line, just to be sent back to weigh your purchase.

# Bag It Yourself . . . and Pay for the Bags

Paper or plastic? Forget about it. You have to pay for a **borsina di plastica** (bohr-*seeh*-nah deeh *plah*-stee-kah) (*plastic bag*). Hence, bringing your own bags is a good idea when shopping. No matter if you have to pay for a bag or you bring your own, you have to bag your own groceries and do it by the time you pay to avoid the annoyed look of the customer in line behind you.

# Free Water? Not Here!

As soon as you sit at a table in a restaurant or a pizzeria, you're used to having a nice (and free!) **bicchiere d'acqua** (beehk-*kyeh*-reh *dah*-kwah) (*glass of water*) full of ice in the United States. Don't expect this in Italy. Water is always bottled, and if you want it, **naturale** (nah-tooh-*rah*-leh) (*still*) or **gassata** (gahs-*sah*-tah) (*sparkling*), you have to order it and pay for it.

# Pepperoni, Cheese on Pasta, and Meatballs

If you're wondering this section counts as three things to remember. If you order a pepperoni pizza, you might be tempted to say pizza con pepperoni using the Italian you learned, Careful! You'll end up getting a pizza with peppers (**peperone** is pepper in Italian). If you want a pepperoni pizza, ask for a **pizza con salame piccante** (*peet*-tsah kohn sah-*lah*-meh peek-*kahn*-teh). Don't ask for **parmigiano** (pahr-mee-*jah*-noh) (*parmesan cheese*) to put on **pasta** (*pah*-stah) with seafood. Mixing fish with cheese is tantamount to eating pickles with milk! And don't be surprised if you don't find spaghetti with **polpette** (pohl-*peht*-teh) (*meatballs*) on the menu. More than likely, you won't find it (and definitely shouldn't ask for it!).

# Tables Are for Diners

Don't sit at a restaurant table to **condividere** (kohn-deeh-*vee*-deh-reh) (*share*) a dish or dessert. Italian restaurants are often small, and the tables are for customers who are having a **pranzo completo** (*prahn*-dzoh kohm-*pleh*-toh) (*full meal*). In bars and cafes, in order to sit down, you have to order something. After you finish, you need to leave and free up the table for other customers. The price of items consumed at the table is often higher.

# The Cappuccino Conundrum . . .

If you're trying to blend in and sound like an Italian, don't order a **cappuccino** (kahp-pooh-*cheeh*-noh) after, say, 11 a.m. Cappuccino is a breakfast drink. If you really have a taste for it after lunch order a **caffè macchiato** (kahf-*feh* mahk-*kyah*-toh), which is an espresso with a little milk.

# Chapter **20**

# Ten Favorite Italian Expressions

Counting how many times a day Italians use some of the following expressions would be an interesting experiment. They're all very typical, and you hear them often in colloquial Italian. So if you remember some of them and use them on the right occasion, you'll come across as Italian. Of course, there are, as in any language, always expressions that sound strange coming from the mouth of a foreigner, but you can use the following without hesitation. Exceptions may be mamma mia and uffa, because they're very spontaneous. But using any or all of the others can make you really sound Italian.

## Mamma mia!

**CULTURAL WISDOM**

**Mamma mia!** (*mahm*-mah *mee*-ah) Please don't think that all Italians are like children just because you notice how often they call for their mommies! In fact, the literal translation is something like "Oh Mama!" and Italians use the exclamation to express surprise, impatience, happiness, sorrow, and so on — in general, a strong emotion. The figurative translation is something like "My goodness!"

# Dai!

**Dai!** (*dah*-ee) (*Come on!* — literally *give!*) Use this word to encourage, to urge someone to do something, or to show disbelief. It's like saying in English "C'mon!" or "No way!"

# Uffa!

**Uffa!** (*oohf*-fah) is a very clear way to show that you're annoyed, bored, angry, or simply fed up with a situation. In English, you'd probably express the same by exhaling in exasperation.

# Che ne so!/Boh!

When Italians want to say that they have no idea about something, they shrug their shoulders and say **Che ne so!** (keh neh soh) (*How should I know?*) or **boh!** (boh). We don't need to tell you that both are quite common expressions.

# Magari!

**Magari!** (mah-*gah*-ree) Just one word, but it expresses so much! It indicates a strong wish or hope. It's a good answer, for instance, if somebody asks you if you'd like to win the lottery. A good translation of this word is "If only!" or "I'd love it!"

# Ti sta bene!

**Ti sta bene!** (tee stah *beh*-neh) This is the Italian way to say "Serves you right!" But this can also mean: "It looks good on you!," depending on the context.

# Non te la prendere!

If you see that somebody is sad, worried, or upset, you can try to console them by saying **Non te la prendere!** (nohn teh lah *prehn*-deh-reh) (*Don't get so upset!*). Sometimes it works.

# Non vedo l'ora!

When you're excited and you just can't wait to see or do something, you say, "**Non vedo l'ora!**" which literally translates as "I don't see the hour." This phrase is more commonly understood as "I can't wait." If you try to say this literally in Italian — **non posso aspettare** — you'll be misunderstood, because it means that you can't wait literally and you must leave.

# Non mi va!

**Non mi va!** (nohn mee vah) is one of the first phrases Italian children learn. It means that you don't want to do something. The best translation is "I don't feel like it!"

# Mi raccomando!

With **Mi raccomando!** (mee rahk-koh-*mahn*-doh), you express a special emphasis in asking for something — like saying "Please, I beg you!" An example is **Telefonami, mi raccomando!** (teh-*leh*-foh-nah-mee mee rahk-koh-*mahn*-doh) ("Don't forget to call me, please!").

# 5
# Appendixes

# Appendix A
# Italian-English Mini Dictionary

## A

**(a) destra**/ah *deh*-strah/(on the) right

**(a) domani**/ah doh-*mah*-nee/see you tomorrow

**(a) dopo**/ah *doh*-poh/see you later

**(a) sinistra**/ah see-*nee*-strah/(on the) left

**abitare (v.)**/ah-bee-*tah*-reh/to live

**abito**/m/*ah*-bee-toh/suit

**acqua**/f/*ah*-kwah/water

**aereo**/m/ah-*eh*-reh-oh/airplane

**aeroporto**/m/ah-eh-roh-*pohr*-toh/ airport

**affittare (v.)**/ahf-feet-*tah*-reh/to rent

**agosto**/m/ah-*gohs*-toh/August

**albergo**/m/ahl-*behr*-goh/hotel

**alto (adj.)**/*ahl*-toh/tall

**amare (v.)**/ah-*mah*-reh/to love

**americano (adj.)**/ah-meh-ree-*kah*-noh/American

**amico**/m/**amica**/f/ah-*mee*-koh/ah-*mee*-kah/friend

**amore**/m/ah-*moh*-reh/love

**anche**/*ahn*-keh/also

**andare (v.)**/ahn-*dah*-reh/to go

**andata**/f/ahn-*dah*-tah/one-way (ticket)

**andata**/f/**e ritorno**/m/ahn-*dah*-tah eh ree-*tohr*-noh/round trip

**anno**/m/*ahn*-noh/year

**antipasto**/m/ahn-tee-*pah*-stoh/ appetizer

**anziano (adj.)**/ahn-*tsyah*-noh/old (for persons)

**appartamento**/m/ahp-pahr-tah-*mehn*-toh/apartment

**aprile**/m/ah-*pree*-leh/April

**architetto**/m/ahr-kee-*teht*-toh/
architect

**arrivare (v.)**/ahr-ree-*vah*-reh/to
arrive

**arrivederci**/ahr-ree-veh-*dehr*-
chee/see you later, good-bye

**assegno**/m/ahs-*seh*-nyoh/check

**autobus**/m/*ow*-toh-boohs/bus

**automobile**/f/*ow*-toh-*moh*-bee-
leh/car

**avere (v.)**/ah-*veh*-reh/to have

**avvocato**/m/ahv-voh-*kah*-toh/lawyer

# B

**bambino**/m/**bambina**/f/bahm-*bee*-
noh/bahm-*bee*-nah/child

**banca**/f/*bahn*-kah/bank

**bello (adj.)**/*behl*-loh/beautiful

**bene (adv.)**/*beh*-neh/well

**bere (v.)**/*beh*-reh/to drink

**bianco (adj.)**/*byahn*-koh/white

**bicchiere**/m/beek-*kyeh*-reh/glass

**bicicletta**/f/bee-chee-*kleht*-tah/
bicycle

**biglietto**/m/bee-*lyeht*-toh/ticket

**birra**/f/*beer*-rah/beer

**blu (adj.)**/blooh/blue

**borsa**/f/*bohr*-sah/bag, handbag

**bottiglia**/f/boht-*tee*-lyah/bottle

**braccio**/m/*brahch*-choh/arm

**buono (adj.)**/*bwoh*-noh/good

**buonanotte**/f/*bwoh*-nah-*noht*-teh/
good-night

**buonasera**/f/*bwoh*-nah-*seh*-rah/good
evening

**buongiorno**/m/bwohn-*johr*-noh/good
morning, good day

# C

**c'è**/cheh/there is

**caffè**/m/kahf-*feh*/coffee

**calcio**/m/*kahl*-choh/soccer

**caldo (adj.)**/*kahl*-doh/warm, hot

**cambiare (v.)**/kahm-*byah*-reh/to
change

**cameriere**/m/**cameriera**/f/kah-meh-
*ryeh*-reh/kah-meh-*ryeh*-rah/
waitress/waiter

**camicia**/f/kah-*mee*-chah/shirt

**campagna**/f/kahm-*pah*-nyah/
countryside

**canadese (adj.)**/kah-nah-*deh*-zeh/
Canadian

**cane**/m/*kah*-neh/dog

**capelli**/m.pl./kah-*pehl*-lee/hair

**cappello**/m/kahp-*pehl*-loh/hat

**cappotto**/m/kahp-*poht*-toh/coat

**caro (adj.)**/*kah*-roh/dear, expensive

**carino (adj.)**/kah-*ree*-noh/nice

**carta di credito**/f/*kahr*-tah dee *kreh*-
dee-toh/credit card

**casa**/f/*kah*-zah/house, home

**cassa**/f/*kahs*-sah/cash register

**cavallo**/m/kah-*vahl*-loh/horse

**cena**/f/*cheh*-nah/dinner

**cento**/*chehn*-toh/hundred

**chi**/kee/who

**chiaro (adj.)**/*kyah*-roh/light-colored,
clear

**ci sono**/chee *soh*-noh/there are

**ciao**/chow/hello, good-bye

**cinema**/m/*chee*-neh-mah/movie
theater

**cinquanta**/cheen-*kwahn*-tah/fifty

**cinque**/*cheen*-kweh/five

**cioccolata**/f/chohk-koh-*lah*-tah/
  chocolate

**città**/f/cheet-*tah*/city, town

**codice postale**/m/*koh*-dee-cheh poh-
  *stah*-leh/zip code

**colazione**/f/koh-lah-*tsyoh*-neh/
  breakfast

**collo**/m/*kohl*-loh/neck

**colore**/m/koh-*loh*-reh/color

**come (adv.)**/*koh*-meh/how

**commesso**/m/**commessa**/f/kohm-
  *mehs*-soh/kohm-*mehs*-sah/sales
  clerk

**comprare (v.)**/kohm-*prah*-reh/to buy

**coro**/m/*koh*-roh/choir

**corto, basso (adj.)**/*kohr*-toh, *bahs*-
  soh/short

**costume da bagno**/m/koh-*stooh*-meh
  dah *bah*-nyoh/bathing suit

**cravatta**/f/krah-*vaht*-tah/tie

**crema**/f/*kreh*-mah/custard

# D

**d'accordo (adv.)**/dahk-*kohr*-doh/all
  right, okay

**dai!**/dahy/come on!

**dare (v.)**/*dah*-reh/to give

**dentista**/m/f/dehn-*tee*-stah/dentist

**dicembre**/m/dee-*chehm*-breh/
  December

**diciannove**/dee-chahn-*noh*-veh/
  nineteen

**diciassette**/dee-chahs-*seht*-teh/
  seventeen

**diciotto**/dee-*choht*-toh/eighteen

**dieci**/*dyeh*-chee/ten

**dire (v.)**/*dee*-reh/to say

**dito**/m/*dee*-toh/finger

**dodici**/*doh*-dee-chee/twelve

**dolce (adj.)**/*dohl*-cheh/sweet

**dolce**/m/*dohl*-cheh/dessert

**domani (adv.)**/doh-*mah*-nee/
  tomorrow

**donna**/f/*dohn*-nah/woman

**dormire (v.)**/dohr-*mee*-reh/to sleep

**dottore**/m/doht-*toh*-reh/doctor

**dove (adv.)**/*doh*-veh/where

**dovere (v.)**/doh-*veh*-reh/to have
  to, must

**due**/*dooh*-eh/two

# E

**emergenza**/f/eh-mehr-*jehn*-tsah/
  emergency

**entrata**/f/ehn-*trah*-tah/entrance

**entrare (v.)**/ehn-*trah*-reh/to enter

**essere (v.)**/*ehs*-seh-reh/to be

**est**/m/ehst/east

# F

**faccia**/f/*fahch*-chah/face

**facile (adj.)**/*fah*-chee-leh/easy

**fame**/f/*fah*-meh/hunger

**fare (v.)**/*fah*-reh/to do

**febbraio**/m/fehb-*brah*-yoh/February

**felice (adj.)**/feh-*lee*-cheh/happy

**festa**/f/*feh*-stah/party, holiday

**figlia**/f/*fee*-lyah/daughter

**figlio**/m/*fee*-lyoh/son

**fine**/f/*fee*-neh/end

**finestra**/f/fee-*neh*-strah/window

**finire (v.)**/fee-*nee*-reh/to finish

**fiore**/m/*fyoh*-reh/flower

**formaggio**/m/fohr-*mahj*-joh/cheese

**fragola**/f/*frah*-goh-lah/strawberry

**fratello**/m/frah-*tehl*-loh/brother
**freddo (adj.)**/*frehd*-doh/cold
**frutta**/f/*frooht*-tah/fruit

## G

**gatto**/m/*gaht*-toh/cat
**gelato**/m/jeh-*lah*-toh/ice cream
**gennaio**/m/jehn-*nah*-yoh/January
**gente**/f/*jehn*-teh/people
**ghiaccio**/m/*gyahch*-choh/ice
**giacca**/f/*jahk*-kah/jacket, blazer
**giallo (adj.)**/*jahl*-loh/yellow
**giardino**/m/jahr-*dee*-noh/garden
**ginocchio**/m/jee-*nohk*-kyoh/knee
**giocare (v.)**/joh-*kah*-reh/to play
**gioco**/m/*joh*-koh/game
**giornale**/m/johr-*nah*-leh/newspaper
**giorno**/m/*johr*-noh/day
**giovane (adj.)**/*joh*-vah-neh/young
**giugno**/m/*jooh*-nyoh/June
**gonna**/f/*gohn*-nah/skirt
**grande (adj.)**/*grahn*-deh/big, large
**grande magazzino**/m/*grahn*-deh mah-gahd-*dzee*-noh/department store
**grazie**/*grah*-tsyeh/thank you
**grigio/(adj.)**/*gree*-joh/gray

## I

**ieri (adv.)**/*yeh*-ree/yesterday
**impermeabile**/m/eem-pehr-meh-*ah*-bee-leh/raincoat
**impiegato**/m/**impiegata**/f/eem-pyeh-*gah*-toh/eem-pyeh-*gah*-tah/employee
**in ritardo**/een ree-*tahr*-doh/late

**indirizzo**/m/een-dee-*reet*-tsoh/address
**infermiera**/f/een-fehr-*myeh*-rah/nurse
**ingegnere**/m.f./een-jeh-*nyeh*-reh/engineer
**insalata**/f/een-sah-*lah*-tah/salad
**invito**/m/een-*vee*-toh/invitation
**io**/*ee*-oh/I
**italiano (adj.)**/ee-tah-*lyah*-noh/Italian

## J

**jeans**/m.pl./jeens/jeans

## L

**lago**/m/*lah*-goh/lake
**lana**/f/*lah*-nah/wool
**largo (adj.)**/*lahr*-goh/wide
**latte**/m/*laht*-teh/milk
**lavoro**/m/lah-*voh*-roh/work
**lei**/ley/she, formal you
**libro**/m/*lee*-broh/book
**loro**/*loh*-roh/they
**luglio**/m/*looh*-lyoh/July
**lui**/*looh*-ee/he
**lungo (adj.)**/*loohn*-goh/long

## M

**ma**/mah/but
**macchina**/f/*mahk*-kee-nah/car
**madre**/f/*mah*-dreh/mother
**maggio**/m/*mahj*-joh/May
**mai (adv.)**/mahy/never
**malato (adj.)**/mah-*lah*-toh/ill

**mamma**/f/*mahm*-mah/mom

**mangiare (v.)**/mahn-*jah*-reh/to eat

**mano**/f/*mah*-noh/hand

**mare**/m/*mah*-reh/sea

**marito**/m/mah-*ree*-toh/husband

**marrone (adj.)**/mahr-*roh*-neh/brown

**marzo**/m/*mahr*-tsoh/March

**me**/meh/me

**medicina**/f/meh-dee-*chee*-nah/
medicine

**medico**/m/*meh*-dee-koh/physician

**mercato**/m/mehr-*kah*-toh/market

**mese**/m/*meh*-zeh/month

**metropolitana**/f/meh-troh-poh-lee-
*tah*-nah/subway

**mettersi (v.)**/*meht*-tehr-see/to put on

**mio (adj.)**/*mee*-oh/my

**mille**/*meel*-leh/thousand

**moglie**/f/*moh*-lyeh/wife

**montagna**/f/mohn-*tah*-nyah/
mountain

# N

**naso**/m/*nah*-zoh/nose

**nebbia**/f/*nehb*-byah/fog

**negozio**/m/neh-*goh*-tsyoh/shop

**nero (adj.)**/*neh*-roh/black

**neve**/f/*neh*-veh/snow

**noi**/noi/we

**noioso (adj.)**/noh-*yoh*-zoh/boring

**nome**/m/*noh*-meh/name

**nord**/m/nohrd/north

**nove**/*noh*-veh/nine

**novembre**/m/noh-*vehm*-breh/
November

**numero**/m/*nooh*-meh-roh/number

**nuoto**/m/*nwoh*-toh/swimming

# O

**occhio**/m/*ohk*-kyoh/eye

**orecchio**/m/oh-*rehk*-kyoh/ear

**ospedale**/m/oh-speh-*dah*-leh/
hospital

**otto**/*oht*-toh/eight

**ottobre**/m/oht-*toh*-breh/October

**ovest**/m/*oh*-vehst/west

# P

**padre**/m/*pah*-dreh/father

**pagare (v.)**/pah-*gah*-reh/to pay

**pane**/m/*pah*-neh/bread

**panna**/f/*pahn*-nah/cream

**pantaloni**/m.pl./pahn-tah-*loh*-nee/
pants

**parlare (v.)**/pahr-*lah*-reh/to talk

**partire (v.)**/pahr-*tee*-reh/to leave

**passaporto**/m/pahs-sah-*pohr*-toh/
passport

**pasticceria**/f/pah-steech-cheh-*ree*-
ah/pastry shop

**per favore (adv.)**/pehr fah-*voh*-reh/
please

**perché**/pehr-*keh*/why, because

**pesce**/m/*peh*-sheh/fish

**piacere (v.)**/pyah-*cheh*-reh/nice to
meet you, to like, pleasure

**piazza**/f/*pyaht*-tsah/square

**piccolo/(adj.)**/*peek*-koh-loh/small,
little

**pioggia**/f/*pyohj*-jah/rain

**piove**/*pyoh*-veh/it's raining

**polizia**/f/poh-lee-*tsee*-ah/police

**potere (v.)**/poh-*teh*-reh/can, may

**pranzo**/m/*prahn*-tsoh/lunch

**preferire (v.)**/preh-feh-*ree*-reh/to
prefer

prego/*preh*-goh/you're welcome

prendere (v.)/*prehn*-deh-reh/to take, to have such as in a bar or restaurant

presentare (v.)/preh-zehn-*tah*-reh/to introduce

# Q

qualcosa/kwahl-*koh*-zah/something

quale/*kwah*-leh/which

quando (adv.)/*kwahn*-doh/when

quanto/quanti (adj.)/*kwahn*-toh/*kwahn*-tee/how much/how many

quattro/m/*kwaht*-troh/four

quattordici/m/kwaht-*tohr*-dee-chee/fourteen

qui (adv.)/kwee/here

quindici/*kween*-dee-chee/fifteen

# R

ragazza/f/rah-*gaht*-tsah/girl

ragazzo/m/rah-*gaht*-tsoh/boy

ridere (v.)/*ree*-deh-reh/to laugh

riso/m/*ree*-zoh/rice, laughter

rosso (adj.)/*rohs*-soh/red

# S

saldi/m.pl./*sahl*-dee/sales

sale/m/*sah*-leh/salt

scarpa/f/*skahr*-pah/shoe

scuro (adj.)/*skooh*-roh/dark

sedici/*seh*-dee-chee/sixteen

segretario/m/segretaria/f/seh-greh-*tah*-ryoh/seh-greh-*tah*-ryah/secretary

sei/sey/six

sempre (adv.)/*sehm*-preh/always

sete/f/*seh*-teh/thirst

sette/*seht*-teh/seven

settembre/m/seht-*tehm*-breh/September

settimana/f/seht-tee-*mah*-nah/week

signora/f/see-*nyoh*-rah/Mrs., Ms., woman

signore/m/see-*nyoh*-reh/Mr., gentleman

soldi/m.pl./*sohl*-dee/money

sole/m/*soh*-leh/sun

solo (adj. and adv.)/*soh*-loh/only, just, alone

sorella/f/soh-*rehl*-lah/sister

spalla/f/*spahl*-lah/shoulder

stanco (adj.)/*stahn*-koh/tired

stazione/f/stah-*tsyoh*-neh/station

strada/f/*strah*-dah/street, road

stretto (adj.)/*streht*-toh/tight, narrow

sud/soohd/south

supermercato/m/sooh-pehr-mehr-*kah*-toh/supermarket

# T

tazza/f/*taht*-tsah/cup

teatro/m/teh-*ah*-troh/theater

telefono/m/teh-*leh*-foh-noh/phone

tempo/m/*tehm*-poh/time, weather

tre/treh/three

tredici/*treh*-dee-chee/thirteen

treno/m/*treh*-noh/train

troppo (adj.)/*trohp*-poh/too much, too many

tu/tooh/you

tutti/*tooht*-tee/everybody

tutto/*tooht*-toh/everything

# U

**ufficio**/m/oohf-*fee*-choh/office
**uno**/*ooh*-noh/one
**uscita**/f/ooh-*shee*-tah/exit
**uomo**/m/*woh*-moh/man

# V

**vacanza**/f/vah-*kahn*-tsah/vacation
**valigia**/f/vah-*lee*-jah/suitcase
**vedere (v.)**/veh-*deh*-reh/to see
**vendere (v.)**/*vehn*-deh-reh/to sell
**venire (v.)**/veh-*nee*-reh/to come
**venti**/*vehn*-tee/twenty
**verde (adj.)**/*vehr*-deh/green
**verdura**/f/vehr-*dooh*-rah/vegetables

**vestito**/m/veh-*stee*-toh/dress, man's suit
**via**/f/*vee*-ah/street
**viaggiare (v.)**/vyahj-*jah*-reh/to travel
**viaggio**/m/*vyahj*-joh/travel
**viale**/m/*vyah*-leh/avenue
**vino**/m/*vee*-noh/wine
**voi**/*voi*/you
**volere (v.)**/voh-*leh*-reh/to want

# Z

**zero**/*dzeh*-roh/zero
**zia**/f/*dzee*-ah/aunt
**zio**/m/*dzee*-oh/uncle
**zucchero**/m/*dzoohk*-keh-roh/sugar

# English-Italian Mini Dictionary

## A

address/**indirizzo**/m/
  een-dee-*reet*-tsoh

airplane/**aereo**/m/ah-*eh*-reh-oh

airport/**aeroporto**/m/
  ah-eh-roh-*pohr*-toh

all right, okay/**d'accordo**/
  dahk-*kohr*-doh

also/**anche**/*ahn*-keh

always/**sempre**/*sehm*-preh

American/**americano**/m/**americana**/f/
  ah-meh-ree-*kah*-noh/
  ah-meh-ree-*kah*-nah

aunt **zia**/f/*dzee*-ah

apartment/**appartamento**/m/
  ahp-pahr-tah-*mehn*-toh

appetizer/**antipasto**/m/
  ahn-tee-*pah*-stoh

April/**aprile**/m/ah-*pree*-leh

architect/**architetto**/m/
  ahr-kee-*teht*-toh

arm/**braccio**/m/*brahch*-choh

arrive (v.)/**arrivare**/ahr-ree-*vah*-reh

August/**agosto**/m/ah-*goh*-stoh

avenue/**viale**/m/*vyah*-leh

## B

bad/**cattivo**/m/**cattiva**/f/kaht-*tee*-
  voh/kaht-*tee*-vah

bag/**borsa**/f/*bohr*-sah

bakery/**pasticceria**/f/
  pah-steech-cheh-*ree*-ah

bank/**banca**/f/*bahn*-kah

bathing suit/**costume da bagno**/m/
  kohs-*tooh*-meh dah *bah*-nyoh

be (v.)/**essere**/*ehs*-seh-reh

beach/**spiaggia**/f/*spyahj*-jah

beautiful/**bello**/m/**bella**/f/*behl*-
  loh/*behl*-lah

because/**perché**/pehr-*keh*

beer/**birra**/f/*beer*-rah

bicycle/**bicicletta**/f/
  bee-chee-*kleht*-tah

big, tall, large/**grande**/m//f/*grahn*-deh

black/**nero**/m/**nera**/f/*neh*-roh/
  neh-rah

blue/**blu**/m/f/*blooh*

book/**libro**/m/*lee*-broh

boring/**noioso**/m/**noiosa**/f/noh-*yoh*-
  zoh/noi-*oh*-zah

bottle/**bottiglia**/f/boht-*tee*-lyah

boy/**ragazzo**/m/rah-*gaht*-tsoh

bread/**pane**/m/*pah*-neh

breakfast/**colazione**/f/
  koh-lah-*tsyoh*-neh

brother/**fratello**/m/frah-*tehl*-loh

brown/**marrone**/m/f/mahr-*roh*-neh

bus/**autobus**/m/*ow*-toh-boohs

but/**ma**/mah

buy (v.)/**comprare**/kohm-*prah*-reh

# C

can, may (v.)/**potere**/poh-*teh*-reh

Canadian/**canadese**/m/f/
kah-nah-*deh*-zeh

car/**automobile**/f/
ow-toh-*moh*-bee-leh

car/**macchina**/*mahk*-kee-nah

cash register/f/**cassa**/*kahs*-sah

cat/**gatto**/m/*gaht*-toh

change (v.)/**cambiare**/kahm-*byah*-reh

check/**assegno**/m/ahs-*seh*-nyoh

cheese/**formaggio**/m/fohr-*mahj*-joh

child (female)/**bambina**/f/
bahm-*bee*-nah

child (male)/**bambino**/m/
bahm-*bee*-noh

chocolate/**cioccolata**/f/
chohk-koh-*lah*-tah

choir/**coro**/m/*koh*-roh

cinema/**cinema**/m/*chee*-neh-mah

city, town/**città**/f/cheet-*tah*

coat/**cappotto**/m/kahp-*poht*-toh

coffee/**caffè**/m/*kahf*-feh

cold/**freddo**/m/**fredda**/f/*frehd*-
doh/*frehd*-dah

color/**colore**/m/koh-*loh*-reh

come on/**dai**/dahy

come (v.)/**venire**/veh-*nee*-reh

countryside/**campagna**/f/
kahm-*pah*-nyah

cream/**panna**/f/*pahn*-nah

credit card/**carta di credito**/f/*kahr*-tah
dee *kreh*-dee-toh

cup/**tazza**/f/*taht*-tsah

custard/**crema**/f/*kreh*-mah

# D

dark/**scuro**/m/**scura**/f/*skooh*-
roh/*skooh*-rah

daughter/**figlia**/f/*fee*-lyah

day/**giorno**/m/*johr*-noh

dear/**caro**/m/**cara**/f/*kah*-roh/*kah*-rah

December/**dicembre**/m/
dee-*chehm*-breh

dentist/**dentista**/m/f/dehn-*tee*-stah

department store/**grande magazzino**/
m/*grahn*-deh mah-gahd-*dzee*-noh

dessert/m/**dolce**/*dohl*-cheh

dinner/**cena**/f/*cheh*-nah

doctor/**dottore**/m/doht-*toh*-reh

dog/**cane**/m/*kah*-neh

dress/**vestito**/m/veh-*stee*-toh

drink (v.)/**bere**/*beh*-reh

# E

ear/**orecchio**/m/oh-*rehk*-kyoh

east/**est**/m/ehst

easy/**facile**/m/f/*fah*-chee-leh

eat (v.)/**mangiare**/mahn-*jah*-reh

eight/**otto**/*oht*-toh

eighteen/**diciotto**/dee-*choht*-toh

eleven/**undici**/*oohn*-dee-chee

emergency/**emergenza**/f/
eh-mehr-*jehn*-tsah

employee/**impiegato**/m/**impiegata**/f/
eem-pyeh-*gah*-toh/
eem-pyeh-*gah*-tah

end/**fine**/f/*fee*-neh

engineer/**ingegnere**/m/
een-jeh-*nyeh*-reh

enter (v.)/**entrare**/ehn-*trah*-reh

entrance/**entrata**/f/ehn-*trah*-tah

everybody/**tutti**/*tooht*-tee

everything/**tutto**/*tooht*-toh

exit/**uscita**/f/ooh-*shee*-tah

expensive/**caro**/m/**cara**/f/*kah*-roh/*kah*-rah

eye/**occhio**/m/*ohk*-kyoh

# F

face/**faccia**/f/*fahch*-chah

father/**padre**/m/*pah*-dreh

February/**febbraio**/m/fehb-*brah*-yoh

fifteen/**quindici**/*kween*-dee-chee

fifty/**cinquanta**/cheen-*kwahn*-tah

finger/**dito**/m/*dee*-toh

finish (v.)/**finire**/fee-*nee*-reh

fish/**pesce**/m/*peh*-sheh

five/**cinque**/*cheen*-kweh

flower/**fiore**/m/*fyoh*-reh

fog/**nebbia**/f/*nehb*-byah

four/**quattro**/*kwaht*-troh

fourteen/**quattordici**/kwaht-*tohr*-dee-chee

friend/**amico**/m/**amica**/f/ah-*mee*-koh/ah-*mee*-kah

fruit/**frutta**/f/*frooht*-tah

# G

garden/**giardino**/m/jahr-*dee*-noh

girl/**ragazza**/f/rah-*gaht*-tsah

give (v.)/**dare**/*dah*-reh

glass/**bicchiere**/m/beek-*kyeh*-reh

go (v.)/**andare**/ahn-*dah*-reh

good/**buono**/m/**buona**/f/*bwoh*-noh/*bwoh*-nah

good-bye/**ciao**/chow

good evening/**buonasera**/*bwoh*-nah-*seh*-rah

good morning, good day/**buongiorno**/bwohn-*johr*-noh

good-night/**buonanotte**/*bwoh*-nah-*noht*-teh

green/**verde**/m/f/*vehr*-deh

gray/**grigio**/m/**grigia**/f/*gree*-joh/*gree*-jah

# H

hair/**capelli**/m.pl./kah-*pehl*-lee

hand/**mano**/f/*mah*-noh

happy/**felice**/m/f/feh-*lee*-cheh

hat/**cappello**/m/kahp-*pehl*-loh

have (v.)/**avere**/ah-*veh*-reh

have, take (at bar, restaurant) (v.)/**prendere**/*prehn*-deh-reh

have to (v.)/**dovere**/doh-*veh*-reh

he/**lui**/*looh*-ee

hello/**ciao**/chow

help/**aiuto**/ah-*yooh*-toh

here/**qui**/kwee

horse/**cavallo**/m/kah-*vahl*-loh

hospital/**ospedale**/m/oh-speh-*dah*-leh

hot/**caldo**/m/**calda**/f/*kahl*-doh/*kahl*-dah

hotel/**albergo**/m/ahl-*behr*-goh

house, home/**casa**/f/*kah*-zah

how/**come**/*koh*-meh

how many/**quanti**/*kwahn*-tee

how much/**quanto**/*kwahn*-toh

hundred/**cento**/*chehn*-toh

hunger/**fame**/f/*fah*-meh

husband/**marito**/m/mah-*ree*-toh

# I

I/**io**/*ee*-oh

ice/**ghiaccio**/m/*gyahch*-choh

ice cream/**gelato**/m/jeh-*lah*-toh

ill/**malato**/m/**malata**/f/mah-*lah*-toh/
mah-*lah*-tah

introduce (v.)/**presentare**/
preh-zehn-*tah*-reh

invitation/**invito**/m/een-*vee*-toh

Italian/**italiano**/m/**italiana**/f/ee-tah-
*lyah*-noh/ee-tah-*lyah*-nah

# J

jacket, blazer/f/**giacca**/*jahk*-kah

January/**gennaio**/m/jehn-*nah*-yoh

jeans/**jeans**/m.pl./jeens

July/**luglio**/m/*looh*-lyoh

June/**giugno**/m/*jooh*-nyoh

# K

knee/**ginocchio**/m/jee-*nohk*-kyoh

knife/**coltello**/m/kohl-*tehl*-loh

# L

lake/**lago**/m/*lah*-goh

large/**largo**/m/**larga**/f/*lahr*-
goh/*lahr*-gah

late/**in ritardo**/een ree-*tahr*-doh

laugh (v.)/**ridere**/*ree*-deh-reh

lawyer/**avvocato**/m/ahv-voh-*kah*-toh

leave (v.)/**partire**/pahr-*tee*-reh

(on the) left/**a sinistra**/ah
see-*nee*-strah

light-colored/**chiaro**/m/**chiara**/f/*kyah*-
roh/*kyah*-rah

live (v.)/**abitare, vivere**/ah-bee-*tah*-
reh, *vee*-veh-reh

long/**lungo**/m/**lunga**/f/*loohn*-
goh/*loohn*-gah

love (v.)/**amare**/ah-*mah*-reh

love/**amore**/m/ah-*moh*-reh

lunch/**pranzo**/m/*prahn*-tsoh

# M

male nurse/**infermiere**/m/
een-fehr-*myeh*-reh

man/**uomo**/m/*woh*-moh

March/**marzo**/m/*mahr*-tsoh

market/**mercato**/m/mehr-*kah*-toh

May/**maggio**/m/*mahj*-joh

me/**me**/meh

meat/**carne**/f/*kahr*-neh

medicine/**medicina**/f/
meh-dee-*chee*-nah

milk/**latte**/m/*laht*-teh

mom/**mamma**/f/*mahm*-mah

money/**soldi**/m/*sohl*-dee

month/**mese**/m/*meh*-zeh

mother/**madre**/f/*mah*-dreh

mountain/**montagna**/f/
mohn-*tah*-nyah

Mr./**signore**/m/see-*nyoh*-reh

Mrs./**signora**/f/see-*nyoh*-rah

my/**mio**/m/**mia**/f/*mee*-oh/*mee*-ah

# N

name/**nome**/m/*noh*-meh

neck/**collo**/m/*kohl*-loh

never/**mai**/mahy

newspaper/**giornale**/m/johr-*nah*-leh

nice/**carino**/m/**carina**/f/kah-*ree*-noh/
kah-*ree*-nah

nice to meet you/**piacere**/
  pyah-*cheh*-reh

nine/**nove**/*noh*-veh

nineteen/**diciannove**/
  dee-chahn-*noh*-veh

north/**nord**/m/nohrd

nose/**naso**/m/*nah*-zoh

November/**novembre**/m/
  noh-*vehm*-breh

number/**numero**/m/nooh-*meh*-roh

nurse/**infermiera**/f/
  een-fehr-*myeh*-rah

# O

October/**ottobre**/m/oht-*toh*-breh

office/**ufficio**/m/oohf-*fee*-choh

old (for persons)/**anziano**/
  m/**anziana**/f/ahn-*tsyah*-noh/
  ahn-*tsyah*-nah

one/**uno**/*ooh*-noh

one-way (ticket)/**andata**/f/
  ahn-*dah*-tah

only, just/**solo**/*soh*-loh

# P

party, holiday/**festa**/f/*feh*-stah

passport/**passaporto**/m/*pahs*-sah-
  *pohr*-toh

pay (v.)/**pagare**/pah-*gah*-reh

people/**gente**/f/*jehn*-teh

phone/**telefono**/m/teh-*leh*-foh-noh

physician/**medico**/m/*meh*-dee-koh

play (v.)/**giocare**/joh-*kah*-reh

play/**gioco**/m/*joh*-koh

please/**per favore**/pehr fah-*voh*-reh

police/**polizia**/f/poh-lee-*tsee*-ah

prefer (v.)/**preferire**/
  preh-feh-*ree*-reh

put on (v.) (clothes/
  accessories)/**mettersi**/
  meht-*tehr*-see

# R

rain/**pioggia**/f/*pyohj*-jah

raincoat/**impermeabile**/m/
  eem-pehr-meh-*ah*-bee-leh

red/**rosso**/m/**rossa**/f/*rohs*-
  soh/*rohs*-sah

rent (v.)/**affittare**/ahf-feet-*tah*-reh

(on the) right/**a destra**/ah *deh*-strah

rice/**riso**/m/*ree*-zoh

round trip/**andata**/f/**e ritorno**/m/ahn-
  *dah*-tah eh ree-*tohr*-noh

# S

salad/**insalata**/f/een-sah-*lah*-tah

sales/**saldi**/m.pl./*sahl*-dee

sales clerk/**commesso**/
  m/**commessa**/f/kohm-*mehs*-soh/
  kohm-*mehs*-sah

salt/**sale**/m/*sah*-leh

say (v.)/**dire**/*dee*-reh

sea/**mare**/m/*mah*-reh

secretary/**segretario**/m/**segretaria**/f/
  seh-greh-*tah*-ryoh/
  seh-greh-*tah*-ryah

see (v.)/**vedere**/veh-*deh*-reh

see you, good-bye/**arrivederci**/
  ahr-ree-veh-*dehr*-chee

see you later/**a dopo**/ah *doh*-poh

see you tomorrow/**a domani**/ah
  doh-*mah*-nee

sell (v.)/**vendere**/vehn-*deh*-reh

September/**settembre**/m/
  seht-*tehm*-breh

seven/**sette**/*seht*-teh

seventeen/**diciassette**/
  dee-chahs-*seht*-teh

she/**lei**/ley

shirt/**camicia**/f/kah-*mee*-chah

shoe/**scarpa**/f/*skahr*-pah

shop/**negozio**/m/neh-*goh*-tsyoh

short/**corto, basso**/m/**corta, bassa**/
  f/*kohr*-toh, *bahs*-soh/*kohr*-tah,
  *bahs*-sah

shoulder/**spalla**/f/*spahl*-lah

sister/**sorella**/f/soh-*rehl*-lah

six/**sei**/sey

sixteen/**sedici**/*seh*-dee-chee

skirt/**gonna**/f/*gohn*-nah

sleep (v.)/**dormire**/dohr-*mee*-reh

small, little/**piccolo**/m/**piccola**/f/*peek*-
  koh-loh/*peek*-koh-lah

snow/**neve**/f/*neh*-veh

soccer/**calcio**/m/*kahl*-choh

something/**qualcosa**/kwahl-*koh*-zah

son/**figlio**/m/*fee*-lyoh

south/**sud**/m/soohd

square/**piazza**/f/*pyaht*-tsah

station/**stazione**/f/stah-*tsyoh*-neh

strawberry/**fragola**/f/*frah*-goh-lah

street, road/**strada**/f/*strah*-dah or
  **via**/f/*vee*-ah

subway/**metropolitana**/f/
  meh-troh-poh-lee-*tah*-nah

sugar/**zucchero**/m/*dzook*-keh-roh

suit/**abito**/m/*ah*-bee-toh

suitcase/**valigia**/f/vah-*lee*-jah

sun/**sole**/m/*soh*-leh

supermarket/**supermercato**/m/
  sooh-pehr-mehr-*kah*-toh

sweet/**dolce**/m/f/*dohl*-cheh

swimming/**nuoto**/m/*nwoh*-toh

# T

take (v.)/**prendere**/*prehn*-deh-reh

talk (v.)/**parlare**/pahr-*lah*-reh

tall/**alto**/m/**alta**/f/*ahl*-toh/*ahl*-tah

tax/**tassa, dazio**/m/*tahs*-sah,
  *dah*-tsyoh

telephone/**telefono**/m/
  teh-*leh*-foh-noh

ten/**dieci**/*dyeh*-chee

thank you/**grazie**/*grah*-tsyeh

theater/**teatro**/m/teh-*ah*-troh

there are/**ci sono**/chee *soh*-noh

there is/**c'è**/cheh

they/**loro**/*loh*-roh

thirst/**sete**/f/*seh*-teh

thirteen/**tredici**/*treh*-dee-chee

thousand/**mille**/*meel*-leh

three/**tre**/treh

ticket/**biglietto**/m/bee-*lyeht*-toh

tie/**cravatta**/f/krah-*vaht*-tah

tight, narrow/**stretto**/m/
  **stretta**/f/*streht*-toh/*streht*-tah

time, weather/**tempo**/m/*tehm*-poh

tired/**stanco**/m/**stanca**/f/*stahn*-
  koh/*stahn*-kah

today/**oggi**/*ohj*-jee

tomorrow/**domani**/doh-*mah*-nee

too much/**troppo**/*trohp*-poh

train/**treno**/m/*treh*-noh

travel (v.)/**viaggiare**/vyahj-*jah*-reh

travel/**viaggio**/m/*vyahj*-joh

trousers/**pantaloni**/m/
  pahn-tah-*loh*-nee

twelve/**dodici**/*doh*-dee-chee

twenty/**venti**/*vehn*-tee

two/**due**/*dooh*-eh

# U

uncle/**zio**/m/*dzee*-oh

# V

vacation/**vacanza**/f/vah-*kahn*-tsah

vegetables/**verdura**/f/vehr-*dooh*-rah

# W

waitress/waiter/**cameriere**/
m/**cameriera**/f/kah-meh-*ryeh*-reh/
kah-meh-*ryeh*-rah

wallet/**portafoglio**/pohr-tah-
*foh*-lyoh

want (v.)/**volere**/voh-*leh*-reh

warm/**caldo**/m/**calda**/f/*kahl*-
doh/*kahl*-dah

water/**acqua**/f/*ah*-kwah

we/**noi**/noi

week/**settimana**/f/seht-tee-
*mah*-nah

well/**bene**/*beh*-neh

west/**ovest**/m/*oh*-vehst

what/**cosa**/*koh*-zah

when/**quando**/*kwahn*-doh

where/**dove**/*doh*-veh

which/**quale**/m/f/*kwah*-leh

white/**bianco**/m/**bianca**/f/*byahn*-
koh/*byahn*-kah

who/**chi**/kee

why/**perché**/pehr-*keh*

wife/**moglie**/f/*moh*-lyeh

window/**finestra**/f/fee-*neh*-strah

wine/**vino**/m/*vee*-noh

woman/**donna**/f/*dohn*-nah

wool/**lana**/f/*lah*-nah

work/**lavoro**/m/lah-*voh*-roh

# Y

year/**anno**/m/*ahn*-noh

yellow/**giallo**/m/**gialla**/f/*jahl*-
loh/*jahl*-lah

yesterday/**ieri**/*yeh*-ree

you (formal)/**Lei**/ley

you (plural, informal/formal)/**voi**/voi

you (singular, informal)/**tu**/tooh

you're welcome/**prego**/*preh*-goh

young/**giovane**/m/f/*joh*-vah-neh

# Z

zero/**zero**/*dzeh*-roh

zip code/**codice postale**/m/*koh*-dee-
cheh poh-*stah*-leh

# Appendix **B**
# Verb Tables
## Italian Regular Verbs

### Regular Verbs Ending with -*are*
For example: parlare *(to speak)*;

Past participle: parlato *(spoken)* (w/avere)

|  | Present | Past | Future |
|---|---|---|---|
| *io (I)* | parlo | ho parlato | parlerò |
| *tu (you, inf.)* | parli | hai parlato | parlerai |
| *lui/lei (he/she/you form.)* | parla | ha parlato | parlerà |
| *noi (we)* | parliamo | abbiamo parlato | parleremo |
| *voi (you)* | parlate | avete parlato | parlerete |
| *loro (they/you form. pl.)* | parlano | hanno parlato | parleranno |

Other common −**are** verbs: **mangiare** *(to eat)*, **studiare** *(to study)*, **imparare** *(to learn)*, **insegnare** *(to teach)*, **suonare** *(to play an instrument)*, **giocare** *(to play a game/ sport)*, **disegnare** *(to draw)*, **cucinare** *(to cook)*, **lavorare** *(to work)*.

# Regular Verbs Ending with *-ere*
### For example: vendere *(to sell)*;
### Past participle: venduto *(sold)* (w/avere)

|  | Present | Past | Future |
|---|---|---|---|
| *io (I)* | vendo | ho venduto | venderò |
| *tu (you, inf.)* | vendi | hai venduto | venderai |
| *lui/lei (he/she/you form.)* | vende | ha venduto | venderà |
| *noi (we)* | vendiamo | abbiamo venduto | venderemo |
| *voi (you)* | vendete | avete venduto | venderete |
| *loro (they/you form. pl.)* | vendono | hanno venduto | venderanno |

Other common **–ere** verbs: **leggere** *(to read)*, **scrivere** *(to write)*, **mettere** *(to put)*, **prendere** *(to take)*, **vivere** *(to live)*, **vedere** *(to see)*, **chiudere** *(to close)*, **ripetere** *(to repeat)*. Unlike the example, most of these past participles are irregular: **letto**, **scritto**, **messo**, **preso**, **vissuto**, **visto/veduto**, **chiuso**. Only **ripetuto** is regular.

# Regular Verbs Ending with *-ire**
### For example: partire *(to leave)*;
### Past participle: partito (left) (w/essere)

|  | Present | Past | Future |
|---|---|---|---|
| *io (I)* | parto | sono partito/a | partirò |
| *tu (you, inf.)* | parti | sei partito/a | partirai |
| *lui/lei (he/she/you form.)* | parte | è partito/a | partirà |
| *noi (we)* | partiamo | siamo partiti/e | partiremo |
| *voi (you)* | partite | siete partiti/e | partirete |
| *loro (they/you form. pl.)* | partono | sono partiti/e | partiranno |

Other common **–ire** verbs: **aprire** *(to open)*, **dormire** *(to sleep)*, **coprire** *(to cover)*, **sentire** *(to hear, feel, taste, touch)*. Note that **aprire** and **coprire** have irregular past participles (**aperto** and **coperto**).

# Regular –ire Verbs with a Special Pattern (-isc-)

**For example: capire** (*to understand*);

**Past participle: capito**

|  | Present | Past | Future |
|---|---|---|---|
| *io (I)* | capisco | ho capito | capirò |
| *tu* | capisci | hai capito | capirai |
| *lui/lei* | capisce | ha capito | capirà |
| *noi* | capiamo | abbiamo capito | capiremo |
| *voi* | capite | avete capito | capirete |
| *loro* | capiscono | hanno capito | capiranno |

**For example: finire** (*to finish*);

**Past participle: finito**

|  | Present | Past | Future |
|---|---|---|---|
| *io* | finisco | ho finito | finirò |
| *tu* | finisci | hai finito | finirai |
| *lui/lei* | finisce | ha finito | finirà |
| *noi* | finiamo | abbiamo finito | finiremo |
| *voi* | finite | avete finito | finirete |
| *loro* | finiscono | hanno finito | finiranno |

**For example: preferire** (*to prefer*);

**Past participle: preferito**

|  | Present | Past | Future |
|---|---|---|---|
| *io* | preferisco | ho preferito | preferirò |
| *tu* | preferisci | hai preferito | preferirai |
| *lui/lei* | preferisce | ha preferito | preferirà |
| *noi* | preferiamo | abbiamo preferito | preferiremo |
| *voi* | preferite | avete preferito | preferirete |
| *loro* | preferiscono | hanno preferito | preferiranno |

Other common **–isc** verbs: **pulire** (*to clean*), **finire** (*to finish, end*), and **costruire** (*to build*).

**Reflexive Verbs**

For example: lavarsi *(to wash oneself)*

**Past participle: lavato *(washed)* (w/essere)**
**(All reflexive verbs take essere in the past)**

|        | Present    | Past              | Future       |
| ------ | ---------- | ----------------- | ------------ |
| *io*      | mi lavo    | mi sono lavato/a  | mi laverò    |
| *tu*      | ti lavi    | ti sei lavato/a   | ti laverai   |
| *lui/lei* | si lava    | si è lavato/a     | si laverà    |
| *noi*     | ci laviamo | ci siamo lavati/e | ci laveremo  |
| *voi*     | vi lavate  | vi siete lavati/e | vi laverete  |
| *loro*    | si lavano  | si sono lavati/e  | si laveranno |

Other common reflexive verbs: **alzarsi** *(to get up)*, **divertirsi** *(to have fun)*, **sentirsi** *(to feel)*, **innamorarsi** *(to fall in love)*, **mettersi** *(to put [clothing/accessories] on)*, **addormentarsi** *(to fall asleep)*, **permettersi** *(to afford)*.

# Avere and Essere

**Verb avere** *(to have)*

**Past participle: avuto *(had)* (w/avere)**

|        | Present | Past         | Future  |
| ------ | ------- | ------------ | ------- |
| *io*      | ho      | ho avuto     | avrò    |
| *tu*      | hai     | hai avuto    | avrai   |
| *lui/lei* | ha      | ha avuto     | avrà    |
| *noi*     | abbiamo | abbiamo avuto | avremo  |
| *voi*     | avete   | avete avuto  | avrete  |
| *loro*    | hanno   | hanno avuto  | avranno |

**Verb *essere* (to be)**

**Past participle: stato *(been)* (w/essere)**

| | Present | Past | Future |
|---|---|---|---|
| *io* | sono | sono stato/a | sarò |
| *tu* | sei | sei stato/a | sarai |
| *lui/lei* | è | è stato/a | sarà |
| *noi* | siamo | siamo stati/e | saremo |
| *voi* | siete | siete stati/e | sarete |
| *loro* | sono | sono stati/e | saranno |

# Other Irregular Verbs

| | | Present | Past | Past Participle |
|---|---|---|---|---|
| **andare** | *io* | vado | andrò | |
| *to go* | *tu* | vai | andrai | |
| | *lui/lei* | va | andrà | andato/a/i/e |
| | *noi* | andiamo | andremo | (w/essere) |
| | *voi* | andate | andrete | |
| | *loro* | vanno | andranno | |

| | | Present | Future | Past Participle |
|---|---|---|---|---|
| | *Io* | bevo | berrò | |
| **bere** | *tu* | bevi | berrai | |
| *to drink* | *lui/lei* | beve | berrà | bevuto (w/avere) |
| | *noi* | beviamo | berremo | |
| | *voi* | bevete | berrete | |
| | *loro* | bevono | berranno | |

| | | Present | Future | Past Participle |
|---|---|---|---|---|
| | io | do | darò | |
| **dare** | tu | dai | darai | |
| *to give* | lui/lei | dà | darà | dato |
| | noi | diamo | daremo | (w/avere) |
| | voi | date | darete | |
| | loro | danno | daranno | |

| | | Present | Future | Past Participle |
|---|---|---|---|---|
| | io | dico | dirò | |
| **dire** | tu | dici | dirai | |
| *to say;* | lui/lei | dice | dirà | detto |
| *to tell* | noi | diciamo | diremo | (w/avere) |
| | voi | dite | direte | |
| | loro | dicono | diranno | |

| | | Present | Future | Past Participle |
|---|---|---|---|---|
| | io | devo | dovrò | |
| **dovere** | tu | devi | dovrai | |
| *to have to;* | lui/lei | deve | dovrà | dovuto |
| *ought to; must* | noi | dobbiamo | dovremo | (w/avere or essere) |
| | voi | dovete | dovrete | |
| | loro | devono | dovranno | |

| | | Present | Future | Past Participle |
|---|---|---|---|---|
| | io | faccio | farò | |
| **fare** | tu | fai | farai | |
| *to do;* | lui/lei | fa | farà | fatto |
| *to make* | noi | facciamo | faremo | (w/avere) |
| | voi | fate | farete | |
| | loro | fanno | faranno | |

| | | Present | Future | Past Participle |
|---|---|---|---|---|
| **piacere** | *mi/ti/gli/le/* | piace | piacerà | |
| *to like* | *ci/vi/gli (loro)* | | | piaciuto/a/i/e |
| | *mi/ti/gli/le/* | piacciono | piaceranno | (w/essere) |
| | *ci/vi/gli (loro)* | | | |

The verb **piacere** takes indirect object pronouns, and usually you only need the third person singular and plural of this verb.

| | | Present | Future | Past Participle |
|---|---|---|---|---|
| | *io* | pongo | porrò | |
| **porre** | *tu* | poni | porrai | |
| *to put* | *lui/lei* | pone | porrà | posto |
| | *noi* | poniamo | porremo | (w/avere) |
| | *voi* | ponete | porrete | |
| | *loro* | pongono | porranno | |

Other verbs conjugated like **porre**: **opporsi** *(to oppose)*, **imporre** *(to impose)*, and **proporre** *(to propose or suggest)*.

| | | Present | Future | Past Participle |
|---|---|---|---|---|
| | *io* | posso | potrò | |
| **potere** | *tu* | puoi | potrai | |
| *can;* | *lui/lei* | può | potrà | potuto |
| *to able to* | *noi* | possiamo | potremo | (w/avere or essere) |
| | *voi* | potete | potrete | |
| | *loro* | possono | potranno | |

|  | | Present | Future | Past Participle |
|---|---|---|---|---|
| **rimanere** | io | rimango | rimarrò | |
| | tu | rimani | rimarrai | |
| *to stay;* | lui/lei | rimane | rimarrà | rimasto/a/i/e |
| *to remain* | noi | rimaniamo | rimarremo | (w/essere) |
| | voi | rimanete | rimarrete | |
| | loro | rimangono | rimarranno | |

|  | | Present | Future | Past Participle |
|---|---|---|---|---|
| | io | salgo | salirò | |
| **salire** | tu | sali | salirai | |
| to go up | lui/lei | sale | salirà | salito/a/i/e |
| | noi | saliamo | saliremo | (w/essere) |
| | voi | salite | salirete | |
| | loro | salgono | saliranno | |

|  | | Present | Future | Past Participle |
|---|---|---|---|---|
| | io | so | saprò | |
| **sapere** | tu | sai | saprai | |
| to know | lui/lei | sa | saprà | saputo |
| | noi | sappiamo | sapremo | (w/avere) |
| | voi | sapete | saprete | |
| | loro | sanno | sapranno | |

|  | | Present | Future | Past Participle |
|---|---|---|---|---|
| | io | scelgo | sceglierò | |
| **scegliere** | tu | scegli | sceglierai | |
| to choose | lui/lei | sceglie | sceglierà | scelto |
| | noi | scegliamo | sceglieremo | (w/avere) |
| | voi | scegliete | sceglierete | |
| | loro | scelgono | sceglieranno | |

| **sedersi** | | Present | Future | Past Participle |
|---|---|---|---|---|
| to sit down | io | mi siedo | mi s(i)ederò | |
| | tu | ti siedi | ti s(i)ederai | |
| | lui/lei | si siede | si s(i)ederà | seduto |
| | noi | ci sediamo | ci s(i)ederemo | (w/essere) |
| | voi | vi sedete | vi s(i)ederete | |
| | loro | si siedono | si s(i)ederanno | |

| | | Present | Future | Past Participle |
|---|---|---|---|---|
| | io | sto | starò | |
| **stare** | tu | stai | starai | |
| to stay; | lui/lei | sta | starà | stato/a/i/e |
| to be | noi | stiamo | staremo | (w/essere) |
| | voi | state | starete | |
| | loro | stanno | staranno | |

| | | Present | Future | Past Participle |
|---|---|---|---|---|
| | io | tengo | terrò | |
| **tenere** | tu | tieni | terrai | |
| to hold | lui/lei | tiene | terrà | tenuto |
| | noi | teniamo | terremo | (w/avere) |
| | voi | tenete | terrete | |
| | loro | tengono | terranno | |

| | | Present | Future | Past Participle |
|---|---|---|---|---|
| | io | tolgo | toglierò | |
| **togliere** | tu | togli | toglierai | |
| to remove; take off; | lui/lei | toglie | toglierà | tolto |
| take away | noi | togliamo | toglieremo | (w/avere) |
| | voi | togliete | toglierete | |
| | loro | tolgono | toglieranno | |

| | | Present | Future | Past Participle |
|---|---|---|---|---|
| | *io* | esco | uscirò | |
| **uscire** | *tu* | esci | uscirai | |
| *to go out* | *lui/lei* | esce | uscirà | uscito/a/i/e |
| | *noi* | usciamo | usciremo | (w/essere) |
| | *voi* | uscite | uscirete | |
| | *loro* | escono | usciranno | |

| | | Present | Future | Past Participle |
|---|---|---|---|---|
| | *io* | vengo | verrò | |
| **venire** | *tu* | vieni | verrai | |
| *to come* | *lui/lei* | viene | verrà | venuto/a/i/e |
| | *noi* | veniamo | verremo | (w/essere) |
| | *voi* | venite | verrete | |
| | *loro* | vengono | verranno | |

| | | Present | Future | Past Participle |
|---|---|---|---|---|
| | *io* | voglio | vorrò | |
| **volere** | *tu* | vuoi | vorrai | |
| *to want* | *lui/lei* | vuole | vorrà | voluto |
| | *noi* | vogliamo | vorremo | (w/avere or essere) |
| | *voi* | volete | vorrete | |
| | *loro* | vogliono | vorranno | |

# Common Irregular Past Participles

In the following table you find a selection of common irregular past participles needed to form compound tenses, such as the **passato prossimo.**

| Verb | Past Participle | English |
|---|---|---|
| **cuocere** *(to cook)* | **cotto** | *cooked* |
| **decidere** *(to decide)* | **deciso** | *decided* |
| **leggere** *(to read)* | **letto** | *read* |
| **mettere** *(to put)* | **messo** | *put* |
| **morire** *(to die)* | **morto** | *died* |
| **nascere** *(to be born)* | **nato** | *born* |
| **perdere** *(to lose)* | **perso, perduto** | *lost* |
| **prendere** *(to take, to have)* | **preso** | *taken, had* |
| **rispondere** *(to reply, to answer)* | **risposto** | *replied, answered* |
| **sciogliere** *(to melt)* | **sciolto** | *melted* |
| **scrivere** *(to write)* | **scritto** | *written* |
| **vedere** *(to see)* | **visto, veduto** | *seen* |
| **vivere** *(to live)* | **vissuto** | *lived* |

For more on Italian verbs and also practice exercises, see *Italian Verbs For Dummies* (John Wiley & Sons, Inc.).

# Appendix **C**
# Answer Keys

The following are the answers to the Fun & Games activities.

## Chapter 2: Jumping Into the Basics of Italian

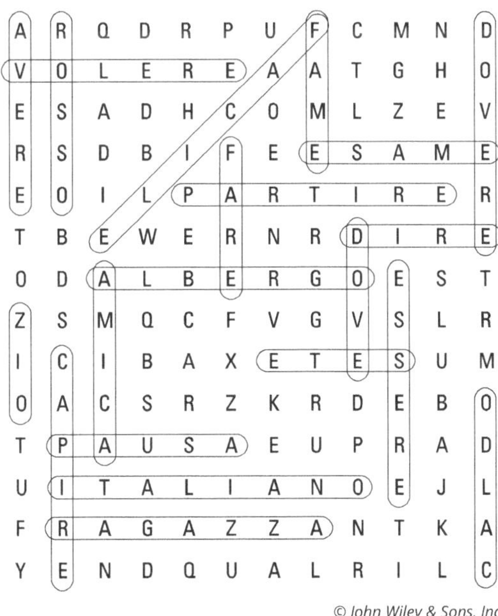

© John Wiley & Sons, Inc.

| albergo | facile |
| amica | fame |
| avere | fare |
| bici | italiano |
| caldo | partire |
| capire | pausa |
| dire | ragazza |
| dove | rosso |
| dovere | sete |
| esame | volere |
| essere | zio |

## Chapter 3: Buongiorno Italia!

| Come sta | conoscerla |
| e Lei | Il piacere |
| Le presento | |

# Chapter 4: Getting Your Numbers and Time Straight

*Illustration by Liz Kurtzman*

# Chapter 5: Casa Dolce Casa (Home Sweet Home)

1. il bagno *(the bathroom)*

2. la camera da letto *(the bedroom)*

3. il letto *(the bed)*

4. il soggiorno *(the living room)*

5. il divano *(the couch)*

6. i fornelli *(the stove-top)*

7. la cucina *(the kitchen)*

8. il tavolo *(the table)*

# Chapter 6: Where Is the Colosseum? Asking Directions

1. Via della Vigna Nuova
2. Ponte Santa Trinità and Ponte Vecchio
3. Arno
4. Palazzo Vecchio
5. Piazza Duomo and Piazza San Giovanni
6. Lungarno
7. Piazza della Repubblica

# Chapter 7: Food Glorious Food — and Don't Forget the Drinks

1. ananas
2. ciliegia
3. uva
4. pera
5. cocomero
6. fragola

# Chapter 8: Shopping Italian Style

1. cappello
2. camicia
3. cravatta
4. completo/vestito
5. pantaloni
6. scarpe
7. gonna
8. camicetta

## Chapter 9: Having Fun Out on the Town

1. festa
2. invitato
3. Sabato
4. ora
5. Verso
6. Dove
7. Perché
8. aspetto

## Chapter 10: From Ring to Ping: Phones, Texts, Emails, & More

1. Pronto
2. parlo
3. amico
4. C'è
5. appena
6. lasciare un messaggio
7. prego
8. chiamato

## Chapter 11: Recreation and the Outdoors

| A | J | A | R | O | C | E | P | O | S |
| U | I | V | S | W | S | O | P | A | B |
| A | H | C | E | M | L | U | Y | O | A |
| C | I | K | R | L | L | U | V | G | D |
| C | G | B | A | E | F | O | L | E | D |
| U | N | V | M | Z | U | I | N | S | D |
| M | A | R | X | J | C | Q | O | I | Y |
| C | G | A | T | T | O | E | I | R | P |
| A | L | B | E | R | O | P | S | T | E |
| F | R | H | O | L | L | E | C | C | U |

© *John Wiley & Sons, Inc.*

cavallo, fiore, uccello, gatto, lupo, quercia, pino, mucca, pecora, albero

## Chapter 12: Planning a Trip

1. b
2. a
3. b
4. c
5. a

# Chapter 13: Money, Money, Money

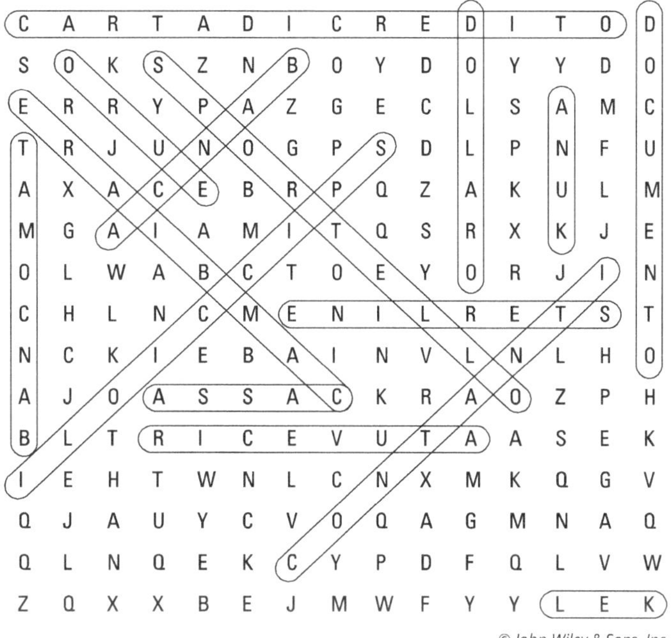



Banca

Bancomat

Cambiare

Carta di credito

Cassa

Contanti

Documento

Dollaro

Euro

Lek

Ricevuta

Spiccioli

Sportello

Sterline

bank

ATM

to change

credit card

cash

identification

dollar

euro

Albanian currency

receipt

small change

door

counter

British pounds

## Chapter 14: Getting Around: Planes, Trains, Taxis, and Buses

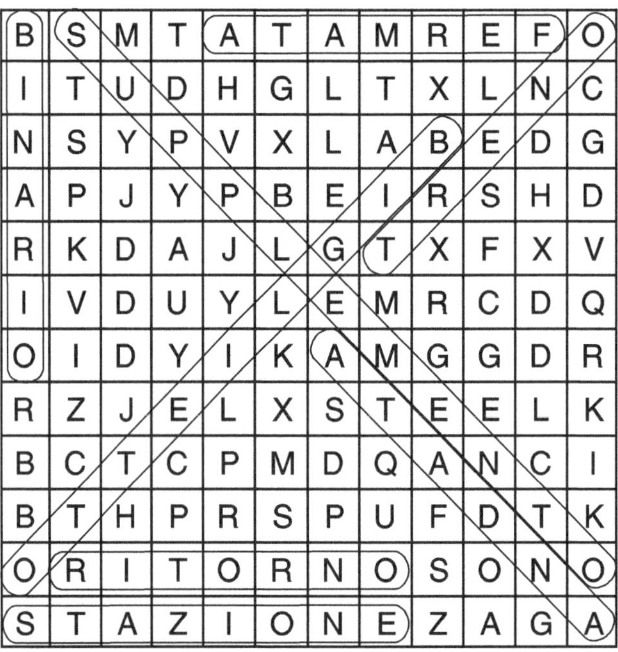

© John Wiley & Sons, Inc.

treno, fermata, stazione, binario, biglietto, andata, ritorno, supplemento

## Chapter 15: Finding a Place to Stay

valigie, cameriere, culla, camera, matrimoniale, letto, piscine, stanza, albergo, prenotazione, pensione, chiave, bagaglio, bagno

# Chapter 16: Handling Emergencies

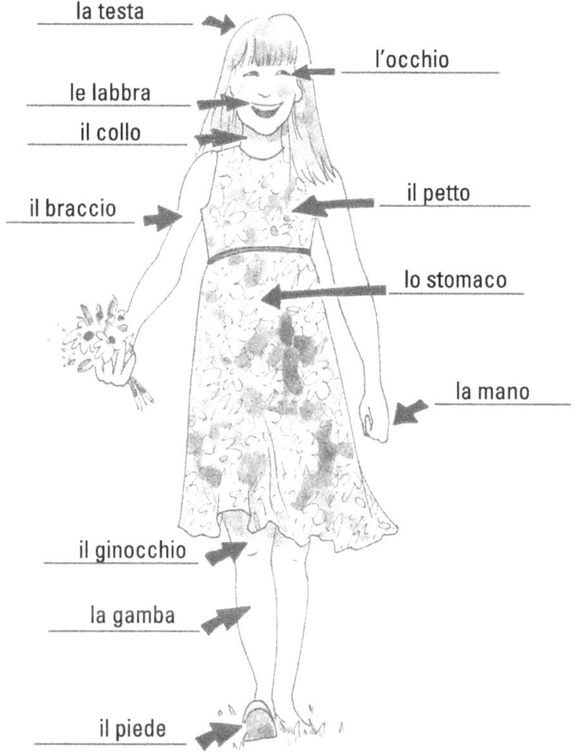


*Illustration by Liz Kurtzman*

# Chapter 17: Small Talk, Wrapping Things Up

1. mio padre **e** mia madre
2. mio fratello
3. i miei nipoti
4. mia nonna
5. mia zia
6. mio cognato
7. mia nuora
8. mia figlia
9. i miei cugini
10. mia suocera

# Index

**casa/case** (house/houses), 20, 23

**casalinghi** (housewares), 137

**cassa** (cash register), 312

**cassaforte** (safe), 255

**castani** (brown), 279

**cattivo** (bad), 24

**cavallo** (horse), 191

cellphones, 170–171

**cellulare** (cellular phone), 170, 174

**cena** (dinner), 15, 115

**centesimi** (cents), 224

**centimetro** (centimeter), 73

**centri commerciali** (shopping malls), 136

**centro** (downtown; city center), 106

**certo** (certainly, of course), 15, 224

**che** (what), 14, 288

**che domanda!** (What a question!), 224

**che è successo** (what happened), 277

**che ne so!** (how should I know), 316

checking in

    to accommodations, 255–261

    for flights, 230–231

**chi** (who?), 288

**chi è il regista?** (who is the director?), 155

**chi sono gli attori?** (who's starring?), 155

**chiacchierare** (to chat), 178

**chiamare** (to call), 178

**chiamarsi** (to call oneself), 44, 191

**chiamata** (call), 178

**chiari** (fair), 279

**chiesa** (church), 16, 110, 113

**chilo/i** (kilo/kilos), 74, 76, 132

**chilogrammo** (kilogram), 74

**chilometro** (kilometer), 73

**chirurgo** (surgeon), 273

**chitarra** (guitar), 202

**ci vediamo!** (see you), 43

**ciambella** (donut), 15

**ciao** (hello, good-bye), 9, 26, 38, 42, 45, 311

**cinema** (cinema, movie theater), 12, 22, 113

**cinquanta centesimi** (50 cents), 74

**cintura** (belt), 144

**cioccolata** (chocolate), 15, 123

**cioccolata calda** (hot cocoa), 117

**circa** (about), 233

**città** (city), 15, 18, 21

**ciuccio** (baby's pacifier), 15

**clarinetto** (clarinet), 202

cognates, 9

**colazione** (breakfast), 115, 254

**collana** (necklace), 144

**collant** (tights), 144

**collo** (neck), 268

**colloquio** (interview), 185

colors, 142–144

**Colosseo** (Colosseum), 100, 309

**colpa** (guilt), 14

**coltello** (knife), 93

**come** (how?), 288

**come al solito** (as usual), 72

**come ti trovi?** (How do you like it?), 293

**come, scusi/a** (pardon/sorry), 109

**cominciare** (to start), 151

communication, 169

    calling for business or pleasure, 172–174

    cellphones, 170–171

    Fun and Games, 186

    human element, 183–184

    missed calls and messages, handling, 175–178

    office equipment, 184–185

    past, talking about, 178–182

    Talkin' the Talk, 171–172, 172–173, 173–174, 175, 176–177, 177, 181, 184–185

    text messaging, 171

    Whatsapp, 171

**compagnia** (company), 183, 300

**compleanno** (birthday), 76

**completo** (outfit), 139

**comprare** (to buy), 180

**comunicazione** (communication), 9

concert, going to, 160–162

**concerto** (concert), 162

**condominio** (apartment building), 83

**coniglio** (rabbit), 129

**cono** (cone), 128

**conoscere** (to know, to meet), 180

**consigliare** (to recommend), 293

consonants, 13–18

**contanti** (cash), 221, 224

**conto** (bill), 122

**conto corrente** (checking account), 219

**controlli l'olio** (check the oil), 240

conventions, explained, 1–2

cooking, 310

cooking at home, 93–95

**coperto** (cover charge, covered), 122

**coppetta** (cup), 128

**coro** (choir), 202

**corriera** (long-distance bus), 244

**corsia di emergenza** (emergency lane), 282

**corti** (short), 279

**corto** (short), 145

**cosa** (what?), 288

**costa di più** (it costs more), 86

**costa meno** (it costs less), 86

**costume da bagno** (bathing suit), 139

**cotone** (cotton), 144

**cotto** (cooked), 345

**cozza** (mussel), 130

**cravatta** (tie), 144

credit cards, using, 221–223

**crema** (custard), 123

**cucchiaio** (spoon), 93

**cucina** (kitchen), 84

**cucinare** (to cook), 93

**cugino/a/i/e** (cousin), 294

**culla** (crib), 254

**cuocere** (to cook), 345

**cuore** (heart), 14

currencies, 224–226

**curriculum vitae** (résumé), 185

customs, going through, 233–234

# D

**d'accordo** (okay, agreed), 38

**da quanto tempo?** (How long?), 293

**dai** (you give), 13, 316

**danno** (damage), 283

**dare** (to give), 13, 32, 34

dates, asking about and giving, 64

**davanti a** (in front of), 90, 102

days of the week, identifying, 61–62

**decidere** (to decide), 345

**deciso** (decided), 345

definite articles, 22–23

demonstrative adjectives and pronouns, 140

dentist, 275

**dentista** (dentist), 273

**dentro** (inside), 90, 103

**denuncia** (report), 283

**denunciare** (to report), 278, 283

department stores and boutiques, 136

**desidera?** (can I help you?), 138

**destinazione** (destination), 238

**di fianco** (on the side), 90

**di fronte a** (opposite), 103

**di mattina** (in the morning), 65

**di media statura** (of medium height), 279

**di pomeriggio** (in the afternoon), 65

**di sera** (in the evening), 65

**dichiarare** (to declare), 236

**diciannove** (nineteen), 58

**diciassette** (seventeen), 58

**diciotto** (eighteen), 58

**dietro** (behind), 90, 102

**dietro l'angolo** (around the corner), 103

dining out, 120

   paying for meal, 122

   reservations, making, 120–121

dinner, 126–129

**dire** (to say, tell), 32, 180

directions, asking, 99

   distances identification when walking, 102–103

   Fun and Games, 114

   giving and receiving directions, 103–106

   location, 110–113

   specific places, asking for, 99–101

   Talkin' the Talk, 101, 104, 105–106, 108–109, 111, 112–113

   verbs, 106–109

**direttore** (manager, director), 183, 301, 303

**discesa** (descent), 18

distance, 73

distances identification when walking, 102–103

**finire** (to finish/end), 29, 151

**fino a** (up to), 103

**fiore** (flower), 188

fish shop, 130

**fiume** (river), 190

**flauto** (flute), 202

**focaccia** (focaccia), 131

**fodera** (lining), 144

**fon** (blow dryer), 255

food labels, reading, 307

food, 115

    beverages, 118–120

    breakfast, 123

    dining out, 120–122

    dinner, 126–129

    drinking, 116–120

    Fun and Games, 134

    lunch, 124–126

    ordering in Italian, 307–308

    shopping for, 129–133

    Talkin' the Talk, 118–119, 119–120, 121, 123, 127, 128–129, 131–132

**forchetta** (fork), 93

**Formula 1** (Formula One car racing), 196

**fornelli** (stovetop), 91

**forno** (oven), 91

**foto** (photo), 22

**fotocopia** (photocopy), 184

**fotocopiatrice** (photocopier), 184

**francobolli** (stamps), 214

**frappé** (milkshake), 129

**frigorifero** (refrigerator), 91, 255

fruits and vegetables, 133

**frullati** (smoothie), 129

**frullatore** (blender), 91

**frutta** (fruit), 13, 132

**frutta e verdura** (fruits and vegetables), 312

**frutta fresca** (fresh fruit), 124

**frutti di mare** (shellfish), 130

**fruttivendoli** (greengrocers), 132

Fun and Games

    accommodations, 265

    basics, 39

    communication, 186

    directions, asking, 114

    emergencies, 286

    food, 134

    greeting and saying good-bye, 56

    home, 97

    money, 227–228

    nightlife, 168

    numbers and time, 77

    recreation and the outdoors, 203

    shopping, for clothing, 148

    small talk, 304

    transportation, 249

    trip planning, 216

**funghi** (mushrooms), 15

**funghi porcini** (porcini mushrooms), 74

**funzionare** (to work; to function), 224

**fuori** (outside), 90, 103

**furto** (theft), 278

**fusilli** (spiral pasta), 125

future tense, 36–37

**futuro semplice** (simple future), 214

# G

**gallina** (chicken), 191

**gallo** (rooster), 191

**gamba** (leg), 15, 268

**gamberetto** (small shrimp), 130

**gambero** (prawn), 130

garage (car park, garage), 261

**garage** (garage), 84

**gassata** (sparkling [water]), 313

**gatto** (cat), 191

**gelateria** (ice cream shop), 128, 129

**gelato** (ice cream), 15, 38, 128

**gelato artigianale** (artisanal ice cream), 128

**gelosia** (jealousy), 16

**gemello/a** (twin), 293

gender and number, 20–22

    adjectives, 23–25

    definite articles, 22–23

    indefinite articles, 22

**genero** (son-in-law), 294

**genitori** (parents), 294

# O

**occhio** (eye), 17, 269

office equipment, 184–185

**oggi** (today), 61

**ombrello** (umbrella), 144

**ombrellone** (umbrella), 213

**ondulati** (wavy), 279

**operaio** (factory worker), 301

**orario** (timetable), 247

**orario di apertura** (business hours), 136

**orata** (sea bream), 130

ordering food in Italian, 307–308

ordinal numbers, practicing, 81–83

**orecchini** (earrings), 144

**ospedale** (hospital), 110, 113, 272

**ovest** (west), 102

# P

**padel** (padel), 187

**padre** (father), 14, 294

**padrone** (boss, owner), 301

**pagare** (to pay), 236

**paio di scarpe** (pair of shoes), 145

**pallacanestro** (basketball), 187

**pallavolo** (volleyball), 187

**palline** (scoops), 128

**pancia** (belly), 269

**pane** (bread), 131

**panetteria** (bakery), 131

**panorama** (view), 188

**pantaloni** (pants), 139

**pantofole** (slippers), 145

**parlare** (to speak), 27

**parrucchiere** (hairdresser), 256

**partenza/e** (departure/s), 238, 247

**partire** (to leave), 27, 182, 212

**partita** (game), 293

party, going to, 162–166

**passaporto** (passport), 211, 231

**passatempo** (pastime), 198

passport, lost or stolen, 283–285

past tense, 36–37

past, talking about, 178

   avere, 179–181

   errere, 181–182

**pasta** (pasta, pastry), 16, 123, 124, 313

**pasta all'uovo** (egg pasta), 125

**pasta fatta in casa** (homemade pasta), 125

**pasticciere** (baker), 301

**pastore** (shepherd), 76

**patente** (driver's license), 238, 283

**pecora** (sheep), 191

**pedalò** (paddle boat), 213

**pelle** (leather), 144

**penne** (penne pasta), 125

**pensione completa** (full board), 255

**pensioni** (small hotels/guesthouses), 251

**per favore** (please), 10, 16, 256

**perché** (why), 18, 167, 288

**perdere** (to lose), 345

**perduto** (lost), 345

**periferia** (suburban area), 83

**permesso?** (may I pass/come in?), 10

**però** (but), 18

**perso** (lost), 345

personal pronouns, 25–26

**pesce** (fish), 124, 130

**pesce spada** (swordfish), 130

**pescheria** (fish shop), 130

**pescivendolo** (fishmonger), 130

**peso** (weight), 12

**pettinarsi** (to comb one's hair), 192

**petto** (chest), 269

pharmacy, 274–275

phone, making arrangements over, 174–175

**piacere** (to like), 45, 198

**piano** (piano), 162

**pianoforte** (piano), 202

**pianta** (plant), 188

**piantina** (map), 38

**piatto** (dish), 93

**piazza** (square), 101, 103, 106, 149

**piccola** (small), 120

**piccolo** (little; small), 13, 139

**piede** (foot), 269

**volere** (to want), 35, 36, 126

**volo** (flight), 212, 233

**vongola** (clam), 130

**vorrei** (I would like), 126, 293

vowels, 12–13

# W

walking, distances identification when, 102–103

watching Italian movies, 308

water, 312–313

weather, chatting about, 67–72

weight, 74

Whatsapp, 171

# X

**xenofobia** (xenophobia), 14

**xilofono** (xylophone), 14

# Y

**yogurt** (yogurt), 129

# Z

**zanzara** (mosquito), 16

**zia/e** (aunt/s), 22, 23, 24, 294

**zio/i** (uncle/s), 22, 23, 24, 294

# About the Authors

**Giuseppe Cavatorta** is professor of Italian at the University of Arizona. Born in Parma in 1964, where he received is B.A, he completed his MA at the University of Virginia (1997) and his PhD at UCLA (2005). His research spans experimental writing, Italian Futurism and the neo-avant-garde, World War II in literature and film, pedagogy, and translation theory. His essays have appeared in journals such as *Studi Novecenteschi*, *Rivista di studi italiani*, *Il Verri*, *Italica*, and *Italian Culture*. He has edited numerous volumes, including *The Promised Land* (2000), Adriano Spatola's *The Composition of Things* (2008), Luigi Ballerini's *Poesie 1972–2015* (2017), *Those Who from Afar Look Like Flies* (2017), and Maria Grazia Calandrone's *The seed and Other Poems* (2025). He is the author of *Scrivere contro* (2010), a critical study of 20th-century Italian experimental writing, and has translated works by Anne Sexton, Emilio Zucchi, Sergio Atzeni, and several American poets for the Mondadori series "Nuova Poesia Americana." His poetry collections include *La stanza sgombra* (*The Empty Room*, 2020) and *Istantanee di un amor de lonh* (*Snapshots of an Amor de Lonh*, 2020). He is also co-author of the textbook *Ponti. Italiano terzo millennio* (with Elissa Tognozzi) and the open educational platform *Italian in Wonderland* (with Letizia Bellocchio and Borbala Gaspar).

**Teresa Picarazzi** graduated with a BA from Skidmore College and an MA/PhD in Italian Literature from Rutgers University. For many years she taught Italian language, literature, and culture at several universities, including the University of Arizona, Wesleyan University, and Dartmouth College. She also directed the Italian language and study abroad programs at some of these. She recently taught Italian at The Hopkins School in New Haven, Connecticut. In her spare time, Teresa likes to cook and read. She lives in Fairfield, Connecticut, with her daughter, her husband, Toby the dog, and Mittens and Governor the cats. The family spends every summer in Ravenna, Italy.

# Dedication

I dedicate this book to my mom Loredana.

—Giuseppe Cavatorta

# Authors' Acknowledgments

I thank Teresa Picarazzi for recommending me to Wiley, trusting me in "messing about" with her book, and my students, present and past, for their curiosity and love for all things Italian, who on a daily basis made me a better teacher. My gratitude as well to the team at Wiley for making this book come true: executive editor Lindsay Berg and senior editorial assistant Hanna Sytsma, for contacting me; project editor Chad Sievers, with his profound knowledge of the *Dummies* ins and outs, who carefully guided me step by step through the process; and technical editor Beatrice (Bijou) D'Arpa. With her eye that misses nothing and a mind attuned to the finest details of language and logic, Beatrice has not only been a vigilant editor but also a quiet co-architect — helping me shape the tone, flow, and readability of every page. I am endlessly grateful for her rigor, patience, and discerning feedback, all delivered with grace and generosity. This book is better because of her — immeasurably so.

## Publisher's Acknowledgments

**Acquisition Editor:** Lindsay Berg and Hanna Sytsma

**Project Manager and Copy Editor:** Chad R. Sievers

**Managing Editor:** Kristie Pyles

**Technical Editor:** Beatrice (Bijou) D'Arpa

**Production Editor:** Tamilmani Varadharaj

**Cover Image:** © Chris/stock.adobe.com